ADULTS, COMPUTERS AND PROBLEM SOLVING: WHAT'S THE PROBLEM?

OECD

BETTER POLICIES FOR BETTER LIVES

This work is published on the responsibility of the Secretary-General of the OECD. The opinions expressed and arguments employed herein do not necessarily reflect the official views of the OECD member countries.

This document and any map included herein are without prejudice to the status of or sovereignty over any territory, to the delimitation of international frontiers and boundaries and to the name of any territory, city or area.

Please cite this publication as:
OECD (2015), *Adults, Computers and Problem Solving: What's the Problem?*, OECD Publishing.
http://dx.doi.org/10.1787/9789264236844-en

ISBN 978-92-64-23683-7 (print)
ISBN 978-92-64-23684-4 (PDF)

Series: OECD Skills Studies
ISSN 2307-8723 (print)
ISSN 2307-8731 (online)

The statistical data for Israel are supplied by and under the responsibility of the relevant Israeli authorities. The use of such data by the OECD is without prejudice to the status of the Golan Heights, East Jerusalem and Israeli settlements in the West Bank under the terms of international law.

Photo credits:
© iStockphoto.com/aleksandr-mansurov.ru/.
Lightspring

Foreword

Information and communication technologies (ICT) permeate every aspect of our lives, from how we "talk" with friends to how we participate in the political process. The volume of information now accessible at the click of a mouse or the touch of a fingertip is overwhelming. But how skilled are we at using these technologies, and the information we can collect through them, to solve problems we encounter in daily life, such as using e-mail to communicate with a friend or knowing how to work with a spreadsheet?

Based on results from the 2012 Survey of Adult Skills, a product of the OECD Programme for the International Assessment of Adult Competencies (PIAAC), this report reveals the extent to which today's adults can and do use computers to solve problems in their work and personal lives. The report shows that the ability to use computers is not only becoming an essential skill, but proficiency in computer use has an impact on the likelihood of participating in the labour force and on workers' wages. It also shows that there are many adults in all countries that participated in the Survey of Adult Skills who do not possess sufficient skills in managing information in digital environments and are not comfortable using ICT to solve the kinds of problems that they are likely to encounter at work or in everyday life. These adults are at a considerable disadvantage in 21st-century societies.

As this detailed examination makes clear, adults' proficiency in problem solving using ICT includes both proficiency in the cognitive skills needed to solve problems and the ability to use digital devices and functionality to access and manage information. Governments need to ensure that all adults have access to digital technologies and networks, and are given opportunities to develop their proficiency in using them, whether in formal education, on-the-job training, or through lifelong learning activities. Opting out of this increasingly wired world is no longer a viable option.

Andreas Schleicher

Director
Directorate for Education and Skills

Acknowledgements

The Survey of Adult Skills, a product of the OECD Programme for the International Assessment of Adult Competencies (PIAAC), was developed collaboratively by the participating countries, the OECD Secretariat, the European Commission and an international consortium led by Educational Testing Service (ETS). This report was prepared by Ji Eun Chung and Stuart Elliott, under the supervision of William Thorn, with assistance from Veronica Borg, Vanessa Denis and François Keslair. Editorial assistance was provided by Marilyn Achiron and Célia Braga-Schich. Administrative assistance was provided by Sabrina Leonarduzzi.

This document is one of a series of thematic reports prepared as part of the analytical work programme of the PIAAC Board of Participating Countries jointly chaired by Dan McGrath (United States) and Patrick Bussière (Canada).

Table of Contents

BOXES

FIGURES

This book has...

StatLinkS

A service that delivers Excel® files from the printed page!

Look for the *StatLinks* at the bottom left-hand corner of the tables or graphs in this book.
To download the matching Excel® spreadsheet, just type the link into your Internet browser, starting with the *http://dx.doi.org* prefix.
If you're reading the PDF e-book edition, and your PC is connected to the Internet, simply click on the link. You'll find *StatLinks* appearing in more OECD books.

Executive Summary

Problem solving is an important part of work and daily life. The labour market now places a premium on higher-order cognitive skills that involve processing, analysing and communicating information. Meanwhile, citizens are daily confronted with a plethora of choices concerning such important matters as retirement planning and saving, health care, and schools for their children that require managing and evaluating multiple and competing sources of information. In addition, the widespread diffusion of information and communication technologies (ICT) has transformed ways of working, learning and interacting. As a result, the capacity to manage information and solve problems using digital devices, applications and networks has become essential for life in the 21st century.

To understand how well-equipped adults are to manage information in digital environments, the Survey of Adult Skills, a product of the OECD Programme for the International Assessment of Adult Competencies (PIAAC), includes an assessment of problem solving in technology-rich environments. This assessment measures the ability of adults to solve the types of problems they commonly face as ICT users in modern societies. The assessment includes problem-solving tasks that require the use of computer applications, such as e-mail, spreadsheets, word-processing applications and websites, that adults often encounter in daily life. The survey also collects information on the frequency with which adults use different types of ICT applications, both at work and in their daily lives.

ONE IN THREE ADULTS IS HIGHLY PROFICIENT IN USING ICT, ON AVERAGE, ALTHOUGH RESULTS VARY ACROSS COUNTRIES

- Across the OECD countries that participated in the survey, one-third of adults score at the highest levels on the proficiency scale (Level 2 or 3). These adults can solve problems that require the co-ordinated use of several different applications, can evaluate the results of web searches, and can respond to occasional unexpected outcomes.

- The Nordic countries and the Netherlands have the largest proportions of adults (around 40%) who score at the highest levels of proficiency. In contrast, Ireland, Poland and the Slovak Republic have the smallest proportions of adults (around 20%) who score at these levels.

HAVING GOOD LITERACY OR NUMERACY SKILLS AND BEING YOUNGER HAVE THE STRONGEST RELATIONSHIPS TO HIGH PROFICIENCY IN PROBLEM SOLVING IN TECHNOLOGY-RICH ENVIRONMENTS

- On average, adults with good literacy or numeracy skills as well as younger adults (16-24 years old) have better skills in problem solving in technology-rich environments. Having tertiary qualifications and being a regular user of ICT are also factors that are strongly and positively related to proficiency in problem solving using ICT, even after accounting for other factors. Being an immigrant and speaking a language other than the test language as a child have no effect on proficiency after other factors are accounted for.

- Younger adults and those with tertiary qualifications are more likely to have some computer experience. However, after other factors are taken into account, the likelihood of having experience with computers is unrelated to literacy proficiency.

PROFICIENCY IN PROBLEM-SOLVING IN TECHNOLOGY-RICH ENVIRONMENTS IS IMPORTANT FOR WORK

- Adults who score at the highest levels of proficiency in problem solving in technology-rich environments are more likely than other adults to be in the labour force and to have higher wages, although proficiency in literacy and numeracy, as well as frequency of ICT use also play a large role in explaining these outcomes. As the nature of work continues to evolve, it is likely that the rewards for proficiency in this domain will continue to increase.

THE PROPORTION OF ADULTS WHO USE ICT FREQUENTLY AT AND OUTSIDE OF WORK VARIES CONSIDERABLY ACROSS COUNTRIES

- Across participating OECD countries, two out of three adults use e-mail and the Internet in their everyday lives, outside of work, at least once a month. Almost half of the workforce uses e-mail daily at work and almost half use word-processing programmes at least once a month. These regular users of ICT thus have opportunities to continue to develop their skills in problem solving in technology-rich environments.

- Differences in the degree of Internet access and ICT use explain much of the variation in proficiency in problem solving in technology-rich environments across countries. The Netherlands and the Nordic countries show the most frequent ICT use, with over 80% of adults using e-mail at least once a month and over 70% using the Internet to understand issues with the same frequency. By contrast, in Japan less than 50% of adults use e-mail or use the Internet to understand issues at least once a month, and less than 30% use the Internet to conduct transactions at least once a month. Korea, Poland and the Slovak Republic also show infrequent use of ICT: around 60% of adults or less use e-mail and the Internet to understand issues at least once a month and less than 40% of adults in Poland and the Slovak Republic use the Internet to conduct transactions at least once a month.

ACROSS ALL PARTICIPATING COUNTRIES, MANY ADULTS STILL HAVE NO EXPERIENCE WITH COMPUTERS AT ALL

- Across participating OECD countries, 8% of adults had no computer experience prior to their participation in the survey. The percentages range from less than 3% of 16-65 year-olds in the Netherlands, Norway and Sweden to around 15% or higher in Italy, Korea, Poland, the Slovak Republic and Spain. In addition, 5% of adults have such limited computer experience that they lack basic computer skills, such as the ability to highlight text.

- Governments should consider their population's proficiency in solving problems using ICT when they provide access to government services through e-mail and the Internet. To encourage widespread use of such "e-government" services, governments can provide assistance to adults with low proficiency in problem solving in technology-rich environments, and ensure that websites intended for the general public are user-friendly.

- Government policies can also encourage those adults who have limited proficiency in ICT skills to participate in adult education and training programmes that aim to help adults to develop these skills.

About The Survey of Adult Skills

The Survey of Adult Skills, a product of the OECD Programme for the International Assessment of Adult Competencies (PIAAC), assesses the proficiency of adults aged 16-65 in literacy, numeracy and problem solving in technology-rich environments. These three domains are key information-processing competencies that are relevant to adults in many social contexts and work situations. They are necessary for fully integrating and participating in the labour market, education and training, and social and civic life.

The Survey of Adult Skills also collects information about a number of factors in each respondent's background and context. This information includes participation in activities that use the competencies assessed in the three domains, such as the frequency of reading different kinds of material or using different types of information and communication technologies (ICT). The survey includes questions about the use of various generic skills at work, such as collaborating with others and organising one's time. Respondents are also asked whether their skills and qualifications match their work requirements and whether they have autonomy with respect to key aspects of their work.

The first survey was conducted in 2011-2012 in 24 countries and sub-national regions: 22 OECD member countries or regions – Australia, Austria, Belgium (Flanders), Canada, the Czech Republic, Denmark, Estonia, Finland, France, Germany, Ireland, Italy, Japan, Korea, the Netherlands, Norway, Poland, the Slovak Republic, Spain, Sweden, the United Kingdom (England and Northern Ireland), and the United States; and two partner countries – Cyprus* and the Russian Federation**. Around 166 000 adults were surveyed during this first cycle. Additional countries will be participating in the survey in the coming years.

The survey is administered under the supervision of trained interviewers, most often in the respondent's home. It starts with a background questionnaire, delivered in Computer-Aided Personal Interview format by the interviewer, and typically takes 30-45 minutes to complete. The assessment of the domain competencies is conducted either on a laptop computer or by completing a paper version, depending on the respondent's computer skills. The respondents usually take 50 minutes to complete the assessments, but there is no time limit. To reduce the time required for the survey, respondents are assessed in only one or two of the three domains, not in all of them. Respondents with very low literacy skills take an alternate assessment of basic reading skills.

The problem-solving and basic-reading assessments are optional for countries; in the first cycle, several countries declined to participate in those parts of the survey (Cyprus*, France, Italy and Spain). The survey is given in the official language or languages of each participating country, sometimes also including a widely-spoken minority or regional language. Sample sizes depend on the number of cognitive domains assessed, the number of languages used, and country decisions about whether to increase the sample sizes to allow more precise estimates for individual geographic regions or population subgroups. In the first cycle of the survey, the samples ranged from about 4 500 to about 27 300 adults.

During the process of scoring the assessment, a difficulty score is assigned to each task, based on the proportion of respondents who complete it successfully. These scores are represented on a 500-point scale. Respondents are placed on the same 500-point scale, using the information about the number and difficulty of the questions they answer correctly. At each point on the scale, an individual with a proficiency score of that particular value has a 67% chance of successfully completing test items located at that point. This individual will also be able to complete more difficult items with a lower probability of success and easier items with a greater chance of success. To help interpret the results, the reporting scales are divided into four proficiency levels (Below Level 1 through Level 3) in the problem solving in technology-rich environments domain. In addition to the four proficiency levels, there are three additional categories (no computer experience, failed ICT core, and opted out) for those adults who were not able to demonstrate their proficiency in this domain due to lack of basic computer skills necessary to sit the assessment.

* Notes regarding Cyprus

Note by Turkey: The information in this document with reference to "Cyprus" relates to the southern part of the Island. There is no single authority representing both Turkish and Greek Cypriot people on the Island. Turkey recognises the Turkish Republic of Northern Cyprus (TRNC). Until a lasting and equitable solution is found within the context of the United Nations, Turkey shall preserve its position concerning the "Cyprus issue".

Note by all the European Union Member States of the OECD and the European Union: The Republic of Cyprus is recognised by all members of the United Nations with the exception of Turkey. The information in this document relates to the area under the effective control of the Government of the Republic of Cyprus.

** A note regarding the Russian Federation

Readers should note that the sample for the Russian Federation does not include the population of the Moscow municipal area. The data published, therefore, do not represent the entire resident population aged 16-65 in Russia but rather the population of Russia *excluding* the population residing in the Moscow municipal area.

More detailed information re garding the data from the Russian Federation as well as that of other countries can be found in the *Technical Report of the Survey of Adult Skills* (OECD, 2014).

Reader's Guide

Data underlying the figures

Detailed data tables corresponding to the figures presented in the main body of the report can be found in Annex A. These figures and tables share a common reference number and are numbered according to the corresponding chapters.

Annex B includes other detailed data tables that correspond either to figures included in boxes or to citations in the main body of the report, but for which no figure was provided.

Unless otherwise stated, the population underlying each of the figures and tables covers adults aged 16-65.

Web package

A comprehensive set of tables (and figures, when available) used in the report can be found on the web at *www.oecd.org/site/piaac/*. The package consists of Excel workbooks that can be viewed and downloaded by chapter.

StatLinks

A *StatLink* URL address is provided under each figure and table. Readers using the pdf version of the report can simply click on the relevant *StatLink* URL to either open or download an Excel® workbook containing the corresponding figures and tables. Readers of the print version can access the Excel® workbook by typing the *StatLink* address in their Internet browser.

Calculating cross-country averages (means)

Most figures and tables presented in this report and in the web package include a cross-country average in addition to values for individual countries or sub-national entities. The average in each figure or table corresponds to the arithmetic mean of the respective estimates for each of the OECD member countries that participated in the assessment of problem solving in technology-rich environments. For England (UK) and Northern Ireland (UK), the weighted average of the two separate entities is used for the overall cross-country average. OECD countries that did not participate in this assessment domain (France, Italy and Spain) are not included in the "Average" presented in the figures and are not discussed in the main text; however, averages including these countries can be found associated with the term "Average-22" in Annex A tables whenever the data are available. The results for partner countries Cyprus* and the Russian Federation** are also not included in the cross-country averages presented in any of the figures or tables.

Standard error (S.E.)

The statistical estimates presented in this report are based on samples of adults, rather than values that could be calculated if every person in the target population in every country had answered every question. Therefore, each estimate has a degree of uncertainty associated with sampling and measurement error, which can be expressed as a standard error. The use of confidence intervals provides a way to make inferences about the population means and proportions in a manner that reflects the uncertainty associated with the sample estimates. In this report, confidence intervals are stated at 95% confidence level. In other words, the result for the corresponding population would lie within the confidence interval in 95 out of 100 replications of the measurement on different samples drawn from the same population.

Statistical significance

Differences considered to be statistically significant from either zero or between estimates are based on the 5% level of significance, unless otherwise stated. In the figures, statistically significant estimates are denoted in a darker tone.

Symbols for missing data and abbreviations

a   Data are not applicable because the category does not apply.

c   There are too few observations or no observation to provide reliable estimates (i.e. there are fewer than 30 individuals). Also denotes unstable odds ratios which may occur when probabilities are very close to 0 or 1.

m   Data are not available. The data are not submitted by the country or were collected but subsequently removed from the publication for technical reasons.

w   Data has been withdrawn at the request of the country concerned.

S.E.   Standard Error

S.D.   Standard Deviation

Score dif.   Score-point difference between x and y

% dif.   Difference in percentage points between x and y

GDP   Gross Domestic Product

ISCED   International Standard Classification of Education

ISCO   International Standard Classification of Occupations

Country coverage

This publication features data on 20 OECD countries: Australia, Austria, Canada, the Czech Republic, Denmark, Estonia, Finland, France, Germany, Ireland, Italy, Japan, Korea, the Netherlands, Norway, Poland, the Slovak Republic, Spain, Sweden and the United States, and three OECD sub-national entities: Flanders (Belgium), England (United Kingdom), and Northern Ireland (United Kingdom). In addition, two partner countries participated in the survey: Cyprus* and the Russian Federation**.

Data estimates for England (UK) and Northern Ireland (UK) are presented separately as well as combined in the data tables, but only as combined (i.e. England/N. Ireland [UK]) in the figures.

Data estimates for France, Italy and Spain are not included in this report as these countries did not participate in the assessment of problem solving in technology-rich environments. However, ICT use-related data for these countries, collected through the background questionnaire, and the results for the ICT core test are both available in tables in Annex A.

The Survey of Adult Skills is conducted in nine additional countries: Chile, Greece, Indonesia, Israel, Lithuania, New Zealand, Singapore, Slovenia and Turkey. Data collection took place in 2014 and the results will be released in 2016. A third round of the survey, with additional countries, is planned for the 2015-19 period.

Rounding

Data estimates, including mean scores, proportions, odds ratios and standard errors, are generally rounded to one decimal place. Therefore, even if the value (0.0) is shown for standard errors, this does necessarily imply that the standard error is zero, but that it is smaller than 0.05.

Further documentation and resources

The details of the technical standards guiding the design and implementation of the Survey of Adult Skills (PIAAC) can be found at *www.oecd.org/site/piaac/*. The first results from the Survey of Adult Skills can be found in the report *OECD Skills Outlook 2013: First Results from the Survey of Adult Skills* (OECD, 2013a). Information regarding the design, methodology and implementation of the Survey of Adult Skills can be found in summary form in the *Reader's Companion to the survey* (OECD, 2013b) and, in detail, in the *Technical Report of the Survey of Adult Skills* (OECD, 2014) (*www.oecd.org/site/piaac/*).

*Notes regarding Cyprus

Readers should note the following information provided by Turkey and by the Member States of the OECD and the European Union regarding the status of Cyprus:

A. Note by Turkey

The information in this document with reference to "Cyprus" relates to the southern part of the Island. There is no single authority representing both Turkish and Greek Cypriot people on the Island. Turkey recognizes the Turkish Republic of Northern Cyprus (TRNC). Until a lasting and equitable solution is found within the context of United Nations, Turkey shall preserve its position concerning the "Cyprus issue".

B. Note by all the European Union Member States of the OECD and the European Union

The Republic of Cyprus is recognized by all members of the United Nations with the exception of Turkey. The information in this document relates to the area under the effective control of the Government of the Republic of Cyprus.

Throughout this report, including the main body, boxes, and annexes, references to Cyprus are accompanied by a symbol pointing to a footnote that refers readers to notes A and B above.

**A note regarding the Russian Federation

Readers should note that the sample for the Russian Federation does not include the population of the Moscow municipal area. The data published, therefore, do not represent the entire resident population aged 16-65 in Russia but rather the population of Russia excluding the population residing in the Moscow municipal area. More detailed information regarding the data from the Russian Federation as well as that of other countries can be found in the *Technical Report of the Survey of Adult Skills* (OECD, 2014).

References

OECD (2014), *Technical Report of the Survey of Adult Skills*, www.oecd.org/site/piaac/_Technical%20Report_17OCT13.pdf, pre-publication copy.

OECD (2013a), *OECD Skills Outlook 2013: First Results from the Survey of Adult Skills*, OECD Publishing, Paris, http://dx.doi.org/10.1787/9789264204256-en.

OECD (2013b), *The Survey of Adult Skills: Reader's Companion*, OECD Publishing, Paris, http://dx.doi.org/10.1787/9789264204027-en.

1

Problem solving in technology-rich environments and the Survey of Adult Skills

The ability to manage information and solve problems using digital devices, applications and networks has become an essential 21st-century skill. This chapter provides the rationale for assessing adults' ability to solve problems in technology-rich environments in the Survey of Adult Skills.

As the demand for non-routine, high-skilled jobs grows, and information and communications technologies (ICT) permeate every aspect of life, the capacity to manage information and solve problems using digital technology and communication tools has become crucial. In this context, policy makers need to be able to determine adults' proficiency in using these technologies to solve common problems in their work and daily lives. This chapter describes the rationale for assessing adults' proficiency in problem solving in technology-rich environments – that is, their capacity to solve problems using ICT – in the Survey of Adult Skills, a product of the OECD Programme for the International Assessment of Adult Competencies (PIAAC).

THE IMPORTANCE OF PROBLEM-SOLVING SKILLS

Problem solving is an integral part of work and daily life. Problems are often defined as situations in which people do not immediately know what to do to achieve their goals due to obstacles or challenges of some kind (OECD, 2012). To solve problems, individuals must thus be able to access and process information, evaluate the consequences of possible choices, and learn from previous steps. Problem solving tends to be required whenever people encounter a new situation. As our home and work environments frequently change, our routine behaviours quickly become outmoded, and it often becomes necessary to find new ways to achieve our goals. Given the pace of economic and social change in contemporary society, most adults now need higher levels of problem-solving skills than were called for in the past.

A seminal set of studies has analysed information on the activities carried out in different occupations and found a systematic shift over time in the mix of tasks carried out across the workforce in several countries. These studies show that the proportion of jobs requiring relatively non-routine cognitive skills has been increasing for several decades in the United States, Germany and Japan, while the proportion of jobs requiring relatively routine tasks and skills has been decreasing (Autor, Levy and Murnane, 2003; Spitz-Oener, 2006; Ikenaga and Kambayashi, 2010). More recent analyses have shown that the declines in the proportion of jobs requiring relatively routine tasks and skills continued in the United States during the first decade of this century (Levy and Murnane, 2013). The growing importance of non-routine cognitive skills in the workforce means that a growing share of the workforce will be called upon to find solutions to unforeseen problems. Similar conclusions can be drawn from the European Working Conditions Survey (Eurofound, 2012).

On average across the countries shown in Figure 1.1, more than 80% of adults reported that they work in jobs that require solving unforeseen problems. In Denmark, the Netherlands, Norway and Sweden, the rate exceeds 90%. By contrast, in Austria, the Netherlands and Norway, less than 30% of workers reported that they are in jobs that largely involve routine tasks. Problem-solving skills are clearly becoming important at work while routine tasks are becoming less prevalent.

PROBLEM SOLVING USING ICT

As ICT hardware and software both change at a breakneck pace, users of these technologies must be able to adjust quickly to new ICT devices or programs or to ICT devices or programs that now function differently than before. As a result, ICT users regularly need to solve problems as they carry out tasks using these technologies both at work and at home.

The importance of ICT in modern life is often described in terms of the diffusion of access to the technology itself. On average across OECD countries in 2011, 77% of households had access to computers compared to 46% in 2000 (Table B1.1 in Annex B) and 75% had access to the Internet at home compared to 28% in 2000 (Table B1.2). In Denmark, Iceland, Korea, Luxembourg, the Netherlands, Norway and Sweden, more than 90% of households had access to the Internet (Table B1.2). Adults are also increasingly accessing the Internet using portable devices such as laptops, netbooks, tablet computers or smart phones, in addition to traditional desktop computers. For example, more than 50% of individuals in Denmark, Norway, Sweden and the United Kingdom used a handheld device to access the Internet in 2012 (Table B1.3). Many middle-income and developing countries are a decade or two behind OECD countries in the process of gaining access to these technologies, but recent trends suggest that many of these countries will approach current OECD-levels of ICT access in a decade or so (Table B1.4). Chapter 5 discusses the role of government policy in promoting access to ICT and the Internet, including providing computers and digital networks in public institutions.

■ Figure 1.1 ■
Jobs involving routine tasks or solving unforeseen problems
Percentage of workers aged 16-74

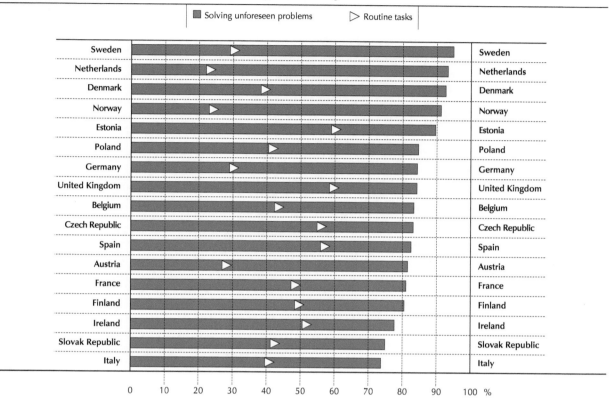

■ Solving unforeseen problems   ▷ Routine tasks

Countries are ranked in descending order of the percentage of individuals in jobs that require solving unforeseen problems.
Source: European Working Conditions Survey (2010). See Table A1.1.

StatLink ᗑᑭ http://dx.doi.org/10.1787/888933231444

LIVING WITH ICT

The near-universal access to ICT devices and applications is, in turn, driving a transformation in the way that people in OECD countries live. Figure 1.2 shows how using the Internet to buy goods increased from 2005 to 2013 in a number of countries. Additional examples of trends in using ICT for everyday tasks – such as banking and exchanging e-mails – are shown in Tables B1.5 and B1.6 in Annex B. These trends demonstrate how ICT has become an integral part of everyday life for many adults in most OECD countries.

The proportion of adults using ICT for these tasks has increased dramatically – by 20 to 40 percentage points in most countries – from 2005 to 2013. The vast majority of adults in the Nordic countries (Denmark, Finland, Norway and Sweden) reported that they use ICT to carry out everyday tasks: more than 80% used Internet banking in 2014 (Table B1.5) and more than 70% made online purchases in 2013 (Table A1.2). If these growth rates continue, many other OECD countries will move towards these near-universal levels of ICT use within the next decade.

As a consequence of using ICT for everyday tasks, offline purchases and practices have been transformed. Box 1.1 discusses some of the innovations that have taken place over the past decade in the travel sector as a growing proportion of adults in OECD countries obtain travel information and make reservations through the Internet.

In addition, more and more people are using the Internet to apply for jobs. As information is becoming increasingly digitised and shared on line, most job openings are now posted on line and many employers accept applications only through special online platforms. As a result, for many adults in OECD countries, the ability to use such platforms has become a required skill for landing a job.

■ Figure 1.2 ■

Evolution of online purchases

Percentage of 25-64 year-olds, 2005 and 2013

■ 2005   ► 2013

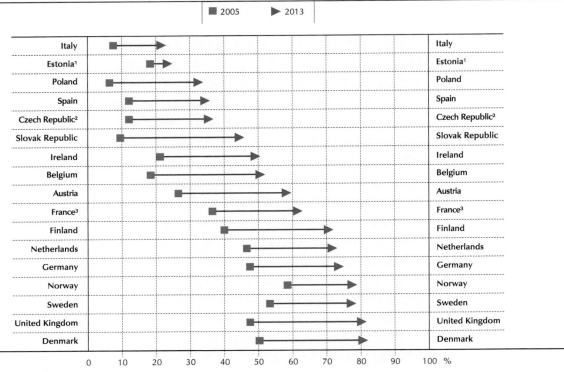

1. Year of reference 2009 instead of 2005.
2. Year of reference 2006 instead of 2005.
3. Year of reference 2007 instead of 2005.
Note: Within the 12 months prior to the Eurostat Community Survey.
Countries are ranked in ascending order of the percentage of individuals who made purchases in the 12 months prior to the Community Survey on ICT usage in households and by individuals.
Source: Eurostat, Community Survey on ICT usage in households and by individuals. See Table A1.2.
StatLink ⬛ http://dx.doi.org/10.1787/888933231457

Box 1.1 Transformation in making travel reservations

Information and communication technologies (ICT) have transformed the way we live. One of the more visible changes is in the travel industry. Nowadays, it is hard to imagine booking travel without comparing flight prices and hotel room rates on line. However, online flight bookings were not available outside airline terminals until the mid-1970s.[1] Only a few domestic airlines allowed licensed travel agents to access the reservation system at that time (McKenney and Copeland, 1995).

Airlines and hotel companies realised that approaching consumers directly, through the Internet, could reduce their fees to travel agents and Computer Reservation Systems operators. As a result, since 1997, many airlines and other travel companies gradually started to sell airline tickets directly to travellers. Travel agencies also started to develop their own travel websites with online flight booking options. For example, in 1996, CheapTickets was founded in the United Kingdom, offering airfare-pricing comparisons and partnering with airlines to offer low Internet rates. Microsoft launched the Expedia online travel booking site the same year. In the years since, many other online travel agencies have emerged, including Orbitz, Opodo, Travelocity and Voyages-sncf (Hockenson, 2012).

Consumers no longer need to call or travel to an offline travel agency to make travel reservations but can easily go on line and book their own travel. Since 2010, more travel arrangements are booked on line than off line, and in 2012, 60% of all travel reservations were made on line. In 2010, 79% of all hotel bookings were either booked on line or influenced by the Internet (Mullin, 2013).

Consumer spending on online travel has grown rapidly in recent years, reflecting continued increases in total travel spending and the growing portion of online bookings. In 2012, online travel sales reached USD 524 billion globally. Online travel spending is growing by 17% per year (Rossini, 2013).

...

Various ICT, problem-solving, literacy and numeracy skills are required to book airline tickets, reserve hotel rooms or purchase package tours. These travel transactions usually involve navigating through many different sites, evaluating the information presented, clicking on boxes, making payments on line and checking booking confirmations via e-mail. These activities are similar to the types of tasks included in the problem solving in technology-rich environments assessment.

With the latest advances in technology, it has become easier to make shopping and travel reservations with smartphones and other mobile devices. Consumers can receive travel alerts and suggestions, store their boarding card on their smartphones, book their own seats, and check in on line using their smartphone. Some 30% of individuals around the world reported that they use mobile apps to find hotel deals, and 29% of travellers have used mobile apps to find cheaper flights (Rossini, 2013).

Note:

1. The online travel evolution-infographic available at *www.staywyse.org/2012/07/02/the-online-travel-evolution-infographic/* [Accessed 1 March 2015].

Figure 1.3 shows the degree to which unemployed adults in Europe use the Internet to search or apply for jobs. As the figure shows, there was a substantial increase in the use of the Internet for this purpose between 2005 and 2013. During this eight-year period, Austria, Ireland, the Netherlands and Norway saw an increase of more than 40 percentage points in the use of the Internet to search for jobs or send job applications. More than 80% of unemployed adults in the Netherlands, Norway and Sweden searched for jobs on line or submitted job applications via the Internet. The Survey of Adult Skills reflects this new reality by including a task in the problem solving in technology-rich environments domain related to accessing and evaluating job-search information in a simulated web environment (see Annex Box 2.2).

■ Figure 1.3 ■

Evolution of using the Internet to search or apply for a job

Percentage of unemployed individuals aged 16-74, 2005 and 2013

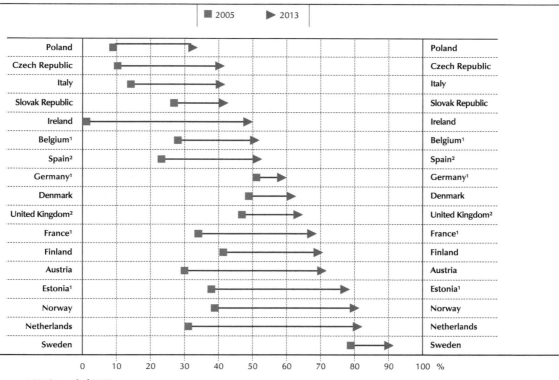

1. Year of reference 2006 instead of 2005.
2. Year of reference 2007 instead of 2005.

Note: Within the 3 months prior to the Eurostat Community Survey.

Countries are ranked in ascending order of the percentage of unemployed individuals who used the Internet to look for a job or sent a job application within the three months prior to the Community Survey on ICT usage in households and by individuals.

Source: Eurostat, Community Survey on ICT usage in households and by individuals. See Table A1.3.

StatLink ᴍᴤᴾ http://dx.doi.org/10.1787/888933231461

WORKING WITH ICT

Digital technologies have also changed business and work practices. For example, as shown in Table B1.7 in Annex B, many enterprises send and receive business invoices on line. ICT applications are transforming work in many industries, and employees in many occupations must be able to use them.

Intensity in the use of ICT differs across different sectors of the economy. As shown in Figure 1.4, only about 15% of workers employed in agriculture across European countries use ICT. By contrast, more than 90% of workers in the financial sector use ICT frequently, as do more than 70% of workers in public administration/defence and education. Many of the sectors with high levels of ICT use, such as financial services and health care, are also those that have increased their share of employment over the past several decades (OECD, 2013). Therefore, having an adequate level of ICT skills to handle various tasks at work is likely to become even more prized by employers in the future.

USING ICT TO INTERACT WITH PUBLIC AUTHORITIES

The increase in access to and use of ICT by individuals and businesses has been accompanied by an increase in the online provision of public services across many OECD countries. As shown in Figure 1.5, between 2008 and 2013 there was a substantial increase in the percentage of adults interacting with public authorities through digital channels. For example, over the past four years, Denmark saw an increase of 36 percentage points in the proportion of adults interacting with public authorities through ICT.

■ Figure 1.4 ■

Using technology, by sector of work

Percentage of workers reporting frequent use of ICT*, EU27 average

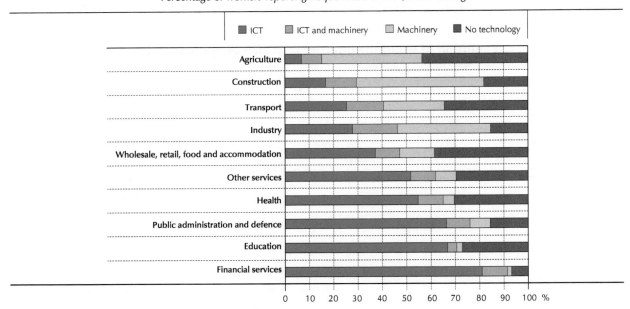

* Use is considered frequent if the technology is used more than 75% of the time.
Sectors are ranked in ascending order of the percentage of workers who reported using ICT frequently at work.
Source: European Working Conditions Survey (2010). See Table A1.4.

StatLink http://dx.doi.org/10.1787/888933231479

Public services provided on line are more convenient for users, which usually means that more people can access those services, and the services are less costly to both users and providers. For these reasons, many countries are looking for ways to provide more public services on line and are investing substantial resources in developing them. Of course, online services often require the user to find and interpret information and, as later chapters of this report make clear, many adults still do not have adequate skills for accessing such services. It is thus critical that governments ensure that public services are equally accessible to those who do not yet have access to computers or who lack the skills to use them. Chapter 5 discusses the issues related to adopting e-government services, including those to consider before designing related policies.

CHALLENGES IN WORKING WITH ICT

Working with ICT involves much more than providing access to the technologies themselves. The differences between access and use are shown in the figures above, where the adoption of ICT hardware – computers, Internet connections, and mobile subscriptions – is substantially larger than the adoption of ICT as the means of carrying out the various tasks described in Figures 1.2, 1.3 and 1.5. There is ample literature on the diffusion of technology that examines the complexity of fully integrating new methods and techniques into work and everyday life (Rogers, 2003). A number of factors determine the pace and extent of diffusion, including not only the characteristics of the innovations themselves, but also the ways that information about innovation is communicated and the obstacles encountered when incorporating the innovations into current work practices and social systems.

Using ICT adds another layer of complexity for users who are more accustomed to performing tasks using more traditional methods. For most adults in OECD countries, using a pencil and paper, calling someone on the telephone, or visiting a store or office involves a set of skills that they have developed and perfected over a number of decades. These skills have become almost automatic: they are applied appropriately with almost no conscious thought or effort. As a result, users of these older techniques can focus on the details of the task they are trying to accomplish – what words to use, how to respond to a difficult conversation, which products to buy – rather than on how to manipulate the physical equipment they use to complete the task.

■ Figure 1.5 ■
Evolution of using the Internet to interact with public authorities
Percentage of 16-74 year-olds, 2008 and 2013

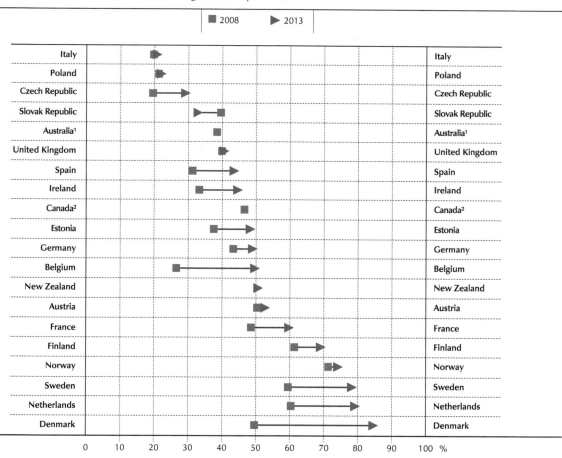

1. Year of reference 2010 instead of 2008.
2. Year of reference 2009 instead of 2008.

Countries are ranked in ascending order of the percentage of adults who used the Internet to interact with public authorities in 2013.

Note: Within the 12 months prior to the surveys, for private purposes. Derived variable on use of e-government services. Individuals used the Internet for at least one of the following: to obtain services from public authorities' websites; to download official forms; and/or to send completed forms. Data for Canada and New Zealand refer only to obtaining services from public authorities' wedsites but does not include other activities such as townlegding or completing official forms.

Source: Eurostat, Community Survey on ICT usage in households and by individuals; OECD ICT database. See Table A1.5.

StatLink http://dx.doi.org/10.1787/888933231480

By contrast, using ICT to accomplish the same tasks places an additional burden on users who are not yet proficient in using these technologies. As a result, it often becomes more difficult to carry out the task – at least for some time – because users must consciously learn how to make the technology function as they intend, in addition to figuring out the substantive details of the task. Many adults who have only recently begun using ICT have had the frustrating – and sometimes embarrassing – experience of accidentally deleting the draft of a sensitive document or accidentally sending the draft of a sensitive e-mail too soon.

References

Autor, D.H., **F. Levy** and **R.J. Murnane** (2003), "The skill content of recent technological change: An empirical exploration", *The Quarterly Journal of Economics*, Vol. 118, pp. 1278-1333.

Eurofound (2012), *Fifth European Working Conditions Survey*, Publications Office of the European Union, Luxembourg.

Hockenson, L. (2012), The Evolution of Online Travel [infographic], Mashable, Social Travel Series, *http://mashable.com/2012/02/21/online-travel-infographic/*.

Ikenaga, T. and **R. Kambayashi** (2010), "Long-term trends in the polarization of the Japanese labor market: The increase of non-routine task input and its valuation in the labor market", *Hitotsubashi University Institute of Economic Research Working Paper*.

Levy, F. and **R.J. Murnane** (2013), *Dancing with Robots: Human Skills for Computerized Work*, Third Way, *http://content.thirdway.org/publications/714/Dancing-With-Robots.pdf* [accessed 16 May 2014].

McKenney, J. and **D. Copeland** (1995), *Waves of Change: Business Evolution through Information Technology*, Harvard Business School Publishing, Boston.

Mullin, M. (2013), Online and Offline Travel Agents in the Age of Digital Travel, TourismLink, *www.tourismlink.eu/2013/03/onlineandoffline-travel-agents-in-the-age-of-digital-travel/*.

OECD (2013a), *OECD Skills Outlook 2013: First Results from the Survey of Adult Skills*, OECD Publishing, Paris, *http://dx.doi.org/10.1787/9789264204256-en*.

OECD (2012), *Literacy, Numeracy and Problem Solving in Technology-Rich Environments: Framework for the OECD Survey of Adult Skills*, OECD Publishing, Paris, *http://dx.doi.org/10.1787/9789264128859-en*.

Rogers, E. M. (2003), *Diffusion of Innovations*, Free Press, New York.

Rossini, A. (2013), "Sustained growth but tougher competition", *WTM Business* 2013, pp. 88-89.

Spitz-Oener, A. (2006), "Technical change, job tasks, and rising educational demands: Looking outside the wage structure", *Journal of Labor Economics*, Vol. 24, pp. 235-270.

2

Proficiency in problem solving in technology-rich environments

This chapter describes the main features of the assessment of problem solving in technology-rich environments included in the Survey of Adult Skills. It also presents the results of the adult survey and information on how frequently adults use ICT devices and applications in their daily lives. The results show a close relationship, across countries, between proficiency in problem solving in technology-rich environments and the degree of access to and use of ICT.

The domain of problem solving in technology-rich environments captures the intersection between the set of cognitive capacities required to solve problems and the use of information and communication technologies (ICT). Proficiency in this skill reflects the capacity to use ICT devices and applications to solve the types of problems adults commonly face as ICT users in modern societies. The domain assesses adults' ability to use "digital technology, communication tools, and networks to acquire and evaluate information, communicate with others and perform practical tasks" (OECD 2012, p. 47). In order to display proficiency in this domain, adults must have the basic computer skills needed to undertake an assessment on a computer: the capacity to type, manipulate a mouse, drag and drop content, and highlight text.

While the definition of the domain encompasses the full range of digital devices, interfaces and applications, the assessment of problem solving in technology-rich environments in the first cycle of the Survey of Adult Skills, a product of the OECD Programme for the International Assessment of Adult Competencies (PIAAC) is restricted to an environment involving computers and computer networks. The tasks in this first assessment involve "solv[ing] problems for personal, work or civic purposes by setting up appropriate goals and plans, and accessing and making use of information through computers and computer networks" (OECD 2012, p. 47). The tasks require respondents to access, interpret, and integrate information from multiple sources in order to construct a solution to a problem.

Of the 24 participating countries and sub-national regions, Cyprus[1], France, Italy and Spain did not participate in the assessment of problem solving in technology-rich environments. Since a measure of proficiency in this domain is not available for these countries, the text, figures and the averages focus on the results of countries that participated in this domain. However, some information for these countries, relevant to this report, is available from other sections of the survey, including information from the background questionnaire on computer experience and on the use of ICT devices and applications, both at and outside of work, and information on adults' basic level of ICT skills, as assessed through the ICT core test. This information for these countries can be found in the tables in the Annex.

Key findings

- On average, 8% of adults indicate that they had no prior experience with computers.
- Across countries, an average of one in three adults performs at the higher levels of problem solving, ranging from 19% in Poland to 44% in Sweden.
- In the Nordic countries and the Netherlands, over 80% of adults use e-mail at least once a month and over 70% use the Internet with similar frequency to understand issues and conduct transactions. By comparison, around 60% of adults or less in Korea, Poland and the Slovak Republic use e-mail and the Internet (to understand issues) at least once a month, and less than 40% of adults in Poland and the Slovak Republic use the Internet to conduct transactions at least once a month.
- Differences in the levels of Internet access and ICT use explain much of the variation in proficiency in problem solving in technology-rich environments across countries.

Fourteen tasks, presented in two assessment modules, were used to assess adults' proficiency in this skill. The results are presented on a 500-point scale that is divided into four proficiency levels that describe the difficulty of the tasks and the specific capabilities of the adults who can perform them. Table A2.1 in the Annex lists the 14 tasks in increasing order of difficulty, clustered into proficiency Levels 1 through 3. The fourth proficiency level, Below Level 1, is used for those adults who cannot reliably perform the tasks at Level 1.

Tasks below Level 1 have clear goals, few steps and familiar environments. Adults who score below Level 1 in proficiency can successfully complete fewer than one in six Level 1 tasks. Adults at this level have passed the ICT core, which means that they can use basic computer functions, such as typing, manipulating a mouse, dragging and dropping content, and highlighting text.

At Level 1, adults can complete tasks in which the goal is explicitly stated and for which a small number of operations are performed in a single familiar environment. The tasks that are rated at this level involve locating an item in a spreadsheet and communicating the result by e-mail, using e-mail to send information to several people, and categorising e-mail messages into existing folders.

At Level 2, adults can complete problems that have explicit criteria for success, a small number of applications, several steps and operators, and occasional unexpected outcomes that need to be addressed. The tasks that are rated at this level involve organising information in a spreadsheet, categorising e-mail messages into new folders, evaluating search engine results according to a set of criteria, completing a multi-step consumer request using a website and e-mail, and evaluating multiple websites to identify the most trustworthy site.

At Level 3, adults can complete tasks involving multiple applications, a large number of steps, occasional impasses, and the discovery and use of ad hoc commands in a novel environment. The tasks that are rated at this level involve evaluating search engine results with a set of criteria, solving a scheduling problem by combining information from an Internet application and several e-mail messages, determining the proper folder destination for categorising a subset of e-mail messages, and transforming information in an e-mail message into a spreadsheet and performing computations with it.

Further information about the overall design and administration of the Survey of Adult Skills is provided on page 15 of this report and in chapter 3 of *The Survey of Adult Skills: Reader's Companion* (OECD, 2013b). A sample task that was used during field testing is described in Box 2.2.

INFORMATION ON ADULTS WHO LACK BASIC ICT SKILLS

Some adults were not able to demonstrate their proficiency in problem solving in technology-rich environments because they lacked the basic computer skills necessary to sit the assessment. Given its nature, the assessment must be delivered on a computer. Unlike the assessments of literacy and numeracy, respondents could not complete the assessment using a paper test booklet. Thus, estimates of the proficiency in this domain are available only for those adults who completed the assessment on computer.

There are three main reasons why some respondents did not complete the assessment on computer and, thus, did not have a score in problem solving using ICT. First, some adults indicated in the background questionnaire that they had never used a computer. Second, among the adults who had used a computer, some did not pass the ICT core test, which was designed to assess whether respondents had sufficient skill in the use of computers and computer networks (including the ability to use a mouse, type, scroll through text, highlight text, use drag and drop functionality, and use pull-down menus) to complete the assessment on a computer. Third, a number of respondents opted to complete the assessment in its paper-based format rather than on a computer without first taking the ICT core test.

Opting out of the computer-based assessment may reflect either respondents' lack of familiarity with computers, their unwillingness to use a computer for an assessment, or different field work practices across countries. The technical standards guiding the design and implementation of the survey (PIAAC, 2011) offered countries no guidance on the procedure to be followed in the event that a respondent expressed a preference to complete the assessment using pencil and paper without first taking the ICT core test. As a result, it is possible that practices in managing this situation varied among countries and among interviewers within countries. The existence of the "opt-out" group (for more information about this group, see Box 2.1) thus adds some uncertainty to both the estimates of the proportions of adults with very poor computer skills (i.e. those who could not meet the minimum requirements for completing the test on computer) and the proportion of adults at the different levels of proficiency in problem solving in technology-rich environments.

Thus, the Survey of Adult Skills provides two different pieces of information about the ability of adults to manage information using ICT. The first is the proportion of adults who have or do not have sufficient familiarity with computers to use them to perform information-processing tasks. The second is the level of proficiency in solving problems commonly encountered in work and everyday life in a technology-rich world. The various pathways through the assessment and the proportions of adults taking these pathways are presented in Figure 2.1.

▪ Figure 2.1 ▪

Pathways to completing the Survey of Adult Skills

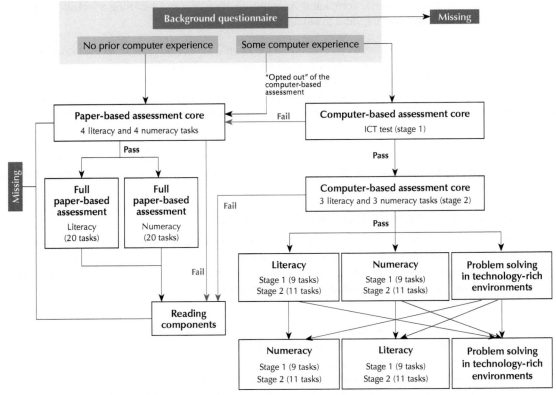

StatLink ⟨⟩ http://dx.doi.org/10.1787/888933231498

Box 2.1 **Adults who "opted out" of taking the computer-based assessment**

Some respondents decided to take the paper-and-pencil version of the assessment rather than taking the computer-based assessment on their own initiative. These individuals also did not take a simple test of their ability to use the basic functionality required to take the full computer-based assessment (the ICT core test). Information about their level of computer proficiency is therefore unknown, as is their ability to solve problems using ICT devices, since this assessment was only computer-based. Nevertheless, a range of information collected through the background questionnaire provides some indication about the characteristics of those who opted out of the computer-based assessment, as well as information suggesting differences in field practices in certain countries related to opting out.

As shown in Figure "a" in Box 2.10 of the first international report (OECD, 2013a), respondents who opted out of the computer-based assessment are more likely to be older (45+), have lower educational attainment, and work in semi-skilled blue-collar or white-collar occupations, and they are less likely to use ICT in everyday life. This group shares similar characteristics with the adults who failed the ICT core test, though they are even more likely to be older and even less likely to use ICT in everyday life than the adults who failed the ICT core test. This suggests that lack of familiarity with computers might have influenced their decision to take the assessment on paper, even if they might have had the skills to take the computer-based assessment.

In some countries, the proportion of adults opting out of the computer-based assessment is substantially larger than it is in other countries. As shown in Figure "a" below, more than 15% of adults opted out of the computer-based assessment in Estonia, Ireland, Japan and Poland. In some of these countries, an unexpectedly large proportion of adults opted out of the computer-based assessment from the subgroups of the population that, in other countries, generally have low rates of opting out. This is particularly true in Poland, where 28% of adults who scored at Level 4 or 5 in literacy, 18% of adults who frequently use e-mail outside of work, 19% of adults with tertiary education, and 12% of young adults opted out of the computer-based assessment. Ireland and Japan also show similar patterns. These results suggest that in these countries, the field practices used to encourage adults to take the computer-based assessment may have

...

functioned differently than in other countries. As a result, the estimates of proficiency in solving problems in technology-rich environments may be biased in these countries because some adults who could have taken the computer-based assessment chose to take the paper-and-pencil version instead.

■ Figure 2.a ■

Percentage of adults who opted out of taking the computer-based assessment, by various characteristics

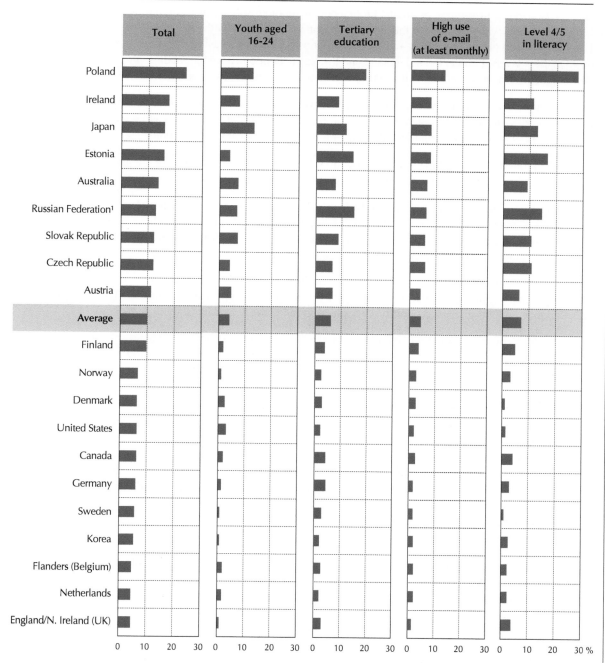

1. See note at the end of this chapter.
Countries are ranked in descending order of the percentage of adults who opted out of taking the computer-based assessment.
Source: Survey of Adults Skills (PIAAC) (2012), Table B2.1 in Annex B.

StatLink ᵐˢᵖ http://dx.doi.org/10.1787/888933231556

PROFICIENCY ACROSS COUNTRIES

Given the variation, across countries, in the proportion of adults who were able and willing to complete the assessment in problem solving in technology-rich environments, results of the assessment are presented in terms of the proportions of adults who perform at the four levels of proficiency rather than by mean scores. There is no information on proficiency for three groups of adults: those who have no computer experience; those who have some computer experience but "opted out" of taking the computer-based assessment; and those who agreed to complete the computer-based assessment but failed the ICT core test that assesses basic computer skills.

Figure 2.2 provides an overview of adults' proficiency in problem solving in technology-rich environments and the proportion of adults without scores in this domain. Countries are ranked by the proportion of adults who are proficient at Level 2 or 3. The Nordic countries and the Netherlands stand out as having the largest proportions of adults who perform at these levels. Estonia, Ireland, Poland and the Slovak Republic have the smallest proportions. Even in the best-performing countries, less than half of the adult population has skills at these levels.

Figure 2.3 shows the proportions of adults attaining Level 2 or 3 across countries, indicating where the differences between countries are statistically significant. The proportion of adults at these levels is significantly larger in Sweden than in any other country, and is significantly smaller in Poland than in any other country.

Nearly one in four adults across participating countries was not able or willing to take the assessment on a computer. Even in the Nordic countries, one in seven adults did not take the assessment on a computer.

On average, 8% of adults indicate that they had no prior experience with computers. The Nordic countries, along with Australia, Canada, the Netherlands, the United Kingdom and the United States, show the smallest proportions of adults with no computer experience, ranging from 1% to 5%. Korea, Poland and the Slovak Republic have much larger proportions of adults with no computer experience, ranging from 15.5% to 22%.

Some 4.9% of adults, on average, had poor computer skills and failed the ICT core test. Japan and Korea have the largest proportions of the population in this category (11% and 9%, respectively), while the Czech Republic and the Slovak Republic had the smallest proportion of adults who failed the ICT core test (both 2.2%).

On average, 9.9% of adults opted out and did not participate in the assessment of problem solving in technology-rich environments. The opt-out rate was more than 14% in Estonia, Ireland, Japan and Poland and was less than 6% in England/N. Ireland (UK), Flanders (Belgium), Korea, the Netherlands and Sweden.

DIFFERENCES IN FREQUENCY OF ICT USE

In addition to assessing proficiency in problem solving in technology-rich environments, the Survey of Adult Skills collected a range of information about how adults use ICT devices and applications. Information was sought on the frequency with which respondents used common applications (e-mail, the Internet, word processing and spreadsheets) or engaged in certain activities, such as programming or participating in real-time interactions, such as chat sessions, both at and outside of work. This chapter focuses on using ICT in daily life outside of work, covering both respondents who work and those who do not.[2] The analysis focuses on the use of e-mail, the Internet (either to understand issues or to conduct transactions), spreadsheets and word processing because they are closely related to the types of tasks that are included in the assessment of problem solving in technology-rich environments.

Figure 2.4 shows the average frequency with which adults use[3] e-mail, the Internet (both to understand issues and to conduct transactions), spreadsheets and word processing in their daily lives outside of work across participating countries.[4] Not surprisingly, the two most frequently occurring practices are using e-mail and using the Internet to understand issues, with over two-thirds of respondents across participating OECD countries using these applications at least once a month. On average, almost half of respondents across participating OECD countries reported they use e-mail daily in their private life (Table A2.4a). Adults use these technologies less frequently for the other activities. More than one in two reported they use the Internet to conduct transactions at least once a month. Roughly two in five respondents use ICT for word processing in their daily lives at least once a month, and around one in five use spreadsheets that often.

In some countries, monthly use of e-mail and the Internet is approaching universality. In the Nordic countries and the Netherlands, over 80% of adults use e-mail at least once a month and over 70% use the Internet, to understand issues and conduct transactions, with similar frequency (Tables A2.4a, b and c). In contrast, in Japan less than 50% of adults use e-mail or use the Internet to understand issues, and less than 30% use the Internet to conduct transactions at least once a month (Tables A2.4a, b and c). Korea, Poland and the Slovak Republic also show infrequent use: around 60% of adults or less use e-mail and the Internet (to understand issues) at least once a month, and less than 40% of adults in Poland and the Slovak Republic use the Internet to conduct transactions at least once a month (Tables A2.4a, b and c).

▪ Figure 2.2 ▪

Proficiency in problem solving in technology-rich environments

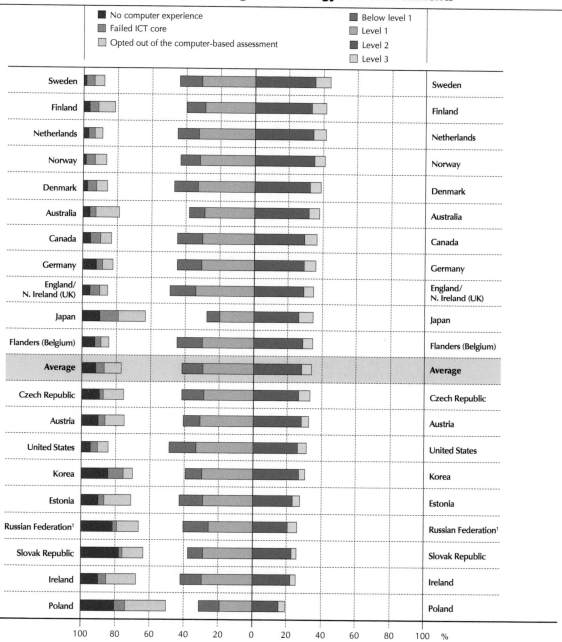

1. See note at the end of this chapter.

Countries are ranked in descending order of the percentage of adults scoring at Level 2 or 3 in problem solving in technology-rich environments.

Source: Survey of Adult Skills (PIAAC) (2012), Table A2.2.

StatLink ᴍꜱᴾ http://dx.doi.org/10.1787/888933231500

▪ Figure 2.3 ▪

Country comparison of proficiency in problem solving in technology-rich environments

Percentage of adults scoring at Level 2 or 3

Significantly **above** the average
Not significantly different from the average
Significantly **below** the average

%	Comparison country	Countries whose % is NOT significantly different from the comparison country
44	Sweden	
42	Finland	Netherlands, Norway
42	Netherlands	Finland, Norway
41	Norway	Finland, Netherlands
39	Denmark	Australia
38	Australia	Canada, Denmark, Germany
37	Canada	Australia, Germany, England/N. Ireland (UK)
36	Germany	Australia, Canada, Japan, Flanders (Belgium), England/N. Ireland (UK)
35	England/N. Ireland (UK)	Canada, Czech Republic, Germany, Japan, Flanders (Belgium)
35	Japan	Austria, Czech Republic, Germany, Flanders (Belgium), England/N. Ireland (UK)
35	Flanders (Belgium)	Austria, Czech Republic, Germany, Japan, England/N. Ireland (UK)
34	Average	Austria, Czech Republic, Japan, Flanders (Belgium), England/N. Ireland (UK)
33	Czech Republic	Austria, Japan, Korea, United States, Flanders (Belgium), England/N. Ireland (UK)
32	Austria	Czech Republic, Japan, Korea, United States, Flanders (Belgium)
31	United States	Austria, Czech Republic, Korea
30	Korea	Austria, Czech Republic, United States, Russian Federation[1]
28	Estonia	Slovak Republic, Russian Federation[1]
26	Russian Federation[1]	Estonia, Ireland, Korea, Slovak Republic
26	Slovak Republic	Estonia, Ireland, Russian Federation[1]
25	Ireland	Slovak Republic, Russian Federation[1]
19	Poland	

1. See note at the end of this chapter.
Countries are ranked in descending order of the percentage of adults scoring at Level 2 or 3 in problem solving in technology-rich environments.
Source: Survey of Adult Skills (PIAAC) (2012), Table A2.3.

StatLink ▪▪▪ http://dx.doi.org/10.1787/888933231513

The estimates from the Survey of Adult Skills regarding ICT use for e-mail and Internet transactions are in line with data from other sources, such as Eurostat. Figure 2.6 compares data from the survey and from Eurostat on the frequency with which adults in the EU countries that participated in the Survey of Adult Skills use e-mail and the Internet to conduct transactions.

▪ Figure 2.4 ▪

Using information technologies in everyday life

Percentage of users of ICT applications in everyday life at least once a month (country average*)

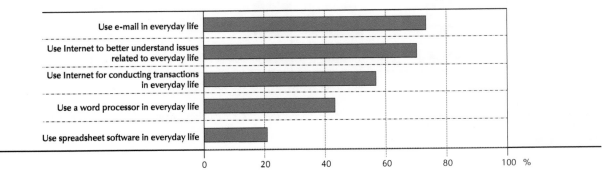

* Country average: average of 19 participating OECD countries and entities.
Source: Survey of Adult Skills (PIAAC)(2012), Tables A2.4a, b, c, d and e.

StatLink ▪▪▪ http://dx.doi.org/10.1787/888933231525

PROFICIENCY AND ICT ACCESS AND USE

While the assessment of problem solving in technology-rich environments measures more than the skill in using ICT devices and applications, one would expect a close relationship between proficiency in this domain and access to and use of ICT. Access to ICT devices and networks makes it possible for adults to use them, and frequent use of ICT is likely to help in developing proficiency in the domain. At the same time, greater proficiency in these skills is likely to encourage more frequent use of ICT, which, in turn, is likely to prompt investments to increase access. Chapter 5 of this report offers some policy pointers to consider in increasing access to ICT for the general public.

Figure 2.5 looks at the relationship between proficiency in problem solving in technology-rich environments and ICT access and use at the country level. The first panel compares the proportion of adults who score at proficiency Level 2 or 3 to the proportion of households with Internet access, by country. The comparison suggests that Internet access explains about two-fifths of the variation in proficiency across countries. The second panel then compares the proportion of adults who score at proficiency Level 2 or 3 to the proportion of adults who use e-mail at least once a month. It shows that monthly use of e-mail explains about three-fifths of the variation in proficiency across countries. When considering ICT access and e-mail use together, these variables explain 70% of the variation in proficiency across countries. The measures of access and use are closely correlated with country performance in problem solving in technology-rich environments, even though the assessment measures much more than adults' familiarity with computers.

▪ Figure 2.5 ▪

Relationship between proficiency in problem solving in technology-rich environments and access to or use of ICT

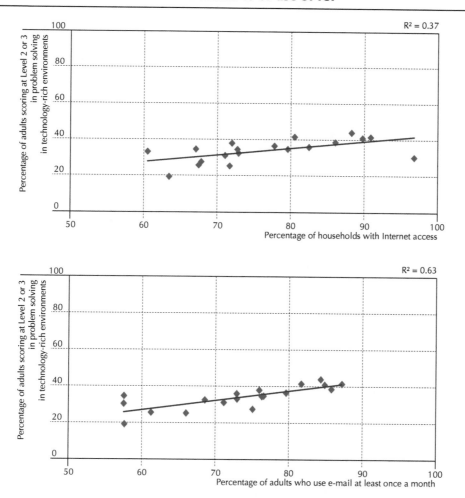

Source: Survey of Adult Skills (PIAAC) (2012) and OECD, ICT Database and Eurostat, Community Survey on ICT usage in housholds and by individuals, November 2011. See Tables A2.1 and A2.5.

StatLink 🔗 http://dx.doi.org/10.1787/888933231538

■ Figure 2.6 ■

Relationship between ICT use in the Survey of Adult Skills and in the Eurostat Community Survey

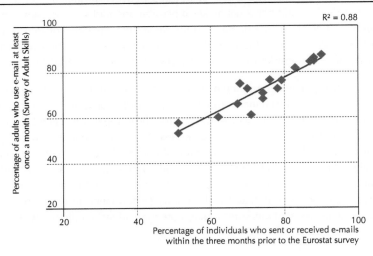

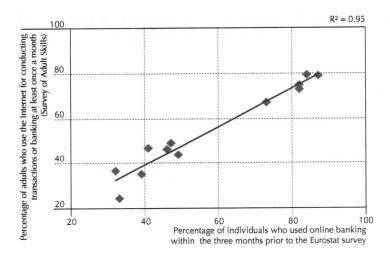

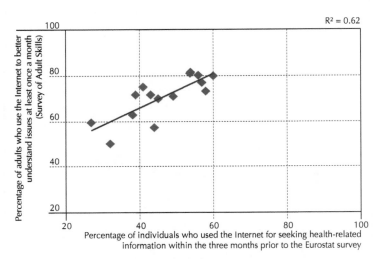

Source: Survey of Adult Skills (PIAAC) (2012), Eurostat Community Survey on ICT usage in households and by individuals. See Tables B1.5, B1.6 and B2.2 in Annex B and Tables A2.4a, b and c.

StatLink ᴍᴤᴤ▸ http://dx.doi.org/10.1787/888933231542

Box 2.2 **Sample task in problem solving in technology-rich environments**

An example of a problem-solving item is provided below. This item involves a scenario in which the respondent assumes the role of a job-seeker. Respondents access and evaluate information relating to job search in a simulated web environment. This environment includes tools and functionalities similar to those found in real-life applications. Users are able to:

- click on links on both the results page and associated web pages;
- navigate, using the back and forward arrows or the Home icon; and
- bookmark web pages and view or change those bookmarks.

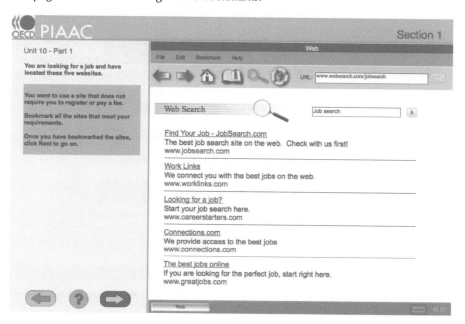

The first test figure presented above is the results page of the search-engine application, which lists five employment agency websites. To complete the task successfully, respondents have to search through the pages of the listed websites to identify whether registration or the payment of a fee is required in order to gain further information about available jobs. Respondents can click on the links on the search page to be directed to the websites identified. For example, by clicking on the "Work Links" link, the respondent is directed to the home page of "Work Links".

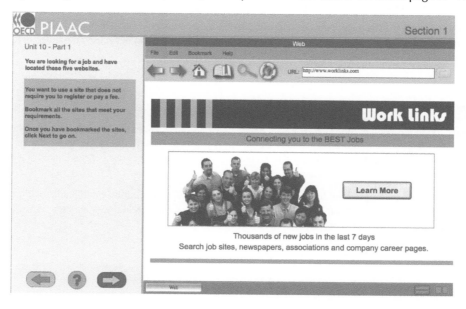

...

In order to discover whether access to the information on available jobs requires registration with the organisation or payment of a fee, the respondent must click the "Learn More" button which opens the following page. The respondent must then return to the search results page to continue evaluating the sites in terms of the specified criteria, using the back arrows without bookmarking the page (correct answer) or having bookmarked the page (incorrect answer).

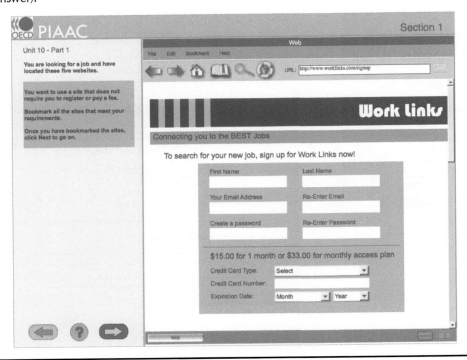

Notes

1. See notes regarding Cyprus below.

2. The discussion in Chapter 4 on proficiency in problem solving in technology-rich environments at work examines responses to the questions related to the use of ICT at work.

3. Respondents who have never used a computer were not asked about the frequency with which they use different ICT applications. The analysis assumes that those respondents who have never used a computer have also never used the different ICT applications.

4. Country-specific figures are available in Tables A2.4a, b, c, d and e.

Notes regarding Cyprus

Note by Turkey: The information in this document with reference to "Cyprus" relates to the southern part of the Island. There is no single authority representing both Turkish and Greek Cypriot people on the Island. Turkey recognises the Turkish Republic of Northern Cyprus (TRNC). Until a lasting and equitable solution is found within the context of the United Nations, Turkey shall preserve its position concerning the "Cyprus issue".

Note by all the European Union Member States of the OECD and the European Union: The Republic of Cyprus is recognised by all members of the United Nations with the exception of Turkey. The information in this document relates to the area under the effective control of the Government of the Republic of Cyprus.

A note regarding the Russian Federation

Readers should note that the sample for the Russian Federation does not include the population of the Moscow municipal area. The data published, therefore, do not represent the entire resident population aged 16-65 in Russia but rather the population of Russia *excluding* the population residing in the Moscow municipal area.

More detailed information regarding the data from the Russian Federation as well as that of other countries can be found in the *Technical Report of the Survey of Adult Skills* (OECD, 2014).

References

OECD (2014), *Technical Report of the Survey of Adult Skills*, *www.oecd.org/site/piaac/_Technical%20Report_17OCT13.pdf*, pre-publication copy.

OECD (2013a), *OECD Skills Outlook 2013: First Results from the Survey of Adult Skills*, OECD Publishing, Paris, *http://dx.doi.org/10.1787/9789264204256-en*.

OECD (2013b), *The Survey of Adult Skills: Reader's Companion*, OECD Publishing, Paris, *http://dx.doi.org/10.1787/9789264204027-en*.

OECD (2012), *Literacy, Numeracy and Problem Solving in Technology-Rich Environments: Framework for the OECD Survey of Adult Skills*, OECD Publishing, Paris, *http://dx.doi.org/10.1787/9789264128859-en*.

PIAAC (2011), *PIAAC Technical Standards and Guidelines*, OECD Programme for the International Assessment of Adult Competencies [PIAAC].

3

Differences within countries in proficiency in problem solving in technology-rich environments

This chapter explores the ways in which proficiency in problem solving in technology-rich environments varies within countries across various socio-demographic groups. It looks at differences in proficiency related to age, education, gender, parents' education, immigrant and language background, and participation in adult education and training. In addition, the chapter examines the association among proficiency in these skills, the use of ICT, and literacy proficiency.

With the widespread diffusion of information and communication technologies (ICT) in all areas of life, the ability to manage information in digital environments and solve problems that involve the use of digital devices, applications and networks is becoming essential for adults of all ages. This chapter examines the relationships between different socio-demographic characteristics and proficiency in problem solving in technology-rich environments, as measured by the 2012 Survey of Adult Skills, a product of the OECD Programme for the International Assessment of Adult Competencies (PIAAC). The analyses help to identify the groups that are most likely to encounter difficulties in using ICT to solve problems. This information can then be used to inform government policies that aim to develop these specific skills in particular segments of the population. In addition, some of the characteristics examined – such as those related to education, participation in adult education and training, and ICT use – provide insights into the types of activities that are likely to lead to better performance in problem solving using ICT. Chapter 5 explores the policy implications of these different relationships.

Of the eight characteristics examined, six are strongly related to the probability of being highly proficient in problem solving in technology-rich environments (Figure 3.1). In particular, being highly proficient in literacy, being younger, having a parent with tertiary qualifications, having tertiary qualifications oneself, being a regular user of ICT, and participating in adult education and training are all strongly associated with the probability of performing at high levels in the problem-solving assessment. Men are found to have a small advantage over women in these skills. The observed differences in proficiency related to immigrant and language background are not significant across OECD countries; however, there are significant differences within some countries.

Key findings

- Literacy proficiency and age have the strongest relationships to proficiency in problem solving in technology-rich environments. Educational attainment and ICT use are strongly related to proficiency, after accounting for other factors.

- Gender is weakly related to proficiency in problem solving in technology-rich environments, while immigrant and language background do not have a significant relationship with proficiency in technology-rich environments, after accounting for other factors.

- Age and educational attainment both have a strong relationship with whether or not an adult has experience using a computer.

When adjustments are made to take account of the impact of other factors, the relationships between many of the characteristics and performance in this domain weaken considerably.[1] However, age and literacy proficiency are still associated with large differences in proficiency. Even when other characteristics are taken into account, a person scoring at Level 4 or 5 on the literacy scale of the Survey of Adult Skills is 69 percentage points more likely to be highly proficient in problem solving in technology-rich environments than someone who scores at Level 2 on the literacy scale. Similarly, a 16-24 year-old is 28 percentage points more likely than a 55-65 year-old to be perform at a high level in the problem-solving domain.

Each of the characteristics, except gender and immigrant and language background, is also associated with the probability of having no computer experience (Figure 3.2).[2] However, when other socio-demographic characteristics and literacy proficiency are taken into account, only age and educational attainment are strongly related to the probability that an adult has no experience in using computers. After accounting for other variables, literacy is not strongly related to computer use.

PROFICIENCY IN PROBLEM SOLVING IN TECHNOLOGY-RICH ENVIRONMENTS, AND COMPUTER EXPERIENCE, RELATED TO VARIOUS SOCIO-DEMOGRAPHIC CHARACTERISTICS

Differences related to age

The personal computer and the Internet have been widely used only since the 1990s. Consequently, different cohorts of individuals were first exposed to these technologies at very different ages. These cohorts first developed skills in using these technologies under different conditions (if at all), and tend to have somewhat different relationships with the technologies. In most of the countries that participated in the Survey of Adult Skills, 16-24 year-olds can be considered to be "digital natives", in that they were brought up in an environment in which digital technologies were in widespread use in homes and in school. At the other extreme, most adults aged 55-65 were first exposed to these technologies in their 30s, at the earliest. Given that familiarity with ICT is a precondition for displaying proficiency in problem solving in technology-rich environments, it would be expected that there are strong age-related differences in proficiency in these skills, and that the differences would be greatest in countries in which diffusion of digital technologies has been slowest.

■ Figure 3.1 ■

Differences in problem solving in technology-rich environments proficiency between various groups

Percentage differences between groups of adults who score at Level 2 or 3 in problem solving in technology-rich environments, before and after accounting for various characteristics

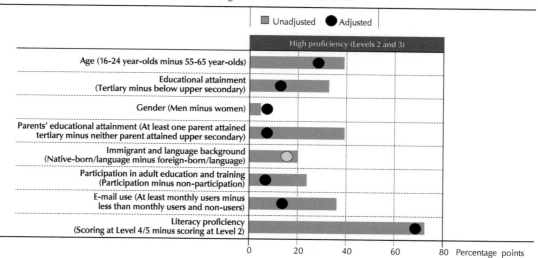

Note: Adjusted results include controls for age, educational attainment, gender, parents' educational attainment, immigrant and language background, participation in adult education and training, e-mail use, and literacy proficiency. Statistically significant differences are marked in a darker tone. Results for each country are available in Table B3.3 in Annex B.

Source: Survey of Adult Skills (PIAAC) (2012), Table A3.1

StatLink ⟨⟩ http://dx.doi.org/10.1787/888933231566

■ Figure 3.2 ■

Differences in computer experience between various groups

Percentage differences between various groups of adults who have no computer experience, before and after accounting for various characteristics

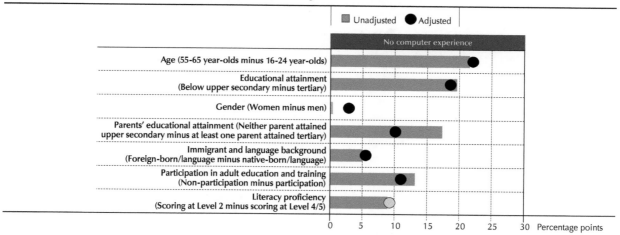

Note: Adjusted results include controls for age, educational attainment, gender, parents' educational attainment, immigrant and language background, participation in adult education and training (AET), and literacy proficiency. Statistically significant differences are marked in a darker tone. Results for each country are available in Table B3.5 in Annex B.

Source: Survey of Adult Skills (PIAAC) (2012), Table A3.2

StatLink ⟨⟩ http://dx.doi.org/10.1787/888933231577

As expected, there is a strong correlation between age and proficiency in problem solving in technology-rich environments across participating countries. At the same time, the strength of the correlation varies considerably across countries. On average, 51% of 16-24 year-olds, but only 12% of 55-65 year-olds, perform at Level 2 or 3 in the domain, a difference of 39 percentage points (Figure 3.3). The gap between the youngest and oldest age groups ranges from 18 percentage points in the United States to 59 percentage points in Korea. Between countries, there is also greater variation in proficiency among the youngest adults than among the oldest. For example, the proportion of 16-24 year-olds who score at Level 2 or 3 ranges from 38% (the United States) to 63% (Korea), while the proportion of 55-65 year-olds who perform at those levels ranges from only 3% (Poland) to 20% (the United States).

Denmark, Finland, the Netherlands, Norway and Sweden have larger proportions of adults who score at Level 2 or 3 in problem solving in technology-rich environments, with larger proportions of adults of all age groups who score at these levels compared to the average. This suggests that most adults in these countries generally had better opportunities to develop these skills, regardless of their age. By contrast, in some other countries, some of the age groups have relatively smaller proportions of adults who score at Level 2 or 3, which pulls down the country average. For example, despite the fact that Korea has the largest proportion of young adults who perform at Level 2 or 3 in the domain (63%), Korea has a smaller-than-average proportion of adults who perform at those levels. This largely reflects the fact that only a tiny proportion (4%) of 55-65 year-old Koreans perform at Level 2 or 3 (the second smallest proportion after that observed in Poland). By contrast, the United States has the largest proportion of 55-65 year-olds who score at Level 2 or 3, but the smallest proportion of 16-24 year-olds who score at those levels.

Computer experience is also related to age. On average, less than 1% of 16-24 year-olds, but 22% of 55-65 year-olds, have no experience with computers (Figure 3.3). The gap between the two age groups ranges from only 5 percentage points in Norway and Sweden to over 50 percentage points in Korea. The variation across countries is much larger among members of the oldest group than among members of the youngest group. The chance that a 16-24 year-old has no computer experience is less than 5% in all countries, whereas the probability that a 55-65 year-old has no computer experience ranges from 5% in Sweden to 52% in Korea.

In most countries, only a small proportion of the youngest cohort does not have computer experience, except for the Slovak Republic, where 4.8% of 16-24 year-olds lack computer experience compared to the average of 0.8% across participating OECD countries. However, large proportions of the oldest age group have no computer experience. Across countries, except Denmark, the Netherlands, Norway and Sweden, more than 10% of adults in oldest age group lack computer experience. In Korea, more than one in two 55-65 year-olds do not have computer experience, nor do more than 45% of adults that age in Poland and the Slovak Republic.

■ Figure 3.3 ■

Problem-solving proficiency and computer experience, by age

Percentage of adults who score at Level 2 or 3 in problem solving in technology-rich environments or have no computer experience

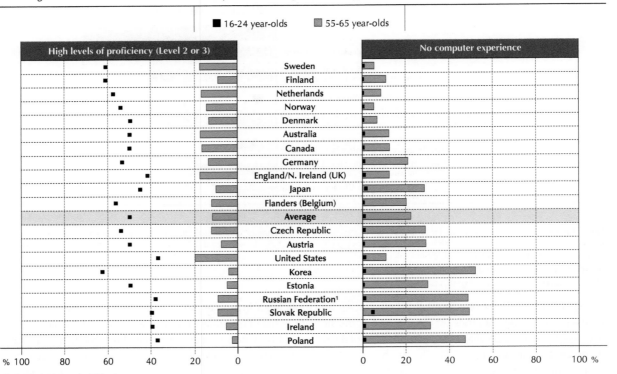

1. See note at the end of this chapter.
Countries are ranked in descending order of the percentage of adults aged 16-65 scoring at Level 2 or 3 in problem solving in technology-rich environments.
Source: Survey of Adult Skills (PIAAC) (2012), Table A3.3.
StatLink ━━ http://dx.doi.org/10.1787/888933231586

Differences related to educational attainment

Given that many types of skills, including problem-solving skills, are developed in formal education, it is reasonable to expect that higher levels of education will be associated with higher levels of proficiency in problem solving in technology-rich environments. However, a positive association between education and proficiency in these skills does not mean that formal education is directly responsible for the higher levels of proficiency observed. It is also likely that adults with higher levels of education have other experiences, such as work in particular occupations or training opportunities later on, that have a more direct impact on proficiency in this domain.

On average, an adult with tertiary education is 33 percentage points more likely than an adult with less than secondary education to perform at Level 2 or 3 in the assessment of problem solving in technology-rich environments (Figure 3.4). However, there are large variations in this difference across countries, ranging from less than 20 percentage points in Estonia to over 40 percentage points in the Netherlands and the United Kingdom.

Educational attainment is also correlated with computer experience. On average, adults with less formal education are more likely to lack experience with computers than those with more education. Only 1% of adults with tertiary education lack experience with computers compared to 21% of those with less than secondary education. The difference between high- and low-educated adults in the probability that they have no experience with computers ranges from 4 percentage points in Norway to 49 percentage points in the Slovak Republic. In every country, few adults with tertiary education lack computer experience. The largest differences between countries are thus found in the proportion of adults with less than secondary education who have no experience with computers. The countries with fewer of these adults are generally also the countries with larger proportions of adults who perform at Level 2 or 3 in problem solving in technology-rich environments.

▪ Figure 3.4 ▪

Problem-solving proficiency and computer experience, by educational attainment

Percentage of adults who score at Level 2 or 3 in problem solving in technology-rich environments or have no computer experience

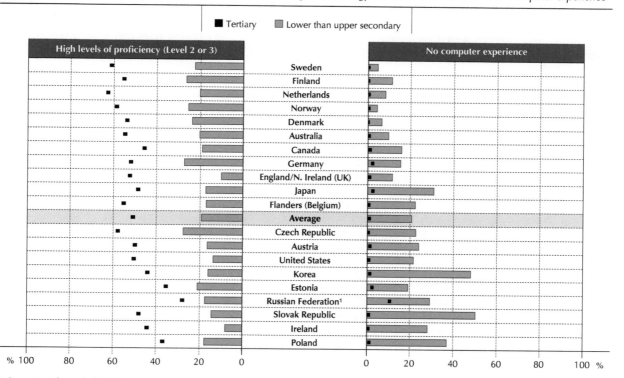

1. See note at the end of this chapter.
Countries are ranked in descending order of the percentage of adults aged 16-65 scoring at Level 2 or 3 in problem solving in technology-rich environments.
Source: Survey of Adult Skills (PIAAC) (2012), Table A3.4.

StatLink ⫘ http://dx.doi.org/10.1787/888933231590

Differences related to adult education and training

Adult education and training, like compulsory education, can provide opportunities to develop proficiency in problem solving in technology-rich environments. For example, many adults are likely to have had at least some training in the use of word-processing software or spreadsheets that would then have an impact on their performance in the problem solving in technology-rich environments assessment, although the type of training would largely depend on adults' occupations and individual needs. It is also likely that people who are more proficient in these skills will avail themselves of learning opportunities through adult education and training. The Survey of Adult Skills found that, on average across participating OECD countries, 52% of respondents had participated in adult education and training in the year prior to the survey.[3]

Not surprisingly, recent participation in adult education and training activities is associated with greater proficiency in problem solving in technology-rich environments. Across OECD countries, 42% of adults who participated in adult education and training during the previous year were proficient at Level 2 or 3 in this domain, compared to only 18% of adults who had not participated in adult education and training during that period (Table B3.6).

Adult education and training is also associated with computer experience. Only 3% of adults who had recently participated in adult education and training activities lack computer experience compared to 16% of those who had not recently participated in such activities (Table B3.6). Across countries, only a small proportion of adults who had recently participated in adult education and training lack computer experience, from near zero in Sweden to 7% in Korea and the Slovak Republic. There is a much wider variation among countries in the proportion of adults who had not recently participated in adult education and training and who have no computer experience: from 4% in Norway to 34% in the Slovak Republic.

Differences related to gender

Surveys commonly find that men use computers somewhat more frequently than women do. For example, Eurostat found that, in 2011, 77% of men aged 16-74 used a computer in the 12 months prior to the survey compared to 73% of women that age.[4] Given that proficiency in problem solving in technology-rich environments requires basic computer skills, it would not be surprising if there were some differences between men's and women's performance in the domain that are similar to the modest differences in men's and women's rates of computer use. In the PISA 2012 problem-solving assessment, which was delivered exclusively in computer-based format, 15-year-old boys had a slight advantage (of 7 score points) over girls (OECD, 2013b).

Indeed, in the 2012 Survey of Adult Skills, men perform slightly better than women in problem solving in technology-rich environments. On average across OECD countries, the proportion of men who are proficient at Level 2 or 3 in this domain is 5 percentage points bigger than that of women (Figure 3.5). In all participating countries, a larger share of men than women performs at these levels, but the differences are not statistically significant in all cases. The largest gender difference (11 percentage points) is observed in Japan. Interestingly, in countries that are most proficient in these skills, men's performance advantage over women is larger than average. Among young adults aged 16-24, there is virtually no difference, on average, in the proportions of men and women who are proficient at Level 2 or 3 in problem solving in technology-rich environments (Table A3.5).

Men and women who participated in the 2012 Survey of Adult Skills reported similar levels of experience with computers.[5] On average across OECD countries, the proportion of women who lack computer experience is slightly larger (0.4 percentage points) than the proportion of men who do (Figure 3.5). In roughly half of the participating countries, men are more likely than women to have no computer experience, while the reverse is true in the remainder of the countries. In Austria, the Czech Republic, Germany, Japan and Korea, more women than men reported that they have no computer experience, though in none of those countries is the gap larger than 5 percentage points. In Estonia, Ireland and Poland, men were more likely than women to report that they have no computer experience, but again the difference is small (between 2 and 4 percentage points). There is almost no gender difference, in any country, in the likelihood that a 16-24 year-old has no experience in using a computer (Table A3.5).

▪ Figure 3.5 ▪

Problem-solving proficiency and computer experience, by gender

Percentage of adults who score at Level 2 or 3 in problem solving in technology-rich environments or have no computer experience

■ Men   ▢ Women

High levels of proficiency (Level 2 or 3)		No computer experience
	Sweden	
	Finland	
	Netherlands	
	Norway	
	Denmark	
	Australia	
	Canada	
	Germany	
	England/N. Ireland (UK)	
	Japan	
	Flanders (Belgium)	
	Average	
	Czech Republic	
	Austria	
	United States	
	Korea	
	Estonia	
	Russian Federation¹	
	Slovak Republic	
	Ireland	
	Poland	

% 100 80 60 40 20 0   0 20 40 60 80 100 %

1. See note at the end of this chapter.
Countries are ranked in descending order of the percentage of adults aged 16-65 scoring at Level 2 or 3 in problem solving in technology-rich environments.
Source: Survey of Adult Skills (PIAAC) (2012), Table A3.5.
StatLink ⬛🔢 http://dx.doi.org/10.1787/888933231605

Differences related to socio-economic status

Given that socio-economic status has a significant impact on many life outcomes, policy makers need to understand the relationship between socio-economic status and skills development and consider whether that relationship reflects inequities in opportunities that could be addressed by policy. The Survey of Adult Skills uses parents' education as an indicator of the socio-economic status of respondents. In the literacy and numeracy domains, the survey revealed a statistically significant difference of about 40 score points between adults with at least one parent who had attained tertiary education and adults with neither parent having attained upper secondary education (OECD 2013a, Table A3.6[L]).

There is a strong correlation between parents' education and the probability that an adult performs at Level 2 or 3 in problem solving in technology-rich environments. On average across OECD countries, the share of adults who are proficient at these levels is 38 percentage points larger among those with at least one parent who had attained tertiary education than it is among adults with neither parent having attained upper secondary education (Table B3.7). The differences in these proportions range from 30 percentage points in Australia to 52 percentage points in the Czech Republic.

There is also a strong correlation between parents' education and computer experience. On average, adults with at least one parent who had attained tertiary education are 17 percentage points less likely to lack computer experience than adults with neither parent having attained upper secondary education (Table B3.7). The size of this gap varies substantially across countries, from 3 percentage points in Norway and Sweden to 50 percentage points in the Slovak Republic. Across all countries, few adults with at least one parent who attained tertiary education lack computer experience; so most of the between-country variation in computer experience associated with parents' education comes from disparities in experience with computers among adults with neither parent having attained upper secondary education.

Differences related to immigrant and language background

In most of the countries that participated in the Survey of Adult Skills, a significant share of the population is of foreign origin; in many cases, immigrants represent over 10% of the total population of these countries. Immigrants often face special challenges in developing information-processing skills in the language(s) of their country of residence. On average, immigrants who did not speak the language of their host country in their childhood have lower proficiency in literacy than native-born, native-language adults (OECD 2013a, Table A3.15 [L]). Policy makers need to understand how well – or poorly – immigrants can manage information in digital environments, in the language(s) of their country of residence, so that sufficient assistance is offered to enable immigrants to integrate more smoothly into the labour market and into society more broadly.

Information about immigrant and language background is combined in the analysis of their relationship with proficiency in problem solving in technology-rich environments. In all countries, most adults were born in-country ("native-born") and most grew up speaking the language(s) in which the survey was delivered ("native language"). Across participating OECD countries, 86% of adults fall into the category "native-born, native language" (OECD 2013a, Table B3.11). The next-largest group is composed of adults who migrated into the country ("foreign-born") and did not grow up speaking the language(s) in which the survey was delivered ("foreign language"). On average, 7% of adults fall into this category, "foreign-born, foreign language". The remainder of adults can be classified into two other categories: adults born in-country who did not grow up speaking the language(s) of the survey ("native-born, foreign language"), and immigrants who grew up speaking the language(s) of the survey ("foreign-born, native language"). These groups represent 2% and 4% of the adult population, respectively, across participating OECD countries. There is substantial variation in these proportions across countries, however. For example, the size of the foreign-born, foreign-language population ranges from near zero in Poland and Japan to 17% in Canada.

Immigrant and language background is correlated with the probability of performing at Level 2 or 3 in the problem solving in technology-rich environments assessment, and this correlation is significant. Some 36% of native-born, native-language adults are proficient at Level 2 or 3 in the domain compared to 17% of foreign-born, foreign-language adults (Figure 3.6). The difference in the proportions of native-born, native-language adults and foreign-born, foreign-language adults who perform at those levels ranges from 5 percentage points in Ireland to 31 percentage points in Sweden. There is much greater between-country variation in the proportion of native-born, native-language adults who are proficient at Level 2 or 3 than there is in the proportion of foreign-born, foreign-language adults who perform at these levels. For example, foreign-born, foreign-language adults in Ireland and Sweden have very similar chances of performing at Level 2 or 3 in the domain – 20% and 18%, respectively – but the chances that native-born, native-language adults in the two countries perform at those levels are very different – 25% and 49%, respectively.

■ Figure 3.6 ■

Problem-solving proficiency and computer experience, by immigrant and language status

Percentage of adults who score at Level 2 or 3 in problem solving in technology-rich environments or have no computer experience

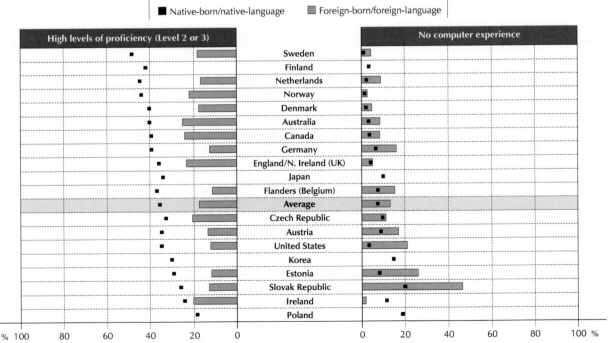

Notes: Estimates based on low sample sizes are not shown. Estimates for the Russian Federation are missing due to the lack of language variables.
Countries are ranked in descending order of the percentage of adults aged 16-65 scoring at Level 2 or 3 in problem solving in technology-rich environments.
Source: Survey of Adult Skills (PIAAC) (2012), Table A3.6.
StatLink http://dx.doi.org/10.1787/888933231610

Immigrant and language background is also weakly associated with computer experience. On average, native-born, native-language adults (8%) are less likely than foreign-born, foreign-language adults (13%) to lack computer experience (Table A3.6). In Estonia, the Slovak Republic and the United States, the gap between these two groups in the probability that an adult lacks computer experience is over 17 percentage points. In contrast, in Ireland, native-born, native-language adults are more likely to lack computer experience than foreign-born, foreign-language adults.

Differences related to ICT use

The frequency with which adults use ICT is likely to be closely related to proficiency in problem solving in technology-rich environments, both because more frequent use of ICT is likely to improve proficiency in this domain, and because people with greater proficiency are likely to use ICT more often. In the cross-country analyses in Chapter 2, frequency of ICT use (measured here as the frequency with which adults use e-mail in their daily lives) is strongly correlated with proficiency in problem solving in technology-rich environments; thus it is reasonable to expect a similar relation to hold within countries.

The more frequently adults use e-mail, the better their performance in the domain. The probability of performing at Level 2 or 3 in problem solving in technology-rich environments is 36 percentage points greater among adults who use e-mail at least once a month than for those who use e-mail less often or not at all (Table B3.8). The difference ranges from a low of 29 percentage points in Poland to a high of 42 percentage points in Finland and the Netherlands.

Differences related to literacy proficiency

As the tasks included in the assessment of problem solving in technology-rich environments involve understanding and interpreting written texts, a reasonably strong relationship between proficiency in literacy and proficiency in the problem-solving domain is expected[6] – and is, in fact, observed in the survey. On average across OECD countries, 83% of adults who are highly proficient in literacy (Level 4 or 5 in the assessment) are also highly proficient (Level 2 or 3) in problem solving in technology-rich environments (Figure 3.7). However, the proportion of adults at these levels of proficiency varies widely across countries, from 57% in Poland to 94% in Sweden. In contrast, only 11% of adults who attain Level 2 in literacy proficiency (on average, one in three adults perform at this level) are highly proficient (Level 2 or 3) in the problem-solving domain, and in no country does this share exceed 15%.

▪ Figure 3.7 ▪
Problem-solving proficiency and computer experience, by level of literacy proficiency

Percentage of adults scoring at Level 2 or 3 in problem solving in technology-rich environments or have no computer experience

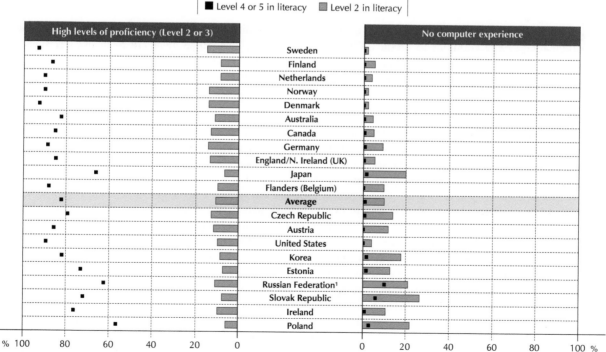

1. See note at the end of this chapter.
Countries are ranked in descending order of the percentage of adults aged 16-65 scoring at Level 2 or 3 in problem solving in technology-rich environments.
Source: Survey of Adult Skills (PIAAC) (2012), Table A3.7.
StatLink ⧉ http://dx.doi.org/10.1787/888933231629

Literacy proficiency is also related to computer experience. On average, only 1% of adults who perform at Level 4 or 5 in the literacy assessment lack computer experience, compared with 10% of adults proficient at Level 2 in literacy (Figure 3.7). There is greater between-country variation in computer experience among adults who are less proficient in literacy than among adults who are more proficient. Few adults who perform at Level 4 or 5 in the literacy assessment lack computer experience, with the exception of those in the Slovak Republic (6%). In contrast, the proportion of adults who perform at Level 2 in literacy who have no computer experience ranges from 2% in Sweden to 26% in the Slovak Republic.

DIFFERENCES IN PROFICIENCY RELATED TO SPECIFIC CHARACTERISTICS, AFTER ACCOUNTING FOR OTHER VARIABLES

Most of the characteristics discussed above have a close relationship with the probability of performing at Level 2 or 3 in problem solving in technology-rich environments and the probability of having no computer experience. But these characteristics are often related to one another (e.g. older adults have lower educational attainment, on average in most countries); thus it is important to know how each of the characteristics is associated with proficiency in problem solving in technology-rich environments when the other characteristics are held constant.

This section details the results when logistic regressions are used to calculate the probability of performing at Level 2 or 3 in problem solving in technology-rich environments if an adult has a certain characteristic, after accounting for the other variables under consideration. These regressions produce odds ratios (see Box 3.1 for a discussion of odds ratios) that reflect the relative increase in the probability that a particular group, say 55-65 year-olds, will perform at Level 2 or 3 in the domain compared to a reference group with different demographic characteristics, say 16-24 year-olds.

Because of the close relationship between proficiency in problem solving in technology-rich environments and the frequency of ICT use, as well as the high correlation of proficiency among the three domains (literacy, numeracy and problem solving in technology-rich environments) covered in the Survey of Adult Skills, the regressions are conducted in stages, with three versions of analysis. Version 1 examines the relationship between proficiency and socio-demographic characteristics, without including information on frequency of ICT use and literacy proficiency. Version 2 adds frequency of ICT use (e-mail) as an additional explanatory variable to distinguish between the relationships with proficiency in problem solving in technology-rich environments from relationships with the frequency of computer use. Version 3 adds literacy proficiency to the regression to distinguish between relationships with proficiency in the problem-solving domain and relationships with literacy proficiency. To distinguish between literacy proficiency and general cognitive ability, Version 3 also includes analyses that use proficiency in numeracy rather than in literacy.

The logistic regressions are performed for each country, and the resulting country coefficients are then averaged across all participating OECD countries to produce OECD average coefficients. Since there are relatively few statistically significant differences between the individual estimates and the OECD average, the OECD averages are used in the following discussion. Figure 3.8 summarises the results of the three different stages of the analysis.

Opportunities to develop skills

The cognitive skills needed to solve problems and ICT skills are acquired and developed in both formal education and in adult education and training activities. As expected, educational attainment and participation in adult education and training during the 12 months prior to the survey are both found to be independently related to proficiency in problem solving in technology-rich environments, even after accounting for other factors.

The probability of performing at Level 2 or 3 in the problem-solving assessment is 39 percentage points higher for adults with tertiary education than it is for adults with less than upper secondary education, after accounting for socio-demographic characteristics (Version 1), somewhat larger than the difference of 33 percentage points that was observed before accounting for the other factors. The difference increases because controlling for age takes into account the large proportion of young adults with low education – and thus corrects for the way low educational attainment among young adults reduces the observed difference in proficiency in problem solving in technology-rich environments that is associated with education. Adding frequency of ICT use (Version 2) to the regression brings the difference back to 33 percentage points. When proficiency in literacy is added (Version 3), the adjusted difference drops substantially to 13 percentage points. If proficiency in numeracy is added instead of proficiency in literacy, the reduction is similar. Thus much of the relationship between educational attainment and proficiency in the problem-solving domain is explained by the higher cognitive proficiency of better-educated adults, as measured by the literacy or numeracy assessments.

After accounting for socio-demographic characteristics (Version 1), the probability of performing at Level 2 or 3 in problem solving in technology-rich environments is 12 percentage points higher for adults who have participated in adult education and training activities in the 12 months prior to the survey than it is for adults who have not recently participated in those activities – half the difference (24 percentage points) observed before taking other socio-economic characteristics into account. Adding frequency of e-mail use to the regression (Version 2) reduces this difference to 9 percentage points, and adding literacy proficiency (Version 3) reduces the difference to 7 percentage points.

■ Figure 3.8 ■

How problem-solving proficiency and lack of computer experience are affected by various characteristics

Differences in the percentage of adults scoring at Level 2 or 3 in problem solving in technology-rich environments or those without computer experience, before and after accounting for various characteristics

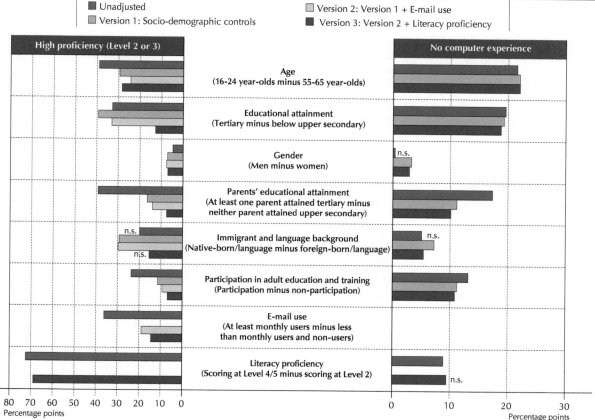

n.s: not significantly different from zero.
Note: Version 1 adjusts for socio-demographic characteristics (age, educational attainment, gender, parents' educational attainment and immigrant and language background). Version 2 adds frequency of ICT use (e-mail) as an adjustment to Version 1. Version 3 adds literacy proficiency to the regression of Version 2 to adjust for cognitive ability.
Results for each country are available in Tables B3.1, 2, 3, 4 and 5 in Annex B.
Source : Survey of Adult Skills (PIAAC)(2012), Tables 3.1 and 3.2.
StatLink ﹍ http://dx.doi.org/10.1787/888933231637

Background characteristics

The analyses include four background characteristics that are not specifically linked to opportunities for skills development: age, gender, parents' level of education, and immigrant status and language background.

Of these four characteristics, age has the strongest relationship with proficiency in problem solving in technology-rich environments, a relationship that is only slightly affected when other factors are taken into account. In Version 3 of the regression, adults aged 16-24 are 28 percentage points more likely than 55-65 year-olds to perform at Level 2 or 3 in the problem-solving assessment. The difference was 39 percentage points before taking other factors into account.

The probability that men, rather than women, perform at Level 2 or 3 in the assessment of problem solving in technology-rich environments increases by two percentage points after other factors are taken into account: from a 5 percentage-point difference before taking other factors into account to a 7 percentage-point difference (in all three versions).[7] This is because more women have tertiary education than men, and accounting for education widens the gender gap by correcting for the extra benefit women have from their higher level of education.

The probability that adults with highly educated parents perform at Level 2 or 3 in the problem-solving domain is 7 percentage points greater than that for adults whose parents have low educational attainment, after accounting for socio-demographic variables, e-mail use and literacy proficiency. This is substantially less than the difference of 39 percentage points before accounting for these other factors. Much of the advantage of having better-educated parents disappears after other socio-demographic factors are taken into account (Version 1) and, to a lesser extent, when literacy proficiency is also taken into account (Version 3).[8] Adding numeracy instead of literacy proficiency in Version 3 produces a similar result.

Before accounting for other factors, the difference in probability that a native-born, native-language adult performs at Level 2 or 3 in problem solving in technology-rich environments compared with a foreign-born, foreign-language adult is 20 percentage points; after taking those other factors into account (Version 1), the difference increases to 29 percentage points.[9] This is because foreign-born, foreign-language adults are relatively younger and more educated than native-born, native-language adults. Taking age and education into account adjusts for those advantages for foreign-born, foreign-language adults and thus widens the gap between them and native-born, native-language adults in proficiency in the problem-solving domain. After accounting for literacy proficiency in addition to socio-demographic factors and e-mail use (Version 3), the advantage associated with native-born, native-language adults shrinks to 16 percentage points and is no longer significant. If numeracy proficiency is considered instead of literacy proficiency, the result is similar (14 percentage points and not significant). This means that the disparity in proficiency in problem solving in technology-rich environments between native-born, native-language adults and foreign-born, foreign-language adults is largely explained by differences in their general cognitive proficiency in the language of their country of residence as assessed through either the literacy or numeracy assessment in the Survey of Adult Skills.

ICT use

A minimum level of familiarity and comfort with computers and common computer applications is required to display proficiency in problem solving in technology-rich environments. Given that the difficulty of the tasks in the problem-solving assessment reflects both the cognitive demands placed on the respondents and more complex uses of technology, it is expected that there would be a relationship between the frequency with which common computer applications are used and proficiency in problem solving in technology-rich environments. In line with expectations, adults who use e-mail at least once a month have a 15 percentage point greater probability of scoring at Level 2 or 3 in the problem-solving domain than less regular users, after taking into account other socio-demographic characteristics and literacy proficiency (Version 3). This suggests that there is a mutually reinforcing relationship between the capacity to solve problems in digital environments and using computer applications, as represented here by e-mail.

Literacy proficiency

After taking account of other factors (Version 3), the probability of performing at Level 2 or 3 in problem solving in technology-rich environments is 69 percentage points higher for adults who are highly proficient in literacy (performing at Level 4 or 5 in the literacy assessment) than it is for adults with lower literacy proficiency (performing at Level 2). This difference is almost as large as that observed before other factors are taken into account (72 percentage points). Using numeracy proficiency in place of literacy proficiency, the difference between the two groups is similar. This suggests that the relationship between literacy proficiency and proficiency in problem solving reflects a relationship between general cognitive proficiency and problem solving using ICT, rather than a relationship specific to literacy proficiency.

The close relationship between general cognitive proficiency and the capacity to solve problems in digital environments is not surprising. The upper levels of performance on both the literacy and the numeracy assessments in the Survey of Adult Skills involve cognitive tasks that include an element of problem solving. Tasks at Levels 4 and 5 in literacy involve multi-step operations to interpret and synthesise multiple texts, including evaluating subtle evidence to accomplish the tasks. Similarly, tasks at Levels 4 and 5 in numeracy involve complex contexts, multiple steps, choosing relevant problem-solving strategies, and communicating explanations of the solutions. The results confirm that adults who can perform such tasks in literacy and numeracy are often able to perform the kinds of tasks, using digital tools and applications, that are assessed in the survey.[10]

In summary, literacy proficiency and age have the strongest independent relationships to proficiency in problem solving in technology-rich environments, after accounting for other factors. Education and ICT use have moderately strong relationships.

DIFFERENCES IN EXPERIENCE WITH COMPUTERS RELATED TO SPECIFIC CHARACTERISTICS, AFTER ACCOUNTING FOR OTHER VARIABLES

A similar analysis was conducted to examine the relationships among background characteristics, educational and labour market factors, literacy proficiency and the probability that an adult has no computer experience. The results differ to some extent from those observed for proficiency in problem solving in technology-rich environments. Age and educational attainment both have strong relationships with the probability of whether or not an adult has experience in using a computer. After taking other factors into account, younger adults are less likely than older adults to have no prior computer experience, as are adults with higher levels of educational attainment. For example, after taking other socio-demographic factors and literacy proficiency into account, a 16-24 year-old is less likely to have no computer experience, by 25 percentage points, than an adult aged 55-65. In addition to age and educational attainment, only parents' education and recent participation in adult education and training had large and statistically significant relationships with the probability of having no computer experience. Interestingly, numeracy proficiency has a significant relationship with the lack of computer experience after taking other factors into account. This contrasts with the analyses of proficiency in problem solving in technology-rich environments, where literacy and numeracy have similar effects.

Box 3.1 **Using odds ratios when comparing a group to a reference group**

Odds ratios reflect the relative likelihood of an event occurring for a particular group relative to a reference group. An odds ratio of 1 represents equal chances of an event occurring for the group vis-à-vis the reference group. Coefficients with a value below 1 indicate that there is less chance of an event occurring for the particular group compared to the reference group, and coefficients greater than 1 represent greater chances. The odds ratios are calculated from logistic regressions that take a number of other factors into account.

The definition of the odds ratio is used to calculate an adjusted percentage point difference associated with each characteristic, using the proficiency in problem solving in technology-rich environments proportion for the corresponding reference category.

For example, for the relationship of age with higher-level proficiency in problem solving in technology-rich environments, the reference category is adults aged 55-65. For this reference category, the proportion of adults with proficiency in Levels 2 or 3 is 11.681%, which corresponds to odds of

$$\frac{0.11681}{1 - 0.11681} = 0.13226$$

Version 3 of the model results in an average coefficient of 1.6214 across OECD countries among adults aged 16-24, which corresponds to an odds ratio of

$$e^{1.6214} = 5.0602$$

The odds ratio of 5.0602 implies that the odds associated with the contrast group – adults aged 16-24 – when the other factors are held constant will be the following:

$$0.13226 * 5.0602 = 0.66926$$

Odds of 0.66926 for the contrast group can be transformed into the corresponding probability p as follows:

$$0.66926 = \frac{p}{1 - p} \quad \Rightarrow \quad p = \frac{0.66926}{1 + 0.66926} \quad \Rightarrow \quad p = 0.40093$$

As a result, in Version 3 of the model, the adjusted difference in the proportion of 16-24 year-old adults with proficiency Level 2 or 3 compared to adults aged 55 to 65 is the difference between 11.681% and 40.093%, or 28.412 percentage points.

Notes

1. The adjustments include a set of socio-demographic characteristics, along with ICT (e-mail) use and literacy proficiency.

2. ICT use is omitted from Figure 3.2 because the questions related to ICT use were not asked of respondents with no computer experience.

3. OECD 2013a, Table A5.9 (L). The analysis combines separate measures of job-related and non-job-related adult education and training, and includes both formal and non-formal types of education and training.

4. *http://ec.europa.eu/eurostat/data/database?node_code=isoc_ci_cfp_cu*, Series on Individuals – computer use.

5. The contrast with the Eurostat figures cited earlier may reflect differences in the countries represented.

6. Because of the high correlation between literacy and numeracy, the correlation between numeracy and problem solving using ICT is similar.

7. In some versions of the models, the relationship between proficiency and gender is significantly smaller than the OECD average in Australia, Canada and the Slovak Republic, and is not significantly different from zero.

8. In all versions of the models, the relationship between proficiency and parents' education is significantly smaller than the OECD average in Denmark, Japan and the Netherlands; in Version 3, the relationship is not significantly different from zero in these countries.

9. In some versions of the models, the relationship between proficiency and immigrant and language status is significantly smaller than the OECD average in Estonia, and is not significantly different from zero.

10. The Adult Literacy and Life Skills Survey (ALL) also assessed problem-solving skills, although the construct for problem solving did not focus specifically on problem solving in technology-rich environments. ALL found a relationship between problem-solving skills and literacy, but did not report on whether there was a similar relationship between problem solving and numeracy (OECD/Statistics Canada, 2011, Chapter 5).

References

OECD (2013a), *OECD Skills Outlook 2013: First Results from the Survey of Adult Skills*, OECD Publishing, Paris, *http://dx.doi.org/10.1787/9789264204256-en*.

OECD (2013b), *PISA 2012 Results: Excellence through Equity (Volume II): Giving Every Student the Chance to Succeed*, PISA, OECD Publishing, Paris, *http://dx.doi.org/10.1787/9789264201132-en*.

OECD/Statistics Canada (2011), *Literacy for Life: Further Results from the Adult Literacy and Life Skills Survey*, OECD Publishing, Paris, *http://dx.doi.org/10.1787/9789264091269-en*.

4

Proficiency in problem solving in technology-rich environments, the use of skills and labour market outcomes

This chapter examines the relationship among proficiency in problem solving in technology-rich environments, the use of ICT at work and labour market outcomes. The analysis first considers the proficiency of the labour force in using ICT to solve problems and reviews data from the Survey of Adult Skills about the frequency with which adults use ICT and solve problems at work, and whether adults believe that their ICT skills are sufficient for work. The chapter then discusses the relationship between proficiency in problem solving in technology-rich environments and labour force participation, unemployment, wages and labour productivity.

How proficient are workers and non-workers in problem solving using information and communication technologies (ICT)? To what extent are workers in different countries using ICT and problem-solving skills at work? Do these adults believe that they have sufficient ICT skills to do their jobs? Are higher proficiency in problem solving using ICT and more frequent use of ICT associated with higher rates of participation in the labour market, lower unemployment, higher wages and higher labour productivity? This chapter examines the relationship between proficiency in problem solving in technology-rich environments, the use of ICT at work, and labour market outcomes.

Key findings

- Workers are more likely than non-workers to be highly proficient in problem solving in technology-rich environments, and workers in skilled occupations are more likely to be highly proficient than workers in elementary occupations.

- In most countries, few workers are concerned that they lack the computer skills needed to do their jobs well, and few workers say that a lack of computer skills has affected their chances of getting a job, promotion or pay raise.

- Proficiency in problem solving in technology-rich environments and use of ICT (e-mail) are associated with higher rates of labour force participation and higher wages, even after accounting for other factors. Adults with no computer experience are less likely to participate in the labour force and are paid less.

- The relationship between proficiency in problem solving in technology-rich environments and wages is more closely related to skills use than the relationship between wages and either literacy or numeracy proficiency.

A PROFILE OF WORKERS' SKILLS IN PROBLEM SOLVING AND USING ICT

Current and recent workers' proficiency in problem solving in technology-rich environments

In most countries, workers who were employed at the time of the Survey of Adult Skills (a product of the OECD Programme for the International Assessment of Adult Competencies, or PIAAC) or who had worked in the 12 months prior to the survey were more likely than non-workers[1] to perform at Level 2 or 3 in the assessment of problem solving in technology-rich environments, and less likely than non-workers to lack computer experience. On average, 37% of current and recent workers are proficient at Level 2 or 3 in the domain. The proportion ranges between 21% in Poland and 47% in Sweden. On average, few current and recent workers (6%) lack computer experience. The proportion is around 1% in the Nordic countries and 2% in Australia and the Netherlands, and rises to 8% in Japan, 14% in Poland and Korea, and 16% in the Slovak Republic.

Compared to the 37% of current and recent workers who perform at the higher levels of proficiency in problem solving in technology-rich environments, only 24% of non-workers attain the same levels of proficiency in the assessment, a difference of 14 percentage points (Figure 4.1). The difference in the probability of performing at those levels between adults who have worked in the past year and those who have not, reaches a high of 26 percentage points in the Netherlands. In Korea, the gap is not significantly different from zero. Computer experience is also related to participation in the labour force. On average, the difference in having experience using computers between adults who had worked in the year prior to the survey and those who had not is 11 percentage points. In Estonia, the difference reaches 20 percentage points.

Proficiency in problem solving in technology-rich environments related to occupation

Different occupations require different skills; they also provide different opportunities to exercise and develop skills. For both reasons, there is likely to be an association between occupation and proficiency in problem solving using ICT. Across OECD participating countries and across those respondents who provided information about their occupation, 39% are in skilled occupations, 28% are in semi-skilled, white-collar occupations, 21% are in semi-skilled, blue-collar occupations, and 9% are in elementary occupations[2] (Table B4.14).

Differences in proficiency related to occupation are examined by comparing adults employed in skilled and elementary occupations. Adults in these two broad occupational groups would be expected to be at the top and the bottom, respectively, of the distribution of cognitive skills. Across OECD countries, 50% of adults in skilled occupations are proficient at Level 2 or 3 on the problem solving in technology-rich environments scale compared to only 20% of adults in elementary occupations, a difference of 30 percentage points (Table B4.1). This difference ranges from 21 percentage points in Poland to 40 percentage points in the United Kingdom.

■ Figure 4.1 ■

Problem-solving proficiency and computer experience, by employment status

Percentage of adults scoring at Level 2 or 3 in problem solving in technology-rich environments or having no computer experience, for workers* and non-workers

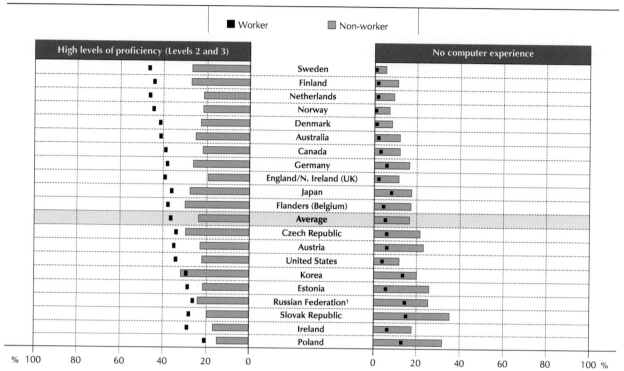

1. See note at the end of this chapter.
* Workers are defined as adults who were employed when the survey was conducted or whose most recent work experience occurred during the 12 months prior to the survey.
Countries are ranked in descending order of the percentage of adults aged 16-65 scoring at Level 2 or 3 in problem solving in technology-rich environments.
Source: Survey of Adult Skills (PIAAC) (2012), Table A4.1.

StatLink ⬛⬛⬛ http://dx.doi.org/10.1787/888933231644

Countries with higher proficiency in this domain, in general, tend to exhibit larger differences in proficiency between occupations. For example, in Sweden, which has the highest proportion of adults who are proficient at Level 2 or 3 in problem solving in technology-rich environments, the probability of scoring at Level 2 or 3 is 61% for adults in skilled occupations and 27% for adults in elementary occupations, a difference of 34 percentage points. By contrast, in Poland, which has the smallest proportion of adults who are proficient at Level 2 or 3, the probability is 33% for adults in skilled occupations and 12% for adults in elementary occupations, a difference of only 21 percentage points.

In many countries there are also large differences in computer experience related to occupation. Across the OECD countries that participated in the Survey of Adult Skills, only 1% of adults in skilled occupations lack computer experience compared to 17% of adults in elementary occupations, a difference of 16 percentage points (Table B4.1). This difference ranges from less than 5 percentage points in the Nordic countries and Australia, to 44 percentage points in the Slovak Republic. The variation across countries in the magnitude of this difference is primarily due to the variation in the computer experience of adults in elementary occupations, because almost no adults in skilled occupations lack computer experience.

Frequency of ICT use at work

The Survey of Adult Skills includes a set of questions about the frequency of ICT use at work. These questions are identical to those that are asked about the frequency of ICT use in everyday life, as discussed in Chapter 2. As in Chapter 2, the analysis in this chapter focuses on the questions related to the use of e-mail, the Internet for understanding issues or conducting transactions, and the use of spreadsheets and word processing.

About 70% of workers use computers[3] at work while about 28% do not use a computer at work, on average across participating countries. In Norway and Sweden, more than 80% of workers reported using computer at work, while more than 40% of workers in Italy, Poland, the Slovak Republic and Spain said that they do not use a computer at work. Among the ICT applications discussed in the survey, e-mail is the most frequently used at work (Figure 4.2). Almost half of workers use e-mail every day at work, which is close to the proportion of adults who use e-mail daily outside of work (Tables A2.4a and A4.2a). In addition, a third of workers use the Internet daily to understand issues, and half use it at least once a month for the same purpose (Figure 4.2, Table A4.2b). As with using e-mail and the Internet for understanding issues outside of work, the greatest frequency of use is found in the Nordic countries and the Netherlands, with the proportion of workers using these technologies at least once a month approaching 70% for e-mail and surpassing 60% for the Internet. In contrast, in Poland, only 43% of workers use e-mail and the Internet frequently for understanding issues.

Adults use the Internet to conduct transactions at work much less frequently. Across OECD countries, 24% of workers use the Internet for transactions at least once a month, compared to 57% of adults who use the Internet for this purpose outside of work (Figures 4.2 and 2.4). This is not surprising, since many workers are not in jobs where they are authorised to make transactions at work, which are defined in the survey as tasks that involve buying, selling or banking. In contrast, most adults have some responsibility for banking and purchases in their daily lives, and Internet services for carrying out such tasks are broadly available.

■ Figure 4.2 ■

Using information technologies at work

Percentage of adults who use information technology applications at work at least once a month (country average*)

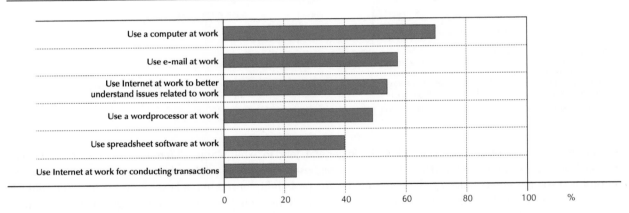

* Country average: average of 19 participating OECD countries and entities.
Source: Survey of Adult Skills (PIAAC) (2012), Tables A4.2a, b, c, d and e.

StatLink ⬛⬛⬛ http://dx.doi.org/10.1787/888933231659

Across OECD countries, 40% of adults use spreadsheets at work compared to 21% of adults who use them outside of work at least once a month. One in five workers, on average across OECD countries, reported using a spreadsheet every day. Some 49% of workers said that they use word processing at least once a month. In the Netherlands, almost 60% of workers use word processing at least that often.

Information on the use of different ICT applications both at work and outside of work is also available for employed adults. Many workers use ICT with similar frequency both at and outside of work (Tables B4.2 through B4.6). Among those workers for whom the pattern of ICT use differs between the two spheres, most use e-mail and the Internet more frequently outside of work than at work. When it comes to using spreadsheets and word processing, the opposite pattern is observed: these are used more frequently at work than outside of work. Japan shows particularly large proportions of workers who use ICT frequently at work but infrequently outside of work for all the applications considered, except transactions on the Internet.

Problem solving at work

The Survey of Adult Skills asks respondents how often they encounter situations in their job that involve "more complex problems that take at least 30 minutes to find a good solution". Overall, 34% of workers report that they engage in complex problem solving at least once a month (Table B4.7).

Workers who undertake complex problem solving at least once a month are more likely than other workers to perform at higher levels in the assessment of problem solving in technology-rich environments. Some 45% of workers who engage in complex problem solving that frequently are proficient at Level 2 or 3 in the domain, compared to 28% of workers who engage in complex problem solving less than once a month or never (Figure 4.3). Although few workers lack computer experience in general, a relationship can still be found between complex problem solving at work and computer experience, with only 3% of workers lacking computer experience if they engage in complex problem solving at work at least once a month compared to 9% of workers who engage in complex problem solving less than once a month or never.

■ Figure 4.3 ■

Problem-solving proficiency and computer experience, by frequency of complex problem solving

Percentage of workers scoring at Level 2 or 3 in problem solving in technology-rich environments or having no computer experience

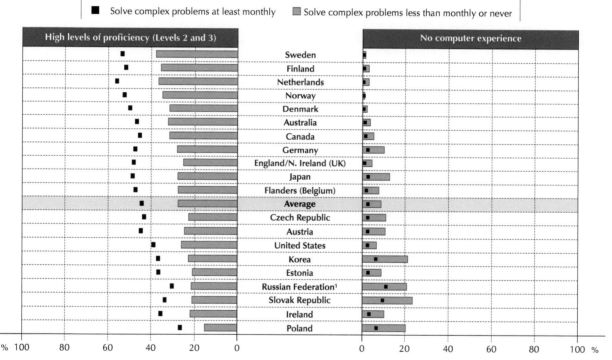

1. See note at the end of this chapter.
Note: Complex problems are defined as those that take at least 30 minutes to find a good solution.
Countries are ranked in descending order of the percentage of adults aged 16-65 scoring at Level 2 or 3 in problem solving in technology-rich environments.
Source: Survey of Adult Skills (PIAAC) (2012), Table A4.3.
StatLink ⟲ http://dx.doi.org/10.1787/888933231662

Adequacy of ICT skills for work

The survey's background questionnaire includes two questions related to the adequacy of ICT skills for work. These are asked of all workers who have used a computer in their current or previous job. The first asks whether the respondent has "the computer skills needed to do [his/her] job well" and the second asks whether "a lack of computer skills affected your chances of being hired for a job or getting a promotion or pay raise". Both of these questions involve self-reports and subjective judgements, which might be influenced by cultural factors. However, the second question suggests some objective criteria to consider (job-related outcomes) when determining the effects of having limited computer skills.

In most countries, relatively few workers believe they lack the computer skills needed to do their jobs well (Figure 4.4). On average, only 7% of workers report lacking the necessary computer skills, with that share ranging from 2% in the Czech Republic to 26% in Japan.

Similarly, few workers (5% on average across OECD countries) believe that a lack of computer skills has affected their chances of being hired, promoted or paid more (Figure 4.4). This proportion ranges from 2% in Korea to 16% in Japan; and again, the proportion of workers who believe this is more than twice as large in Japan as in any other country.

■ Figure 4.4 ■

Workers who reported insufficient computer skills

Percentage of workers* who reported that they lack the computer skills to do their job well or that their lack of computer skills has affected their chances of getting a job, promotion or pay raise

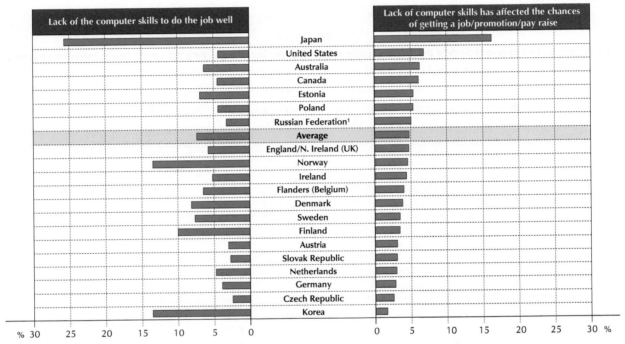

* Workers are defined as adults who were employed when the survey was conducted or whose most recent work experience occurred during the 12 months prior to the survey.
1. See note at the end of this chapter.
Countries are ranked in descending order of the percentage of workers who reported that their lack of computer skills has affected their chances of getting a job, promotion or pay raise.
Source: Survey of Adult Skills (PIAAC)(2012), Tables A4.4a and b.
StatLink ⧫ http://dx.doi.org/10.1787/888933231674

Although closely related, the two questions cover different aspects of the adequacy of respondents' skills. Indeed, some workers may have adequate computer skills for their current job precisely because their lack of computer skills prevented them from moving to another job requiring more advanced computer skills or because a failure to be hired, promoted or paid more in the past prompted them to improve their computer skills. On average, only 19% of adults who report that their employment has been affected at some point by their lack of computer skills feel that they lack the computer skills they need for their current job (Figure 4.5). A smaller percentage (7%) of the workers whose employment has not been affected by their lack of computer skills feels that they do, in fact, lack the computer skills they need for their current job.

Older workers are more likely to feel they lack the computer skills needed to do their job well, with 10% of 55-65 year-olds expressing this concern compared to 2% of 16-24 year-olds. (Table B4.8). This finding is consistent with the generally lower proficiency in problem solving in technology-rich environments that is observed among older adults (see Chapter 3). In contrast, there is little variation by age in the perception that a lack of computer skills has affected the chances of being hired or promoted or getting a pay raise (Table B4.9).

■ Figure 4.5 ■

Workers who reported insufficient computer skills, by the effect on employment

Percentage of workers (working at the time of the survey or had worked in the 12 months prior to it) who reported that they lack the computer skills to do their job well

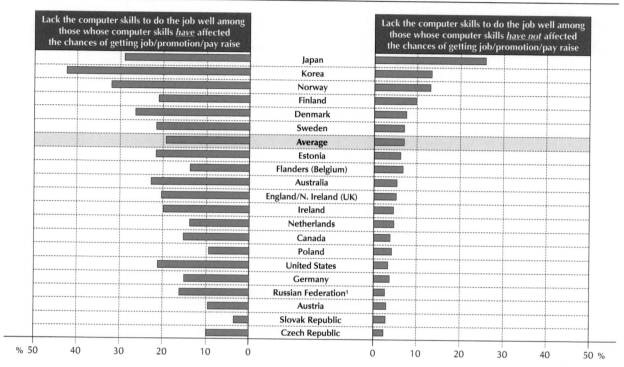

1. See note at the end of this chapter.
Countries are ranked in descending order of the percentage of workers who reported a lack of computer skills to do the job well among those whose computer skills have not affected the chances of getting a job/promotion/pay raise.
Source: Survey of Adult Skills (PIAAC) (2012), Table A4.5.
StatLink ᐧᐧ http://dx.doi.org/10.1787/888933231682

Concern about having adequate computer skills also varies by the level of proficiency in problem solving in technology-rich environments. On average, 5% of adults who perform at proficiency Level 2 or 3 in the assessment believe that they lack the computer skills needed for their jobs, compared to 8% of adults who score below Level 1 or who did not take the assessment on the computer (Table B4.10). However, there is little association between proficiency in the domain and the perception that a lack of computer skills has affected the chances of being hired, promoted or paid more (Table B4.11).

RELATIONSHIPS AMONG ADULTS' PROBLEM-SOLVING AND ICT SKILLS, FREQUENCY OF ICT USE AND VARIOUS ECONOMIC OUTCOMES

The following sections examine how proficiency in problem solving in technology-rich environments, frequency of ICT use, frequency of problem solving, and the level of adequacy of ICT skills for work are related to labour market outcomes. The discussion in this first section focuses on the relationship of each of these variables with labour market outcomes *before* accounting for other variables. The following sections examine the relationships *after* taking account of other factors that are related to the outcomes.

Relationship with labour force participation

On average across OECD countries, 80% of adults aged 25-65 participate in the labour force.[4] Some 90% of adults who are proficient at Level 2 or 3 in the assessment of problem solving in technology-rich environments participate in the labour force compared to 84% of those who are proficient at Level 1 and 76% of those who are proficient below Level 1 (Figure 4.6 and Table A4.6). There is notable variation among countries in the difference in labour force participation rates between adults performing at Level 2 or 3 and those who perform below Level 1: from 5 percentage points in Korea to 25 percentage points in the Netherlands. In most of the countries that are highly proficient in problem solving in technology-rich environments (Denmark, the Netherlands, Norway and Sweden), the gap in the rates of labour force participation between adults performing at Level 2 or 3 and those performing below Level 1 is relatively large. In these countries, adults who score below Level 1 have lower rates of labour force participation while those with high proficiency have higher rates of labour force participation compared to the OECD average.

The labour force participation rates of adults who failed the ICT core test (73%) or opted out of the computer assessment (69%) are, on average, lower than that of adults who took the computer assessment. Only 47% of adults with no computer experience participate in the labour market. All OECD countries show a wide gap between the labour force participation rates for adults with no computer experience and the overall population, ranging from 12 percentage points in Korea to 53 percentage points in Norway. The labour market seems to prefer workers who have some familiarity with a computer. At the same time, those who are employed would also have more opportunities to develop or maintain their skills in problem solving using ICT so the relationship between problem solving proficiency and labour force participation like goes in both directions.

■ Figure 4.6 ■
Labour force participation, by problem-solving proficiency
Adults aged 25-65

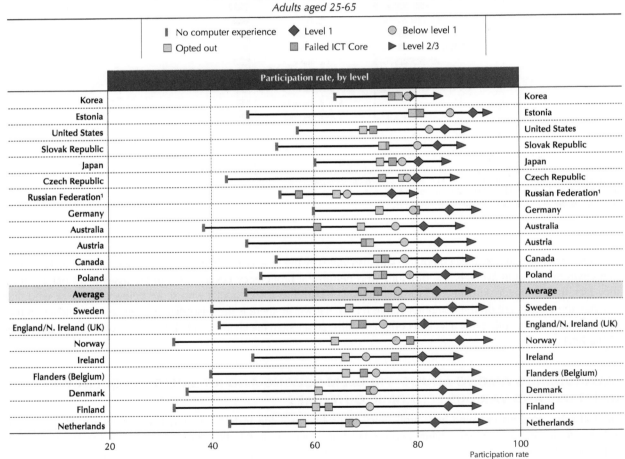

1. See note at the end of this chapter.
Countries are ranked in ascending order of the difference in participation rates (Level 2/3 minus Below Level 1).
Source: Survey of Adult Skills (PIAAC) (2012), Table A4.6.
StatLink ⬛⬛⬛ http://dx.doi.org/10.1787/888933231693

Frequency of ICT use is also related to labour force participation. On average, 85% of 25-65 year-olds who use e-mail at least once a month outside of work participate in the labour force, compared to only 66% of adults who use e-mail less often or never (Figure 4.7). This difference ranges from 7 percentage points in Japan to 27 percentage points in Finland.

■ Figure 4.7 ■
Labour force participation, by e-mail use in everyday life
Adults aged 25-65

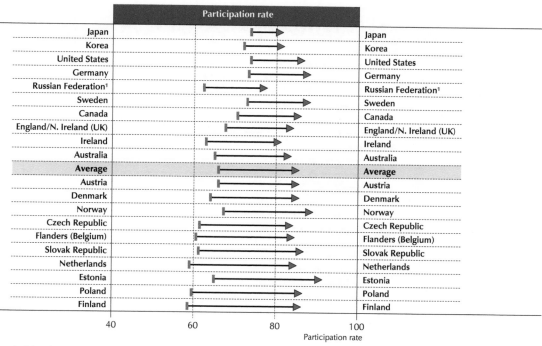

1. See note at the end of this chapter.
Note: Frequent use of e-mail means using e-mail at least once a month.
Countries are ranked in ascending order of the unadjusted difference in participation rates (frequent minus infrequent use of e-mail).
Source: Survey of Adult Skills (PIAAC) (2012), Table A4.7.

StatLink ⬛ http://dx.doi.org/10.1787/888933231708

Relationship with unemployment

Across OECD countries, proficiency in problem solving in technology-rich environments is negatively correlated with unemployment: adults who have the capacity to take the assessment have a lower rate of unemployment (4.6%) than the average for all labour force participants (5.3%). Some 3.6% of labour force participants who perform at Level 2 or 3, 5.1% of those who perform at Level 1, and 6.2% of those who are proficient below Level 1 are unemployed (Figure 4.8). By contrast, 7.8% of labour force participants who fail the ICT core test and 8.3% of participants who have no computer experience are unemployed. A number of countries, including Estonia and the Slovak Republic have particularly high levels of unemployment among adults who have no computer experience. The average unemployment rate among adults who opt out of the computer assessment is 6.8%, close to the average for all labour force participants. However, this pattern is not observed in a few countries. For example, in Korea, unemployment rates are generally low, regardless of adults' level of proficiency in problem solving in technology-rich environments. However, unemployment rates among adults who perform at Level 2 or 3 are slightly higher than those among adults who perform at lower levels of proficiency.

The overall unemployment rate is highly influenced by the economic conditions in each country, and it is likely that economic conditions affect the unemployment rate differently for workers at different proficiency levels. Therefore, when comparing unemployment rate results across countries it is important to remember that in 2011-2012, when the data for the Survey of Adult Skills were collected, the countries participating in the survey were affected to different degrees by the economic crisis.

■ Figure 4.8 ■

Unemployment rate, by problem-solving proficiency

Adults aged 25-65

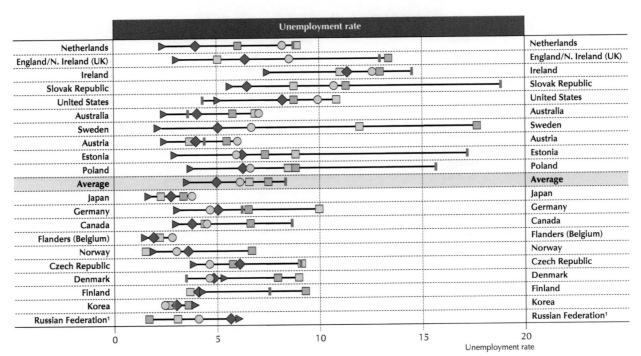

1. See note at the end of this chapter.
Countries are ranked in ascending order of the difference in unemployment rates (Level 2/3 minus Below Level 1).
Source: Survey of Adult Skills (PIAAC) (2012), Table A4.8.
StatLink ⟨⟩ http://dx.doi.org/10.1787/888933231714

Frequency of ICT use is also somewhat related to unemployment. On average, 4.9% of labour force participants aged 25-65 who use e-mail at least once a month in everyday life are unemployed, compared to 6.2% of labour force participants who use e-mail less often or never (Figure 4.9). In some countries with relatively low unemployment rates, this relationship is reversed: unemployment rates are higher among adults who use e-mail more frequently.

Relationship with wages

In all participating countries, higher levels of proficiency in problem solving in technology-rich environments are associated with higher wages. On average across OECD countries, hourly wages for workers who perform at proficiency Level 2 or 3 are 26% higher than mean hourly wages for workers who perform below Level 1 (Figure 4.10). This premium ranges from 9% in Korea to 56% in the United States. Hourly wages for workers at proficiency Level 1 are 11% higher than those of workers who perform below Level 1. Computer experience is also associated with wages. Hourly wages for workers with no computer experience are 18% lower than those of workers with Below Level 1 proficiency, and range from 9% in Sweden to 34% in Estonia. On average across OECD countries, the hourly wages for workers who failed the ICT core test or who opted out of the computer assessment are close to those of workers who perform below Level 1 in the assessment.

Frequency of ICT use has a strong relationship with wages. On average across OECD countries, hourly wages for workers who use e-mail at work at least once a month are 51% higher than those of workers who do not use e-mail at work that frequently (Figure 4.11). This difference in wages ranges from 24% in Sweden to 85% in the United States.

■ Figure 4.9 ■
Unemployment rate, by e-mail use in everyday life
Adopts aged 25-65

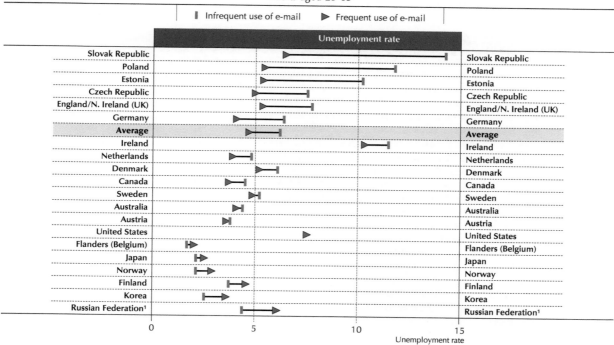

1. See note at the end of this chapter.
Note: Frequent use of e-mail means using e-mail at least once a month.
Countries are ranked in ascending order of the difference in unemployment rates (frequent minus infrequent use of e-mail).
Source: Survey of Adult Skills (PIAAC) (2012), Table A4.9.
StatLink http://dx.doi.org/10.1787/888933231728

■ Figure 4.10 ■
Wage premium, by problem-solving proficiency
Percentage difference in mean hourly wages relative to Below Level 1, by problem solving in technology-rich environments levels

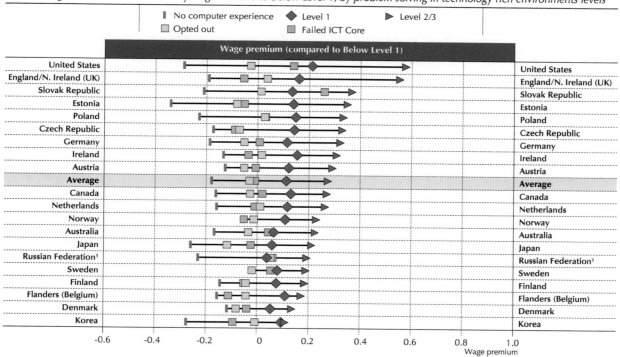

1. See note at the end of this chapter.
Countries are ranked in descending order of the wage premium for Level 2/3.
Source: Survey of Adult Skills (PIAAC) (2012), Table A4.10.
StatLink http://dx.doi.org/10.1787/888933231738

■ Figure 4.11 ■

Wage premium associated with e-mail use at work

Percentage difference in mean hourly wages between frequent* and less frequent use of e-mail at work

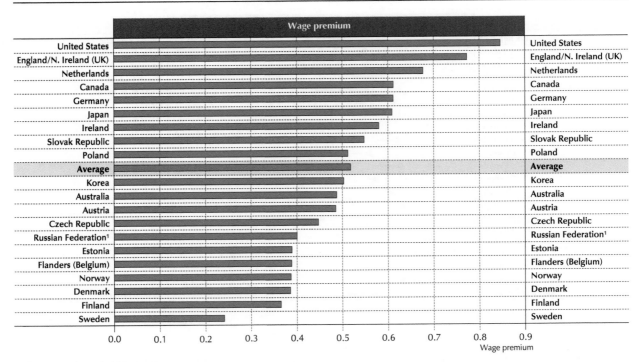

1. See note at the end of this chapter.
* Frequent use refers to use of e-mail at least once a month; less-frequent use refers to use of e-mail less than once a month or never.
Note: All differences are statistically significant.
Countries are ranked in descending order of the wage premium for workers using e-mail at work frequently.*
Source: Survey of Adult Skills (PIAAC) (2012), Table A4.11.

StatLink ᴹˢᴾ http://dx.doi.org/10.1787/888933231745

Engaging in complex problem solving at work is also associated with higher wages. On average across OECD countries, hourly wages for workers who engage in complex problem solving at work at least once a month are 34% higher than those of workers who do not engage in this activity that frequently (Figure 4.12). This difference in wages ranges from 19% in Flanders (Belgium) to 53% in England/N. Ireland (UK).

Across participating countries, believing that one lacks the computer skills necessary to do one's job does not have a clear relationship with wages. On average across OECD countries, there is no wage penalty for workers who believe that they lack the computer skills necessary for their jobs (Table A4.13). Consistent with expectations, workers who use computers but believe they lack the necessary computer skills for their jobs are paid at least 10% less than workers who believe they have the necessary skills in the Czech Republic, the Slovak Republic and Japan where statistically significant differences are found. In Norway, the opposite is observed as workers who believe that they lack the computer skills to do their jobs are paid 6% more than workers who say they have the skills necessary to do their jobs.

A clearer relationship is found between wages and having employment difficulties due to inadequate computer skills. On average across OECD countries, workers who report that their limited computer skills have caused difficulties in being hired, promoted or paid more are paid 10% less than workers who have not encountered such difficulties (Figure 4.13). In England/N.Ireland (UK), Germany and Ireland workers who report having employment difficulties due to limited computer skills are paid 15% less than workers who report having encountered no such difficulties from a lack of computer skills.

▪ Figure 4.12 ▪

Wage premium associated with regular use of complex problem-solving skills

Percentage difference in mean hourly wages between frequent* use of complex problem-solving skills and less frequent use of those skills at work

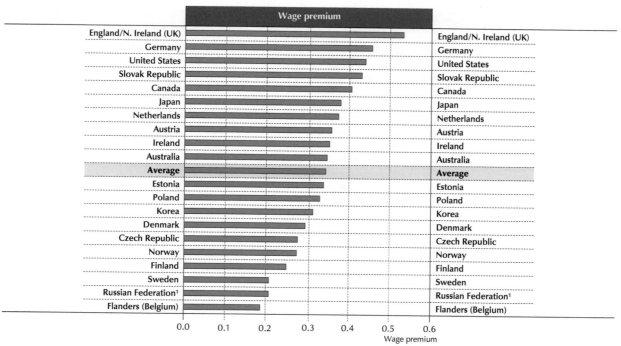

1. See note at the end of this chapter.
* Frequent use refers to the use of complex problem-solving skills at least once a month; less-frequent use refers to the use of complex problem-solving skills less than once a month or never.
Note: All differences are statistically significant. Complex problems are defined as those that take at least 30 minutes to find a good solution.
Countries are ranked in descending order of the wage difference between workers who frequently use complex problem-solving skills and workers who use those skills less often or never.
Source: Survey of Adult Skills (PIAAC) (2012), Table A4.12
StatLink ᐧᒧᔕᐤ http://dx.doi.org/10.1787/888933231750

RELATIONSHIPS AMONG ADULTS' PROBLEM-SOLVING AND ICT SKILLS, FREQUENCY OF ICT USE AND VARIOUS ECONOMIC OUTCOMES, AFTER ACCOUNTING FOR OTHER FACTORS

As the preceding sections show, there are clear associations between the various measures related to proficiency in problem solving in technology-rich environments and ICT use and labour market outcomes. However, it is also well-documented that such outcomes also tend to be affected by workers' socio-demographic characteristics, such as age, educational attainment and work experience. To adjust for the effect of these other factors, the analyses in this section take account of the following characteristics of workers: age, educational attainment, gender, marital status, immigrant status, and work experience.

In order to identify the relationships between proficiency in problem solving in technology-rich environments and the use of ICT and economic outcomes, after accounting for the influence of other factors, the relationships are modelled in several stages. Version 1 analyses proficiency in problem solving in technology-rich environments and membership in the different groups of adults who did not take the assessment on the computer as a function of socio-demographic characteristics alone. Version 2 takes account of proficiency in literacy and numeracy, as measured in the Survey of Adult Skills, in order to distinguish proficiency in problem solving using ICT from other types of cognitive proficiency. Version 3 adds the frequency of e-mail use to distinguish proficiency in problem solving using ICT from simple use of ICT.[5] For the wage regression, Version 3 also adds the other factors related to problem solving in technology-rich environments: how frequently adults solve complex problems at work, and the two measures related to the adequacy of computer skills for work. Version 4 adds measures of skills use that are not related to problem solving in technology-rich environments – specifically, measures of the use of reading, writing and numeracy skills[6] – to distinguish the use of ICT skills from the use of skills in general. Finally, for the wage regression, Version 5 also accounts for occupation.

■ Figure 4.13 ■

Wage premium associated with reported employment difficulties due to lack of computer skills

Percentage difference in mean hourly wages between adults who reported employment difficulties due to lack of computer skills and adults who reported no effect on their employment

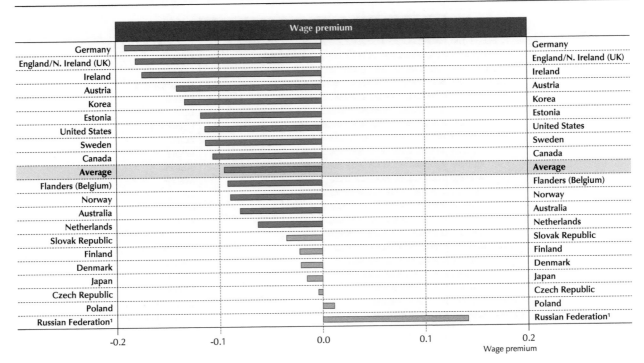

1. See note at the end of this chapter.
Note: Statistically significant differences are marked in a darker tone.
Countries are ranked in descending order of the wage premium associated with a lack of computer skills causing employment difficulties, compared to a lack of computer skills having no effect on employment.
Source: Survey of Adult Skills (PIAAC) (2012), Table A4.13.

StatLink ᴍᔕᔎ http://dx.doi.org/10.1787/888933231764

The regressions are estimated for each country and the resulting country coefficients are averaged across all participating OECD countries to produce OECD average coefficients. As in Chapter 3, the discussion focuses on the OECD average results because there are relatively few statistically significant differences between the individual country estimates and the OECD average.

Relationships with labour force participation, after accounting for other factors

Proficiency in problem solving in technology-rich environments is positively related to greater labour force participation when socio-demographic factors are accounted for (Version 1), although the relationship is weaker than that observed before taking these factors into account. After taking socio-demographic factors into account, the labour force participation rate of adults who are proficient at Level 2 or 3 is 9 percentage points higher than that of adults who are proficient below Level 1, and the participation rate of adults who are proficient at Level 1 is 4 percentage points higher (Figure 4.14).[7] However, these relationships are weakened further when proficiency in literacy and numeracy are also taken into account (Version 2), although only the coefficient on numeracy is significant. This suggests that a large part of the relationship between proficiency in the domain and labour force participation before taking account of socio-demographic factors and literacy and numeracy proficiency reflects an association with numeracy proficiency rather than problem solving in technology-rich environments. When adjusted for proficiency in literacy and numeracy, the labour force participation rate of adults who are proficient at Level 2 or 3 in the domain is 5 percentage points higher than that among adults who are proficient below Level 1, and there is no significant difference for adults who are proficient at Level 1. The results for the analyses that add frequency of ICT use and the use of other types of skills (Versions 3 and 4) are similar to the results for Version 2.[8]

There are also significant differences in labour force participation associated with whether or not respondents took the assessment on the computer, after accounting for other factors. The largest effect is for adults with no computer experience, whose labour force participation rate is 14-16 percentage points lower than that of adults proficient below Level 1, after taking account of other factors. Results are similar in all four versions of the analysis. Adults who failed the ICT core test have labour force participation rates that are 3-4 percentage points lower than adults who are proficient below Level 1, after accounting for other factors, and adults who opted out of the computer assessment have participation rates that are 4-5 percentage points lower.[9]

In the versions of the model that include ICT use, there are also significant differences in labour force participation between adults who use e-mail at least once a month and adults who use e-mail less often or never. Adults who use e-mail at least once a month have a participation rate that is 2-6 percentage points higher than adults who do not in most countries, after other factors are accounted for (Versions 3-4). Flanders (Belgium), Japan and Sweden show a relationship between ICT use and labour force participation that is significantly different from the OECD average and is usually not significantly different from zero.

▪ Figure 4.14 ▪

How labour force participation is affected by problem-solving proficiency and lack of computer experience

Differences in the rate of labour force participation between various groups, before and after accounting for various characteristics

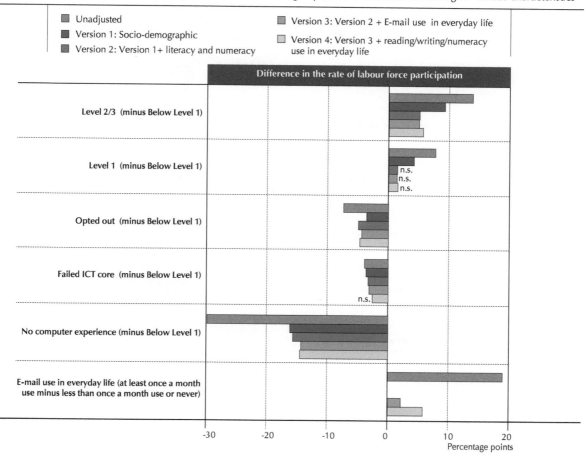

n.s: not significant.
Note: Version 1 adjusts for socio-demographic characteristics (age, gender, foreign-born status, years of education and marital status). Version 2 adds literacy and numeracy proficiency to the regression of Version 1. Version 3 adds frequency of ICT use (e-mail) in everyday life as an adjustment to Version 2. Version 4 adds use of reading/writing/numeracy skills in everyday life as an additional adjustment to Version 3.
Source: Survey of Adult Skills (PIAAC) (2012), Tables A4.6, A4.7 and A4.14.

StatLink ⬛🔗 http://dx.doi.org/10.1787/888933231775

Relationships with unemployment, after accounting for other factors

After accounting for other relevant factors, the relationships between proficiency in problem solving in technology-rich environments, ICT use and unemployment are no longer significant (Figure 4.15). Adults who are proficient at Level 2 or 3 in the domain have an unemployment rate that is significantly lower than that of adults who are proficient below

Level 1 only in the analysis that does not include proficiency in literacy and numeracy (Version 1). When literacy and numeracy are taken into account, being proficient at Level 2 or 3 no longer has a significant relation with unemployment, whereas the relationships with literacy and numeracy are significant (Versions 2-4).[10] This suggests that a large part of the relationship between proficiency in problem solving in technology-rich environments and unemployment, before taking other factors into account, reflects an association with cognitive proficiency, in general, rather than proficiency in this domain. Adults who are proficient at Level 1 and adults who did not take the assessment on the computer do not have significantly different unemployment rates in any version of the analysis. In addition, e-mail use is associated with a higher rate of unemployment when other types of skills use are not included (Version 3), but that relationship disappears after also accounting for the use of reading, writing and numeracy skills outside of work (Version 4).

■ Figure 4.15 ■

How unemployment rates are affected by problem-solving proficiency and lack of computer experience

Differences in the rate of unemployment between various groups, before and after accounting for various characteristics

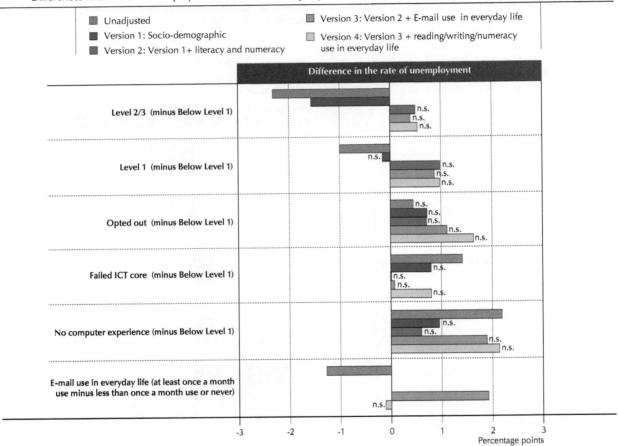

n.s: not significant.

Note: Version 1 adjusts for socio-demographic characteristics (age, gender, foreign-born status, years of education and marital status). Version 2 adds literacy and numeracy proficiency to the regression of Version 1. Version 3 adds frequency of ICT use (e-mail) in everyday life as an adjustment to Version 2. Version 4 adds use of reading/writing/numeracy skills in everyday life as an additional adjustment to Version 3.

Source: Survey of Adult Skills (PIAAC) (2012), Tables A4.7, A4.8 and A4.15.

StatLink ⬛⬛⬛ http://dx.doi.org/10.1787/888933231788

Relationship with wages, after accounting for other factors

After accounting for socio-demographic characteristics (Version 1), the relationship between proficiency in problem solving in technology-rich environments and wages weakens (Figure 4.16): workers proficient at Level 2 or 3 in the domain are paid 18% more than workers below Level 1, and workers proficient at Level 1 are paid 8% more (before accounting for socio-demographic factors, the differences in wages are 26% and 11%, respectively). When literacy and numeracy proficiency are also taken into account (Version 2), the two adjusted wage premiums shrink to 8% and 4%; and when use of ICT, problem solving at work, and adequacy of computer skills are also taken into account (Version 3) they decrease further to 4% and 1%. The wage premium for workers proficient at Level 1 is not significant once ICT use, problem solving at work and computer adequacy are also accounted for (Version 3). The wage premium for workers proficient at Level 2 or 3 is no longer significant once the use of other skills is accounted for (Version 4), while the wage premiums associated with literacy and numeracy proficiency are still statistically significant for the OECD average.[11] The results of the analysis indicate that the relationship between proficiency in problem solving in technology-rich environments and wages, before accounting for these other factors, reflects general cognitive proficiency (particularly numeracy) and the various types of skills use, rather than a relationship with proficiency in problem solving using ICT itself.[12]

▪ Figure 4.16 ▪

How wages are affected by problem-solving proficiency and lack of computer experience

Percentage differences in wages between various groups, before and after accounting for various characteristics

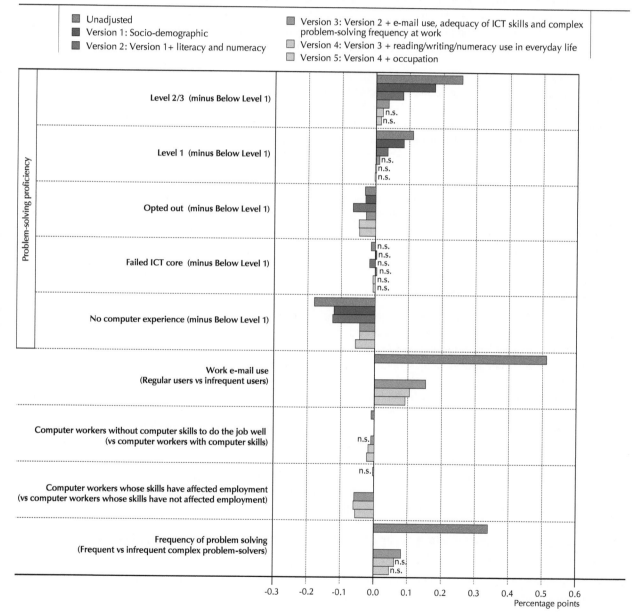

n.s: not significant.

Note: Version 1 adjusts for socio-demographic characteristics (age, gender, foreign-born status, years of education, marital status and years of experience). Version 2 adds literacy and numeracy proficiency to the regression of Version 1. Version 3 adds the frequency of ICT use (e-mail) at work, the two adequacy measures of computer skills for work and the frequency of complex problem solving at work as an adjustment to Version 2. Version 4 adds use of reading/ writing/numeracy skills at work as an additional adjustment to Version 3. Version 5 adds occupation as an additional adjustment to Version 4.
Source: Survey of Adult Skills (PIAAC) (2012), Tables A4.10, A4.11, A4.12, A4.13 and A4.16.

StatLink ⟐⟐⟐ http://dx.doi.org/10.1787/888933231799

Belonging to two of the categories of workers who did not take the computer assessment has a significant negative relationship with wages, after other factors are taken into account. The wages of workers who opted out of the computer assessment are 3-7% lower than those of workers who perform below Level 1, with the negative wage effect similar across all versions of the model. The wages of workers with no computer experience are 12-13% lower than those of workers with proficiency below Level 1, before ICT use and the other variables related to problem solving in technology-rich environments are taken into account (Versions 1-2) and 4-6% lower after those variables are accounted for (Versions 3-5).[13] There is no significant difference between the wages of workers who failed the ICT core test and workers who perform below Level 1 on the assessment.[14]

When ICT (e-mail) use is added to the analysis (Version 3), it is associated with a wage premium of 15%, which is substantially smaller than the difference of 51% observed before taking other factors into account. Also accounting for the use of reading, writing and numeracy skills (Version 4) reduces the adjusted wage premium for e-mail use to 10%.[15] Engaging in complex problem solving at work is associated with a wage premium of 8% (Version 3), which is reduced to 6% after taking account of the use of reading, writing and numeracy skills (Version 4).[16] These wage premiums for solving complex problems at work are thus substantially less than the difference of 34% that was observed before taking other factors into account.

The two measures of adequacy of computer skills show some relationship with wages when other factors are considered. With all of the factors taken into account, the wages of workers who believe they lack the necessary computer skills for their job are 2% lower than those of workers who believe they do have the necessary skills (Version 5), although there is not a significant effect in the analyses without taking into account the use of reading, writing and numeracy skills or occupation (Versions 3-4).[17] The wages of workers who have had employment difficulties because of their limited computer skills are 6% lower than those of workers who have not had such difficulties (Versions 3-5).[18]

Overall, the wage analysis shows several relationships between computer use and wages, including negative wage effects for workers who have no computer experience or who opt out of the computer assessment, and positive wage effects for workers who use e-mail at least once a month. Solving complex problems at work also has a positive relationship with wages after other factors are taken into account. Proficiency in problem solving in technology-rich environments does not show a relationship with wages that is distinct from general cognitive proficiency as measured by the literacy and numeracy assessments.

RELATIONSHIP WITH LABOUR PRODUCTIVITY

Across countries, there is a relationship between average labour productivity and a country's average proficiency in problem solving in technology-rich environments and using e-mail frequently (Figures 4.17 and 4.18).[19] The proportion of workers who are proficient at Level 2 or 3 explains 41% of the variation in labour productivity, while the proportion of workers who use e-mail at work at least once a month explains 48% of that variation. When proficiency in problem solving in technology-rich environments and e-mail use are used together to explain cross-country differences in labour productivity, the addition of proficiency in the domain does not help to explain the variation any more than e-mail use alone does, since e-mail use, itself, explains much of the variation of proficiency in problem solving in technology-rich environments. These simple correlations at the country level do not imply a direct causal relationship between proficiency in the domain, ICT use and labour productivity. Proficiency in problem solving in technology-rich environments and ICT use are only used as proxies of a complex set of factors reflecting the mix of occupations, industries and work practices that are themselves significant determinants of aggregate labour productivity. Still, these relationships do exist at the country level. In contrast, country averages of proficiency in literacy and numeracy are not correlated with average labour productivity, although there is a correlation with the use of reading skills.

THE COMPLEX RELATIONSHIP BETWEEN PROBLEM SOLVING USING ICT AND LABOUR MARKET OUTCOMES

The analyses above suggest that computer use is closely associated with labour market outcomes. Adults who lack computer experience are less likely to participate in the labour force and are paid lower wages than those who have experience with computers. In addition, adults who use e-mail at least once a month at home are more likely to participate in the labour force; and those who use e-mail at least once a month at work are paid higher wages. These relationships remain significant even after accounting for the use of other types of information-processing skills. Although it is unclear whether frequent computer use results in better work outcomes or vice versa – since computer experience is now required for many jobs, but many jobs also provide adults with opportunities to gain computer experience – the results show a clear link between work and computer use.

■ Figure 4.17 ■

Labour productivity and high performance in problem solving in technology-rich environments

In GDP per hour worked, percentage of workers scoring at Level 2 or 3 in problem solving in technology-rich environments

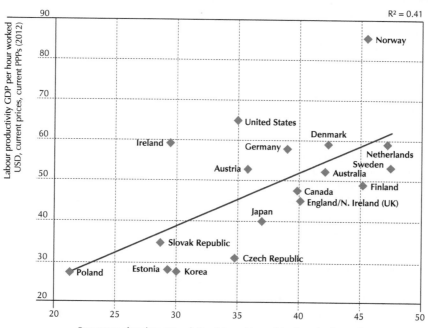

Source: Survey of Adult Skills (PIAAC) (2012), Table A4.1 and OECD.Stat.

StatLink ᯔᡰᡏ http://dx.doi.org/10.1787/888933231803

■ Figure 4.18 ■

Labour productivity and frequent use of e-mail

In GDP per hour worked, percentage of adults who use e-mail at least once a month at work

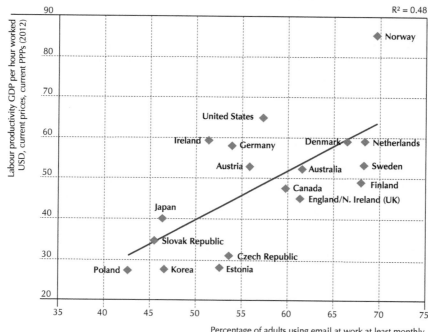

Source: Survey of Adult Skills (PIAAC)(2012), Table A4.2a and OECD.Stat.

StatLink ᯔᡰᡏ http://dx.doi.org/10.1787/888933231813

The relationship between proficiency in problem solving using ICT and work is more complex. The relationships between higher proficiency in this skill and all three labour market outcomes are significant after accounting for only socio-demographic factors. However, when proficiency in literacy and numeracy are accounted for as well, there is no longer a significant relationship with unemployment, and when the use of non-ICT skills are accounted for, the relationship with wages is no longer significant either.[20]

The analyses reinforce the finding from Chapter 3 that there are important areas of commonality across the three different proficiency measures. What matters for labour market outcomes, in part, is cognitive proficiency, in general, more than the different areas of cognitive proficiency, as measured in the three different assessments – literacy, numeracy and problem solving in technology-rich environments – in the Survey of Adult Skills. In addition, the higher levels of proficiency in literacy and numeracy include an element of problem solving that is somewhat similar to the kind of problem solving assessed in the survey.

The analyses also suggest that proficiency in problem solving using ICT has a closer relationship with the use of related skills than either literacy or numeracy proficiency does. When considering labour force participation and wages, accounting for skills use reduces the strength and significance of the relationships with proficiency in problem solving in technology-rich environments, for both the use of ICT skills and the use of reading, writing and numeracy skills. In contrast, the associations with proficiency in literacy and numeracy are not affected by accounting for skills use. A contrast between proficiency in problem solving in technology-rich environments and proficiency in literacy and numeracy is also seen in the cross-country correlations with labour productivity, where proficiency in problem solving using ICT is correlated with labour productivity, but proficiency in literacy and numeracy are not. In this way, proficiency in problem solving in technology-rich environments is similar to the skills-use variables – both ICT skills and reading skills – which are correlated with labour productivity. These relationships with skills use are an important way that proficiency in problem solving in technology-rich environments differs from proficiency in literacy and numeracy.

The relationship between proficiency in problem solving in technology-rich environments and the use of skills may reflect the way that adults developed this proficiency. Proficiency in these skills includes both the cognitive skills necessary to solve problems and the ability to use digital devices and functionality to access and manage information. Unlike proficiency in literacy and numeracy, which reflect years of development in formal education, many adults have developed ICT skills largely on their own at work and at home, with informal help from family, friends and colleagues. Since the demand for these skills in the labour market arose relatively recently, many adults have not had the opportunity to develop them during formal education. As a result, the part of proficiency in this domain that is related specifically to ICT skills is likely to be closely linked to opportunities and requirements for the use of these skills. And given the fact that, for most adults, ICT skills are largely self-taught, it is precisely those adults with higher cognitive proficiency in general who have had the capacity to develop proficiency in problem solving using ICT on their own, outside of formal education. Over time, this relationship between general cognitive proficiency and skills use may weaken if more adults acquire proficiency in the domain during their formal education – and that, in turn, may be necessary as proficiency in problem solving in technology-rich environments becomes increasingly important, both at and outside of work.

Notes

1. "Non-workers" refers to adults who were not working at the time of the survey, or who have not worked in the 12 months prior to it.

2. Table B4.14 in Annex B. Skilled occupations include managers (ISCO 1); professionals (ISCO 2); and technicians and associate professions (ISCO 3). Semi-skilled white-collar occupations include clerical support workers (ISCO 4); and service and sales workers (ISCO 5). Semi-skilled blue-collar occupations include skilled agricultural, forestry and fishery workers (ISCO 6); craft and related trades workers (ISCO 7); and plant and machine operators and assemblers (ISCO 8). Elementary occupations (ISCO 9) include cleaners, labourers, and similar unskilled occupations.

3. A "computer" included a mainframe, desktop or laptop computer, or any other device, such as a cell phone or tablet, that can be used to send or receive e-mail messages, process data or text, or find things on the Internet.

4. The analysis excludes adults below 25 years of age since many young adults are not yet in the labour force but still in school.

5. The results are similar for regressions that use a more comprehensive ICT use index that aggregates across the different ICT use questions.

6. These measures are for skills use outside of work for the analyses of labour force participation and unemployment, and for skills use at work for the analysis of wages.

7. There are few significant country differences in the size of these adjusted relationships.

8. The overall pattern of results is the same if only literacy or numeracy alone is used in Version 2, instead of both used together. In addition, if the frequency of ICT use and the use of other types of skills is added to the model before literacy and numeracy, the relationship between proficiency and labour force participation is still substantially weakened by the addition of literacy and numeracy, not by the addition of the various measures of skills use.

9. For all four versions of the model, the relationship between failing the ICT core and labour force participation is significantly weaker than the OECD average in the Czech Republic and Ireland, and is not significantly different from zero in either country. For all four versions of the model, the relationship between opting out and labour force participation is significantly weaker than the OECD average in the Czech Republic and is not significantly different from zero. In general, the overall pattern of results is the same if only literacy or numeracy alone is used in Version 2, or if the various skills-use variables are added to the model before literacy and numeracy.

10. This result is not substantially affected by using literacy or numeracy alone in Version 2 instead of both together, or by adding the various skills-use variables to the model before literacy and numeracy. For Denmark, in Versions 2-4, the relationship between Level 2 or 3 and unemployment is significantly different from the OECD average and positive, with the unemployment rate among workers who are proficient at Level 2 or 3 higher than that among workers who perform below Level 1.

11. The overall pattern of results in Versions 2-5 is not substantially affected by using literacy or numeracy alone instead of both together, except that the small remaining relationships between proficiency and wages in Versions 4 and 5 are still statistically significant when only literacy or numeracy are used separately.

12. Hanushek et al. (2013) also find that the inclusion of literacy and numeracy in a wage analysis substantially reduces the strength the relationship with proficiency in problem solving in technology-rich environments, and that the relationships between literacy and numeracy and wages are stronger than the relationship between proficiency in problem solving in technology-rich environments and wages. Their analysis does not consider the additional effect of skill use on these relationships.

13. In some versions of the models for the Czech Republic and Sweden, the wage penalty for having no computer experience is significantly smaller than the OECD average and not significantly different than zero. In some versions of the models, Ireland has a reversed relationship, with workers who have no computer experience receiving a significant wage benefit compared to workers who perform below Level 1.

14. The relationship between failing the ICT core and wages is significantly different in some countries than the OECD average. In some versions of the model, the Slovak Republic or Sweden are significantly different than the OECD and show a significant wage benefit, with workers who fail the ICT core receiving higher wages than those who perform below Level 1. In some versions of the model, Estonia and Korea are significantly different than the OECD and show a significant wage penalty, with workers who fail the ICT core receiving lower wages that those who perform below Level 1.

15. In Version 4, Sweden has a wage benefit associated with email use that is significantly smaller than the OECD average and is not significantly different than zero; in Version 5, this is true for Finland and Norway, in addition to Sweden.

16. In some versions of the model, Flanders (Belgium), Japan and Ireland have a wage benefit from engaging in complex problem solving at work that is significantly smaller than the OECD average and is not significantly different than zero.

17. In all versions of the model, Canada has a relationship between workers' beliefs that they lack the necessary computer skills for their job and wages that is significantly different than the OECD average and in the opposite direction: on average, workers in Canada who believe they lack the necessary computer skills receive higher wages than similar workers who do not believe they lack the necessary computer skills.

18. Denmark and the Slovak Republic are significantly different than the OECD average in some versions of the analysis and do not show a significant wage penalty from employment difficulties related to limited computer skills.

19. Note that the measure of labour productivity used (GDP per hour worked) does not reflect the contribution of other productive factors, unlike the analyses of wages.

20. For both unemployment and wages, there are significant relationships with either numeracy alone or with both literacy and numeracy. So the lack of significance with respect to proficiency in problem solving in technology-rich environments is not simply a reflection of the multicollinearity resulting from the use of several highly correlated measures of proficiency.

Reference

Hanushek, E., G. Schwerdt, S. Wiederhold and L. Woessmann (2013), "Returns to Skills Around the World: Evidence from PIAAC," *OECD Education Working Papers*, No. 101, OECD Publishing, Paris, *http://dx.doi.org/10.1787/5k3tsjqmvtq2-en*.

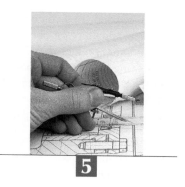

5

Some pointers for policy

In all countries, there are many adults who are not proficient in solving problems using ICT; in most, some groups of adults are more likely than others to struggle with these skills. This chapter suggests how governments can help their citizens to develop these skills and what governments should consider when designing e-government services. The chapter also presents several case studies of countries in which large proportions of the population are skilled in problem solving using ICT.

Given the widespread and growing presence of information and communication technology (ICT) in all areas of social and economic life, as described in Chapter 1, it is important for adults to be able to manage information in digital environments both at work and in daily life. The findings presented in Chapter 4 confirm the importance of these skills by showing how proficiency in problem solving using ICT is related to such economic outcomes as employment and earnings, while also showing that these relationships are sensitive to general cognitive proficiency and opportunities to use skills, both at work and at home. Policy makers, businesses, and education providers thus need to be aware of adults' proficiency in these 21st-century skills and to consider how they can help adults who have not yet developed these skills.

One of the major findings of this study is that there are many adults in all countries that participated in the 2012 Survey of Adult Skills, a product of the OECD Programme for the International Assessment of Adult Competencies (PIAAC), who do not possess sufficient skills in managing information in digital environments and are not comfortable using ICT to solve the kinds of problems that they are likely to encounter at work or in everyday life (see Chapter 2). This could slow the uptake of digital technologies at work, limit the utility of electronic platforms that deliver services, whether public (e.g. e-government, e-education) or private (e-commerce), and create inequalities in access to the digital world.

While the large number of adults with low proficiency in these skills is worrying, many adults, in all countries, have acquired greater proficiency in these skills over the past decade or two. It is only comparatively recently that the general public has been regularly exposed to technology-rich environments and expected to become proficient in problem solving using ICT. In historical terms, the acquisition of these skills by so many people, in such a short time is remarkable, even if considerable inequalities still exist in both access to digital technologies and proficiency in using them.

ADULTS WITH LOW PROFICIENCY IN PROBLEM SOLVING USING ICT

In all countries, low proficiency in problem solving in technology-rich environments is concentrated in certain groups of the population. Adults who are aged 55-65 years, adults with less than upper secondary education, adults with neither parent having attained upper secondary education, foreign-born adults who did not grow up speaking the language(s) in which the Survey of Adult Skills was delivered, and adults with low proficiency in literacy are particularly at risk of performing poorly in the problem-solving assessment.

The proportion of adults without any computer experience is of particular concern. Overall, 8% of adults in the OECD countries that participated in the survey have no computer experience. Again, certain groups are much more likely than others to lack computer experience. For example, 22% of adults aged 55-65, 21% of adults with less than upper secondary education, 19% of adults with neither parent having attained upper secondary education, and 13% of foreign-born, foreign-language adults have no computer experience. Lack of computer experience is associated with substantially lower labour force participation and wages, even after accounting for other relevant factors.

The fact that a relatively large proportion of adults either has low proficiency in problem solving in technology-rich environments or lacks familiarity with ICT and computers poses significant challenges to governments. Governments need to ensure broader access to digital technologies and networks and provide opportunities for adults with no or low skills in this domain to develop their proficiency. Governments also need to consider the level of their population's skills when developing initiatives to deliver services and information through digital technologies and networks. For example, initiatives designed to make the Internet the default medium of access to and interaction with public administrations may run the risk of excluding certain subgroups of the population unless alternative access points are provided and websites are designed to be used by adults with low literacy, numeracy or ICT skills.

Some countries may face special challenges that need to be addressed in particular ways. For example, countries with large immigrant populations – such as Canada and Sweden – may have a particularly large portion of their population with limited proficiency in problem solving in technology-rich environments that is foreign-born with foreign language. For such countries, it may be important to develop policies to increase proficiency in problem solving in technology-rich environments that reflect the special circumstances of their specific immigrant populations.

THE IMPORTANCE OF ACCESS TO AND USE OF ICT AND PROBLEM-SOLVING SKILLS AT WORK

Increasing access to ICT

In order to develop the skills in managing information in technology-rich environments that are measured by the Survey of Adult Skills, adults must first have access to computers and the Internet. It is striking that a simple measure of access to the Internet explains one third of the variation in proficiency in problem solving in technology-rich environments across countries (see Chapter 2). Ensuring that all citizens have access to ICT is a necessary, though of course not sufficient, condition for ensuring that these skills are developed across the population. Thus governments should adopt policies that maximise access to ICT and connectivity to information networks.

Government policy can play an active role in promoting access to ICT and the Internet, as has been seen throughout the introduction of broadband technologies. For example, over the past decade OECD countries have adopted policies that structure the market for broadband service, including policies to remove barriers to entry by competing firms and to provide tax incentives to suppliers for new investments. The regulatory framework that governs the provision of telecommunications services is a key determinant of access to digital networks through its influence on the price and quality of the ICT services that are available to the public and the affordability of ICT access. In addition, governments have encouraged the adoption of broadband through programmes to increase awareness of the technology and policies to provide incentives to specific groups of users, such as disabled people, unemployed individuals, rural residents and new PC owners. Such policies are likely to have led to substantial increases in the rate of broadband takeup (OECD, 2008). For example, the government of Canada undertook a number of projects and initiatives to increase ICT access for Canadians in rural and remote communities.[1]

Governments could also expand access by making computers and digital networks available in public institutions, such as existing government offices that interact with the public, including libraries, post offices, medical and social services, tax offices, and schools and universities. These institutions already use ICT in their operations, and they often provide ways for citizens to use their services on line or with computer kiosks. For example, Figure 1.5 in Chapter 1 shows an estimate of the proportion of adults who use the Internet to interact with public authorities in some way. Government institutions could build on this by identifying adults who do not access services using ICT and providing assistance for them to do so; and government agencies that interact with the public could take a more active role in encouraging and supporting the adults who are not yet comfortable using ICT.

This approach of government actively providing access to ICT and encouraging the use of it is similar to the role that some governments have played in making ICT available in compulsory education and encouraging teachers to use the technology to improve instruction. Box 5.1 describes the role that the government has played in Korea to provide ICT access in the public schools. The Korea case underlines the importance of providing both technology access and appropriate support to encourage its use, since access is necessary but not sufficient to encourage the development of proficiency in problem solving using ICT.

Policies to encourage greater use of ICT and problem-solving skills

When it comes to developing ICT skills, use is as important as access. As discussed in Chapter 3, there is a clear relationship between ICT use and proficiency in problem solving in technology-rich environments, both across and within countries. The association of proficiency in this domain with frequency of ICT use reinforces the common observation that many people acquire proficiency in these skills informally, through trial and error and with the help of family, friends and colleagues. Part of the relationship between ICT use and proficiency in problem solving using ICT stems from the opportunities to develop skills that regular ICT use affords. Across all countries, the proportion of adults who use e-mail regularly is roughly double the proportion of adults who perform at high levels in problem solving in technology-rich environments. Regular use of ICT both at and outside of work is likely to improve proficiency in these skills by providing more opportunities to solve problems using the technology. Governments' use of e-mail and Internet websites to communicate with citizens is likely to encourage citizens who are less comfortable using ICT to develop their skills in this area.

But using ICT even daily will not necessarily improve an adult's ability to solve problems in technology-rich environments: higher-order cognitive skills are also required. As discussed in Chapter 4, workers who are confronted with complex problems to solve at least once a month are more likely than other workers to be highly proficient in problem solving using ICT. The Finnish working life 2020 programme[2], the workplace innovation fund in Ireland, and the workplace productivity project in New Zealand (Buchanan et al., 2010) all envisage a redesign of the working environment so that workers can use their skills more.

DEVELOPING PROFICIENCY IN PROBLEM SOLVING USING ICT IN FORMAL EDUCATION

The analyses in Chapter 3 show that proficiency in problem solving in technology-rich environments is related to education. Even after accounting for other factors, an individual with tertiary education is 13 percentage points more likely to perform at Level 2 or 3 in the assessment than an adult who lacks upper secondary education. In addition, an adult who recently participated in adult education and training is 7 percentage points more likely to perform at those levels in the assessment than an adult who had not recently participated in adult education and training.

Yet formal education may not be the primary context in which these skills are developed. Education may lead to later opportunities to develop proficiency in problem solving using ICT, or the level of education an adult attains may reflect certain personal characteristics that also tend to be associated with greater proficiency in those skills. Still, formal education helps to develop more sophisticated approaches to solving problems, including the capacity to assess the quality of information gathered from different sources and synthesize that information into a coherent whole. Educational settings are also likely to develop proficiency in the more difficult aspects of computer programmes – such as the spreadsheet and word processing programmes that are a focus of the assessment of problem solving in technology-rich environments.

The PISA 2012 report on problem solving (OECD, 2014) discusses some possible approaches to improving 15-year-old students' skills in problem solving, including encouraging teachers and students to reflect on solution strategies when dealing with subject-specific problems in the classroom. When teachers ask students to describe the steps they took to solve a problem, they encourage students' metacognition, which, in turn, improves general problem-solving skills. Problem-solving skills cannot be taught in a traditional classroom setting alone where a set of rules-based solutions are taught. As Levy (2010) argues, when solutions are taught in classes, it is difficult to improve students' ability to solve unforeseen problems in real life. Exposure to diverse real-world problems and contexts seems to be essential for developing problem-solving skills. Countries can also do more to improve students' access to ICT at school. Across OECD countries, PISA reports that only two in three 15-year-olds attend schools where there is adequate access to computers for instruction (OECD 2013, Vol. IV, Figure IV.3.8).

Adult education and training is another promising route for developing proficiency in problem solving in technology-rich environments. Among other benefits, adult education and training courses are usually much more accessible to adults: they are generally offered in more flexible schedules and are specifically targeted to address the interests and needs of their students. For example, adult learning courses can be targeted to help adults who have low proficiency in these skills, while formal education tends to reach primarily younger adults who may already be very proficient. In addition, adult education and training can be used to reach specific populations, such as older adults, immigrants or adults with less formal education, who may already be receiving some support with targeted government programmes. Box 5.2 describes examples of adult education programmes offered in the Nordic countries – countries that show some of the highest levels of proficiency in problem solving in technology-rich environments, particularly among older adults.

In addition, on-the-job training provided by employers, either in formal settings, such as training sessions or workshops, or in informal settings, such as learning from supervisors or peers, is a good way to help employees to develop various work-related skills as well as proficiency in problem solving using ICT. During on-the-job training, cognitive skills, including problem-solving skills and ICT skills, can be both developed and used to do the job better, which can also be beneficial for employers.

E-GOVERNMENT AND PROFICIENCY IN PROBLEM SOLVING USING ICT

For over a decade, many governments have been providing citizens with access to government services through e-mail and the Internet. The move toward e-government has been prompted by the dual goals of decreasing cost and increasing service (OECD, 2009). Using ICT can allow government agencies to function more efficiently internally while also providing more coherent external interactions with the public. For example, between 2008 and 2013, Denmark showed a remarkable increase in the use of the Internet for interacting with public authorities: in 2008, 49% of Danish adults used e-government services; in 2013, 85% of adults did (see Figure 1.5 in Chapter 1).

However, in many countries, progress in expanding e-government has been limited by the public's slow uptake. Results from the Survey of Adult Skills provide one explanation for the slow pace of adoption: many adults do not have sufficient proficiency in computer skills to feel confident in using e-government services.

An OECD report on the adoption of e-government services recommends that these services need to be more focused on user needs in order to be successful (OECD, 2009). Among other things, the report recommends the use of a simple organisation of e-government websites and common architectures across all content areas for navigation and search within websites. Such changes would make it easier for people with low proficiency in computer skills to use e-government websites. Without such effort, government services can create a digital divide among the citizens. Government policies need to be carefully designed to bridge the gap between those with access to and the ability to use the services and those without such capacity.

Once a sufficient level of proficiency is reached among the population, governments can then begin to require e-government use, which strongly encourages all adults to develop at least minimal levels of proficiency in problem solving using ICT. Denmark has taken this approach with respect to some e-government services, including mandatory registration of unemployed adults on a public website for job-seekers and mandatory use of electronic transfers for all government payments (OECD, 2009, Box 3.32). This approach is only feasible in a country whose citizens have high levels of proficiency in computer skills.

HIGH-PERFORMING COUNTRIES

The Nordic countries and the Netherlands show particularly high levels of proficiency in problem solving in technology-rich environments, with many adults performing at Level 2 and 3 in the assessment and few adults who have no computer experience. The high average performance in these countries is a reflection of the better results among the population subgroups that tend to perform poorly in other countries. For example, fewer older or less-educated adults in these countries have no computer experience, and more adults who have less-educated parents or who work in elementary occupations perform at Level 2 or 3. The high average performance in the Nordic countries and the Netherlands tends to reflect high performance across the full population, not just among particular groups.

The high levels of performance in problem solving in technology-rich environments in these countries is paired with high levels of ICT use. Over 80% of adults in these countries use e-mail frequently, with most doing so daily. At the same time, most of these countries show larger-than-average numbers of workers who have had difficulties in getting a job or a promotion because of their limited computer skills. This suggests that, in these societies, there is a widespread expectation that everyone will have some level of proficiency in these skills.

To some extent, the high performance in the Nordic countries and the Netherlands may be associated with achieving high levels of access to computers and the Internet earlier than occurred in other countries. In 2005, 76% of the households across these five countries had access to a computer at home – a proportion 17 percentage points larger than the OECD average; and 69% of the households in the five countries had access to the Internet – a proportion 20 percentage points larger than the OECD average.[3] In addition, greater equity of opportunities in the access to formal education and adult education and training, both at and outside of work, might have contributed to their high performance. When it comes to developing skills in Nordic countries, socio-economic status matters little or not at all.

Box 5.1 **Korea: The largest proportion of highly proficient young adults**

Among all OECD countries, Korea has the largest proportion of 16-24 year-olds who scored at Level 2 or 3 (63.4%) and the smallest proportion of young adults who scored below Level 1 (2.6%) in problem solving in technology-rich environments in the 2012 Survey of Adult Skills. In a related finding, the OECD Programme for International Student Assessment (PISA) shows that 15-year-old students in Korea are highly proficient in digital reading skills, including evaluating information on the Internet, assessing its credibility, and navigating webpages. In fact, Korean students performed significantly better in digital reading than in print reading, (as did students in Australia, Iceland, Macao-China, New Zealand and Sweden) (OECD, 2011). In addition, 15-year-old Korean students also had the highest performance in PISA's computer-based creative problem-solving assessment among the 44 countries and economies that participated in that assessment (OECD, 2014).

Considering that a high level of cognitive skills and frequent use of ICT are linked to high performance in problem solving in technology-rich environments (see Chapter 3), it is not surprising to find that young Korean adults are highly proficient in these skills. These young adults also performed very well in both literacy and numeracy in the Survey of Adult Skills. Technology is pervasive in both public and private settings (for example, high-speed Internet connections are available in subways and trains), so a certain level of ICT skills is required to conduct everyday tasks. In universities, it is common to find students using their mobile devices to reserve library seats, mark their attendance in classes, and check their grades.[1]

According to the Korea Internet and Security Agency (KISA, 2013), 99% of junior high and high school students use the Internet more than once a day, spending an average of about two hours per day on line. Most Korean students use computers and the Internet outside of school rather than at school, with only half of students reporting that they use the Internet at school. Some 68% of 15-year-olds reported that they do not have time to use the Internet at school, according to PISA 2012 results. Most Korean students reported that they use the Internet to search for information, communicate with friends, and access educational content. More students access the Internet through mobile devices, such as smartphones, tablet PCs and laptops. In fact, ownership of smart devices tripled among Korean youth between 2011 and 2012, rising from 21% to 65% of young people who own such devices. As of 2013, about 85% of junior high and high school students owned smartphones, according to the Korean Ministry of Education.

...

The Korean government continues to invest in ICT in schools. In 2011, the Korean government launched the "Smart Education" initiative, which aims to make digital versions of textbooks and assessments, increase the number of online classes, promote the use of Internet Protocol Television in class, allow easy and free access to a variety of educational materials, improve school infrastructure and standard platforms for a Smart Education cloud system, and strengthen teacher competencies with training courses and smart devices (Ministry of Education, Science and Technology, 2011).

ICT is frequently used at the tertiary level of education. In 2001, the Ministry of Education and Human Resource Development enacted the "Cyber University Foundation Law", which spawned the creation of 17 cyber universities by 2004 and another four by 2012. In addition, there are nine cyber graduate schools across the country, as of 2013, offering distance and e-learning degree courses, such as MBAs, education and information-security programmes.[2]

Notes:

1. "In South Korea, All of Life is Mobile", *The New York Times*, www.nytimes.com/2009/05/25/technology/25iht-mobile.html?pagewanted=all&_r=0, [accessed 26 November 2014].

2. Cyber University Statistics, available at www.cuinfo.net/home/eudc/statistics.sub.action?gnb=55, [accessed 9 September 2014].

Box 5.2 The Nordic Countries: High proficiency, particularly among older adults

Denmark, Finland, Norway and Sweden have the largest proportion of adults aged 16-65 who scored at Level 2 or 3 in problem solving in technology-rich environments, and the smallest proportion of adults who have no computer experience or basic ICT skills among all the OECD countries that participated in the Survey of Adult Skills. The Nordic countries have highly sophisticated ICT infrastructures in place that make it easy to access the Internet anywhere. In 2011, more than 85% of adults in Denmark, Finland, Norway and Sweden had access to the computer (Table B1.1), and more than 85% of adults in those countries had access to the Internet. For example, almost 92% of Swedish adults have access to a computer and about 91% have access to the Internet at home.

Participation in adult education and training is above 60%, on average across Nordic countries, with high rates even among the least-skilled adults. ICT has been used as a tool to support and complement formal education, giving learners access to educational resources anywhere, any time. Some 35 universities and university colleges in Sweden offer distance higher education courses.[1] Similarly, Norway offers online adult education and training through the NKI Distance Education and through Norwaynet with IT for Open Learning (NITOL).[2]

There have been several policy efforts to increase participation in adult learning and training for disadvantaged groups in Nordic countries. In Finland, study vouchers (Opintoseteli) are provided to cover the costs of developing ICT skills among retirees, immigrants and unemployed adults. These groups can use vouchers to pay for any courses in Adult Education Centres.[3]

The high average performance in problem solving in technology-rich environments that is observed among the Nordic countries is a reflection of the high performance of older adults in these countries. This high proficiency among older adults seems to be associated with high employment rates among these age groups. As the findings in this report suggest, using ICT skills and other cognitive skills at work helps to maintain and develop these skills. For example, Norway has one of the highest employment rates and the lowest unemployment rate among older adults among all OECD countries. The Norwegian government works with business to establish policies that create comfortable working conditions for older adults while reforming the pension system to provide stronger economic incentives for older people to remain employed. When older adults stay longer in the labour force, they can learn new skills through colleagues or work-based training. According to an employers' survey conducted in 2011, 29% of Norwegian companies with 10 or more employees reported that they offer training and career-development opportunities to older employees (Eironline, 2013).

In addition to high-performing older adults, less-educated adults and low-skilled workers with no computer experience in the Nordic countries also performed relatively well in the assessment. In Denmark, adult vocational training programmes (arbejdsmarkedsuddannelser or AMU) provide vocational training for both low-skilled and skilled workers, as well as unemployed adults, immigrants and refugees. The programmes aim to improve vocational and other skills, including ICT, literacy and numeracy skills. In 2006, 617 000 adults participated in these programmes.[4]

Notes:

1. Eurostat, extracted September 2014, Community Survey on ICT usage in households and by individuals, http://epp.eurostat.ec.europa.eu/tgm/table.do?tab=table&init=1&plugin=1&language=en&pcode=tin00134

2. NITOL, available at www2.tisip.no/nitol/english/nitol.html [accessed 9 September 2014].

3. Training Vouchers, available at www.hel.fi/www/sto/fi/opiskelu/maahanmuuttajat-immigrants/opintosetelit [accessed 9 September 2014].

4. Adult vocational training in Denmark, available at http://eng.uvm.dk/Education/Adult-Education-and-Continuing-Training/Adult-vocational-training-in-Denmark [accessed 9 September 2014].

Notes

1. Statistics Canada (2008) found that significantly fewer Canadians in remote and rural areas have access to the Internet. As a response, federal, provincial and territorial governments of Canada have undertaken a number of projects and initiatives to increase the use of ICT in rural and remote communities. For example, Connecting Canadians, a plan to bring high-speed Internet to 280 000 Canadian households as part of Digital Canada 150 (a comprehensive approach to ensure that all Canadian citizens can benefit from the digital age) was launched in the summer of 2014. The government of Canada will be investing up to CAD 305 million over five years to extend access to high-speed Internet (five megabits per second) to 98% of Canadian households, mainly in rural and remote communities. *www.ic.gc.ca/eic/site/028.nsf/eng/50009.html*.

2. Working Life 2020 as part of Liideri programme, available at *www.tekes.fi/en/programmes-and-services/tekes-programmes/liideri/*.

3. OECD Key ICT Indicators, available at *www.oecd.org/internet/broadband/oecdkeyictindicators.htm* [accessed 1 August 2014].

References

Buchanan, J., L. Scott, S. Yu, H. Schutz and **M. Jakubauskas** (2010), *"Skills Demand and Utilisation: An International Review of Approaches to Measurement and Policy Development"*, OECD Local Economic and Employment Development (LEED) Working Papers, No. 2010/04, OECD Publishing, Paris, *http://dx.doi.org/10.1787/5km8zddfr2jk-en*.

Eironline (2013), Norway: The Role of Governments and Social Partners in Keeping Older Workers in the Labour Market, *www.eurofound.europa.eu/eiro/studies/tn1210012s/no1210019q.htm*.

KISA (2013), 2013 Survey on the Internet usage, *http://isis.kisa.or.kr/eng/board/fileDown.jsp?pageId=040100&bbsId=10&itemId=326&athSeq=1*.

Levy, F. (2010), *"How Technology Changes Demands for Human Skills"*, OECD Education Working Papers, No.45, OECD Publishing, Paris, *http://dx.doi.org/10.1787/5kmhds6czqzq-en*.

Ministry of Education, Science and Technology (2011), 스마트교육 추진 전략 실행계획 *(Action plan for Korea's Smart Education Initiative)*, *www.moe.go.kr/web/110501/ko/board/view.do?bbsId=348&boardSeq=23930*.

OECD (2014), *PISA 2012 Results: Creative Problem Solving (Volume V): Students' Skills in Tackling Real-Life Problems*, PISA, OECD Publishing, Paris, *http://dx.doi.org/10.1787/9789264208070-en*.

OECD (2013), *PISA 2012 Results: What Makes Schools Successful?* (Volume IV): Resources, Policies and Practices, PISA, OECD Publishing, Paris, *http://dx.doi.org/10.1787/9789264201156-en*.

OECD (2011), *PISA 2009 Results: Students on Line: Digital Technologies and Performance* (Volume VI), PISA, OECD Publishing, Paris, *http://dx.doi.org/10.1787/9789264112995-en*.

OECD (2009), *Rethinking e-Government Services: User-Centred Approaches*, OECD Publishing, Paris, *http://dx.doi.org/10.1787/9789264059412-en*.

OECD (2008), *Broadband Growth and Policies in OECD Countries*, OECD Publishing, Paris, *http://dx.doi.org/10.1787/9789264046764-en*.

Statistics Canada (2008), *How Canadians' Use of the Internet Affects Social Life and Civic Participation*, Connectedness Series, No. 16, Statistics Canada.

Wood, S. (2004), *Fully on-the-job Training: Experiences and Steps Ahead*, National Centre for Vocational Education Research, Adelaide.

Annex A

TABLES OF RESULTS

All tables in Annex A are available on line.

Notes regarding Cyprus

Note by Turkey: The information in this document with reference to "Cyprus" relates to the southern part of the Island. There is no single authority representing both Turkish and Greek Cypriot people on the Island. Turkey recognises the Turkish Republic of Northern Cyprus (TRNC). Until a lasting and equitable solution is found within the context of the United Nations, Turkey shall preserve its position concerning the "Cyprus issue".

Note by all the European Union Member States of the OECD and the European Union: The Republic of Cyprus is recognised by all members of the United Nations with the exception of Turkey. The information in this document relates to the area under the effective control of the Government of the Republic of Cyprus.

A note regarding the Russian Federation

Readers should note that the sample for the Russian Federation does not include the population of the Moscow municipal area. The data published, therefore, do not represent the entire resident population aged 16-65 in Russia but rather the population of Russia *excluding* the population residing in the Moscow municipal area.

More detailed information re garding the data from the Russian Federation as well as that of other countries can be found in the *Technical Report of the Survey of Adult Skills* (OECD, 2014).

[Part 1/1]

Table A1.1 **Percentage of workers aged 16-74 who are in jobs that require solving unforeseen problems or conducting routine tasks**

	Solving unforeseen problems	Routine tasks
Austria	81.8	27.5
Belgium	83.6	44.7
Czech Republic	83.4	57.3
Denmark	92.9	39.5
Estonia	89.9	59.7
Finland	80.8	48.9
France	81.3	48.0
Germany	84.6	31.3
Ireland	77.9	53.0
Italy	74.0	42.0
Netherlands	93.5	24.4
Norway	91.5	25.3
Poland	84.9	43.0
Slovak Republic	75.2	43.6
Spain	82.8	58.3
Sweden	95.2	31.4
United Kingdom	84.5	59.4
Average	84.6	43.4

Source: European Working Conditions Survey, 2010.

StatLink ⟡ http://dx.doi.org/10.1787/888933231824

[Part 1/1]

Table A1.2 **Percentage of 25-64 year-olds who made online purchases, 2005 and 2013**

	2005	2013
Austria	26	58
Belgium	18	51
Czech Republic[1]	13	36
Denmark	51	81
Estonia[3]	18	24
Finland	40	71
France[2]	36	62
Germany	47	74
Ireland	22	49
Italy	7	22
Netherlands	46	72
Norway	58	77
Poland	6	33
Slovak Republic	9	45
Spain	13	35
Sweden	54	77
United Kingdom	47	80
Average	30	56

Notes:
1. Year of reference 2006.
2. Year of reference 2007.
3. Year of reference 2009.

Note: Within the 12 months prior to the Eurostat Community Survey.

Source: Eurostat, Community Survey on ICT usage in households and by individuals.

StatLink ⟡ http://dx.doi.org/10.1787/888933231831

[Part 1/1]

Percentage of unemployed individuals aged 16-74 who used the Internet to look for a job or send
Table A1.3   **a job application**

	2005	2013
Austria	29	71
Belgium[1]	27	51
Czech Republic	10	40
Denmark	48	62
Estonia[1]	37	76
Finland	42	69
France[1]	35	67
Germany[1]	52	58
Ireland	2	48
Italy	15	41
Netherlands	32	81
Norway	38	80
Poland	8	33
Slovak Republic	26	42
Spain[2]	24	52
Sweden	78	90
United Kingdom[2]	46	64
Average	32	60

Notes:
1. Year of reference 2006.
2. Year of reference 2007.
Note: Within the 3 months prior to the Eurostat Community Survey.
Source: Eurostat, Community Survey on ICT usage in households and by individuals.
StatLink ᴍᴤᴘ http://dx.doi.org/10.1787/888933231845

[Part 1/1]

Table A1.4   **Percentage of workers reporting frequent use* of technology, by sector of work, EU 27 average**

	ICT	ICT and machinery	Machinery	No technology
Financial services	81	10	2	7
Education	67	4	2	27
Public administration and defence	66	10	8	16
Health	55	10	5	30
Other services	52	10	9	30
Wholesale, retail, food and accommodation	37	10	14	38
Industry	28	19	38	15
Transport	26	15	25	34
Construction	17	13	52	18
Agriculture	7	8	41	44

* Use is considered frequent if the technology is used more than 75% of the time.
Source: European Working Conditions Survey, 2010.
StatLink ᴍᴤᴘ http://dx.doi.org/10.1787/888933231853

[Part 1/1]

Table A1.5 **Percentage of individuals aged 16-74 who used the Internet to interact with public authorities**

	2008	2013
Australia[2]	38	m
Austria	51	54
Belgium	26	50
Canada[1]	46	m
Czech Republic	19	29
Denmark	49	85
Estonia	37	48
Finland	62	69
France	48	60
Germany	44	49
Ireland	34	45
Italy	20	21
Netherlands	61	79
New Zealand	m	51
Norway	72	76
Poland	22	23
Slovak Republic	40	33
Spain	32	44
Sweden	59	78
United Kingdom	40	41
Average	42	52

Notes:

1. Year of reference 2009.

2. Year of reference 2010.

Note: Within the 12 months prior to the surveys, for private purposes. Derived variable on use of e-government services. Individuals used the Internet for at least one of the following: to obtain services from public authorities websites; to download official forms; and/or to send completed forms.

Data for Canada and New Zealand refer only to obtaining services from public authorities websites but does not include other activities such as downloading or completing official forms.

Source: Eurostat, Community Survey on ICT usage in households and by individuals; OECD ICT database.

StatLink ⊡≋⊡ http://dx.doi.org/10.1787/888933231860

[Part 1/1]

Table A2.1 Tasks in the problem solving in technology-rich environments assessment

Proficiency level	Score	Item name	Description
Level 1: 241-290 Tasks in which the goal is explicitly stated and for which a small number of operations are performed in a single familiar environment.	268	Club Membership – Member ID	Locate an item within a large amount of information in a multiple-column spread-sheet based on a single explicit criterion; use e-mail to communicate the result.
	286	Reply All	With a defined goal and explicit criteria, use e-mail and send information to three people.
	286	Party Invitations – Can / Cannot Come	Categorise a small number of messages in an e-mail application into existing folders according to one explicit criterion.
Level 2: 291-340 Tasks that have explicit criteria for success, a small number of applications, several steps and operators, and occasional unexpected outcomes.	296	Club Membership – Eligibility for Club President	Organise large amounts of information in a multiple-column spreadsheet using multiple explicit criteria; locate and mark relevant entries.
	299	Party Invitations Accommodations	Categorise a small number of messages in an e-mail application by creating a new folder; evaluate the contents of the entries based on one criterion in order to file them in the proper folder.
	305	Digital Photography Book Purchase	Choose an item on a webpage that best matches a set of given criteria from a search engine results page; the information can be made available only by clicking on links and navigating through several webpages; based on a search engine results page, navigate through several Internet sites in order to choose an item on a webpage that best matches a set of given criteria.
	316	CD Tally	Organise large amounts of information in a multiple-column spreadsheet and determine a value based on a single explicit criterion; use a dropdown menu in a novel Internet application to communicate the result.
	320	Tickets	Use a novel Internet-based application involving multiple tools to complete an order based on a combination of explicit criteria.
	321	Lamp Return	Enact a plan to navigate through a website to complete an explicitly specified consumer transaction. Monitor the progress of submitting a request, retrieving an e-mail message, and filling out a novel online form.
	325	Sprained Ankle – Reliable / Trustworthy Source	Apply evaluation criteria and then navigate through multiple websites to infer the most reliable and trustworthy site. Monitoring throughout the process is required.
Level 3: 341 or more Tasks involving multiple applications, a large number of steps, occasional impasses, and the discovery and use of ad hoc commands in a novel environment.	342	Sprained Ankle – Site Evaluation Table	Evaluate several entries in a search engine results page given an explicit set of separate reliability criteria.
	346	Meeting Rooms	Using information from a novel Internet application and several e-mail messages, establish and apply criteria to solve a scheduling problem where an impasse must be resolved, and communicate the outcome.
	355	Local E-mail – File 3 E-mails	Infer the proper folder destination in order to transfer a subset of incoming e-mail messages based on the subject header and the specific contents of each message.
	374	Class Attendance	Using information embedded in an e-mail message, establish and apply the criteria to transform the e-mail information to a spreadsheet. Monitor the progress of correctly organising information to perform computations through novel built-in functions.

StatLink ⬛⬛⬛ http://dx.doi.org/10.1787/888933231879

[Part 1/1]

Table A2.2 **Percentage of adults scoring at each proficiency level in problem solving in technology-rich environments**

OECD	Below level 1		Level 1		Level 2		Level 3		No computer experience		Failed ICT core		Opted out of the computer-based assessment		Missing	
	%	S.E.	%	S.E.	%	S.E.	%	S.E.	%	S.E.	%	S.E.	%	S.E.	%	S.E.
National entities																
Australia	9.2	(0.6)	28.9	(0.8)	31.8	(1.0)	6.2	(0.5)	4.0	(0.3)	3.5	(0.3)	13.7	(0.6)	2.7	(0.3)
Austria	9.9	(0.5)	30.9	(0.9)	28.1	(0.8)	4.3	(0.4)	9.6	(0.4)	4.0	(0.3)	11.3	(0.5)	1.8	(0.2)
Canada	14.8	(0.4)	30.0	(0.7)	29.4	(0.5)	7.1	(0.4)	4.5	(0.2)	5.9	(0.2)	6.3	(0.3)	1.9	(0.1)
Czech Republic	12.9	(0.9)	28.8	(1.3)	26.5	(1.1)	6.6	(0.6)	10.3	(0.5)	2.2	(0.3)	12.1	(0.8)	0.6	(0.2)
Denmark	13.9	(0.6)	32.9	(0.8)	32.3	(0.7)	6.3	(0.4)	2.4	(0.2)	5.3	(0.2)	6.4	(0.3)	0.4	(0.1)
Estonia	13.8	(0.5)	29.0	(0.7)	23.2	(0.6)	4.3	(0.4)	9.9	(0.3)	3.4	(0.2)	15.8	(0.4)	0.5	(0.1)
Finland	11.0	(0.5)	28.9	(0.8)	33.2	(0.7)	8.4	(0.6)	3.5	(0.3)	5.2	(0.3)	9.7	(0.4)	0.1	(0.1)
France	m	m	m	m	m	m	m	m	10.5	(0.3)	6.0	(0.3)	11.6	(0.4)	m	m
Germany	14.4	(0.8)	30.5	(0.8)	29.2	(0.8)	6.8	(0.6)	7.9	(0.5)	3.7	(0.4)	6.1	(0.5)	1.5	(0.2)
Ireland	12.6	(0.7)	29.5	(0.9)	22.1	(0.8)	3.1	(0.3)	10.1	(0.4)	4.7	(0.4)	17.4	(0.7)	0.6	(0.1)
Italy	m	m	m	m	m	m	m	m	24.4	(0.8)	2.5	(0.3)	14.6	(0.9)	m	m
Japan	7.6	(0.6)	19.7	(0.8)	26.3	(0.8)	8.3	(0.5)	10.2	(0.5)	10.7	(0.7)	15.9	(0.9)	1.3	(0.1)
Korea	9.8	(0.5)	29.6	(0.9)	26.8	(0.8)	3.6	(0.3)	15.5	(0.4)	9.1	(0.4)	5.4	(0.3)	0.3	(0.1)
Netherlands	12.5	(0.6)	32.6	(0.7)	34.3	(0.8)	7.3	(0.4)	3.0	(0.2)	3.7	(0.3)	4.5	(0.3)	2.3	(0.2)
Norway	11.4	(0.6)	31.8	(0.8)	34.9	(0.9)	6.1	(0.4)	1.6	(0.2)	5.2	(0.3)	6.7	(0.4)	2.2	(0.2)
Poland	12.0	(0.6)	19.0	(0.7)	15.4	(0.7)	3.8	(0.3)	19.5	(0.5)	6.5	(0.4)	23.8	(0.7)	0.0	(0.0)
Slovak Republic	8.9	(0.5)	28.8	(0.9)	22.8	(0.7)	2.9	(0.3)	22.0	(0.7)	2.2	(0.2)	12.2	(0.4)	0.3	(0.1)
Spain	m	m	m	m	m	m	m	m	17.0	(0.5)	6.2	(0.3)	10.7	(0.5)	m	m
Sweden	13.1	(0.5)	30.8	(0.8)	35.2	(0.9)	8.8	(0.6)	1.6	(0.2)	4.8	(0.3)	5.7	(0.3)	0.1	(0.0)
United States	15.8	(0.9)	33.1	(0.9)	26.0	(0.9)	5.1	(0.4)	5.2	(0.4)	4.1	(0.4)	6.3	(0.6)	4.3	(0.6)
Sub-national entities																
Flanders (Belgium)	14.8	(0.6)	29.8	(0.8)	28.7	(0.8)	5.8	(0.4)	7.4	(0.3)	3.5	(0.3)	4.7	(0.3)	5.2	(0.2)
England (UK)	15.1	(0.8)	33.8	(1.1)	29.3	(0.9)	5.7	(0.5)	4.1	(0.3)	5.8	(0.4)	4.6	(0.4)	1.6	(0.2)
Northern Ireland (UK)	16.4	(1.5)	34.5	(1.2)	25.0	(1.2)	3.7	(0.6)	10.0	(0.6)	5.8	(0.4)	2.3	(0.3)	2.2	(0.3)
England/N. Ireland (UK)	15.1	(0.8)	33.9	(1.0)	29.1	(0.9)	5.6	(0.5)	4.3	(0.3)	5.8	(0.3)	4.5	(0.4)	1.6	(0.2)
Average[1]	12.3	(0.1)	29.4	(0.2)	28.2	(0.2)	5.8	(0.1)	8.0	(0.1)	4.9	(0.1)	9.9	(0.1)	1.5	(0.0)
Average-22[2]	m	m	m	m	m	m	m	m	9.3	(0.1)	4.9	(0.1)	10.2	(0.1)	m	m

Partners

Cyprus[3]	m	m	m	m	m	m	m	m	18.4	(0.4)	1.9	(0.2)	18.0	(0.5)	m	m
Russian Federation[4]	14.9	(2.2)	25.6	(1.3)	20.4	(1.4)	5.5	(1.1)	18.3	(1.7)	2.5	(0.6)	12.8	(1.6)	0.0	(0.0)

1. Average of 19 participating OECD countries and entities.
2. Average of 22 OECD countries and entities: average of 19 countries with France, Italy and Spain.
3. See notes at the beginning of this Annex.
4. See note at the beginning of this Annex.
Source: Survey of Adult Skills (PIAAC) (2012).
StatLink http://dx.doi.org/10.1787/888933231884

[Part 1/1]

Table A2.3 Percentage of adults with high proficiency in problem solving in technology-rich environments

OECD	High proficiency	
	%	S.E.
National entities		
Australia	38.0	(1.0)
Austria	32.5	(0.8)
Canada	36.6	(0.6)
Czech Republic	33.1	(1.1)
Denmark	38.7	(0.7)
Estonia	27.6	(0.7)
Finland	41.6	(0.7)
France	m	m
Germany	36.0	(0.8)
Ireland	25.3	(0.8)
Italy	m	m
Japan	34.6	(0.8)
Korea	30.4	(0.8)
Netherlands	41.5	(0.8)
Norway	41.0	(0.8)
Poland	19.2	(0.8)
Slovak Republic	25.6	(0.8)
Spain	m	m
Sweden	44.0	(0.7)
United States	31.1	(1.0)
Sub-national entities		
Flanders (Belgium)	34.5	(0.8)
England (UK)	35.0	(0.9)
Northern Ireland (UK)	28.7	(1.3)
England/N. Ireland (UK)	34.8	(0.9)
Average[1]	34.0	(0.2)
Average-22[2]	m	m
Partners		
Cyprus[3]	m	m
Russian Federation[4]	25.9	(2.2)

1. Average of 19 participating OECD countries and entities.
2. Average of 22 OECD countries and entities: average of 19 countries with France, Italy and Spain.
3. See notes at the beginning of this Annex.
4. See note at the beginning of this Annex.
Note: High proficiency is defined as scoring at Level 2 or 3 in problem solving in technology-rich environments.
Source: Survey of Adult Skills (PIAAC) (2012).
StatLink ⧉ http://dx.doi.org/10.1787/888933231895

[Part 1/1]

Table A2.4a **Frequency of e-mail use in everyday life**

OECD	Never		Less than once a month		Less than once a week but at least once a month		At least once a week but not everyday		Everyday	
	%	S.E.	%	S.E.	%	S.E.	%	S.E.	%	S.E.
National entities										
Australia	18.6	(0.6)	3.5	(0.3)	4.4	(0.3)	20.1	(0.6)	51.4	(0.7)
Austria	23.6	(0.6)	5.9	(0.4)	9.3	(0.5)	25.2	(0.6)	34.1	(0.6)
Canada	16.6	(0.4)	2.8	(0.2)	4.1	(0.2)	15.9	(0.4)	59.7	(0.5)
Czech Republic	24.6	(1.0)	1.8	(0.2)	3.7	(0.4)	23.1	(1.0)	46.2	(1.2)
Denmark	10.0	(0.4)	3.8	(0.2)	6.6	(0.4)	21.1	(0.6)	58.2	(0.6)
Estonia	21.9	(0.4)	2.6	(0.2)	4.9	(0.2)	18.9	(0.5)	51.3	(0.5)
Finland	13.8	(0.4)	4.4	(0.3)	7.8	(0.4)	29.6	(0.6)	44.4	(0.6)
France	24.6	(0.4)	3.3	(0.2)	4.0	(0.2)	16.1	(0.5)	51.2	(0.5)
Germany	20.1	(0.6)	5.5	(0.4)	7.1	(0.4)	24.2	(0.7)	41.7	(0.7)
Ireland	29.0	(0.5)	4.5	(0.3)	5.0	(0.3)	19.7	(0.6)	41.3	(0.6)
Italy	40.9	(0.8)	5.1	(0.4)	4.5	(0.4)	17.5	(0.8)	31.4	(0.8)
Japan	35.4	(0.7)	5.8	(0.3)	6.8	(0.4)	14.2	(0.5)	36.5	(0.7)
Korea	33.8	(0.6)	8.4	(0.4)	12.2	(0.4)	22.7	(0.5)	22.7	(0.6)
Netherlands	8.5	(0.4)	2.0	(0.2)	3.2	(0.2)	16.7	(0.6)	67.4	(0.6)
Norway	8.6	(0.4)	4.3	(0.3)	7.3	(0.4)	25.3	(0.6)	52.3	(0.7)
Poland	37.7	(0.5)	4.7	(0.3)	5.5	(0.3)	18.1	(0.5)	34.1	(0.5)
Slovak Republic	34.9	(0.6)	3.6	(0.3)	5.2	(0.3)	20.1	(0.6)	36.0	(0.6)
Spain	36.6	(0.6)	2.4	(0.2)	3.6	(0.3)	14.9	(0.6)	41.8	(0.7)
Sweden	10.9	(0.5)	4.7	(0.3)	7.1	(0.4)	23.8	(0.6)	53.4	(0.8)
United States	21.4	(0.7)	3.2	(0.4)	3.4	(0.4)	14.2	(0.5)	53.5	(1.0)
Sub-national entities										
Flanders (Belgium)	14.9	(0.5)	3.5	(0.3)	3.9	(0.3)	21.3	(0.6)	51.1	(0.7)
England (UK)	17.2	(0.6)	4.4	(0.4)	5.4	(0.3)	21.9	(0.7)	49.7	(0.8)
Northern Ireland (UK)	27.8	(0.9)	6.4	(0.5)	7.1	(0.5)	19.2	(0.7)	37.3	(0.8)
England/N. Ireland (UK)	17.5	(0.6)	4.4	(0.3)	5.4	(0.3)	21.8	(0.6)	49.3	(0.8)
Average[1]	21.2	(0.1)	4.2	(0.1)	5.9	(0.1)	20.8	(0.1)	46.5	(0.2)
Average-22[2]	22.9	(0.1)	4.1	(0.1)	5.7	(0.1)	20.2	(0.1)	45.9	(0.1)

Partners

	Never		Less than once a month		Less than once a week but at least once a month		At least once a week but not everyday		Everyday	
Cyprus[3]	36.0	(0.6)	5.5	(0.3)	4.3	(0.3)	11.4	(0.5)	25.2	(0.6)
Russian Federation[4]	45.9	(2.5)	10.2	(0.9)	5.5	(0.5)	15.5	(1.2)	22.8	(1.8)

1. Average of 19 participating OECD countries and entities.
2. Average of 22 OECD countries and entities: average of 19 countries with France, Italy and Spain.
3. See notes at the beginning of this Annex.
4. See note at the beginning of this Annex.
Source: Survey of Adult Skills (PIAAC) (2012).

StatLink ⌗ http://dx.doi.org/10.1787/888933231906

[Part 1/1]

Frequency of Internet use to better understand issues related to everyday life (e.g. health, financial matters, or environmental issues)

Table A2.4b

OECD	Frequency of use									
	Never		Less than once a month		Less than once a week but at least once a month		At least once a week but not everyday		Everyday	
	%	S.E.	%	S.E.	%	S.E.	%	S.E.	%	S.E.
National entities										
Australia	20.2	(0.6)	6.3	(0.4)	9.1	(0.4)	27.9	(0.7)	34.6	(0.7)
Austria	21.5	(0.6)	5.9	(0.3)	13.0	(0.5)	31.1	(0.6)	26.7	(0.7)
Canada	18.0	(0.4)	6.6	(0.2)	10.7	(0.3)	27.5	(0.4)	36.1	(0.5)
Czech Republic	22.7	(1.1)	1.6	(0.3)	3.1	(0.4)	21.5	(0.7)	50.4	(1.2)
Denmark	11.3	(0.3)	7.5	(0.4)	13.8	(0.5)	30.8	(0.6)	36.3	(0.7)
Estonia	20.8	(0.4)	7.2	(0.3)	13.4	(0.4)	28.9	(0.5)	29.2	(0.5)
Finland	12.0	(0.4)	7.8	(0.3)	16.4	(0.4)	35.5	(0.7)	28.0	(0.6)
France	24.4	(0.5)	3.8	(0.2)	6.7	(0.3)	22.0	(0.5)	42.1	(0.5)
Germany	18.5	(0.6)	6.8	(0.4)	13.2	(0.5)	33.6	(0.6)	26.4	(0.7)
Ireland	30.0	(0.5)	6.7	(0.3)	9.5	(0.4)	24.1	(0.8)	29.2	(0.7)
Italy	40.2	(0.9)	9.3	(0.6)	8.6	(0.6)	19.9	(0.7)	21.4	(0.7)
Japan	35.4	(0.8)	15.0	(0.6)	17.9	(0.5)	20.3	(0.6)	10.2	(0.5)
Korea	29.3	(0.6)	9.8	(0.4)	19.9	(0.6)	28.0	(0.6)	12.7	(0.5)
Netherlands	12.0	(0.4)	8.7	(0.4)	14.2	(0.6)	29.2	(0.7)	33.6	(0.6)
Norway	8.7	(0.4)	7.4	(0.4)	15.6	(0.5)	35.5	(0.6)	30.5	(0.7)
Poland	34.3	(0.6)	6.0	(0.3)	8.5	(0.4)	21.6	(0.5)	29.5	(0.6)
Slovak Republic	34.7	(0.7)	6.8	(0.4)	7.5	(0.3)	23.0	(0.7)	27.6	(0.7)
Spain	37.3	(0.6)	4.9	(0.3)	7.9	(0.4)	20.4	(0.5)	28.7	(0.7)
Sweden	12.5	(0.5)	7.4	(0.4)	12.6	(0.4)	32.2	(0.7)	35.3	(0.7)
United States	21.9	(0.8)	6.6	(0.4)	10.4	(0.5)	23.8	(0.6)	33.1	(1.0)
Sub-national entities										
Flanders (Belgium)	15.9	(0.5)	7.7	(0.4)	13.5	(0.5)	31.1	(0.6)	26.7	(0.6)
England (UK)	19.1	(0.6)	9.2	(0.5)	13.3	(0.6)	28.3	(0.8)	28.7	(0.9)
Northern Ireland (UK)	29.2	(0.9)	10.4	(0.6)	12.4	(0.6)	24.1	(1.0)	21.7	(0.7)
England/N. Ireland (UK)	19.4	(0.6)	9.2	(0.5)	13.3	(0.5)	28.2	(0.8)	28.4	(0.9)
Average[1]	21.0	(0.1)	7.4	(0.1)	12.4	(0.1)	28.1	(0.1)	29.7	(0.2)
Average-22[2]	22.8	(0.1)	7.2	(0.1)	11.8	(0.1)	27.1	(0.1)	29.9	(0.1)
Partners										
Cyprus[3]	33.1	(0.6)	7.4	(0.5)	6.8	(0.4)	15.2	(0.5)	19.9	(0.6)
Russian Federation[4]	41.8	(1.7)	11.0	(0.8)	10.1	(0.8)	16.6	(1.0)	20.3	(1.4)

1. Average of 19 participating OECD countries and entities.
2. Average of 22 OECD countries and entities: average of 19 countries with France, Italy and Spain.
3. See notes at the beginning of this Annex.
4. See note at the beginning of this Annex.
Source: Survey of Adult Skills (PIAAC) (2012).

StatLink http://dx.doi.org/10.1787/888933231915

[Part 1/1]

Table A2.4c **Frequency of Internet use for conducting transactions (e.g. buying or selling products or services, or banking)**

OECD	Never %	Never S.E.	Less than once a month %	Less than once a month S.E.	Less than once a week but at least once a month %	Less than once a week but at least once a month S.E.	At least once a week but not everyday %	At least once a week but not everyday S.E.	Everyday %	Everyday S.E.
National entities										
Australia	28.8	(0.7)	9.0	(0.5)	13.3	(0.6)	34.6	(0.8)	12.5	(0.4)
Austria	42.3	(0.7)	12.0	(0.6)	19.9	(0.5)	21.0	(0.6)	2.9	(0.2)
Canada	29.8	(0.5)	10.3	(0.3)	18.8	(0.4)	30.1	(0.5)	10.0	(0.3)
Czech Republic	37.6	(1.1)	14.8	(0.8)	20.7	(1.0)	22.0	(1.0)	4.2	(0.5)
Denmark	15.4	(0.4)	11.5	(0.4)	31.7	(0.6)	35.6	(0.6)	5.4	(0.3)
Estonia	24.7	(0.5)	7.8	(0.3)	33.0	(0.5)	28.2	(0.6)	5.7	(0.2)
Finland	15.5	(0.4)	5.3	(0.4)	31.9	(0.7)	44.8	(0.6)	2.4	(0.2)
France	39.4	(0.5)	19.7	(0.5)	21.3	(0.5)	15.0	(0.4)	3.7	(0.2)
Germany	35.0	(0.7)	14.2	(0.6)	21.3	(0.7)	23.7	(0.7)	4.3	(0.3)
Ireland	40.5	(0.7)	12.8	(0.5)	15.6	(0.5)	23.4	(0.7)	7.3	(0.4)
Italy	67.7	(0.8)	12.6	(0.6)	8.5	(0.5)	7.1	(0.4)	3.4	(0.4)
Japan	52.2	(0.6)	18.3	(0.5)	18.2	(0.5)	8.4	(0.4)	1.7	(0.2)
Korea	34.4	(0.6)	10.8	(0.4)	25.2	(0.6)	24.2	(0.5)	5.2	(0.3)
Netherlands	15.2	(0.5)	8.6	(0.4)	24.1	(0.6)	43.4	(0.8)	6.4	(0.4)
Norway	11.2	(0.5)	7.6	(0.4)	31.0	(0.6)	45.0	(0.7)	3.0	(0.2)
Poland	49.4	(0.6)	13.8	(0.5)	17.6	(0.5)	15.3	(0.5)	3.8	(0.3)
Slovak Republic	51.2	(0.8)	13.3	(0.5)	17.4	(0.6)	14.3	(0.5)	3.5	(0.4)
Spain	61.4	(0.7)	13.4	(0.5)	10.9	(0.4)	9.3	(0.4)	4.2	(0.3)
Sweden	16.4	(0.5)	8.7	(0.4)	47.0	(0.9)	25.6	(0.9)	2.2	(0.3)
United States	30.5	(0.9)	11.5	(0.6)	16.8	(0.5)	25.1	(0.7)	11.8	(0.6)
Sub-national entities										
Flanders (Belgium)	30.0	(0.6)	8.7	(0.4)	17.9	(0.5)	34.2	(0.6)	4.1	(0.3)
England (UK)	25.2	(0.6)	10.6	(0.5)	19.7	(0.7)	33.7	(0.8)	9.4	(0.6)
Northern Ireland (UK)	35.5	(1.0)	13.1	(0.7)	17.2	(0.8)	23.6	(0.9)	8.3	(0.5)
England/N. Ireland (UK)	25.6	(0.6)	10.7	(0.5)	19.6	(0.7)	33.3	(0.8)	9.4	(0.5)
Average[1]	30.8	(0.1)	11.0	(0.1)	23.2	(0.1)	28.0	(0.2)	5.6	(0.1)
Average-22[2]	34.3	(0.1)	11.6	(0.1)	21.9	(0.1)	25.6	(0.1)	5.3	(0.1)
Partners										
Cyprus[3]	53.9	(0.6)	11.5	(0.5)	8.7	(0.5)	5.5	(0.4)	2.7	(0.3)
Russian Federation[4]	80.0	(1.1)	10.7	(0.8)	4.6	(0.4)	3.4	(0.4)	1.2	(0.2)

1. Average of 19 participating OECD countries and entities.
2. Average of 22 OECD countries and entities: average of 19 countries with France, Italy and Spain.
3. See notes at the beginning of this Annex.
4. See note at the beginning of this Annex.
Source: Survey of Adult Skills (PIAAC) (2012).

StatLink http://dx.doi.org/10.1787/888933231923

[Part 1/1]
Table A2.4d **Frequency of spreadsheet software use (e.g. Excel)**

OECD	Never		Less than once a month		Less than once a week but at least once a month		At least once a week but not everyday		Everyday	
	%	S.E.	%	S.E.	%	S.E.	%	S.E.	%	S.E.
National entities										
Australia	62.1	(0.9)	17.4	(0.6)	10.2	(0.5)	6.5	(0.4)	1.9	(0.2)
Austria	57.2	(0.5)	20.1	(0.5)	11.9	(0.5)	7.2	(0.4)	1.8	(0.2)
Canada	57.4	(0.5)	18.9	(0.4)	11.2	(0.3)	8.8	(0.3)	2.8	(0.2)
Czech Republic	54.3	(1.0)	20.9	(1.0)	11.1	(0.8)	10.0	(0.8)	3.0	(0.4)
Denmark	50.5	(0.6)	22.4	(0.5)	15.0	(0.5)	9.2	(0.4)	2.5	(0.2)
Estonia	57.8	(0.5)	20.3	(0.4)	12.4	(0.3)	7.5	(0.3)	1.5	(0.1)
Finland	54.4	(0.6)	27.0	(0.6)	12.7	(0.5)	4.7	(0.3)	0.9	(0.1)
France	63.7	(0.5)	17.0	(0.4)	9.8	(0.3)	6.3	(0.3)	2.3	(0.2)
Germany	54.7	(0.7)	21.1	(0.6)	13.0	(0.6)	8.1	(0.5)	1.6	(0.2)
Ireland	71.9	(0.6)	12.7	(0.5)	6.7	(0.4)	5.8	(0.3)	2.4	(0.2)
Italy	69.5	(0.8)	12.2	(0.5)	6.6	(0.5)	7.8	(0.4)	3.1	(0.3)
Japan	68.4	(0.6)	16.4	(0.4)	8.3	(0.4)	4.1	(0.3)	1.5	(0.2)
Korea	66.2	(0.7)	11.5	(0.4)	12.6	(0.4)	7.1	(0.3)	2.3	(0.2)
Netherlands	51.3	(0.6)	19.9	(0.5)	14.1	(0.6)	9.9	(0.5)	2.5	(0.2)
Norway	49.7	(0.7)	26.4	(0.6)	14.3	(0.5)	6.4	(0.3)	0.8	(0.1)
Poland	67.0	(0.4)	16.5	(0.4)	8.7	(0.3)	6.4	(0.3)	1.4	(0.2)
Slovak Republic	62.8	(0.8)	15.2	(0.6)	8.3	(0.3)	10.4	(0.5)	2.9	(0.3)
Spain	71.1	(0.6)	12.0	(0.5)	7.0	(0.4)	6.3	(0.4)	2.8	(0.3)
Sweden	56.2	(0.7)	24.4	(0.6)	12.8	(0.5)	5.1	(0.4)	1.4	(0.2)
United States	57.5	(0.8)	17.7	(0.6)	10.6	(0.4)	7.1	(0.4)	2.9	(0.3)
Sub-national entities										
Flanders (Belgium)	52.6	(0.8)	18.4	(0.6)	12.6	(0.5)	9.1	(0.4)	2.1	(0.2)
England (UK)	62.2	(0.9)	16.1	(0.6)	10.1	(0.6)	8.0	(0.4)	2.3	(0.3)
Northern Ireland (UK)	70.0	(0.9)	13.4	(0.7)	6.9	(0.5)	5.7	(0.5)	1.8	(0.3)
England/N. Ireland (UK)	62.5	(0.9)	16.0	(0.6)	10.0	(0.5)	7.9	(0.4)	2.2	(0.3)
Average[1]	58.7	(0.2)	19.1	(0.1)	11.4	(0.1)	7.4	(0.1)	2.0	(0.0)
Average-22[2]	60.0	(0.1)	18.4	(0.1)	10.9	(0.1)	7.4	(0.1)	2.1	(0.0)
Partners										
Cyprus[3]	60.7	(0.7)	10.6	(0.5)	4.3	(0.3)	4.5	(0.4)	2.2	(0.2)
Russian Federation[4]	73.4	(1.8)	13.1	(1.0)	5.6	(0.6)	5.7	(0.6)	2.1	(0.3)

1. Average of 19 participating OECD countries and entities.
2. Average of 22 OECD countries and entities: average of 19 countries with France, Italy and Spain.
3. See notes at the beginning of this Annex.
4. See note at the beginning of this Annex.
Source: Survey of Adult Skills (PIAAC) (2012).
StatLink ᴍᴙᴨ http://dx.doi.org/10.1787/888933231933

[Part 1/1]

Table A2.4e **Frequency of a word processor use (e.g. Word)**

OECD	Frequency of use									
	Never		Less than once a month		Less than once a week but at least once a month		At least once a week but not everyday		Everyday	
	%	S.E.	%	S.E.	%	S.E.	%	S.E.	%	S.E.
National entities										
Australia	38.7	(0.8)	17.2	(0.6)	14.3	(0.5)	17.9	(0.6)	10.0	(0.4)
Austria	33.4	(0.6)	19.3	(0.6)	20.5	(0.5)	18.9	(0.5)	6.2	(0.3)
Canada	34.2	(0.5)	19.5	(0.4)	16.2	(0.4)	19.1	(0.4)	10.0	(0.3)
Czech Republic	38.1	(1.1)	16.3	(0.8)	16.3	(0.8)	20.6	(1.0)	8.0	(0.8)
Denmark	22.4	(0.5)	17.7	(0.5)	20.6	(0.5)	23.8	(0.5)	15.2	(0.5)
Estonia	44.5	(0.5)	18.3	(0.4)	16.9	(0.4)	15.2	(0.4)	4.5	(0.2)
Finland	28.9	(0.6)	28.9	(0.6)	23.3	(0.5)	15.7	(0.5)	2.9	(0.2)
France	44.3	(0.5)	21.4	(0.4)	15.6	(0.3)	12.3	(0.4)	5.6	(0.3)
Germany	28.8	(0.7)	18.2	(0.5)	22.4	(0.6)	21.2	(0.6)	7.9	(0.4)
Ireland	48.9	(0.6)	15.6	(0.6)	11.7	(0.5)	15.1	(0.5)	8.2	(0.4)
Italy	53.6	(0.8)	13.6	(0.6)	9.6	(0.5)	15.1	(0.6)	7.4	(0.5)
Japan	61.5	(0.8)	20.3	(0.6)	9.8	(0.5)	5.3	(0.3)	1.7	(0.2)
Korea	53.9	(0.8)	13.7	(0.4)	16.1	(0.5)	12.3	(0.5)	3.7	(0.3)
Netherlands	22.2	(0.6)	17.3	(0.6)	18.9	(0.6)	26.0	(0.6)	13.3	(0.5)
Norway	20.7	(0.5)	24.0	(0.6)	23.4	(0.5)	21.0	(0.6)	8.5	(0.4)
Poland	48.6	(0.6)	13.9	(0.5)	13.7	(0.4)	17.0	(0.5)	6.8	(0.4)
Slovak Republic	45.4	(0.8)	13.0	(0.5)	11.1	(0.5)	20.7	(0.5)	9.6	(0.5)
Spain	52.1	(0.6)	11.6	(0.5)	10.8	(0.5)	15.9	(0.5)	8.8	(0.4)
Sweden	26.8	(0.7)	25.5	(0.7)	21.0	(0.6)	19.6	(0.5)	7.1	(0.4)
United States	36.9	(0.8)	15.6	(0.6)	16.7	(0.5)	16.6	(0.4)	9.9	(0.5)
Sub-national entities										
Flanders (Belgium)	32.0	(0.7)	18.4	(0.5)	17.8	(0.5)	19.5	(0.5)	7.1	(0.4)
England (UK)	34.3	(0.8)	19.9	(0.7)	16.5	(0.6)	19.7	(0.7)	8.1	(0.5)
Northern Ireland (UK)	44.9	(1.0)	17.9	(0.8)	11.9	(0.5)	14.8	(0.7)	8.3	(0.6)
England/N. Ireland (UK)	34.7	(0.8)	19.8	(0.7)	16.4	(0.6)	19.5	(0.7)	8.2	(0.5)
Average[1]	36.9	(0.2)	18.5	(0.1)	17.2	(0.1)	18.2	(0.1)	7.8	(0.1)
Average-22[2]	38.7	(0.1)	18.1	(0.1)	16.5	(0.1)	17.7	(0.1)	7.8	(0.1)
Partners										
Cyprus[3]	45.4	(0.6)	11.4	(0.4)	7.6	(0.4)	10.9	(0.5)	7.0	(0.4)
Russian Federation[4]	55.6	(2.4)	15.0	(1.2)	7.8	(0.5)	13.1	(1.0)	8.4	(1.0)

1. Average of 19 participating OECD countries and entities.
2. Average of 22 OECD countries and entities: average of 19 countries with France, Italy and Spain.
3. See notes at the beginning of this Annex.
4. See note at the beginning of this Annex.
Source: Survey of Adult Skills (PIAAC) (2012).

StatLink http://dx.doi.org/10.1787/888933231945

[Part 1/1]

Table A2.5 **Literacy proficiency, frequent e-mail use and access to the Internet at home**

OECD	Literacy mean score		Percentage of adults with frequent e-mail use (at least once a month)		Households with Internet access at home (2010 or latest available year)
	Score	S.E.	%	S.E.	%
National entities					
Australia	280.4	(0.9)	76.0	(0.6)	72.0
Austria	269.5	(0.7)	68.6	(0.7)	72.9
Canada	273.5	(0.6)	79.6	(0.4)	77.8
Czech Republic	274.0	(1.0)	72.9	(1.0)	60.5
Denmark	270.8	(0.6)	85.8	(0.4)	86.1
Estonia	275.9	(0.7)	75.1	(0.4)	67.8
Finland	287.5	(0.7)	81.7	(0.5)	80.5
France	262.1	(0.6)	71.2	(0.5)	73.6
Germany	269.8	(0.9)	72.9	(0.6)	82.5
Ireland	266.5	(0.9)	66.0	(0.6)	71.7
Italy	250.5	(1.1)	53.4	(0.8)	59.0
Japan	296.2	(0.7)	57.6	(0.8)	67.1
Korea	272.6	(0.6)	57.5	(0.6)	96.8
Netherlands	284.0	(0.7)	87.2	(0.4)	90.9
Norway	278.4	(0.6)	84.9	(0.5)	89.8
Poland	266.9	(0.6)	57.6	(0.6)	63.4
Slovak Republic	273.8	(0.6)	61.2	(0.6)	67.5
Spain	251.8	(0.7)	60.2	(0.7)	59.1
Sweden	279.2	(0.7)	84.3	(0.6)	88.3
United States	269.8	(1.0)	71.2	(0.9)	71.1
Sub-national entities					
Flanders (Belgium)	275.5	(0.8)	76.3	(0.5)	72.7
England (UK)	272.6	(1.1)	77.0	(0.7)	m
Northern Ireland (UK)	268.7	(1.9)	63.6	(0.9)	m
England/N. Ireland (UK)	272.5	(1.0)	76.6	(0.7)	79.6
Average[1]	275.6	(0.2)	73.3	(0.1)	76.8
Average-22[2]	272.8	(0.2)	71.7	(0.1)	75.0

Partners

Cyprus[3]	268.8	(0.8)	40.9	(0.6)	m
Russian Federation[4]	275.2	(2.7)	43.8	(2.7)	m

1. Average of 19 participating OECD countries and entities.
2. Average of 22 OECD countries and entities: average of 19 countries with France, Italy and Spain.
3. See notes at the beginning of this Annex.
4. See note at the beginning of this Annex.
Source: Survey of Adult Skills (PIAAC) (2012); OECD, ICT Database; Eurostat, Community Survey on ICT usage in housholds and by individuals, November 2011.

StatLink ⬛⬛ http://dx.doi.org/10.1787/888933231952

[Part 1/2]

Table A3.1

Percentage differences between groups of adults who score at Level 2 or 3 in problem solving in technology-rich environments, before and after accounting for various characteristics (country average)

	Version 1 (socio-demographic variables)						Version 2 (socio-demographic variables + e-mail use)					
	Coef.	S.E.	Unadjusted %	Adjusted %	Unadjusted % dif	Adjusted % dif	Coef.	S.E.	Unadjusted %	Adjusted %	Unadjusted % dif	Adjusted % dif
Age (ref. value is 55-65 year-olds)												
16-24 year-olds	1.7 ***	(0.1)	50.7	41.2	39.0	29.5	1.5 ***	(0.1)	50.7	36.1	39.0	24.4
25-34 year-olds	1.8 ***	(0.0)	49.2	44.3	37.5	32.7	1.6 ***	(0.1)	49.2	39.8	37.5	28.1
35-44 year-olds	1.4 ***	(0.0)	38.1	34.4	26.4	22.7	1.2 ***	(0.0)	38.1	31.3	26.4	19.6
45-54 year-olds	0.8 ***	(0.0)	24.0	21.9	12.3	10.2	0.7 ***	(0.0)	24.0	20.9	12.3	9.2
Educational attainment (ref. value is lower than upper secondary)												
Upper secondary	0.8 ***	(0.0)	30.5	34.4	11.5	15.4	0.7 ***	(0.0)	30.5	31.6	11.5	12.5
Tertiary	1.8 ***	(0.0)	51.8	58.3	32.8	39.3	1.5 ***	(0.0)	51.8	52.2	32.8	33.1
Gender (ref. value is women)												
Men	0.3 ***	(0.0)	36.3	38.8	4.7	7.1	0.3 ***	(0.0)	36.3	39.2	4.7	7.6
Parents' educational attainment (ref. value is neither parent attained upper secondary)												
At least one parent attained upper secondary	0.5 ***	(0.0)	37.6	24.2	21.8	8.4	0.4 ***	(0.0)	37.6	22.6	21.8	6.8
At least one parent attained tertiary	0.9 ***	(0.0)	55.0	32.2	39.3	16.5	0.8 ***	(0.0)	55.0	29.8	39.3	14.0
Immigrant and language background (ref. value is foreign-born and foreign language)												
Native-born and native language	1.5 **	(0.6)	36.4	45.9	19.9	29.4	1.5 ***	(0.6)	36.4	46.4	19.9	29.8
Native-born and foreign language	0.8 ***	(0.1)	29.4	31.1	12.8	14.6	0.8 ***	(0.1)	29.4	30.9	12.8	14.4
Foreign-born and native language	1.2 **	(0.6)	33.6	38.9	17.0	22.3	1.2 **	(0.6)	33.6	39.1	17.0	22.5
Participation in adult education and training (ref. value is did not participate)												
Participated	0.6 ***	(0.0)	42.3	30.0	23.8	11.5	0.5 ***	(0.0)	42.3	27.8	23.8	9.3
Frequency of e-mail use (ref. value is low frequency/irregular use)												
High frequency/regular use							1.5 ***	(0.0)	43.5	26.2	36.2	18.9
Level of literacy proficiency (ref value is Level 2)												
At or below Level 1												
Level 3												
Level 4/5												

* Significant estimate p ≤ 0.10.
** Significant estimate p ≤ 0.05.
*** Significant estimate p ≤ 0.01.

Notes: The reference category for problem solving in technology-rich environments is Below Level 1. Adjusted results include controls for age, educational attainment, gender, parents' educational attainment, immigrant and language background, participation in adult education and training, e-mail use, and literacy proficiency. Results for each country are available in Tables B3.1, B3.2, B3.3 in Annex B.

Source: Survey of Adult Skills (PIAAC) (2012).

StatLink ⬛⬛⬛ http://dx.doi.org/10.1787/888933231964

[Part 2/2]

Table A3.1 **Percentage differences between groups of adults who score at Level 2 or 3 in problem solving in technology-rich environments, before and after accounting for various characteristics (country average)**

	Version 3 (socio-demographic variables + e-mail use + literacy proficiency)					
	Coef.	S.E.	Unadjusted %	Adjusted %	Unadjusted % dif	Adjusted % dif
Age (ref. value is 55-65 year-olds)						
16-24 year-olds	1.6 ***	(0.1)	50.7	40.1	39.0	28.4
25-34 year-olds	1.6 ***	(0.1)	49.2	38.6	37.5	26.9
35-44 year-olds	1.1 ***	(0.1)	38.1	28.5	26.4	16.8
45-54 year-olds	0.6 ***	(0.0)	24.0	19.5	12.3	7.9
Educational attainment (ref. value is lower than upper secondary)						
Upper secondary	0.3 ***	(0.0)	30.5	23.5	11.5	4.5
Tertiary	0.7 ***	(0.1)	51.8	31.9	32.8	12.9
Gender (ref. value is women)						
Men	0.3 ***	(0.0)	36.3	38.7	4.7	7.0
Parents' educational attainment (ref. value is neither parent attained upper secondary)						
At least one parent attained upper secondary	0.3 ***	(0.0)	37.6	20.2	21.8	4.4
At least one parent attained tertiary	0.5 ***	(0.0)	55.0	23.2	39.3	7.5
Immigrant and language background (ref. value is foreign-born and foreign language)						
Native-born and native language	0.9	(0.6)	36.4	32.1	19.9	15.5
Native-born and foreign language	0.4 ***	(0.1)	29.4	22.7	12.8	6.1
Foreign-born and native language	0.8	(0.6)	33.6	30.1	17.0	13.6
Participation in adult education and training (ref. value is did not participate)						
Participated	0.4 ***	(0.0)	42.3	25.3	23.8	6.9
Frequency of e-mail use (ref. value is low frequency/irregular use)						
High frequency/regular use	1.3 ***	(0.0)	43.5	21.9	36.2	14.5
Level of literacy proficiency (ref value is Level 2)						
At or below Level 1	-3.6 ***	(1.3)	0.4	0.3	-10.1	-10.2
Level 3	2.0 ***	(0.0)	50.1	46.3	39.5	35.8
Level 4/5	3.5 ***	(0.1)	83.0	79.5	72.4	68.9

* Significant estimate p ≤ 0.10.
** Significant estimate p ≤ 0.05.
*** Significant estimate p ≤ 0.01.

Notes: The reference category for problem solving in technology-rich environments is Below Level 1. Adjusted results include controls for age, educational attainment, gender, parents' educational attainment, immigrant and language background, participation in adult education and training, e-mail use, and literacy proficiency. Results for each country are available in Tables B3.1, B3.2, B3.3 in Annex B.

Source: Survey of Adult Skills (PIAAC) (2012).

StatLink ⬛🔗 http://dx.doi.org/10.1787/888933231964

[Part 1/1]

Table A3.2 **Percentage differences between various groups of adults who have no computer experience, before and after accounting for various characteristics (country average)**

	Version 1 (socio-demographic variables)						Version 2 (socio-demographic variables + literacy proficiency)					
	Coef.	S.E.	Unadjusted %	Adjusted %	Unadjusted % dif	Adjusted % dif	Coef.	S.E.	Unadjusted %	Adjusted %	Unadjusted % dif	Adjusted % dif
Age (ref. value is 55-65 year-olds)												
16-24 year-olds	-4.9 ***	(1.8)	0.7	0.2	-21.6	-22.0	-4.9 ***	(1.8)	0.7	0.2	-21.6	-22.0
25-34 year-olds	-3.3 ***	(1.2)	1.7	1.1	-20.5	-21.1	-3.2 ***	(1.2)	1.7	1.2	-20.5	-21.1
35-44 year-olds	-1.9 ***	(0.1)	4.1	4.3	-18.2	-17.9	-1.8 ***	(0.1)	4.1	4.6	-18.2	-17.7
45-54 year-olds	-0.7 ***	(0.0)	10.8	12.0	-11.4	-10.2	-0.7 ***	(0.0)	10.8	12.4	-11.4	-9.8
Educational attainment (ref. value is lower than upper secondary)												
Upper secondary	-1.3 ***	(0.0)	7.1	6.7	-13.5	-13.9	-1.1 ***	(0.0)	7.1	7.9	-13.5	-12.7
Tertiary	-3.0 ***	(0.1)	1.0	1.2	-19.6	-19.4	-2.6 ***	(0.1)	1.0	1.8	-19.6	-18.8
Gender (ref. value is women)												
Men	-0.5 ***	(0.1)	7.8	5.0	-0.4	-3.2	-0.5 ***	(0.1)	7.8	5.4	-0.4	-2.9
Parents' educational attainment (ref. value is neither parent attained upper secondary)												
At least one parent attained upper secondary	-0.6 ***	(0.1)	4.4	11.7	-14.3	-7.1	-0.5 ***	(0.1)	4.4	12.6	-14.3	-6.2
At least one parent attained tertiary	-1.0 ***	(0.1)	1.4	7.6	-17.3	-11.2	-0.9 ***	(0.1)	1.4	8.6	-17.3	-10.1
Immigrant and language background (ref. value is foreign-born and foreign language)												
Native-born and native language	-0.9 ***	(0.1)	7.7	5.5	-5.0	-7.2	-0.6 ***	(0.1)	7.7	7.3	-5.0	-5.4
Native-born and foreign language	-2.6	(2.1)	7.1	1.0	-5.6	-11.7	-2.5	(2.3)	7.1	1.2	-5.6	-11.5
Foreign-born and native language	-1.4	(1.4)	10.5	3.5	-2.2	-9.2	-1.2	(1.5)	10.5	4.4	-2.2	-8.4
Participation in adult education and training (ref. value is did not participate)												
Participated	-1.4 ***	(0.1)	2.6	4.5	-13.1	-11.2	-1.3 ***	(0.1)	2.6	4.9	-13.1	-10.8
Level of literacy proficiency (ref value is Level 2)												
At or below Level 1							0.7 *	(0.1)	23.9	17.7	14.1	7.9
Level 3							-0.6 ***	(0.3)	3.6	5.8	-6.2	-4.1
Level 4/5							-3.5	(2.4)	0.9	0.3	-8.9	-9.5

* Significant estimate p ≤ 0.10.

** Significant estimate p ≤ 0.05.

*** Significant estimate p ≤ 0.01.

Notes: The reference category for problem solving in rich-environments is Below Level 1. Adjusted results include controls for age, educational attainment, gender, parents' educational attainment, immigrant and language background, participation in adult education and training, e-mail use, and literacy proficiency. Results for each country are available in Tables B3.4 and B3.5 in Annex B.

Source: Survey of Adult Skills (PIAAC) (2012).

StatLink ⌐⌐⌐ http://dx.doi.org/10.1787/888933231979

[Part 1/2]

Percentage of adults who score at Level 2 or 3 in problem solving in technology-rich environments or have no computer experience, by age

Table A3.3

OECD	16-24 year-olds				25-34 year-olds				35-44 year-olds			
	No computer experience		Level 2/3		No computer experience		Level 2/3		No computer experience		Level 2/3	
	%	S.E.	%	S.E.	%	S.E.	%	S.E.	%	S.E.	%	S.E.
National entities												
Australia	0.4	(0.3)	50.7	(2.6)	1.0	(0.3)	47.9	(2.0)	1.8	(0.3)	42.0	(1.7)
Austria	0.2	(0.2)	50.7	(2.0)	1.6	(0.4)	49.1	(1.7)	4.8	(0.7)	36.9	(1.9)
Canada	0.2	(0.1)	50.8	(1.8)	0.8	(0.2)	49.0	(1.7)	1.7	(0.3)	42.0	(1.3)
Czech Republic	0.6	(0.3)	54.7	(2.9)	3.1	(1.0)	51.5	(2.2)	2.8	(0.5)	31.8	(2.6)
Denmark	0.1	(0.1)	50.4	(1.9)	1.1	(0.4)	57.7	(1.9)	1.0	(0.3)	47.9	(1.9)
Estonia	0.1	(0.1)	50.4	(2.1)	0.8	(0.2)	43.8	(1.6)	4.8	(0.6)	27.3	(1.1)
Finland	0.0	(0.0)	61.9	(2.4)	0.0	(0.0)	67.5	(2.1)	0.0	(0.0)	52.7	(1.9)
France	1.4	(1.4)	m	m	1.7	(0.4)	m	m	5.4	(0.5)	m	m
Germany	0.5	(0.3)	54.2	(1.7)	1.2	(0.4)	52.9	(1.8)	4.6	(0.8)	39.1	(1.8)
Ireland	0.6	(0.3)	40.3	(2.6)	1.6	(0.3)	36.0	(1.6)	6.3	(0.8)	26.2	(1.3)
Italy	1.4	(1.4)	m	m	7.3	(1.2)	m	m	17.8	(1.4)	m	m
Japan	1.6	(0.6)	45.8	(2.4)	1.8	(0.4)	53.7	(2.0)	3.5	(0.6)	44.6	(1.6)
Korea	0.7	(0.3)	63.4	(2.1)	1.0	(0.3)	48.6	(2.4)	4.4	(0.5)	29.1	(1.4)
Netherlands	0.0	(0.0)	58.3	(2.2)	0.5	(0.2)	57.6	(2.2)	1.4	(0.4)	49.5	(2.1)
Norway	0.2	(0.1)	54.9	(1.8)	0.3	(0.2)	56.3	(1.8)	0.3	(0.2)	48.4	(1.7)
Poland	0.7	(0.2)	37.9	(1.2)	3.6	(0.5)	29.9	(1.9)	13.3	(1.3)	18.3	(1.8)
Slovak Republic	4.8	(0.7)	40.5	(1.8)	9.4	(0.9)	34.9	(2.1)	16.4	(1.2)	26.3	(2.1)
Spain	1.4	(1.4)	m	m	4.2	(0.6)	m	m	9.4	(0.7)	m	m
Sweden	0.4	(0.3)	61.7	(2.1)	0.5	(0.3)	60.5	(1.8)	0.5	(0.3)	50.5	(1.8)
United States	0.8	(0.3)	37.6	(2.5)	1.9	(0.7)	38.9	(2.1)	4.9	(0.8)	34.3	(1.9)
Sub-national entities												
Flanders (Belgium)	0.2	(0.1)	57.1	(1.9)	2.2	(0.5)	51.8	(2.0)	3.1	(0.5)	38.9	(1.9)
England (UK)	0.7	(0.4)	42.3	(2.6)	0.4	(0.1)	47.4	(1.8)	1.7	(0.5)	39.0	(1.9)
Northern Ireland (UK)	c	c	44.2	(3.3)	2.8	(0.9)	42.1	(2.3)	6.9	(1.0)	28.8	(2.2)
England/N. Ireland (UK)	0.7	(0.4)	42.4	(2.5)	0.4	(0.1)	47.2	(1.7)	1.8	(0.4)	38.6	(1.9)
Average[1]	0.7	(0.1)	50.7	(0.5)	1.7	(0.1)	49.2	(0.4)	4.1	(0.1)	38.1	(0.4)
Average-22[2]	0.8	(0.1)	m	m	2.1	(0.1)	m	m	5.0	(0.1)	m	m
Partners												
Cyprus[3]	1.5	(0.5)	m	m	4.4	(0.7)	m	m	13.4	(0.9)	m	m
Russian Federation[4]	0.8	(0.4)	38.8	(4.4)	3.6	(0.9)	33.8	(4.2)	12.4	(2.4)	22.0	(3.2)

1. Average of 19 participating OECD countries and entities.
2. Average of 22 OECD countries and entities: average of 19 countries with France, Italy and Spain.
3. See notes at the beginning of this Annex.
4. See note at the beginning of this Annex.
Source: Survey of Adult Skills (PIAAC) (2012).

StatLink 🔗 http://dx.doi.org/10.1787/888933231980

[Part 2/2]

Table A3.3 **Percentage of adults who score at Level 2 or 3 in problem solving in technology-rich environments or have no computer experience, by age**

OECD	45-54 year-olds				55-65 year-olds			
	No computer experience		Level 2/3		No computer experience		Level 2/3	
	%	S.E.	%	S.E.	%	S.E.	%	S.E.
National entities								
Australia	4.9	(0.7)	30.8	(2.0)	12.3	(1.0)	17.2	(1.3)
Austria	11.3	(1.1)	22.6	(1.5)	29.2	(1.5)	7.5	(1.0)
Canada	6.1	(0.5)	28.2	(1.1)	12.5	(0.6)	16.4	(1.0)
Czech Republic	14.2	(1.5)	18.7	(2.2)	29.0	(1.9)	12.1	(1.9)
Denmark	2.5	(0.4)	30.0	(1.6)	6.8	(0.6)	13.2	(1.0)
Estonia	13.3	(0.9)	13.1	(1.2)	30.0	(1.1)	4.8	(0.7)
Finland	3.8	(0.8)	30.1	(1.6)	10.9	(0.9)	8.9	(0.9)
France	13.5	(0.9)	m	m	27.8	(1.0)	m	m
Germany	10.2	(1.0)	27.3	(1.7)	20.9	(1.7)	13.4	(1.6)
Ireland	16.1	(1.4)	13.8	(1.2)	31.2	(1.5)	5.3	(0.8)
Italy	33.6	(2.2)	m	m	53.8	(2.1)	m	m
Japan	9.6	(0.9)	26.8	(1.7)	28.6	(1.5)	9.9	(1.1)
Korea	24.2	(1.2)	11.3	(1.2)	52.0	(1.4)	4.1	(0.7)
Netherlands	3.3	(0.5)	32.3	(1.8)	8.6	(0.8)	16.6	(1.2)
Norway	1.8	(0.5)	31.7	(1.5)	5.3	(0.8)	14.2	(1.3)
Poland	31.9	(1.6)	7.9	(1.2)	47.3	(1.7)	2.5	(0.6)
Slovak Republic	30.4	(1.6)	17.4	(1.6)	49.2	(1.5)	9.2	(1.3)
Spain	23.0	(1.2)	m	m	42.6	(1.7)	m	m
Sweden	1.1	(0.4)	34.7	(1.8)	5.5	(0.8)	17.4	(1.2)
United States	7.5	(0.8)	25.6	(1.8)	10.8	(0.9)	19.7	(1.9)
Sub-national entities								
Flanders (Belgium)	7.4	(0.7)	24.7	(1.5)	20.2	(1.1)	12.0	(1.2)
England (UK)	6.1	(0.8)	28.5	(1.5)	12.0	(1.2)	17.6	(1.8)
Northern Ireland (UK)	15.8	(1.4)	17.0	(1.6)	25.1	(2.1)	9.5	(1.7)
England/N. Ireland (UK)	6.4	(0.8)	28.1	(1.5)	12.4	(1.1)	17.4	(1.7)
Average[1]	10.8	(0.2)	24.0	(0.4)	22.2	(0.3)	11.7	(0.3)
Average-22[2]	12.6	(0.2)	m	m	24.9	(0.3)	m	m
Partners								
Cyprus[3]	30.1	(1.4)	m	m	48.9	(1.6)	m	m
Russian Federation[4]	26.7	(3.8)	25.4	(2.8)	48.6	(3.8)	9.0	(1.9)

1. Average of 19 participating OECD countries and entities.
2. Average of 22 OECD countries and entities: average of 19 countries with France, Italy and Spain.
3. See notes at the beginning of this Annex.
4. See note at the beginning of this Annex.
Source: Survey of Adult Skills (PIAAC) (2012).

StatLink http://dx.doi.org/10.1787/888933231980

[Part 1/1]

Table A3.4

Percentage of adults who score at Level 2 or 3 in problem solving in technology-rich environments or have no computer experience, by educational attainment

OECD	Lower than upper secondary				Upper secondary				Tertiary			
	No computer experience		Level 2/3		No computer experience		Level 2/3		No computer experience		Level 2/3	
	%	S.E.	%	S.E.	%	S.E.	%	S.E.	%	S.E.	%	S.E.
National entities												
Australia	9.7	(0.8)	20.1	(1.4)	2.9	(0.4)	37.3	(1.6)	0.6	(0.2)	55.7	(1.5)
Austria	24.0	(1.3)	16.3	(1.4)	6.8	(0.5)	34.5	(1.1)	1.4	(0.4)	50.8	(2.2)
Canada	15.8	(0.8)	18.8	(1.6)	4.2	(0.3)	32.1	(0.9)	1.1	(0.1)	46.7	(1.0)
Czech Republic	22.6	(2.1)	27.5	(2.8)	10.1	(0.6)	27.9	(1.3)	0.5	(0.2)	58.8	(3.2)
Denmark	6.4	(0.6)	23.6	(1.1)	1.9	(0.2)	35.2	(1.2)	0.0	(0.0)	54.8	(1.2)
Estonia	19.1	(1.0)	20.8	(1.4)	12.3	(0.5)	23.3	(0.9)	2.5	(0.3)	36.4	(1.3)
Finland	11.3	(1.1)	26.3	(1.8)	2.9	(0.4)	36.2	(1.1)	0.1	(0.1)	56.3	(1.1)
France	25.3	(0.9)	m	m	7.3	(0.5)	m	m	0.6	(0.1)	m	m
Germany	15.3	(1.5)	27.1	(1.9)	8.8	(0.7)	30.5	(1.0)	2.4	(0.4)	52.9	(1.6)
Ireland	28.1	(1.2)	7.9	(0.9)	4.7	(0.4)	22.2	(1.5)	0.6	(0.1)	45.1	(1.5)
Italy	40.2	(1.4)	m	m	8.1	(0.7)	m	m	1.8	(0.5)	m	m
Japan	30.8	(1.9)	17.1	(1.7)	10.8	(0.7)	27.2	(1.2)	2.6	(0.3)	49.5	(1.3)
Korea	48.2	(1.3)	15.8	(1.1)	10.7	(0.6)	26.1	(1.3)	1.4	(0.2)	44.9	(1.6)
Netherlands	8.3	(0.7)	20.0	(1.1)	1.0	(0.2)	43.6	(1.5)	0.4	(0.2)	63.8	(1.5)
Norway	4.3	(0.6)	25.3	(1.5)	1.0	(0.3)	37.6	(1.1)	0.3	(0.1)	59.6	(1.5)
Poland	37.0	(1.7)	17.6	(1.4)	22.9	(0.8)	11.5	(0.6)	1.2	(0.3)	37.8	(1.8)
Slovak Republic	50.3	(1.6)	14.3	(1.3)	19.1	(0.7)	22.3	(1.1)	0.9	(0.3)	48.9	(2.2)
Spain	32.4	(0.9)	m	m	5.7	(0.6)	m	m	1.4	(0.3)	m	m
Sweden	4.5	(0.7)	22.4	(1.6)	0.9	(0.2)	44.1	(1.2)	0.2	(0.1)	62.1	(1.2)
United States	21.5	(1.8)	13.6	(1.5)	4.1	(0.4)	24.7	(1.3)	0.8	(0.2)	51.3	(1.7)
Sub-national entities												
Flanders (Belgium)	22.3	(1.2)	16.9	(1.4)	7.1	(0.5)	29.6	(1.2)	0.6	(0.2)	56.2	(1.4)
England (UK)	11.1	(0.9)	10.1	(1.2)	2.7	(0.4)	34.1	(1.4)	1.0	(0.3)	53.5	(1.6)
Northern Ireland (UK)	23.1	(1.5)	7.5	(1.5)	5.1	(0.6)	32.1	(2.2)	0.9	(0.4)	49.4	(2.4)
England/N. Ireland (UK)	11.6	(0.9)	10.0	(1.1)	2.7	(0.4)	34.1	(1.3)	1.0	(0.3)	53.4	(1.6)
Average[1]	20.6	(0.3)	19.0	(0.3)	7.1	(0.1)	30.5	(0.3)	1.0	(0.1)	51.8	(0.4)
Average-22[2]	22.2	(0.3)	m	m	7.1	(0.1)	m	m	1.0	(0.1)	m	m

Partners

Cyprus[3]	38.6	(1.0)	m	m	17.0	(0.9)	m	m	4.3	(0.5)	m	m
Russian Federation[4]	29.1	(4.5)	17.4	(3.2)	29.5	(2.7)	22.6	(2.5)	11.2	(1.3)	28.6	(2.6)

1. Average of 19 participating OECD countries and entities.
2. Average of 22 OECD countries and entities: average of 19 countries with France, Italy and Spain.
3. See notes at the beginning of this Annex.
4. See note at the beginning of this Annex.
Source: Survey of Adult Skills (PIAAC) (2012).
StatLink 🔗 http://dx.doi.org/10.1787/888933231998

[Part 1/1]

Table A3.5 **Percentage of adults who score at Level 2 or 3 in problem solving in technology-rich environments or have no computer experience, by age and gender**

	16-65 year-olds								16-24 year-olds							
	Men				Women				Men				Women			
	No computer experience		Level 2/3		No computer experience		Level 2/3		No computer experience		Level 2/3		No computer experience		Level 2/3	
OECD	%	S.E.	%	S.E.	%	S.E.	%	S.E.	%	S.E.	%	S.E.	%	S.E.	%	S.E.
National entities																
Australia	4.1	(0.4)	38.5	(1.2)	3.8	(0.4)	37.5	(1.5)	0.8	(0.5)	49.4	(3.2)	0.1	(0.1)	52.0	(4.1)
Austria	8.6	(0.5)	36.7	(1.0)	10.6	(0.7)	28.3	(1.2)	0.0	(0.0)	53.4	(2.6)	0.3	(0.3)	47.9	(3.4)
Canada	4.8	(0.3)	37.3	(0.7)	4.2	(0.2)	35.9	(0.8)	0.1	(0.1)	49.7	(2.3)	0.3	(0.2)	51.9	(2.4)
Czech Republic	9.4	(0.7)	35.7	(1.5)	11.2	(0.8)	30.6	(1.5)	1.0	(0.6)	56.6	(3.3)	0.1	(0.2)	52.8	(4.0)
Denmark	2.9	(0.3)	40.0	(1.0)	1.9	(0.2)	37.3	(1.0)	0.1	(0.1)	48.7	(3.2)	0.0	(0.0)	52.1	(2.3)
Estonia	11.1	(0.5)	28.3	(1.1)	8.8	(0.4)	26.9	(0.8)	0.0	(0.0)	49.1	(2.7)	0.1	(0.1)	51.9	(2.6)
Finland	4.0	(0.4)	42.7	(1.1)	3.0	(0.3)	40.4	(1.1)	0.0	(0.0)	65.7	(2.9)	0.0	(0.0)	58.0	(3.4)
France	10.3	(0.5)	m	m	10.6	(0.5)	m	m	0.2	(0.2)	m	m	0.7	(0.4)	m	m
Germany	6.4	(0.5)	39.9	(1.2)	9.5	(0.8)	32.0	(1.1)	0.2	(0.3)	56.2	(2.7)	0.7	(0.4)	52.2	(2.3)
Ireland	11.2	(0.6)	26.8	(1.0)	9.0	(0.5)	23.8	(1.3)	0.5	(0.4)	41.1	(3.6)	0.7	(0.6)	39.5	(3.4)
Italy	19.6	(1.0)	m	m	29.3	(1.1)	m	m	2.4	(0.9)	m	m	2.5	(1.0)	m	m
Japan	7.8	(0.5)	40.0	(1.2)	12.7	(0.7)	29.1	(1.1)	1.7	(0.7)	46.6	(3.1)	1.6	(0.8)	44.9	(3.3)
Korea	13.0	(0.5)	33.3	(1.1)	18.0	(0.6)	27.6	(1.1)	1.3	(0.7)	63.1	(2.8)	0.1	(0.1)	63.6	(3.0)
Netherlands	2.9	(0.3)	45.4	(1.1)	3.0	(0.3)	37.6	(1.0)	0.0	(0.0)	59.5	(2.6)	0.0	(0.0)	56.9	(3.0)
Norway	1.5	(0.2)	44.0	(1.0)	1.8	(0.3)	37.8	(1.1)	0.2	(0.2)	55.1	(2.4)	0.2	(0.2)	54.6	(2.6)
Poland	21.3	(0.8)	20.7	(1.1)	17.7	(0.7)	17.7	(0.9)	0.8	(0.3)	37.1	(1.7)	0.6	(0.2)	38.8	(1.8)
Slovak Republic	22.0	(0.9)	26.5	(1.2)	22.0	(0.8)	24.8	(1.0)	4.7	(1.0)	40.7	(2.9)	4.9	(1.0)	40.3	(2.9)
Spain	16.2	(0.6)	m	m	17.8	(0.7)	m	m	1.1	(0.5)	m	m	1.3	(0.6)	m	m
Sweden	1.3	(0.3)	45.9	(1.1)	1.8	(0.3)	42.0	(1.2)	0.0	(0.0)	62.2	(3.1)	0.7	(0.6)	61.1	(2.6)
United States	5.8	(0.5)	32.7	(1.3)	4.7	(0.6)	29.6	(1.3)	0.9	(0.4)	37.8	(3.1)	0.7	(0.4)	37.4	(3.8)
Sub-national entities																
Flanders (Belgium)	6.8	(0.4)	37.3	(1.0)	8.1	(0.5)	31.7	(1.1)	0.2	(0.2)	56.6	(2.3)	0.2	(0.2)	57.6	(2.7)
England (UK)	3.9	(0.4)	39.1	(1.4)	4.3	(0.4)	30.9	(1.0)	0.4	(0.5)	45.0	(3.8)	0.9	(0.7)	39.6	(2.9)
Northern Ireland (UK)	10.0	(0.9)	33.2	(1.5)	10.1	(0.7)	24.4	(1.6)	0.1	(0.1)	49.6	(4.4)	2.8	(1.3)	38.7	(4.3)
England/N. Ireland (UK)	4.1	(0.4)	38.9	(1.4)	4.5	(0.4)	30.7	(1.0)	0.4	(0.4)	45.2	(3.7)	1.0	(0.6)	39.5	(2.9)
Average[1]	7.8	(0.1)	36.3	(0.3)	8.2	(0.1)	31.6	(0.3)	0.7	(0.1)	51.3	(0.7)	0.7	(0.1)	50.2	(0.7)
Average-22[2]	8.9	(0.1)	m	m	9.7	(0.1)	m	m	0.8	(0.1)	m	m	0.8	(0.1)	m	m
Partners																
Cyprus[3]	17.2	(0.7)	m	m	19.4	(0.6)	m	m	1.9	(0.9)	m	m	1.1	(0.6)	m	m
Russian Federation[4]	18.7	(2.1)	25.6	(2.4)	18.0	(1.6)	26.3	(2.7)	0.6	(0.3)	35.0	(4.5)	1.0	(0.6)	42.9	(5.6)

1. Average of 19 participating OECD countries and entities.
2. Average of 22 OECD countries and entities: average of 19 countries with France, Italy and Spain.
3. See notes at the beginning of this Annex.
4. See note at the beginning of this Annex.
Source: Survey of Adult Skills (PIAAC) (2012).

StatLink ⟨⟩ http://dx.doi.org/10.1787/888933232002

[Part 1/1]

Table A3.6 — **Percentage of adults who score at Level 2 or 3 in problem solving in technology-rich environments or have no computer experience, by immigrant and language status**

OECD	Native-born and native language				Native-born and foreign language				Foreign-born and native language				Foreign-born and foreign language			
	No computer experience		Level 2/3		No computer experience		Level 2/3		No computer experience		Level 2/3		No computer experience		Level 2/3	
	%	S.E.	%	S.E.	%	S.E.	%	S.E.	%	S.E.	%	S.E.	%	S.E.	%	S.E.
National entities																
Australia	3.4	(0.3)	41.1	(1.2)	2.5	(1.4)	37.3	(5.2)	3.1	0.7	40.8	(2.6)	8.5	(1.1)	25.1	(2.1)
Austria	9.2	(0.5)	35.6	(0.9)	1.9	(1.3)	26.8	(4.9)	4.8	2.0	43.3	(4.8)	16.9	(1.8)	13.5	(1.6)
Canada	3.8	(0.2)	40.3	(0.8)	2.7	(0.5)	39.8	(2.3)	3.3	0.6	33.6	(2.2)	8.4	(0.7)	24.0	(1.5)
Czech Republic	10.0	(0.5)	33.6	(1.2)	c	c	c	c	27.2	7.9	34.8	(10.5)	11.1	(3.0)	20.6	(7.3)
Denmark	2.2	(0.2)	41.2	(0.8)	1.0	(1.0)	41.0	(7.7)	3.2	2.0	42.5	(6.3)	4.8	(0.6)	17.6	(1.5)
Estonia	8.5	(0.3)	30.0	(0.7)	10.6	(2.3)	28.0	(4.6)	18.4	1.3	12.4	(1.7)	26.0	(4.2)	11.7	(3.4)
Finland	3.5	(0.3)	42.9	(0.8)	5.2	(2.6)	30.6	(4.6)	1.6	1.6	55.2	(7.3)	3.4	(2.5)	19.5	(5.7)
France	9.3	(0.4)	m	m	6.4	(2.3)	m	m	14.7	1.9	m	m	23.3	(1.8)	m	m
Germany	6.9	(0.5)	40.2	(0.9)	5.9	(3.2)	23.9	(5.6)	13.8	3.3	26.2	(4.1)	16.0	(2.4)	12.6	(1.9)
Ireland	12.0	(0.5)	25.0	(1.0)	24.0	(7.0)	14.7	(5.5)	3.4	0.9	32.8	(2.5)	1.8	(0.6)	20.3	(2.4)
Italy	24.6	(0.8)	m	m	32.2	(8.4)	m	m	12.7	3.8	m	m	25.7	(3.1)	m	m
Japan	10.4	(0.5)	34.9	(0.8)	c	c	c	c	c	c	c	c	c	c	c	c
Korea	15.4	(0.4)	31.0	(0.8)	c	c	c	c	36.2	7.0	15.8	(5.5)	15.6	(7.1)	0.0	(0.0)
Netherlands	2.4	(0.2)	45.6	(0.8)	4.3	(3.0)	27.3	(9.3)	3.6	1.6	41.3	(5.1)	8.9	(1.7)	16.7	(2.2)
Norway	1.5	(0.2)	44.9	(0.8)	1.7	(1.6)	34.8	(6.4)	0.0	0.0	46.7	(7.7)	2.7	(0.8)	22.0	(1.9)
Poland	19.6	(0.5)	19.3	(0.8)	8.8	(3.6)	12.7	(5.4)	c	c	c	c	c	c	c	c
Slovak Republic	20.8	(0.6)	26.8	(0.8)	34.1	(3.4)	11.8	(2.8)	45.5	6.9	12.7	(5.7)	46.4	(8.1)	13.0	(6.1)
Spain	17.5	(0.5)	m	m	21.3	(2.9)	m	m	8.0	1.4	m	m	22.6	(2.8)	m	m
Sweden	1.1	(0.2)	49.3	(0.9)	0.0	(0.0)	41.0	(5.6)	1.4	1.5	37.6	(6.0)	4.4	(0.9)	18.2	(1.6)
United States	3.4	(0.3)	35.7	(1.3)	5.5	(1.6)	32.8	(5.5)	5.5	2.5	24.1	(4.3)	20.9	(3.1)	12.2	(1.9)
Sub-national entities																
Flanders (Belgium)	7.7	(0.4)	37.8	(0.9)	3.5	(1.4)	33.6	(4.3)	2.6	1.3	39.9	(4.9)	15.3	(2.5)	11.4	(2.7)
England (UK)	4.1	(0.3)	37.1	(1.0)	2.4	(2.5)	34.5	(7.0)	4.5	1.3	31.4	(3.9)	5.0	(1.1)	23.4	(2.7)
Northern Ireland (UK)	10.4	(0.6)	29.8	(1.3)	c	c	c	c	9.1	3.2	28.8	(6.6)	4.7	(3.4)	21.2	(4.6)
England/N. Ireland (UK)	4.4	(0.3)	36.8	(1.0)	2.7	(2.4)	34.3	(6.9)	4.7	1.3	31.3	(3.8)	5.0	(1.1)	23.3	(2.7)
Average[1]	7.7	(0.1)	36.4	(0.2)	7.1	(0.7)	29.4	(1.4)	10.5	(0.8)	33.6	(1.3)	12.7	(0.8)	16.6	(0.8)
Average-22[2]	9.0	(0.1)	m	m	9.2	(0.8)	m	m	10.7	(0.7)	m	m	14.4	(0.7)	m	m

Partners

Cyprus[3]	23.5	(0.5)	m	m	c	c	m	m	9.1	1.7	m	m	18.5	(3.7)	m	m
Russian Federation[4]	m	m	m	m	m	m	m	m	m	m	m	m	m	m	m	m

1. Average of 19 participating OECD countries and entities.
2. Average of 22 OECD countries and entities: average of 19 countries with France, Italy and Spain.
3. See notes at the beginning of this Annex.
4. See note at the beginning of this Annex.
Notes: Results for the Russian Federation are missing as no language variables are available for the Russian Federation.
Source: Survey of Adult Skills (PIAAC) (2012).
StatLink ᴍᴎᴤ http://dx.doi.org/10.1787/888933232012

[Part 1/1]

Table A3.7 **Percentage of adults who score at Level 2 or 3 in problem solving in technology-rich environments or have no computer experience, by level of literacy proficiency**

OECD	At or below Level 1				Level 2				Level 3				Level 4/5			
	No computer experience		Level 2/3		No computer experience		Level 2/3		No computer experience		Level 2/3		No computer experience		Level 2/3	
	%	S.E.	%	S.E.	%	S.E.	%	S.E.	%	S.E.	%	S.E.	%	S.E.	%	S.E.
National entities																
Australia	18.1	(1.6)	0.0	(0.0)	4.3	(0.6)	11.2	(1.4)	1.0	(0.2)	52.0	(2.1)	0.2	(0.2)	83.3	(1.9)
Austria	24.5	(2.2)	0.0	(0.0)	11.7	(1.0)	11.6	(1.2)	3.9	(0.9)	55.9	(1.6)	0.0	(0.0)	86.4	(2.4)
Canada	14.8	(1.0)	0.5	(0.2)	4.7	(0.4)	12.9	(0.8)	1.3	(0.3)	55.1	(1.1)	0.4	(0.2)	86.0	(1.3)
Czech Republic	23.7	(3.1)	1.0	(0.9)	13.8	(1.4)	12.7	(1.7)	5.4	(0.8)	51.5	(2.2)	0.7	(0.7)	80.1	(3.8)
Denmark	10.1	(1.0)	0.3	(0.3)	2.1	(0.4)	14.1	(0.9)	0.3	(0.2)	61.3	(1.1)	0.0	(0.0)	93.4	(1.5)
Estonia	23.9	(1.5)	0.6	(0.4)	12.6	(0.8)	7.3	(0.9)	5.6	(0.5)	40.2	(1.1)	1.6	(0.5)	73.9	(2.0)
Finland	15.3	(2.0)	0.4	(0.4)	5.0	(0.8)	8.6	(1.2)	1.3	(0.3)	48.8	(1.5)	0.0	(0.0)	87.4	(1.3)
France	27.0	(1.2)	m	m	9.9	(0.7)	m	m	3.1	(0.4)	m	m	0.8	(0.5)	m	m
Germany	20.7	(2.1)	0.6	(0.3)	9.1	(1.2)	14.2	(1.0)	3.2	(0.6)	59.1	(2.0)	0.7	(0.4)	89.5	(2.1)
Ireland	25.0	(1.9)	0.4	(0.3)	10.6	(0.8)	9.7	(1.1)	4.6	(0.7)	41.7	(1.8)	0.8	(0.6)	77.2	(2.3)
Italy	42.5	(2.3)	m	m	23.7	(1.3)	m	m	9.9	(1.3)	m	m	3.8	(2.9)	m	m
Japan	48.0	(3.8)	0.0	(0.0)	19.8	(1.5)	6.6	(1.1)	6.2	(0.7)	36.9	(1.4)	1.6	(0.4)	67.1	(1.9)
Korea	51.3	(2.1)	0.0	(0.0)	17.7	(0.9)	8.5	(0.7)	5.4	(0.7)	49.2	(1.7)	1.7	(0.8)	82.7	(2.5)
Netherlands	14.5	(1.8)	0.0	(0.0)	3.7	(0.6)	8.6	(1.0)	0.7	(0.2)	54.8	(1.3)	0.0	(0.0)	90.9	(1.4)
Norway	5.9	(1.2)	1.1	(0.7)	2.0	(0.4)	14.0	(1.5)	0.7	(0.2)	58.1	(1.9)	0.0	(0.0)	90.8	(1.4)
Poland	41.8	(1.9)	0.5	(0.3)	21.8	(1.0)	5.9	(0.7)	9.6	(1.0)	32.6	(1.6)	2.9	(1.2)	57.4	(3.2)
Slovak Republic	51.8	(2.8)	0.5	(0.4)	26.3	(1.2)	7.6	(0.9)	13.5	(0.9)	39.1	(1.6)	6.2	(1.7)	72.9	(3.8)
Spain	37.4	(1.5)	m	m	13.8	(0.9)	m	m	4.5	(0.8)	m	m	1.3	(0.9)	m	m
Sweden	7.4	(1.4)	0.7	(0.5)	1.9	(0.6)	15.0	(1.6)	0.1	(0.2)	58.8	(1.6)	0.0	(0.0)	93.8	(1.5)
United States	21.2	(1.9)	0.0	(0.0)	4.0	(0.6)	9.7	(1.3)	0.7	(0.3)	51.3	(1.8)	0.0	(0.0)	90.1	(1.9)
Sub-national entities																
Flanders (Belgium)	24.7	(1.8)	0.4	(0.3)	9.7	(1.0)	9.7	(1.0)	2.6	(0.5)	53.0	(1.6)	0.0	(0.0)	88.9	(1.7)
England (UK)	11.7	(1.3)	1.3	(0.8)	5.0	(0.6)	13.5	(1.3)	1.5	(0.4)	52.9	(2.2)	0.2	(0.2)	85.7	(2.2)
Northern Ireland (UK)	20.2	(2.3)	0.9	(0.7)	13.1	(1.4)	10.4	(2.2)	4.8	(1.0)	47.9	(3.2)	1.6	(1.2)	85.2	(3.1)
England/N. Ireland (UK)	12.0	(1.3)	1.3	(0.8)	5.3	(0.6)	13.3	(1.2)	1.6	(0.4)	52.7	(2.2)	0.3	(0.2)	85.7	(2.2)
Average[1]	23.9	(0.5)	0.4	(0.1)	9.8	(0.2)	10.6	(0.3)	3.6	(0.1)	50.1	(0.4)	0.9	(0.1)	83.0	(0.5)
Average-22[2]	25.5	(0.4)	m	m	10.6	(0.2)	m	m	3.9	(0.1)	m	m	1.0	(0.2)	m	m
Partners																
Cyprus[3]	33.8	(2.3)	m	m	23.7	(1.1)	m	m	18.5	(1.2)	m	m	11.0	(3.0)	m	m
Russian Federation[4]	22.0	(4.9)	2.4	(1.2)	20.9	(2.3)	10.8	(1.6)	16.9	(2.3)	36.4	(2.7)	10.6	(3.6)	63.2	(5.8)

1. Average of 19 participating OECD countries and entities.
2. Average of 22 OECD countries and entities: average of 19 countries with France, Italy and Spain.
3. See notes at the beginning of this Annex.
4. See note at the beginning of this Annex.
Source: Survey of Adult Skills (PIAAC) (2012).

StatLink http://dx.doi.org/10.1787/888933232021

[Part 1/1]

Table A4.1

Percentage of adults scoring at Level 2 or 3 in problem solving in technology-rich environments or have no computer experience, by employment status

OECD	Non-worker				Worker (working at the time of the survey or had worked in the 12 months prior to it)			
	No computer experience		Level 2/3		No computer experience		Level 2/3	
	%	S.E.	%	S.E.	%	S.E.	%	S.E.
National entities								
Australia	12.0	(1.1)	25.0	(2.2)	2.0	0.2	42.1	(1.1)
Austria	23.0	(1.4)	22.8	(1.5)	6.3	0.4	35.8	(1.0)
Canada	12.0	(0.7)	21.7	(1.2)	3.1	0.2	39.9	(0.6)
Czech Republic	21.4	(1.2)	29.5	(2.0)	6.2	0.5	34.8	(1.3)
Denmark	8.3	(0.8)	22.6	(1.7)	1.2	0.1	42.4	(0.8)
Estonia	25.6	(0.9)	21.4	(1.1)	5.8	0.3	29.3	(0.9)
Finland	11.0	(1.0)	27.1	(1.7)	1.7	0.2	45.2	(0.9)
France	17.9	(0.8)	m	m	7.6	0.4	m	m
Germany	16.4	(1.5)	26.1	(1.5)	6.0	0.5	39.0	(1.0)
Ireland	17.6	(0.9)	16.6	(1.2)	6.6	0.4	29.5	(1.1)
Italy	36.3	(1.3)	m	m	17.5	1.0	m	m
Japan	17.4	(1.5)	27.6	(1.7)	8.4	0.5	37.0	(0.9)
Korea	19.8	(0.9)	31.8	(1.4)	14.1	0.5	30.0	(1.0)
Netherlands	9.2	(1.2)	21.3	(1.6)	1.7	0.2	47.2	(0.9)
Norway	7.0	(1.0)	21.5	(1.9)	0.7	0.1	45.5	(0.8)
Poland	31.8	(1.2)	14.7	(0.8)	13.6	0.5	21.3	(1.0)
Slovak Republic	35.1	(1.1)	19.4	(1.2)	15.8	0.7	28.7	(0.9)
Spain	29.6	(0.9)	m	m	11.6	0.5	m	m
Sweden	5.3	(0.9)	26.8	(1.7)	0.8	0.2	47.5	(0.8)
United States	11.8	(1.0)	21.9	(1.7)	4.0	0.4	35.0	(1.3)
Sub-national entities								
Flanders (Belgium)	17.1	(0.9)	29.8	(1.3)	4.6	0.3	38.7	(1.1)
England (UK)	11.1	(0.9)	19.3	(1.6)	2.1	0.3	40.3	(1.0)
Northern Ireland (UK)	18.9	(1.5)	16.7	(1.9)	6.7	0.6	34.7	(1.5)
England/N. Ireland (UK)	11.5	(0.9)	19.2	(1.6)	2.3	0.3	40.1	(1.0)
Average[1]	16.5	(0.2)	23.5	(0.4)	5.5	(0.1)	37.3	(0.2)
Average-22[2]	18.1	(0.2)	m	m	6.4	(0.1)	m	m
Partners								
Cyprus[3]	30.2	(1.0)	m	m	18.8	0.7	m	m
Russian Federation[4]	25.2	(2.7)	23.8	(4.0)	15.2	1.6	26.9	(1.9)

1. Average of 19 participating OECD countries and entities.
2. Average of 22 OECD countries and entities: average of 19 countries with France, Italy and Spain.
3. See notes at the beginning of this Annex.
4. See note at the beginning of this Annex.
Source: Survey of Adult Skills (PIAAC) (2012).
StatLink ᕱᕯᎦ http://dx.doi.org/10.1787/888933232033

[Part 1/1]

Table A4.2a **Frequency of e-mail use at work**

OECD	Frequency of usage											
	Never		Less than once a month		Less than once a week but at least once a month		At least once a week but not everyday		Everyday		Missing	
	%	S.E.	%	S.E.	%	S.E.	%	S.E.	%	S.E.	%	S.E.
National entities												
Australia	33.8	(0.7)	2.3	(0.3)	2.0	(0.2)	6.5	(0.4)	53.1	(0.8)	2.3	(0.2)
Austria	38.5	(0.8)	3.2	(0.3)	2.8	(0.3)	6.8	(0.4)	46.3	(0.8)	2.4	(0.2)
Canada	36.7	(0.6)	2.2	(0.2)	2.3	(0.2)	5.3	(0.3)	52.3	(0.5)	1.2	(0.1)
Czech Republic	44.1	(1.3)	1.4	(0.2)	2.0	(0.3)	7.2	(0.7)	44.4	(1.2)	0.9	(0.3)
Denmark	30.2	(0.6)	2.7	(0.2)	3.4	(0.3)	7.4	(0.4)	55.7	(0.7)	0.6	(0.1)
Estonia	44.9	(0.7)	1.7	(0.2)	1.8	(0.2)	5.0	(0.3)	45.8	(0.7)	0.8	(0.1)
Finland	28.3	(0.6)	3.6	(0.3)	3.4	(0.3)	9.5	(0.5)	55.1	(0.6)	0.1	(0.1)
France	44.8	(0.6)	1.9	(0.2)	1.5	(0.2)	4.5	(0.3)	46.2	(0.5)	1.1	(0.1)
Germany	41.7	(0.8)	2.4	(0.3)	2.8	(0.2)	6.4	(0.5)	44.7	(0.8)	1.9	(0.2)
Ireland	45.5	(1.0)	2.4	(0.3)	2.2	(0.2)	5.9	(0.4)	43.3	(1.0)	0.6	(0.2)
Italy	57.2	(1.0)	1.5	(0.3)	1.2	(0.3)	4.4	(0.4)	34.6	(0.9)	1.1	(0.3)
Japan	47.1	(0.8)	4.6	(0.4)	4.1	(0.3)	7.4	(0.4)	34.9	(0.8)	1.9	(0.2)
Korea	49.9	(0.8)	3.0	(0.3)	5.7	(0.4)	10.6	(0.5)	30.3	(0.6)	0.5	(0.1)
Netherlands	27.1	(0.6)	1.6	(0.2)	2.0	(0.2)	6.2	(0.4)	60.2	(0.6)	2.9	(0.2)
Norway	25.0	(0.5)	2.7	(0.3)	2.8	(0.2)	8.6	(0.4)	58.3	(0.6)	2.7	(0.2)
Poland	55.1	(0.8)	1.8	(0.2)	2.0	(0.2)	7.1	(0.5)	33.6	(0.8)	0.4	(0.1)
Slovak Republic	52.2	(1.1)	1.7	(0.2)	1.7	(0.2)	7.8	(0.5)	36.1	(1.0)	0.5	(0.1)
Spain	53.8	(0.7)	1.5	(0.2)	1.4	(0.2)	4.3	(0.3)	37.5	(0.7)	1.5	(0.2)
Sweden	27.4	(0.7)	4.1	(0.3)	3.6	(0.3)	8.6	(0.5)	56.1	(0.6)	0.2	(0.1)
United States	35.1	(1.0)	2.3	(0.2)	2.6	(0.3)	6.5	(0.4)	48.2	(0.9)	5.2	(0.7)
Sub-national entities												
Flanders (Belgium)	31.3	(0.8)	1.5	(0.2)	1.5	(0.2)	5.0	(0.4)	53.6	(0.8)	7.0	(0.3)
England (UK)	34.1	(0.8)	2.5	(0.3)	2.1	(0.3)	5.7	(0.4)	53.7	(0.9)	1.8	(0.2)
Northern Ireland (UK)	38.3	(1.1)	3.2	(0.4)	2.1	(0.3)	5.4	(0.5)	47.9	(1.2)	3.2	(0.4)
England/N. Ireland (UK)	34.3	(0.8)	2.5	(0.3)	2.1	(0.3)	5.7	(0.4)	53.5	(0.9)	1.8	(0.2)
Average[1]	38.3	(0.2)	2.5	(0.1)	2.7	(0.1)	7.0	(0.1)	47.7	(0.2)	1.8	(0.1)
Average-22[2]	40.2	(0.2)	2.4	(0.1)	2.5	(0.1)	6.7	(0.1)	46.5	(0.2)	1.7	(0.1)
Partners												
Cyprus[3]	43.3	(0.8)	2.5	(0.2)	1.9	(0.2)	4.1	(0.4)	(24.5)	(0.7)	23.8	(0.5)
Russian Federation[4]	66.5	(1.9)	3.9	(0.5)	2.9	(0.6)	6.7	(0.8)	(19.7)	(1.5)	0.3	(0.1)

1. Average of 19 participating OECD countries and entities.
2. Average of 22 OECD countries and entities: average of 19 countries with France, Italy and Spain.
3. See notes at the beginning of this Annex.
4. See note at the beginning of this Annex.
Source: Survey of Adult Skills (PIAAC) (2012).
StatLink 🔗 http://dx.doi.org/10.1787/888933232047

[Part 1/1]

Table A4.2b **Frequency of Internet use to better understand issues related to work**

OECD	Never		Less than once a month		Less than once a week but at least once a month		At least once a week but not everyday		Everyday		Missing	
	%	S.E.	%	S.E.	%	S.E.	%	S.E.	%	S.E.	%	S.E.
National entities												
Australia	35.6	(0.8)	4.2	(0.3)	5.3	(0.3)	13.7	(0.6)	38.8	(0.8)	2.3	(0.2)
Austria	41.6	(0.8)	5.0	(0.4)	5.7	(0.4)	14.3	(0.6)	31.0	(0.8)	2.4	(0.2)
Canada	37.6	(0.6)	5.4	(0.3)	5.7	(0.3)	13.5	(0.4)	36.6	(0.6)	1.2	(0.1)
Czech Republic	46.3	(1.4)	3.6	(0.5)	3.9	(0.5)	9.7	(0.6)	35.7	(1.3)	0.9	(0.3)
Denmark	31.7	(0.6)	5.6	(0.3)	7.3	(0.4)	17.1	(0.5)	37.7	(0.8)	0.6	(0.1)
Estonia	43.9	(0.7)	3.3	(0.2)	4.3	(0.3)	11.5	(0.4)	36.1	(0.6)	0.8	(0.1)
Finland	29.9	(0.6)	7.5	(0.4)	9.5	(0.5)	20.2	(0.7)	32.7	(0.7)	0.1	(0.1)
France	49.7	(0.6)	5.9	(0.3)	5.4	(0.3)	12.6	(0.4)	25.4	(0.6)	1.1	(0.1)
Germany	43.4	(0.9)	4.1	(0.3)	5.6	(0.4)	16.3	(0.7)	28.6	(0.7)	1.9	(0.2)
Ireland	47.5	(0.9)	4.2	(0.4)	4.6	(0.3)	12.4	(0.5)	30.6	(0.9)	0.6	(0.2)
Italy	59.0	(1.0)	2.7	(0.3)	2.4	(0.3)	8.8	(0.6)	26.0	(0.9)	1.1	(0.3)
Japan	42.8	(0.7)	5.6	(0.4)	7.3	(0.5)	15.2	(0.6)	27.3	(0.7)	1.9	(0.2)
Korea	45.3	(0.7)	3.0	(0.3)	5.9	(0.3)	13.9	(0.6)	31.4	(0.7)	0.5	(0.1)
Netherlands	31.9	(0.6)	5.4	(0.4)	6.4	(0.3)	13.5	(0.6)	39.9	(0.8)	2.9	(0.2)
Norway	25.4	(0.6)	7.4	(0.4)	8.5	(0.4)	21.3	(0.5)	34.7	(0.7)	2.7	(0.2)
Poland	54.0	(0.8)	2.5	(0.3)	2.9	(0.3)	11.6	(0.6)	28.6	(0.8)	0.4	(0.1)
Slovak Republic	53.7	(1.0)	3.5	(0.3)	3.7	(0.3)	11.3	(0.5)	27.2	(0.9)	0.5	(0.1)
Spain	55.3	(0.7)	3.1	(0.3)	2.6	(0.3)	8.2	(0.5)	29.4	(0.7)	1.5	(0.2)
Sweden	31.6	(0.7)	8.5	(0.4)	9.4	(0.5)	18.8	(0.7)	31.4	(0.6)	0.3	(0.1)
United States	35.5	(1.0)	4.6	(0.4)	5.4	(0.3)	12.5	(0.5)	36.8	(1.0)	5.2	(0.7)
Sub-national entities												
Flanders (Belgium)	35.1	(0.8)	4.3	(0.3)	5.2	(0.4)	13.9	(0.6)	34.4	(0.7)	7.0	(0.3)
England (UK)	36.2	(0.9)	5.7	(0.5)	5.4	(0.4)	16.0	(0.8)	34.9	(0.8)	1.8	(0.2)
Northern Ireland (UK)	40.5	(1.1)	5.4	(0.5)	5.9	(0.5)	13.7	(0.7)	31.3	(1.1)	3.2	(0.4)
England/N. Ireland (UK)	36.4	(0.9)	5.7	(0.4)	5.4	(0.3)	15.9	(0.7)	34.8	(0.8)	1.8	(0.2)
Average[1]	39.4	(0.2)	4.9	(0.1)	5.9	(0.1)	14.6	(0.1)	33.4	(0.2)	1.8	(0.1)
Average-22[2]	41.5	(0.2)	4.8	(0.1)	5.6	(0.1)	13.9	(0.1)	32.5	(0.2)	1.7	(0.1)
Partners												
Cyprus[3]	45.4	(0.8)	3.4	(0.3)	2.8	(0.3)	6.4	(0.4)	(18.1)	(0.7)	23.8	(0.5)
Russian Federation[4]	64.1	(1.6)	5.8	(0.5)	3.4	(0.5)	9.8	(0.9)	(16.6)	(1.1)	0.3	(0.1)

1. Average of 19 participating OECD countries and entities.
2. Average of 22 OECD countries and entities: average of 19 countries with France, Italy and Spain.
3. See notes at the beginning of this Annex.
4. See note at the beginning of this Annex.
Source: Survey of Adult Skills (PIAAC) (2012).

StatLink ⬛⬛⬛ http://dx.doi.org/10.1787/888933232059

ADULTS, COMPUTERS AND PROBLEM SOLVING: WHAT'S THE PROBLEM?

[Part 1/1]

Table A4.2c Frequency of Internet use for conducting transactions (e.g. buying or selling products or services, or banking) at work

OECD	Frequency of usage											
	Never		**Less than once a month**		**Less than once a week but at least once a month**		**At least once a week but not everyday**		**Everyday**		**Missing**	
	%	S.E.	%	S.E.	%	S.E.	%	S.E.	%	S.E.	%	S.E.
National entities												
Australia	62.2	(0.8)	6.1	(0.4)	5.2	(0.4)	10.0	(0.5)	14.3	(0.6)	2.3	(0.2)
Austria	72.1	(0.6)	5.1	(0.4)	4.9	(0.3)	7.5	(0.4)	8.0	(0.5)	2.4	(0.2)
Canada	68.4	(0.5)	5.7	(0.3)	5.4	(0.3)	7.8	(0.3)	11.4	(0.4)	1.2	(0.1)
Czech Republic	72.2	(1.2)	5.1	(0.5)	4.0	(0.4)	9.0	(0.8)	8.8	(0.6)	0.9	(0.3)
Denmark	62.3	(0.6)	8.6	(0.4)	6.8	(0.3)	11.1	(0.4)	10.5	(0.4)	0.6	(0.1)
Estonia	65.4	(0.7)	4.9	(0.3)	5.0	(0.3)	9.9	(0.4)	14.1	(0.5)	0.8	(0.1)
Finland	66.7	(0.6)	6.7	(0.3)	6.5	(0.4)	13.0	(0.5)	6.8	(0.4)	0.1	(0.1)
France	81.1	(0.4)	4.4	(0.3)	3.3	(0.2)	4.5	(0.3)	5.6	(0.3)	1.1	(0.1)
Germany	76.1	(0.8)	4.1	(0.3)	3.4	(0.3)	7.1	(0.4)	7.5	(0.5)	1.9	(0.2)
Ireland	72.7	(0.8)	5.0	(0.4)	4.1	(0.3)	6.9	(0.4)	10.7	(0.6)	0.6	(0.2)
Italy	82.0	(0.8)	3.8	(0.4)	2.5	(0.3)	4.6	(0.4)	6.0	(0.5)	1.1	(0.3)
Japan	81.4	(0.6)	4.9	(0.3)	3.9	(0.3)	3.5	(0.3)	4.4	(0.3)	1.9	(0.2)
Korea	62.6	(0.7)	4.3	(0.3)	8.3	(0.4)	12.3	(0.5)	12.0	(0.5)	0.5	(0.1)
Netherlands	67.2	(0.7)	6.3	(0.4)	4.8	(0.3)	8.8	(0.4)	10.0	(0.5)	2.9	(0.2)
Norway	62.0	(0.7)	7.5	(0.4)	6.9	(0.4)	12.6	(0.5)	8.3	(0.4)	2.7	(0.2)
Poland	77.7	(0.7)	4.3	(0.3)	3.6	(0.3)	6.4	(0.5)	7.6	(0.5)	0.4	(0.1)
Slovak Republic	75.9	(0.8)	3.7	(0.4)	3.6	(0.3)	7.1	(0.4)	9.1	(0.6)	0.5	(0.1)
Spain	82.2	(0.6)	3.0	(0.2)	2.6	(0.3)	3.5	(0.3)	7.2	(0.4)	1.5	(0.2)
Sweden	69.2	(0.7)	7.2	(0.4)	7.8	(0.4)	9.1	(0.5)	6.4	(0.4)	0.2	(0.1)
United States	60.2	(1.0)	6.7	(0.4)	6.2	(0.4)	8.4	(0.4)	13.3	(0.8)	5.2	(0.7)
Sub-national entities												
Flanders (Belgium)	67.4	(0.8)	4.7	(0.3)	3.9	(0.3)	7.7	(0.4)	9.3	(0.5)	7.0	(0.3)
England (UK)	65.6	(1.0)	6.4	(0.4)	4.8	(0.4)	9.1	(0.5)	12.3	(0.8)	1.8	(0.2)
Northern Ireland (UK)	69.7	(1.0)	6.0	(0.6)	4.1	(0.4)	6.6	(0.5)	10.4	(0.8)	3.2	(0.4)
England/N. Ireland (UK)	65.7	(1.0)	6.4	(0.4)	4.8	(0.4)	9.0	(0.5)	12.2	(0.8)	1.8	(0.2)
Average[1]	68.8	(0.2)	5.7	(0.1)	5.2	(0.1)	8.8	(0.1)	9.7	(0.1)	1.8	(0.1)
Average-22[2]	70.6	(0.2)	5.4	(0.1)	4.9	(0.1)	8.2	(0.1)	9.3	(0.1)	1.7	(0.1)
Partners												
Cyprus[3]	64.1	(0.7)	3.2	(0.3)	2.1	(0.3)	2.1	(0.3)	(4.6)	(0.4)	23.8	(0.5)
Russian Federation[4]	87.2	(1.1)	4.2	(0.5)	2.3	(0.4)	2.4	(0.3)	(3.5)	(0.4)	0.3	(0.1)

1. Average of 19 participating OECD countries and entities.
2. Average of 22 OECD countries and entities: average of 19 countries with France, Italy and Spain.
3. See notes at the beginning of this Annex.
4. See note at the beginning of this Annex.

Source: Survey of Adult Skills (PIAAC) (2012).

StatLink ᴴᴵᴸᴱ http://dx.doi.org/10.1787/888933232064

[Part 1/1]

Table A4.2d Frequency of spreadsheet software (e.g. Excel) use at work

	Frequency of usage											
	Never		Less than once a month		Less than once a week but at least once a month		At least once a week but not everyday		Everyday		Missing	
OECD	%	S.E.	%	S.E.	%	S.E.	%	S.E.	%	S.E.	%	S.E.
National entities												
Australia	45.0	(0.8)	7.1	(0.4)	6.7	(0.3)	13.8	(0.6)	25.1	(0.7)	2.4	(0.2)
Austria	51.4	(0.8)	7.7	(0.5)	7.3	(0.4)	12.6	(0.6)	18.6	(0.7)	2.4	(0.2)
Canada	50.3	(0.5)	6.1	(0.2)	6.6	(0.2)	11.1	(0.3)	24.8	(0.5)	1.2	(0.1)
Czech Republic	50.8	(1.3)	5.7	(0.5)	5.9	(0.6)	14.0	(0.9)	22.8	(1.2)	0.9	(0.3)
Denmark	51.9	(0.7)	8.6	(0.4)	7.7	(0.3)	12.7	(0.5)	18.4	(0.5)	0.6	(0.1)
Estonia	53.4	(0.7)	7.3	(0.3)	6.8	(0.3)	11.6	(0.4)	20.0	(0.5)	0.8	(0.1)
Finland	50.9	(0.6)	11.5	(0.5)	10.3	(0.5)	14.2	(0.5)	12.9	(0.5)	0.2	(0.1)
France	55.5	(0.6)	6.5	(0.3)	5.4	(0.3)	9.8	(0.4)	21.7	(0.5)	1.1	(0.1)
Germany	52.7	(0.8)	7.3	(0.4)	6.3	(0.4)	10.8	(0.5)	20.9	(0.7)	2.0	(0.2)
Ireland	57.7	(0.9)	5.4	(0.4)	4.4	(0.3)	8.2	(0.5)	23.7	(0.8)	0.6	(0.2)
Italy	63.2	(0.9)	4.9	(0.5)	4.2	(0.5)	7.2	(0.5)	19.4	(0.7)	1.1	(0.3)
Japan	48.2	(0.8)	6.5	(0.4)	7.6	(0.4)	13.3	(0.5)	22.6	(0.7)	1.9	(0.2)
Korea	56.7	(0.7)	3.4	(0.3)	7.4	(0.4)	11.0	(0.5)	21.1	(0.6)	0.5	(0.1)
Netherlands	43.4	(0.7)	7.2	(0.4)	8.6	(0.4)	14.2	(0.6)	23.7	(0.7)	2.9	(0.2)
Norway	48.4	(0.7)	10.6	(0.4)	9.3	(0.4)	13.4	(0.5)	15.7	(0.5)	2.7	(0.2)
Poland	64.6	(0.7)	6.3	(0.5)	5.9	(0.4)	8.7	(0.5)	14.2	(0.6)	0.4	(0.1)
Slovak Republic	56.8	(1.1)	6.0	(0.5)	5.2	(0.4)	11.6	(0.7)	19.8	(0.9)	0.5	(0.1)
Spain	64.0	(0.8)	4.1	(0.3)	4.1	(0.4)	7.7	(0.4)	18.7	(0.6)	1.5	(0.2)
Sweden	50.7	(0.7)	10.8	(0.5)	9.0	(0.4)	12.9	(0.5)	16.5	(0.5)	0.2	(0.1)
United States	48.5	(1.0)	6.3	(0.5)	7.2	(0.5)	10.8	(0.6)	21.9	(0.8)	5.2	(0.7)
Sub-national entities												
Flanders (Belgium)	44.5	(0.8)	6.8	(0.4)	5.5	(0.4)	12.2	(0.6)	24.1	(0.7)	7.0	(0.3)
England (UK)	46.3	(0.9)	6.1	(0.4)	6.5	(0.5)	11.9	(0.6)	27.4	(0.9)	1.8	(0.2)
Northern Ireland (UK)	51.5	(1.3)	5.6	(0.5)	6.9	(0.6)	9.7	(0.6)	23.2	(1.0)	3.2	(0.4)
England/N. Ireland (UK)	46.4	(0.9)	6.1	(0.4)	6.5	(0.5)	11.8	(0.5)	27.2	(0.8)	1.9	(0.2)
Average[1]	51.2	(0.2)	7.2	(0.1)	7.1	(0.1)	12.0	(0.1)	20.7	(0.2)	1.8	(0.1)
Average-22[2]	52.5	(0.2)	6.9	(0.1)	6.7	(0.1)	11.5	(0.1)	20.6	(0.1)	1.7	(0.0)
Partners												
Cyprus[3]	49.9	(0.7)	4.2	(0.4)	2.9	(0.3)	5.3	(0.3)	(13.9)	(0.5)	23.8	(0.5)
Russian Federation[4]	67.1	(1.0)	6.8	(0.7)	4.1	(0.5)	7.8	(0.6)	(13.9)	(0.8)	0.3	(0.1)

1. Average of 19 participating OECD countries and entities.
2. Average of 22 OECD countries and entities: average of 19 countries with France, Italy and Spain.
3. See notes at the beginning of this Annex.
4. See note at the beginning of this Annex.
Source: Survey of Adult Skills (PIAAC) (2012).

StatLink ᴍꜱᴾ http://dx.doi.org/10.1787/888933232073

[Part 1/1]

Table A4.2e   **Frequency of a word processor (e.g. Word) use at work**

OECD	Never		Less than once a month		Less than once a week but at least once a month		At least once a week but not everyday		Everyday		Missing	
	%	S.E.	%	S.E.	%	S.E.	%	S.E.	%	S.E.	%	S.E.
National entities												
Australia	41.7	(0.8)	4.5	(0.3)	5.5	(0.4)	12.9	(0.6)	33.2	(0.7)	2.3	(0.2)
Austria	42.3	(0.8)	6.3	(0.4)	7.1	(0.4)	14.4	(0.5)	27.5	(0.8)	2.4	(0.2)
Canada	44.0	(0.6)	5.1	(0.2)	5.9	(0.3)	12.4	(0.4)	31.5	(0.5)	1.2	(0.1)
Czech Republic	46.5	(1.2)	4.3	(0.5)	5.7	(0.5)	15.8	(0.9)	26.9	(1.1)	0.9	(0.3)
Denmark	36.9	(0.6)	5.8	(0.3)	8.5	(0.4)	15.3	(0.6)	32.8	(0.6)	0.7	(0.1)
Estonia	50.7	(0.7)	5.4	(0.3)	6.5	(0.3)	14.2	(0.6)	22.5	(0.5)	0.8	(0.1)
Finland	36.2	(0.5)	10.0	(0.5)	11.9	(0.4)	20.9	(0.6)	20.8	(0.5)	0.2	(0.1)
France	51.3	(0.5)	5.5	(0.3)	5.3	(0.2)	10.6	(0.3)	26.2	(0.5)	1.1	(0.1)
Germany	42.6	(0.9)	4.8	(0.4)	5.6	(0.5)	13.7	(0.6)	31.3	(0.7)	2.0	(0.2)
Ireland	51.2	(1.0)	3.6	(0.3)	3.4	(0.3)	11.2	(0.6)	29.9	(0.8)	0.7	(0.2)
Italy	59.0	(0.9)	4.0	(0.4)	3.2	(0.4)	9.0	(0.6)	23.7	(0.8)	1.1	(0.3)
Japan	47.0	(0.9)	9.1	(0.4)	9.5	(0.6)	14.5	(0.5)	18.0	(0.6)	1.9	(0.2)
Korea	53.4	(0.8)	3.7	(0.3)	7.7	(0.4)	12.8	(0.5)	21.8	(0.5)	0.5	(0.1)
Netherlands	33.8	(0.6)	4.5	(0.3)	5.5	(0.4)	13.1	(0.5)	40.2	(0.7)	2.9	(0.2)
Norway	31.9	(0.5)	8.4	(0.5)	9.1	(0.4)	18.6	(0.6)	29.4	(0.6)	2.7	(0.2)
Poland	57.2	(0.8)	3.4	(0.3)	4.9	(0.4)	11.9	(0.5)	22.2	(0.7)	0.4	(0.1)
Slovak Republic	52.8	(1.0)	3.1	(0.3)	4.0	(0.4)	13.2	(0.6)	26.4	(0.9)	0.5	(0.1)
Spain	57.4	(0.8)	3.1	(0.3)	3.4	(0.3)	8.9	(0.5)	25.8	(0.7)	1.5	(0.2)
Sweden	37.2	(0.8)	10.0	(0.5)	10.3	(0.5)	17.8	(0.7)	24.6	(0.7)	0.2	(0.1)
United States	43.0	(1.0)	5.1	(0.4)	6.3	(0.4)	12.2	(0.6)	28.2	(0.7)	5.2	(0.7)
Sub-national entities												
Flanders (Belgium)	37.6	(0.8)	4.7	(0.3)	5.9	(0.3)	13.9	(0.6)	30.9	(0.7)	7.0	(0.3)
England (UK)	38.6	(0.8)	4.9	(0.3)	4.6	(0.4)	13.5	(0.6)	36.5	(0.9)	1.8	(0.2)
Northern Ireland (UK)	43.9	(1.2)	4.1	(0.4)	5.2	(0.5)	10.6	(0.7)	33.1	(1.0)	3.2	(0.4)
England/N. Ireland (UK)	38.8	(0.7)	4.9	(0.3)	4.6	(0.4)	13.4	(0.6)	36.4	(0.9)	1.8	(0.2)
Average[1]	43.4	(0.2)	5.6	(0.1)	6.7	(0.1)	14.3	(0.1)	28.1	(0.2)	1.8	(0.1)
Average-22[2]	45.1	(0.2)	5.4	(0.1)	6.4	(0.1)	13.7	(0.1)	27.7	(0.2)	1.7	(0.1)
Partners												
Cyprus[3]	43.6	(0.8)	3.3	(0.3)	2.8	(0.3)	6.7	(0.4)	(19.8)	(0.6)	23.8	(0.5)
Russian Federation[4]	62.0	(1.0)	4.1	(0.6)	3.2	(0.4)	9.8	(0.9)	(20.6)	(1.4)	0.3	(0.1)

1. Average of 19 participating OECD countries and entities.
2. Average of 22 OECD countries and entities: average of 19 countries with France, Italy and Spain.
3. See notes at the beginning of this Annex.
4. See note at the beginning of this Annex.
Source: Survey of Adult Skills (PIAAC) (2012).

StatLink ⬛ http://dx.doi.org/10.1787/888933232086

[Part 1/1]

Table A4.2f **Use of a computer at work**

OECD	Yes		No		Missing	
	%	S.E.	%	S.E.	%	S.E.
National entities						
Australia	74.7	(0.7)	23.0	(0.6)	2.3	(0.2)
Austria	69.4	(0.8)	28.2	(0.8)	2.4	(0.2)
Canada	73.4	(0.5)	25.4	(0.5)	1.2	(0.1)
Czech Republic	64.4	(1.2)	34.8	(1.2)	0.9	(0.3)
Denmark	78.7	(0.6)	20.7	(0.6)	0.6	(0.1)
Estonia	63.2	(0.7)	36.0	(0.7)	0.8	(0.1)
Finland	79.7	(0.6)	20.2	(0.6)	0.1	(0.0)
France	64.8	(0.6)	34.2	(0.6)	1.0	(0.1)
Germany	67.8	(0.8)	30.3	(0.8)	1.9	(0.2)
Ireland	64.9	(0.8)	34.5	(0.8)	0.6	(0.2)
Italy	49.4	(1.1)	49.5	(1.1)	1.1	(0.3)
Japan	69.5	(0.7)	28.6	(0.7)	1.9	(0.2)
Korea	62.7	(0.8)	36.9	(0.8)	0.5	(0.1)
Netherlands	77.5	(0.5)	19.7	(0.5)	2.9	(0.2)
Norway	80.7	(0.5)	16.6	(0.5)	2.7	(0.2)
Poland	53.5	(0.8)	46.2	(0.8)	0.4	(0.1)
Slovak Republic	55.7	(1.0)	43.8	(1.0)	0.5	(0.1)
Spain	54.6	(0.8)	43.9	(0.8)	1.5	(0.2)
Sweden	81.9	(0.7)	18.0	(0.7)	0.2	(0.1)
United States	70.4	(0.7)	24.4	(0.8)	5.2	(0.7)
Sub-national entities						
Flanders (Belgium)	69.2	(0.8)	23.9	(0.7)	7.0	(0.3)
England (UK)	73.7	(0.8)	24.5	(0.8)	1.8	(0.2)
Northern Ireland (UK)	69.2	(1.0)	27.6	(1.0)	3.2	(0.4)
England/N. Ireland (UK)	73.6	(0.8)	24.6	(0.8)	1.8	(0.2)
Average[1]	70.0	(0.2)	28.2	(0.2)	1.8	(0.1)
Average-22[2]	68.2	(0.2)	30.1	(0.2)	1.7	(0.0)
Partners						
Cyprus[3]	43.1	(0.8)	33.1	(0.8)	23.8	(0.5)
Russian Federation[4]	45.0	(1.4)	54.8	(1.3)	0.2	(0.1)

1. Average of 19 participating OECD countries and entities.
2. Average of 22 OECD countries and entities: average of 19 countries with France, Italy and Spain.
3. See notes at the beginning of this Annex.
4. See note at the beginning of this Annex.
Source: Survey of Adult Skills (PIAAC) (2012).

StatLink ⬛🖳 http://dx.doi.org/10.1787/888933232095

[Part 1/1]

Table A4.3 **Percentage of workers scoring at Level 2 or 3 in problem solving in technology-rich environments or having no computer experience, by frequency of complex problem solving**

OECD	Less than monthly or never				At least monthly			
	No computer experience		Level 2/3		No computer experience		Level 2/3	
	%	S.E.	%	S.E.	%	S.E.	%	S.E.
National entities								
Australia	3.6	(0.4)	32.3	(1.6)	1.2	(0.2)	47.7	(1.5)
Austria	10.6	(0.8)	24.6	(1.3)	2.5	(0.4)	45.7	(1.5)
Canada	5.2	(0.4)	31.6	(0.9)	1.4	(0.2)	46.3	(0.9)
Czech Republic	10.9	(1.0)	22.7	(1.7)	2.6	(0.6)	44.2	(1.9)
Denmark	2.1	(0.3)	31.6	(1.2)	0.5	(0.1)	50.8	(1.1)
Estonia	8.9	(0.5)	20.9	(1.2)	2.8	(0.3)	37.5	(1.2)
Finland	2.9	(0.5)	35.7	(1.3)	0.7	(0.2)	52.7	(1.2)
France	11.4	(0.6)	m	m	3.4	(0.3)	m	m
Germany	10.1	(0.9)	28.0	(1.3)	2.5	(0.4)	48.4	(1.5)
Ireland	10.2	(0.7)	21.9	(1.4)	3.3	(0.5)	36.5	(1.5)
Italy	27.3	(1.7)	m	m	10.6	(1.0)	m	m
Japan	12.7	(0.9)	27.7	(1.0)	2.7	(0.4)	49.6	(1.7)
Korea	21.1	(0.9)	22.8	(1.1)	6.6	(0.5)	37.7	(1.4)
Netherlands	2.9	(0.4)	36.8	(1.3)	0.5	(0.2)	56.9	(1.2)
Norway	0.9	(0.2)	35.0	(1.3)	0.5	(0.2)	53.4	(1.2)
Poland	20.1	(0.8)	15.2	(1.0)	6.9	(0.5)	27.4	(1.4)
Slovak Republic	23.4	(1.2)	21.1	(1.3)	10.0	(0.8)	34.6	(1.4)
Spain	16.8	(0.8)	m	m	6.3	(0.7)	m	m
Sweden	1.3	(0.3)	38.0	(1.3)	0.5	(0.2)	54.5	(1.1)
United States	6.6	(0.8)	26.1	(1.6)	2.5	(0.4)	39.8	(1.6)
Sub-national entities								
Flanders (Belgium)	7.7	(0.7)	27.6	(1.2)	1.8	(0.3)	48.2	(1.5)
England (UK)	4.1	(0.7)	25.2	(1.6)	0.9	(0.2)	49.3	(1.2)
Northern Ireland (UK)	11.1	(1.2)	23.1	(2.2)	3.5	(0.6)	43.0	(2.0)
England/N. Ireland (UK)	4.4	(0.7)	25.1	(1.6)	1.0	(0.2)	49.1	(1.2)
Average[1]	8.7	(0.2)	27.6	(0.3)	2.7	(0.1)	45.3	(0.3)
Average-22[2]	10.1	(0.2)	m	m	3.2	(0.1)	m	m

Partners

Cyprus[3]	23.7	(1.3)	m	m	14.2	(0.9)	m	m
Russian Federation[4]	20.6	(2.5)	21.5	(2.5)	11.6	(1.8)	31.2	(2.4)

1. Average of 19 participating OECD countries and entities.
2. Average of 22 OECD countries and entities: average of 19 countries with France, Italy and Spain.
3. See notes at the beginning of this Annex.
4. See note at the beginning of this Annex.
Note: Complex problems are defined as problems that take at least 30 minutes to find a good solution.
Source: Survey of Adult Skills (PIAAC) (2012).

StatLink ⟐ http://dx.doi.org/10.1787/888933232106

[Part 1/1]

Table A4.4a **Percentage of workers, by adequacy of reported computer skills to do their job well**

OECD	Lack the computer skills to do the job well		Has the computer skills to do the job well		No use of computer at work	
	%	S.E.	%	S.E.	%	S.E.
National entities						
Australia	6.3	(0.5)	68.3	(0.9)	23.0	(0.6)
Austria	3.0	(0.3)	66.4	(0.9)	28.2	(0.8)
Canada	4.5	(0.2)	68.9	(0.5)	25.4	(0.5)
Czech Republic	2.5	(0.4)	61.8	(1.2)	34.8	(1.2)
Denmark	8.1	(0.4)	70.5	(0.7)	20.7	(0.6)
Estonia	6.9	(0.3)	56.3	(0.7)	36.0	(0.7)
Finland	10.0	(0.5)	69.6	(0.6)	20.2	(0.6)
France	8.6	(0.4)	56.0	(0.6)	34.1	(0.6)
Germany	3.9	(0.4)	63.9	(0.8)	30.3	(0.8)
Ireland	5.2	(0.4)	59.6	(0.8)	34.5	(0.8)
Italy	4.0	(0.4)	45.4	(1.1)	49.5	(1.1)
Japan	25.7	(0.7)	43.8	(0.8)	28.6	(0.7)
Korea	13.6	(0.5)	49.1	(0.6)	36.9	(0.8)
Netherlands	4.8	(0.3)	72.6	(0.7)	19.7	(0.5)
Norway	13.5	(0.5)	67.2	(0.6)	16.6	(0.5)
Poland	4.4	(0.4)	49.0	(0.8)	46.2	(0.8)
Slovak Republic	2.8	(0.3)	52.9	(1.0)	43.8	(1.0)
Spain	5.0	(0.4)	49.6	(0.7)	43.9	(0.8)
Sweden	7.6	(0.4)	74.1	(0.8)	18.0	(0.7)
United States	4.4	(0.3)	66.0	(0.7)	24.4	(0.8)
Sub-national entities						
Flanders (Belgium)	6.5	(0.4)	62.6	(0.8)	23.9	(0.7)
England (UK)	5.8	(0.4)	67.7	(0.9)	24.5	(0.8)
Northern Ireland (UK)	4.6	(0.5)	64.5	(1.0)	27.6	(1.0)
England/N. Ireland (UK)	5.8	(0.4)	67.6	(0.9)	24.6	(0.8)
Average[1]	7.3	(0.1)	62.6	(0.2)	28.2	(0.2)
Average-22[2]	7.1	(0.1)	61.0	(0.2)	30.1	(0.2)

Partners

Cyprus[3]	3.5	(0.3)	39.6	(0.7)	33.1	(0.8)
Russian Federation[4]	3.3	(0.5)	41.4	(1.5)	54.8	(1.3)

1. Average of 19 participating OECD countries and entities.
2. Average of 22 OECD countries and entities: average of 19 countries with France, Italy and Spain.
3. See notes at the beginning of this Annex.
4. See note at the beginning of this Annex.
Source: Survey of Adult Skills (PIAAC) (2012).
StatLink ᴍ╗☞ http://dx.doi.org/10.1787/888933232119

[Part 1/1]

Table A4.4b

Percentage of workers by adequacy of reported computer skills affecting the chances of getting a job, promotion or pay raise

OECD	A lack of computer skills <u>has</u> affected the chances of getting a job/promotion/pay raise		A lack of computer skills <u>has not</u> affected the chances of getting a job/promotion/pay raise		No use of computer at work	
	%	S.E.	%	S.E.	%	S.E.
National entities						
Australia	6.3	(0.4)	68.2	(0.8)	23.0	(0.6)
Austria	3.1	(0.3)	66.3	(0.9)	28.2	(0.8)
Canada	6.1	(0.3)	67.1	(0.5)	25.4	(0.5)
Czech Republic	2.5	(0.4)	61.8	(1.2)	34.8	(1.2)
Denmark	3.9	(0.3)	74.6	(0.6)	20.7	(0.6)
Estonia	5.4	(0.3)	57.7	(0.7)	36.0	(0.7)
Finland	3.5	(0.3)	76.0	(0.7)	20.2	(0.6)
France	4.8	(0.3)	59.4	(0.6)	34.1	(0.6)
Germany	2.8	(0.3)	64.8	(0.9)	30.3	(0.8)
Ireland	4.4	(0.3)	60.4	(0.8)	34.5	(0.8)
Italy	3.6	(0.3)	45.7	(1.1)	49.5	(1.1)
Japan	16.3	(0.6)	53.1	(0.8)	28.6	(0.7)
Korea	1.7	(0.2)	60.9	(0.7)	36.9	(0.8)
Netherlands	3.0	(0.3)	74.4	(0.6)	19.7	(0.5)
Norway	4.6	(0.3)	75.8	(0.5)	16.6	(0.5)
Poland	5.4	(0.3)	48.0	(0.9)	46.2	(0.8)
Slovak Republic	3.0	(0.3)	52.6	(1.0)	43.8	(1.0)
Spain	3.7	(0.4)	50.7	(0.8)	43.9	(0.8)
Sweden	3.5	(0.3)	77.6	(0.6)	18.0	(0.7)
United States	6.9	(0.4)	63.5	(0.8)	24.4	(0.8)
Sub-national entities						
Flanders (Belgium)	4.0	(0.3)	65.0	(0.8)	23.9	(0.7)
England (UK)	4.8	(0.4)	68.8	(0.8)	24.5	(0.8)
Northern Ireland (UK)	3.6	(0.4)	65.5	(1.0)	27.6	(1.0)
England/N. Ireland (UK)	4.7	(0.4)	68.7	(0.8)	24.6	(0.8)
Average[1]	4.8	(0.1)	65.1	(0.2)	28.2	(0.2)
Average-22[2]	4.7	(0.1)	63.3	(0.2)	30.1	(0.2)
Partners						
Cyprus[3]	4.4	(0.4)	38.6	(0.8)	33.1	(0.8)
Russian Federation[4]	5.1	(0.6)	39.6	(1.3)	54.8	(1.3)

1. Average of 19 participating OECD countries and entities.
2. Average of 22 OECD countries and entities: average of 19 countries with France, Italy and Spain.
3. See notes at the beginning of this Annex.
4. See note at the beginning of this Annex.
Source: Survey of Adult Skills (PIAAC) (2012).

StatLink ᴍᴎᴩ http://dx.doi.org/10.1787/888933232126

[Part 1/1]

Percentage of workers who reported that their lack of computer skills either have or have not affected their chances of getting a job, promotion or pay raise

Table A4.5

	A lack of computer skills <u>has not</u> affected the chances of getting a job/promotion/pay raise				A lack of computer skills <u>has</u> affected the chances of getting a job/promotion/pay raise			
	Has the computer skills to do the job well		Lack the computer skills to do the job well		Has the computer skills to do the job wel		Lack the computer skills to do the job well	
OECD	%	S.E.	%	S.E.	%	S.E.	%	S.E.
National entities								
Australia	94.7	(0.4)	5.3	(0.4)	77.2	(3.4)	22.8	(3.4)
Austria	97.0	(0.3)	2.9	(0.3)	90.5	(2.7)	9.5	(2.7)
Canada	96.2	(0.2)	3.8	(0.2)	84.7	(1.4)	15.3	(1.4)
Czech Republic	97.6	(0.4)	2.3	(0.4)	90.2	(3.4)	9.8	(3.4)
Denmark	92.5	(0.4)	7.4	(0.4)	73.5	(3.7)	26.5	(3.7)
Estonia	93.9	(0.3)	6.1	(0.3)	77.9	(2.7)	21.7	(2.7)
Finland	90.3	(0.5)	9.6	(0.5)	78.8	(3.4)	21.2	(3.4)
France	91.9	(0.4)	8.0	(0.4)	79.1	(2.9)	20.9	(2.9)
Germany	96.4	(0.4)	3.6	(0.4)	83.4	(4.3)	15.1	(4.2)
Ireland	95.5	(0.4)	4.5	(0.4)	80.1	(3.5)	19.9	(3.5)
Italy	96.2	(0.4)	3.8	(0.4)	89.7	(3.3)	10.3	(3.3)
Japan	74.4	(0.9)	25.6	(0.9)	70.9	(1.9)	29.1	(1.9)
Korea	86.9	(0.5)	13.1	(0.5)	57.5	(5.4)	42.5	(5.4)
Netherlands	95.4	(0.3)	4.6	(0.3)	86.2	(3.3)	13.8	(3.3)
Norway	87.1	(0.6)	12.9	(0.6)	67.9	(3.0)	32.1	(3.0)
Poland	95.7	(0.4)	4.1	(0.4)	90.6	(2.5)	9.4	(2.5)
Slovak Republic	97.2	(0.3)	2.8	(0.3)	96.5	(1.5)	3.5	(1.5)
Spain	95.5	(0.4)	4.5	(0.4)	80.4	(3.6)	19.6	(3.6)
Sweden	93.0	(0.4)	6.9	(0.4)	78.3	(4.5)	21.7	(4.5)
United States	96.7	(0.3)	3.3	(0.3)	78.4	(2.4)	21.2	(2.4)
Sub-national entities								
Flanders (Belgium)	93.3	(0.4)	6.7	(0.4)	86.2	(2.5)	13.8	(2.5)
England (UK)	94.7	(0.4)	5.2	(0.4)	79.5	(2.7)	20.5	(2.7)
Northern Ireland (UK)	95.7	(0.5)	4.3	(0.5)	81.8	(4.9)	18.2	(4.9)
England/N. Ireland (UK)	94.7	(0.4)	5.1	(0.4)	79.6	(2.7)	20.4	(2.7)
Average[1]	93.1	(0.1)	6.9	(0.1)	80.4	(0.7)	19.4	(0.7)
Average-22[2]	93.3	(0.1)	6.7	(0.1)	80.8	(0.7)	19.1	(0.7)
Partners								
Cyprus[3]	96.0	(0.3)	4.0	(0.3)	85.1	(2.9)	14.9	(2.9)
Russian Federation[4]	97.2	(0.5)	2.6	(0.5)	83.7	(4.6)	16.2	(4.6)

1. Average of 19 participating OECD countries and entities.
2. Average of 22 OECD countries and entities: average of 19 countries with France, Italy and Spain.
3. See notes at the beginning of this Annex.
4. See note at the beginning of this Annex.
Source: Survey of Adult Skills (PIAAC) (2012).
StatLink 🔗 http://dx.doi.org/10.1787/888933232138

[Part 1/1]

Labour force participation rate, by proficiency in problem solving in technology-rich environments among adults aged 25-65

Table A4.6

OECD	No computer experience		Failed ICT core		Opted out		Below Level 1		Level 1		Level 2/3		Total	
	%	S.E.	%	S.E.	%	S.E.	%	S.E.	%	S.E.	%	S.E.	%	S.E.
National entities														
Australia	38.6	(2.9)	60.7	(4.3)	69.1	(1.3)	76.2	(2.7)	81.5	(1.3)	88.6	(0.9)	78.6	(0.3)
Austria	46.8	(2.2)	70.1	(3.9)	70.5	(2.0)	77.7	(3.3)	84.6	(1.5)	90.4	(0.9)	78.7	(0.6)
Canada	52.6	(2.5)	74.1	(1.8)	72.2	(1.7)	77.7	(1.3)	84.2	(0.8)	90.5	(0.7)	82.1	(0.4)
Czech Republic	43.0	(2.5)	73.4	(5.2)	77.1	(2.3)	78.2	(2.5)	79.7	(1.7)	87.7	(1.4)	76.8	(0.2)
Denmark	35.2	(4.1)	71.0	(2.7)	60.5	(2.7)	71.6	(2.0)	85.2	(1.0)	91.8	(0.8)	81.5	(0.4)
Estonia	47.3	(1.9)	80.8	(2.3)	79.1	(1.2)	86.9	(1.5)	91.3	(0.9)	93.9	(0.7)	83.2	(0.4)
Finland	32.6	(3.9)	62.8	(3.3)	59.9	(2.4)	70.8	(1.9)	86.4	(1.0)	91.4	(0.7)	79.6	(0.6)
France	50.0	(1.7)	68.9	(1.9)	72.1	(1.3)	m	m	m	m	m	m	m	m
Germany	59.9	(2.8)	80.1	(3.4)	72.5	(3.0)	79.6	(2.2)	86.6	(1.2)	91.5	(0.8)	83.4	(0.6)
Ireland	48.0	(2.4)	75.7	(3.4)	65.7	(1.8)	70.1	(2.3)	81.1	(1.5)	88.3	(1.3)	73.9	(0.7)
Italy	48.1	(1.7)	71.1	(5.8)	70.1	(2.3)	m	m	m	m	m	m	m	m
Japan	60.2	(2.5)	75.8	(2.1)	72.9	(1.7)	77.4	(2.6)	80.6	(1.8)	86.0	(1.0)	78.0	(0.3)
Korea	64.3	(1.2)	75.8	(1.9)	76.5	(2.3)	78.9	(2.0)	79.0	(1.3)	84.4	(1.4)	77.1	(0.5)
Netherlands	43.3	(4.2)	66.9	(3.9)	57.2	(3.7)	68.0	(2.6)	83.5	(1.1)	92.8	(0.8)	81.4	(0.5)
Norway	32.6	(5.7)	78.7	(2.9)	63.7	(2.9)	76.1	(2.4)	88.4	(1.1)	94.0	(0.7)	85.4	(0.5)
Poland	49.5	(1.6)	73.4	(3.2)	72.2	(1.4)	78.7	(2.2)	85.8	(1.7)	91.8	(1.2)	72.9	(0.6)
Slovak Republic	52.8	(1.6)	73.9	(4.7)	73.2	(1.9)	80.2	(2.3)	84.4	(1.3)	88.8	(1.3)	75.1	(0.6)
Spain	48.3	(1.4)	74.5	(3.0)	71.1	(2.0)	m	m	m	m	m	m	m	m
Sweden	39.9	(7.6)	74.4	(3.7)	66.5	(3.1)	77.2	(2.4)	87.2	(1.3)	92.9	(0.8)	85.0	(0.5)
United States	56.8	(3.0)	71.8	(3.9)	69.4	(2.7)	82.8	(1.6)	85.8	(1.2)	90.0	(0.9)	82.8	(0.7)
Sub-national entities														
Flanders (Belgium)	39.7	(2.2)	69.7	(3.3)	65.9	(3.0)	72.1	(1.7)	83.7	(0.9)	91.7	(0.7)	78.7	(0.3)
England (UK)	40.9	(4.0)	69.6	(3.0)	68.0	(2.8)	73.8	(1.9)	81.8	(1.0)	90.5	(0.8)	79.9	(0.2)
Northern Ireland (UK)	48.0	(3.2)	64.2	(4.2)	51.0	(5.8)	67.2	(2.8)	78.6	(1.7)	90.7	(1.1)	74.1	(0.6)
England/N. Ireland (UK)	41.5	(3.8)	69.4	(2.9)	67.7	(2.7)	73.5	(1.8)	81.7	(0.9)	90.6	(0.8)	79.7	(0.2)
Average[1]	46.6	(0.8)	72.6	(0.8)	69.0	(0.6)	76.5	(0.5)	84.2	(0.3)	90.4	(0.2)	79.7	(0.1)
Average-22[2]	46.9	(0.7)	72.4	(0.7)	69.3	(0.5)	m	m	m	m	m	m	m	m
Partners														
Cyprus[3]	58.2	(1.5)	83.8	(4.9)	82.8	(1.4)	m	m	m	m	m	m	m	m
Russian Federation[4]	53.4	(3.8)	57.1	(5.2)	64.1	(2.1)	66.7	(3.6)	75.1	(2.6)	78.5	(4.5)	67.9	(1.8)

1. Average of 19 participating OECD countries and entities.
2. Average of 22 OECD countries and entities: average of 19 countries with France, Italy and Spain.
3. See notes at the beginning of this Annex.
4. See note at the beginning of this Annex.
Source: Survey of Adult Skills (PIAAC) (2012).

StatLink ▄▄▄▄ http://dx.doi.org/10.1787/888933232147

[Part 1/1]

Table A4.7 Labour force participation rate, by frequency of e-mail use in everyday life among adults aged 25-65

OECD	Low frequency of e-mail use		High frequency of e-mail use		Total	
	%	S.E.	%	S.E.	%	S.E.
National entities						
Australia	65.0	(1.2)	83.1	(0.5)	78.6	(0.3)
Austria	66.0	(1.3)	85.0	(0.7)	78.7	(0.6)
Canada	70.5	(1.0)	85.3	(0.4)	82.1	(0.4)
Czech Republic	61.4	(1.5)	83.5	(0.8)	76.8	(0.2)
Denmark	64.0	(1.7)	84.5	(0.5)	81.5	(0.4)
Estonia	64.9	(1.1)	90.7	(0.4)	83.2	(0.4)
Finland	58.5	(1.7)	85.4	(0.6)	79.6	(0.6)
France	63.4	(0.8)	81.3	(0.4)	75.7	(0.2)
Germany	73.2	(1.4)	87.6	(0.7)	83.4	(0.6)
Ireland	62.9	(1.7)	80.5	(0.8)	73.9	(0.7)
Italy	58.5	(1.1)	82.8	(0.8)	70.4	(0.5)
Japan	73.8	(0.9)	81.2	(0.7)	78.0	(0.3)
Korea	72.0	(0.8)	81.4	(0.8)	77.1	(0.5)
Netherlands	59.0	(2.3)	84.6	(0.5)	81.4	(0.5)
Norway	67.3	1.9	88.4	0.5	85.4	0.5
Poland	59.6	(1.1)	85.8	(0.7)	72.9	(0.6)
Slovak Republic	61.2	(1.2)	86.2	(0.8)	75.1	(0.6)
Spain	63.5	(1.0)	84.9	(0.7)	75.6	(0.5)
Sweden	72.9	1.8	87.6	0.6	85.0	0.5
United States	73.8	(1.5)	86.3	(0.8)	82.8	(0.7)
Sub-national entities						
Flanders (Belgium)	60.5	(1.5)	83.8	(0.4)	78.7	(0.3)
England (UK)	67.8	(1.3)	83.6	(0.4)	79.9	(0.2)
Northern Ireland (UK)	62.8	(1.3)	81.4	(0.9)	74.1	(0.6)
England/N. Ireland (UK)	67.6	(1.2)	83.6	(0.4)	79.7	(0.2)
Average[1]	66.0	(0.3)	85.0	(0.1)	79.7	(0.1)
Average-22[2]	65.4	(0.3)	84.7	(0.1)	78.9	(0.1)
Partners						
Cyprus[3]	70.4	(1.0)	88.4	(0.9)	78.0	(0.7)
Russian Federation[4]	62.3	(2.3)	76.9	(1.3)	67.9	(1.8)

1. Average of 19 participating OECD countries and entities.
2. Average of 22 OECD countries and entities: average of 19 countries with France, Italy and Spain.
3. See notes at the beginning of this Annex.
4. See note at the beginning of this Annex.
Note: High frequency stands for use of e-mail at least once a month.
Source: Survey of Adult Skills (PIAAC) (2012).

StatLink ⬛🖳 http://dx.doi.org/10.1787/888933232156

[Part 1/2]

Table A4.8 Employment and unemployment rates, by proficiency in problem solving in technology-rich environments among adults aged 25-65

OECD	No computer experience				Failed ICT core				Opted out				Below Level 1			
	Employment rate		Unemployment rate		Employment rate		Unemployment rate		Employment rate		Unemployment rate		Employment rate		Unemployment rate	
	%	S.E.	%	S.E.	%	S.E.	%	S.E.	%	S.E.	%	S.E.	%	S.E.	%	S.E.
National entities																
Australia	96.4	(1.8)	3.6	(1.8)	94.2	(2.5)	5.8	(2.5)	93.2	(1.2)	6.8	(1.2)	93.0	(1.7)	7.0	(1.7)
Austria	95.6	(1.8)	4.4	(1.8)	94.5	(2.3)	5.5	(2.3)	96.4	(1.0)	3.6	(1.0)	94.0	(1.7)	6.0	(1.7)
Canada	91.3	(2.3)	8.7	(2.3)	93.4	(1.5)	6.6	(1.5)	95.6	(1.0)	4.4	(1.0)	95.5	(0.7)	4.5	(0.7)
Czech Republic	90.9	(2.1)	9.1	(2.1)	94.2	(2.8)	5.8	(2.8)	90.9	(2.3)	9.1	(2.3)	95.4	(1.5)	4.6	(1.5)
Denmark	96.5	(2.1)	3.5	(2.1)	92.1	(1.7)	7.9	(1.7)	91.0	(2.2)	9.0	(2.2)	94.5	(1.3)	5.5	(1.3)
Estonia	82.8	(1.9)	17.2	(1.9)	92.7	(1.9)	7.3	(1.9)	91.2	(0.9)	8.8	(0.9)	94.1	(0.9)	5.9	(0.9)
Finland	92.4	(3.6)	7.6	(3.6)	90.7	(2.7)	9.3	(2.7)	96.4	(1.1)	3.6	(1.1)	95.8	(1.2)	4.2	(1.2)
France	92.6	(1.2)	7.4	(1.2)	93.0	(1.3)	7.0	(1.3)	91.8	(1.0)	8.2	(1.0)	m	m	m	m
Germany	93.8	(2.2)	6.2	(2.2)	93.4	(2.4)	6.6	(2.4)	90.1	(2.1)	9.9	(2.1)	95.3	(1.2)	4.7	(1.2)
Ireland	85.5	(2.6)	14.5	(2.6)	87.0	(3.6)	13.0	(3.6)	88.9	(1.6)	11.1	(1.6)	87.4	(1.8)	12.6	(1.8)
Italy	81.9	(2.1)	18.1	(2.1)	76.8	(5.8)	23.2	(5.8)	90.8	(1.6)	9.2	(1.6)	m	m	m	m
Japan	98.4	(0.9)	1.6	(0.9)	96.7	(1.2)	3.3	(1.2)	97.7	(0.8)	2.3	(0.8)	96.2	(1.5)	3.8	(1.5)
Korea	97.1	(0.6)	2.9	(0.6)	96.4	(0.9)	3.6	(0.9)	97.3	(1.0)	2.7	(1.0)	97.5	(0.9)	2.5	(0.9)
Netherlands	91.2	(4.4)	8.8	(4.4)	94.0	(2.7)	6.0	(2.7)	91.1	(3.2)	8.9	(3.2)	91.8	(2.0)	8.2	(2.0)
Norway	c	c	c	c	93.4	(1.9)	6.6	(1.9)	98.5	(1.2)	1.5	(1.2)	96.9	(1.2)	3.1	(1.2)
Poland	84.4	(1.6)	15.6	(1.6)	91.2	(2.1)	8.8	(2.1)	91.5	(1.0)	8.5	(1.0)	93.4	(1.5)	6.6	(1.5)
Slovak Republic	81.2	(1.6)	18.8	(1.6)	88.8	(3.8)	11.2	(3.8)	91.3	(1.6)	8.7	(1.6)	89.3	(2.3)	10.7	(2.3)
Spain	75.8	(1.9)	24.2	(1.9)	75.6	(2.9)	24.4	(2.9)	80.6	(2.2)	19.4	(2.2)	m	m	m	m
Sweden	c	c	c	c	82.4	(4.0)	17.6	(4.0)	88.0	(3.5)	12.0	(3.5)	93.3	(1.6)	6.7	(1.6)
United States	95.7	(1.3)	4.3	(1.3)	91.3	(1.7)	8.7	(1.7)	89.1	(2.4)	10.9	(2.4)	90.1	(1.6)	9.9	(1.6)
Sub-national entities																
Flanders (Belgium)	98.1	(1.1)	1.9	(1.1)	98.1	(0.6)	1.9	(0.6)	97.8	(1.1)	2.2	(1.1)	97.2	(0.8)	2.8	(0.8)
England (UK)	86.8	(4.7)	13.2	(4.7)	86.4	(2.6)	13.6	(2.6)	94.9	(2.0)	5.1	(2.0)	91.4	(1.4)	8.6	(1.4)
Northern Ireland (UK)	89.6	(2.3)	10.4	(2.3)	95.8	(2.2)	4.2	(2.2)	93.7	(3.3)	6.3	(3.3)	92.9	(1.6)	7.1	(1.6)
England/N. Ireland (UK)	87.1	(4.3)	12.9	(4.3)	86.7	(2.5)	13.3	(2.5)	94.9	(1.9)	5.1	(1.9)	91.5	(1.4)	8.5	(1.4)
Average[1]	91.7	(0.6)	8.3	(0.6)	92.2	(0.6)	7.8	(0.6)	93.2	(0.4)	6.8	(0.4)	93.8	(0.3)	6.2	(0.3)
Average-22[2]	90.4	(0.5)	9.6	(0.5)	90.7	(0.6)	9.3	(0.6)	92.5	(0.4)	7.5	(0.4)	m	m	m	m
Partners																
Cyprus[3]	88.4	(1.5)	11.6	(1.5)	97.8	(2.1)	2.2	(2.1)	92.5	(1.2)	7.5	(1.2)	m	m	m	m
Russian Federation[4]	94.3	(2.3)	5.7	(2.3)	98.3	(1.7)	1.7	(1.7)	96.9	(0.9)	3.1	(0.9)	95.9	(1.8)	4.1	(1.8)

1. Average of 19 participating OECD countries and entities.
2. Average of 22 OECD countries and entities: average of 19 countries with France, Italy and Spain.
3. See notes at the beginning of this Annex.
4. See note at the beginning of this Annex.
Source: Survey of Adult Skills (PIAAC) (2012).

StatLink ᴹᴾᴬ http://dx.doi.org/10.1787/888933232168

[Part 2/2]

Table A4.8 Employment and unemployment rates, by proficiency in problem solving in technology-rich environments among adults aged 25-65

	Level 1				Level 2/3				Total			
	Employment rate		Unemployment rate		Employment rate		Unemployment rate		Employment rate		Unemployment rate	
OECD	%	S.E.	%	S.E.	%	S.E.	%	S.E.	%	S.E.	%	S.E.
National entities												
Australia	95.9	(0.7)	4.1	(0.7)	97.4	(0.5)	2.6	(0.5)	95.7	(0.2)	4.3	(0.2)
Austria	96.0	(0.8)	4.0	(0.8)	97.4	(0.6)	2.6	(0.6)	96.2	(0.4)	3.8	(0.4)
Canada	96.2	(0.5)	3.8	(0.5)	96.8	(0.4)	3.2	(0.4)	96.0	(0.2)	4.0	(0.2)
Czech Republic	93.9	(1.2)	6.1	(1.2)	96.0	(1.0)	4.0	(1.0)	94.2	(0.2)	5.8	(0.2)
Denmark	95.2	(0.7)	4.8	(0.7)	94.5	(0.7)	5.5	(0.7)	94.5	(0.4)	5.5	(0.4)
Estonia	93.9	(0.6)	6.1	(0.6)	96.9	(0.6)	3.1	(0.6)	93.4	(0.3)	6.6	(0.3)
Finland	95.9	(0.7)	4.1	(0.7)	95.6	(0.6)	4.4	(0.6)	95.5	(0.4)	4.5	(0.4)
France	m	m	m	m	m	m	m	m	92.9	(0.2)	7.1	(0.2)
Germany	95.0	(0.8)	5.0	(0.8)	96.8	(0.5)	3.2	(0.5)	95.2	(0.4)	4.8	(0.4)
Ireland	88.6	(1.2)	11.4	(1.2)	92.4	(1.1)	7.6	(1.1)	89.2	(0.5)	10.8	(0.5)
Italy	m	m	m	m	m	m	m	m	87.7	(0.7)	12.3	(0.7)
Japan	97.2	(0.9)	2.8	(0.9)	98.2	(0.5)	1.8	(0.5)	97.6	(0.2)	2.4	(0.2)
Korea	97.0	(0.6)	3.0	(0.6)	96.1	(0.6)	3.9	(0.6)	96.8	(0.3)	3.2	(0.3)
Netherlands	96.1	(0.7)	3.9	(0.7)	97.4	(0.5)	2.6	(0.5)	95.8	(0.4)	4.2	(0.4)
Norway	96.5	(0.6)	3.5	(0.6)	97.9	(0.4)	2.1	(0.4)	97.1	(0.3)	2.9	(0.3)
Poland	93.7	(1.2)	6.3	(1.2)	96.1	(0.8)	3.9	(0.8)	91.9	(0.5)	8.1	(0.5)
Slovak Republic	93.5	(1.0)	6.5	(1.0)	94.2	(1.0)	5.8	(1.0)	90.7	(0.5)	9.3	(0.5)
Spain	m	m	m	m	m	m	m	m	82.7	(0.6)	17.3	(0.6)
Sweden	95.0	(0.9)	5.0	(0.9)	97.7	(0.5)	2.3	(0.5)	94.9	(0.4)	5.1	(0.4)
United States	91.8	(1.0)	8.2	(1.0)	94.7	(0.7)	5.3	(0.7)	92.5	(0.4)	7.5	(0.4)
Sub-national entities												
Flanders (Belgium)	98.1	(0.4)	1.9	(0.4)	98.4	(0.4)	1.6	(0.4)	98.0	(0.2)	2.0	(0.2)
England (UK)	93.6	(0.8)	6.4	(0.8)	96.8	(0.5)	3.2	(0.5)	94.0	(0.1)	6.0	(0.1)
Northern Ireland (UK)	95.2	(1.0)	4.8	(1.0)	96.1	(1.1)	3.9	(1.1)	94.7	(0.5)	5.3	(0.5)
England/N. Ireland (UK)	93.6	(0.7)	6.4	(0.7)	96.8	(0.5)	3.2	(0.5)	94.0	(0.1)	6.0	(0.1)
Average[1]	94.9	(0.2)	5.1	(0.2)	96.4	(0.2)	3.6	(0.2)	94.7	(0.1)	5.3	(0.1)
Average-22[2]	m	m	m	m	m	m	m	m	93.8	(0.1)	6.2	(0.1)
Partners												
Cyprus[3]	m	m	m	m	m	m	m	m	92.0	(0.6)	8.0	(0.6)
Russian Federation[4]	94.3	(1.7)	5.7	(1.7)	94.0	(1.7)	6.0	(1.7)	94.9	(1.0)	5.1	(1.0)

1. Average of 19 participating OECD countries and entities.
2. Average of 22 OECD countries and entities: average of 19 countries with France, Italy and Spain.
3. See notes at the beginning of this Annex.
4. See note at the beginning of this Annex.
Source: Survey of Adult Skills (PIAAC) (2012).
StatLink ⟐ http://dx.doi.org/10.1787/888933232168

[Part 1/1]

Table A4.9 **Employment and unemployment rates, by frequency of e-mail use in everyday life among adults aged 25-65**

OECD	Low frequency of e-mail use				High frequency of e-mail use				Total			
	Employment rate		Unemployment rate		Employment rate		Unemployment rate		Employment rate		Unemployment rate	
	%	S.E.	%	S.E.	%	S.E.	%	S.E.	%	S.E.	%	S.E.
National entities												
Australia	95.6	(0.8)	4.4	(0.8)	95.7	(0.2)	4.3	(0.2)	95.7	(0.2)	4.3	(0.2)
Austria	96.2	(0.9)	3.8	(0.9)	96.2	(0.4)	3.8	(0.4)	96.2	(0.4)	3.8	(0.4)
Canada	95.6	(0.6)	4.4	(0.6)	96.0	(0.2)	4.0	(0.2)	96.0	(0.2)	4.0	(0.2)
Czech Republic	92.5	(1.0)	7.5	(1.0)	94.8	(0.3)	5.2	(0.3)	94.2	(0.2)	5.8	(0.2)
Denmark	93.9	(1.3)	6.1	(1.3)	94.6	(0.4)	5.4	(0.4)	94.5	(0.4)	5.5	(0.4)
Estonia	89.8	(0.8)	10.2	(0.8)	94.5	(0.4)	5.5	(0.4)	93.4	(0.3)	6.6	(0.3)
Finland	96.3	(0.9)	3.7	(0.9)	95.4	(0.4)	4.6	(0.4)	95.5	(0.4)	4.5	(0.4)
France	92.2	(0.7)	7.8	(0.7)	93.1	(0.3)	6.9	(0.3)	92.9	(0.2)	7.1	(0.2)
Germany	93.6	(1.0)	6.4	(1.0)	95.8	(0.5)	4.2	(0.5)	95.2	(0.4)	4.8	(0.4)
Ireland	88.6	(1.2)	11.4	(1.2)	89.5	(0.6)	10.5	(0.6)	89.2	(0.5)	10.8	(0.5)
Italy	86.4	(1.3)	13.6	(1.3)	88.7	(0.9)	11.3	(0.9)	87.7	(0.7)	12.3	(0.7)
Japan	97.9	(0.5)	2.1	(0.5)	97.4	(0.4)	2.6	(0.4)	97.6	(0.2)	2.4	(0.2)
Korea	97.4	(0.3)	2.6	(0.3)	96.4	(0.4)	3.6	(0.4)	96.8	(0.3)	3.2	(0.3)
Netherlands	95.2	(1.5)	4.8	(1.5)	95.9	(0.4)	4.1	(0.4)	95.8	(0.4)	4.2	(0.4)
Norway	97.9	0.8	2.1	0.8	97.0	0.3	3.0	0.3	97.1	0.3	2.9	0.3
Poland	88.2	(0.9)	11.8	(0.9)	94.4	(0.5)	5.6	(0.5)	91.9	(0.5)	8.1	(0.5)
Slovak Republic	85.8	(1.0)	14.2	(1.0)	93.4	(0.5)	6.6	(0.5)	90.7	(0.5)	9.3	(0.5)
Spain	81.8	(1.1)	18.2	(1.1)	83.2	(0.8)	16.8	(0.8)	82.7	(0.6)	17.3	(0.6)
Sweden	94.8	1.5	5.2	1.5	94.9	0.4	5.1	0.4	94.9	0.4	5.1	0.4
United States	92.7	(1.1)	7.3	(1.1)	92.4	(0.5)	7.6	(0.5)	92.5	(0.4)	7.5	(0.4)
Sub-national entities												
Flanders (Belgium)	98.3	(0.5)	1.7	(0.5)	97.9	(0.2)	2.1	(0.2)	98.0	(0.2)	2.0	(0.2)
England (UK)	92.2	(1.0)	7.8	(1.0)	94.4	(0.3)	5.6	(0.3)	94.0	(0.1)	6.0	(0.1)
Northern Ireland (UK)	93.1	(1.0)	6.9	(1.0)	95.4	(0.6)	4.6	(0.6)	94.7	(0.5)	5.3	(0.5)
England/N. Ireland (UK)	92.3	(0.9)	7.7	(0.9)	94.5	(0.3)	5.5	(0.3)	94.0	(0.1)	6.0	(0.1)
Average[1]	93.8	(0.2)	6.2	(0.2)	95.1	(0.1)	4.9	(0.1)	94.7	(0.1)	5.3	(0.1)
Average-22[2]	92.8	(0.2)	7.2	(0.2)	94.2	(0.1)	5.8	(0.1)	93.8	(0.1)	6.2	(0.1)
Partners												
Cyprus[3]	91.4	(0.8)	8.6	(0.8)	92.5	(0.9)	7.5	(0.9)	92.0	(0.6)	8.0	(0.6)
Russian Federation[4]	95.7	(1.0)	4.3	(1.0)	93.9	(1.3)	6.1	(1.3)	94.9	(1.0)	5.1	(1.0)

1. Average of 19 participating OECD countries and entities.
2. Average of 22 OECD countries and entities: average of 19 countries with France, Italy and Spain.
3. See notes at the beginning of this Annex.
4. See note at the beginning of this Annex.
Note: High frequency stands for use of e-mail at least once a month.
Source: Survey of Adult Skills (PIAAC) (2012).

StatLink ⬛⬛ http://dx.doi.org/10.1787/888933232172

[Part 1/1]

Table A4.10 Mean hourly wage, by proficiency in problem solving in technology-rich environments

OECD	No computer experience		Failed ICT core		Opted out		Below Level 1		Level 1		Level 2/3	
	Mean wage	S.E.	Mean wage	S.E.	Mean wage	S.E.	Mean wage	S.E.	Mean wage	S.E.	Mean wage	S.E.
National entities												
Australia	14.2	(0.5)	17.8	(1.1)	16.5	(0.5)	17.1	(0.6)	18.2	(0.3)	20.7	(0.3)
Austria	14.7	(0.4)	16.8	(0.7)	16.0	(0.4)	16.9	(0.6)	18.9	(0.3)	21.5	(0.4)
Canada	15.0	(0.6)	18.2	(0.6)	17.4	(0.5)	17.9	(0.4)	20.2	(0.3)	22.5	(0.3)
Czech Republic	6.5	(0.3)	7.2	(0.5)	7.3	(0.2)	7.9	(0.3)	9.0	(0.3)	10.4	(0.3)
Denmark	19.6	(0.8)	21.3	(0.7)	20.3	(0.6)	22.2	(0.4)	23.3	(0.3)	25.2	(0.2)
Estonia	5.7	(0.3)	8.2	(0.4)	8.0	(0.2)	8.7	(0.3)	9.9	(0.2)	11.6	(0.2)
Finland	15.0	(0.9)	16.7	(0.8)	16.8	(0.3)	17.6	(0.4)	18.9	(0.2)	20.6	(0.2)
France	12.2	(0.2)	13.9	(0.4)	14.8	(0.3)	m	m	m	m	m	m
Germany	13.4	(0.5)	16.6	(0.8)	15.6	(0.6)	16.5	(0.5)	18.4	(0.4)	21.5	(0.4)
Ireland	16.5	(1.1)	18.2	(1.2)	19.3	(0.6)	19.0	(0.8)	21.9	(0.5)	24.5	(0.6)
Italy	12.9	(0.4)	14.6	(1.4)	14.7	(0.5)	m	m	m	m	m	m
Japan	11.3	(0.5)	14.9	(0.8)	13.5	(0.5)	15.3	(0.9)	16.2	(0.6)	18.3	(0.4)
Korea	12.6	(0.6)	15.7	(0.9)	17.3	(1.6)	17.4	(1.1)	19.0	(0.7)	19.0	(0.6)
Netherlands	15.6	(1.2)	18.4	(0.9)	18.7	(1.0)	18.5	(0.5)	20.7	(0.3)	23.1	(0.3)
Norway	c	c	20.3	0.6	21.1	0.6	21.5	0.5	23.8	0.3	26.0	0.2
Poland	6.7	(0.3)	8.9	(0.5)	8.9	(0.2)	8.7	(0.4)	9.9	(0.3)	11.4	(0.3)
Slovak Republic	6.2	(0.2)	10.0	(1.0)	8.0	(0.3)	7.9	(0.7)	9.0	(0.3)	10.7	(0.3)
Spain	10.8	(0.3)	13.5	(0.7)	13.0	(0.5)	m	m	m	m	m	m
Sweden	c	c	17.7	1.0	16.5	0.6	16.9	0.3	18.1	0.2	19.8	0.2
United States	12.1	(0.6)	19.4	(2.2)	16.6	(0.9)	17.0	(0.8)	20.6	(0.6)	26.6	(0.8)
Sub-national entities												
Flanders (Belgium)	17.3	(0.8)	18.3	(0.7)	19.7	(0.8)	20.6	(0.5)	22.7	(0.3)	23.7	(0.3)
England (UK)	11.4	(0.7)	13.4	(0.7)	14.7	(0.8)	14.2	(0.4)	16.5	(0.3)	22.0	(0.4)
Northern Ireland (UK)	12.1	(0.6)	14.3	(1.3)	c	c	14.1	(0.6)	16.1	(0.5)	18.3	(0.5)
England/N. Ireland (UK)	11.5	(0.7)	13.5	(0.6)	14.7	(0.8)	14.2	(0.4)	16.5	(0.3)	21.9	(0.4)
Average[1]	12.6	(0.2)	15.7	(0.2)	15.4	(0.2)	15.9	(0.1)	17.7	(0.1)	19.9	(0.1)
Average-22[2]	12.5	(0.1)	15.5	(0.2)	15.2	(0.1)	m	m	m	m	m	m
Partners												
Cyprus[3]	14.1	(0.6)	15.5	(1.5)	17.3	(0.5)	m	m	m	m	m	m
Russian Federation[4]	3.6	(0.2)	5.0	(0.6)	5.0	(0.2)	4.7	(0.3)	4.9	(0.2)	5.6	(0.1)

1. Average of 19 participating OECD countries and entities.
2. Average of 22 OECD countries and entities: average of 19 countries with France, Italy and Spain.
3. See notes at the beginning of this Annex.
4. See note at the beginning of this Annex.
Source: Survey of Adult Skills (PIAAC) (2012).

StatLink ⏻ http://dx.doi.org/10.1787/888933232187

[Part 1/1]

Table A4.11   **Mean hourly wage, by frequency of e-mail use at work**

OECD	Less than monthly or never (A)		At least monthly (B)		Wage premium for (B)	
	Mean wage	S.E.	Mean wage	S.E.	% diff.	S.E.
National entities						
Australia	14.5	(0.2)	21.6	(0.3)	48.8	(0.0)
Austria	14.8	(0.2)	22.0	(0.3)	48.5	(0.0)
Canada	14.8	(0.2)	23.9	(0.2)	61.2	(0.0)
Czech Republic	7.3	(0.1)	10.6	(0.2)	44.8	(0.0)
Denmark	18.8	(0.2)	26.0	(0.2)	38.6	(0.0)
Estonia	8.0	(0.1)	11.1	(0.1)	38.9	(0.0)
Finland	15.3	(0.2)	20.8	(0.1)	36.5	(0.0)
France	12.7	(0.1)	17.9	(0.1)	40.7	(0.0)
Germany	14.1	(0.2)	22.8	(0.3)	61.3	(0.0)
Ireland	16.3	(0.3)	25.8	(0.4)	58.0	(0.0)
Italy	13.8	(0.3)	19.4	(0.4)	40.6	(0.0)
Japan	12.4	(0.2)	19.9	(0.3)	60.9	(0.0)
Korea	14.0	(0.4)	21.0	(0.4)	49.8	(0.1)
Netherlands	14.5	(0.2)	24.4	(0.2)	67.7	(0.0)
Norway	18.9	0.2	26.2	0.1	38.7	(0.0)
Poland	7.6	(0.1)	11.5	(0.2)	51.4	(0.0)
Slovak Republic	7.1	(0.1)	10.9	(0.2)	54.8	(0.0)
Spain	11.8	(0.2)	18.6	(0.3)	57.6	(0.0)
Sweden	15.9	0.2	19.7	0.1	24.1	(0.0)
United States	14.1	(0.3)	26.1	(0.6)	84.6	(0.0)
Sub-national entities						
Flanders (Belgium)	17.8	(0.2)	24.8	(0.2)	38.9	(0.0)
England (UK)	12.1	(0.2)	21.5	(0.3)	78.2	(0.0)
Northern Ireland (UK)	12.3	(0.3)	19.0	(0.3)	54.4	(0.0)
England/N. Ireland (UK)	12.1	(0.2)	21.4	(0.3)	77.3	(0.0)
Average[1]	13.6	(0.0)	20.6	(0.1)	51.8	(0.0)
Average-22[2]	13.5	(0.0)	20.3	(0.1)	51.1	(0.0)
Partners						
Cyprus[3]	15.1	(0.3)	19.8	(0.4)	30.6	(0.0)
Russian Federation[4]	4.4	(0.1)	6.1	(0.2)	39.9	(0.1)

1. Average of 19 participating OECD countries and entities.
2. Average of 22 OECD countries and entities: average of 19 countries with France, Italy and Spain.
3. See notes at the beginning of this Annex.
4. See note at the beginning of this Annex.
Source: Survey of Adult Skills (PIAAC) (2012).

StatLink ᵐˢᵖ http://dx.doi.org/10.1787/888933232199

[Part 1/1]

Table A4.12 Mean hourly wage, by frequency of complex problem solving

OECD	Less than monthly or never (A)		At least monthly (B)		Wage premium for (B)	
	Mean wage	S.E.	Mean wage	S.E.	% diff.	S.E.
National entities						
Australia	15.4	(0.2)	20.7	(0.2)	34.8	(0.0)
Austria	15.9	(0.2)	21.6	(0.2)	35.9	(0.0)
Canada	16.5	(0.2)	23.2	(0.2)	40.7	(0.0)
Czech Republic	7.8	(0.1)	9.9	(0.2)	27.7	(0.0)
Denmark	20.3	(0.2)	26.3	(0.2)	29.5	(0.0)
Estonia	8.2	(0.1)	11.0	(0.1)	34.0	(0.0)
Finland	16.7	(0.2)	20.9	(0.2)	25.0	(0.0)
France	13.7	(0.1)	17.3	(0.1)	26.7	(0.0)
Germany	15.2	(0.2)	22.1	(0.3)	45.6	(0.0)
Ireland	18.1	(0.3)	24.5	(0.4)	35.4	(0.0)
Italy	13.7	(0.3)	17.8	(0.3)	30.5	(0.0)
Japan	13.8	(0.2)	19.0	(0.4)	38.1	(0.0)
Korea	15.3	(0.5)	20.0	(0.4)	30.7	(0.0)
Netherlands	17.9	(0.2)	24.6	(0.2)	37.6	(0.0)
Norway	20.9	0.2	26.6	0.2	27.5	(0.0)
Poland	8.0	(0.2)	10.7	(0.2)	33.1	(0.0)
Slovak Republic	7.1	(0.1)	10.2	(0.2)	43.2	(0.0)
Spain	13.1	(0.2)	16.8	(0.3)	27.6	(0.0)
Sweden	16.6	0.2	20.1	0.1	20.8	(0.0)
United States	16.8	(0.5)	24.2	(0.5)	44.1	(0.1)
Sub-national entities						
Flanders (Belgium)	20.2	(0.2)	24.0	(0.2)	18.7	(0.0)
England (UK)	13.6	(0.3)	20.8	(0.3)	53.6	(0.0)
Northern Ireland (UK)	13.4	(0.3)	18.4	(0.3)	36.8	(0.0)
England/N. Ireland (UK)	13.5	(0.3)	20.7	(0.2)	53.4	(0.0)
Average[1]	15.0	(0.1)	20.0	(0.1)	34.5	(0.0)
Average-22[2]	14.8	(0.1)	19.7	(0.1)	33.7	(0.0)
Partners						
Cyprus[3]	15.7	(0.3)	18.5	(0.3)	18.1	(0.0)
Russian Federation[4]	4.4	(0.1)	5.3	(0.2)	20.7	(0.1)

1. Average of 19 participating OECD countries and entities.
2. Average of 22 OECD countries and entities: average of 19 countries with France, Italy and Spain.
3. See notes at the beginning of this Annex.
4. See note at the beginning of this Annex.
Source: Survey of Adult Skills (PIAAC) (2012).
StatLink ᵐˢᵖ http://dx.doi.org/10.1787/888933232209

[Part 1/1]

Mean hourly wage and wage premium, by adequacy of computer skills affecting the chances of getting a job, promotion or pay raise

Table A4.13

OECD	Has the computer skills to do the job well (A)		Lack the computer skills to do the job well (B)		Wage premium for (A)		A lack of computer skills has not affected the chances of getting a job/promotion/pay raise or does not use computer at work (C)		A lack of computer skills has affected the chances of getting a job/promotion/pay raise (D)		Wage premium for (D)		Does not use computer at work	
	Mean wage	S.E.	Mean wage	S.E.	% diff.	S.E.	Mean wage	S.E.	Mean wage	S.E.	% diff.	S.E.	Mean wage	S.E.
National entities														
Australia	20.7	(0.7)	20.2	(0.2)	2.5	(0.0)	20.4	(0.2)	18.7	(0.5)	-8.0	(0.0)	14.7	(0.3)
Austria	21.7	(1.2)	20.7	(0.2)	4.8	(0.1)	20.9	(0.2)	17.9	(0.7)	-14.1	(0.0)	14.4	(0.2)
Canada	23.2	(0.8)	22.1	(0.2)	4.8	(0.0)	22.4	(0.2)	20.0	(0.5)	-10.6	(0.0)	14.6	(0.2)
Czech Republic	8.8	(0.4)	10.1	(0.2)	-12.7	(0.0)	10.0	(0.1)	10.0	(0.7)	-0.4	(0.1)	7.0	(0.1)
Denmark	24.6	(0.3)	25.0	(0.2)	-1.5	(0.0)	25.0	(0.1)	24.4	(0.7)	-2.1	(0.0)	18.8	(0.3)
Estonia	10.0	(0.3)	10.6	(0.1)	-5.5	(0.0)	10.7	(0.1)	9.4	(0.4)	-11.8	(0.0)	8.0	(0.2)
Finland	19.4	(0.4)	20.2	(0.1)	-3.9	(0.0)	20.2	(0.1)	19.7	(0.6)	-2.2	(0.0)	15.1	(0.2)
France	16.8	(0.3)	17.0	(0.1)	-1.1	(0.0)	17.0	(0.1)	16.7	(0.4)	-1.8	(0.0)	12.4	(0.1)
Germany	21.0	(0.7)	21.4	(0.3)	-1.8	(0.0)	21.5	(0.3)	17.4	(0.8)	-19.1	(0.0)	13.3	(0.2)
Ireland	25.7	(1.1)	24.1	(0.3)	6.5	(0.0)	24.5	(0.3)	20.2	(0.8)	-17.5	(0.0)	15.5	(0.3)
Italy	18.9	(1.1)	18.6	(0.3)	1.7	(0.1)	18.7	(0.3)	16.7	(1.2)	-11.0	(0.1)	13.3	(0.3)
Japan	16.6	(0.3)	18.5	(0.4)	-10.3	(0.0)	17.8	(0.3)	17.5	(0.4)	-1.5	(0.0)	11.5	(0.3)
Korea	18.4	(0.7)	19.9	(0.4)	-7.4	(0.0)	19.7	(0.3)	17.0	(1.9)	-13.5	(0.1)	13.8	(0.5)
Netherlands	24.4	(1.0)	23.1	(0.2)	5.3	(0.0)	23.3	(0.2)	21.8	(0.8)	-6.3	(0.0)	14.3	(0.2)
Norway	26.5	0.3	25.0	0.1	6.3	0.0	25.4	0.1	23.1	0.7	-9.0	0.0	19.2	(0.4)
Poland	11.5	(0.7)	10.9	(0.2)	5.1	(0.1)	11.0	(0.2)	11.1	(0.6)	1.0	(0.1)	7.3	(0.1)
Slovak Republic	9.1	(0.6)	10.4	(0.2)	-12.8	(0.1)	10.4	(0.2)	10.0	(0.6)	-3.5	(0.1)	6.8	(0.1)
Spain	16.8	(0.8)	17.6	(0.3)	-4.9	(0.0)	17.7	(0.3)	16.6	(1.2)	-6.2	(0.1)	11.2	(0.2)
Sweden	19.9	0.4	19.1	0.1	4.2	0.0	19.3	0.1	17.1	0.5	-11.3	0.0	15.7	(0.3)
United States	22.9	(1.1)	24.1	(0.5)	-4.8	(0.0)	24.3	(0.6)	21.5	(1.3)	-11.4	(0.1)	13.8	(0.3)
Sub-national entities														
Flanders (Belgium)	25.0	(0.7)	24.0	(0.2)	4.4	(0.0)	24.2	(0.2)	22.0	(0.7)	-9.2	(0.0)	17.1	(0.2)
England (UK)	19.4	(1.0)	20.1	(0.2)	-3.3	(0.0)	20.3	(0.2)	16.6	(0.8)	-18.3	(0.0)	12.0	(0.2)
Northern Ireland (UK)	20.3	(1.1)	17.6	(0.2)	15.1	(0.1)	17.9	(0.2)	15.2	(1.0)	-15.0	(0.1)	12.2	(0.5)
England/N. Ireland (UK)	19.4	(0.9)	20.0	(0.2)	-2.7	(0.0)	20.2	(0.2)	16.5	(0.8)	-18.1	(0.0)	12.0	(0.2)
Average¹	19.4	(0.2)	19.4	(0.1)		(0.0)	19.5	(0.1)	17.7	(0.2)	-8.9	(0.0)	13.3	(0.1)
Average-22²	19.2	(0.2)	19.2	(0.1)		(0.0)	19.3	(0.1)	17.5	(0.2)	-8.5	(0.0)	13.2	(0.1)
Partners														
Cyprus³	20.5	(1.2)	19.2	(0.3)	6.9	(0.1)	19.7	(0.3)	15.7	(0.9)	-20.0	(0.0)	14.0	(0.4)
Russian Federation⁴	4.7	(0.5)	5.7	(0.1)	-17.0	(0.1)	5.6	(0.1)	6.3	(0.9)	13.6	(0.2)	4.3	(0.1)

1. Average of 19 participating OECD countries and entities.
2. Average of 22 OECD countries and entities: average of 19 countries with France, Italy and Spain.
3. See notes at the beginning of this Annex.
4. See note at the beginning of this Annex.
Source: Survey of Adult Skills (PIAAC) (2012).

StatLink 🔗 http://dx.doi.org/10.1787/888933232211

[Part 1/2]
Differences in the rate of labour force participation between various groups after accounting for various characteristics

Table A4.14

OECD	Version 1 (socio-demographic controls)					Version 2 (Version 1 + literacy and numeracy)				
	No computer experience	Failed ICT core	Opted out	Level 1	Level 2/3	No computer experience	Failed ICT core	Opted out	Level 1	Level 2/3
	% point	% point	% point	% point	% point	% point	% point	% point	% point	% point
National entities										
Australia	-24.7 ***	-12.8 *	-2.3	2.1	7.8 *	-23.1 ***	-12.2 *	-2.7	0.4	5.3
Austria	-13.4 **	-6.1	-7.4	2.6	5.3	-14.6 ***	-7.1	-10.2 *	-0.9	-1.1
Canada	-11.7 ***	-5.9 **	-3.2	2.7	7.5 ***	-10.6 ***	-6.3 **	-4.5	-0.3	2.7
Czech Republic	-15.3 ***	7.5	6.0	-0.3	5.3	-15.7 ***	7.2	5.3	-1.3	3.9
Denmark	-27.1 ***	-6.8	-10.1 **	7.2 **	14.6 ***	-26.9 ***	-6.6	-11.6 **	2.1	7.1
Estonia	-25.7 ***	-5.8 *	-5.2 ***	2.0	4.9 **	-26.2 ***	-6.4 *	-6.9 ***	0.0	2.0
Finland	-26.2 ***	-12.9 ***	-7.6 **	11.2 ***	17.7 ***	-27.4 ***	-15.3 ***	-14.6 ***	6.5 **	10.4 **
France	m	m	m	m	m	m	m	m	m	m
Germany	-5.7	1.9	-4.9	3.8	7.2 **	-5.3	2.7	-7.8 *	-1.3	-1.6
Ireland	-11.5 ***	4.5	-4.1	7.1 *	14.5 ***	-11.4 **	4.7	-5.4	5.3	11.8 **
Italy	m	m	m	m	m	m	m	m	m	m
Japan	-8.6 *	-3.1	-2.3	-0.4	3.8	-7.9 *	-2.5	-1.8	-0.3	3.8
Korea	-7.2 ***	-5.1	-1.5	-1.4	4.3	-7.0 **	-4.9	-1.2	-1.5	4.1
Netherlands	-10.1 *	-1.4	-9.0 *	7.9 **	13.7 ***	-10.1	-0.9	-7.7	9.4 **	15.9 ***
Norway	-30.7 ***	0.3	-7.4 *	8.4 **	13.6 ***	-30.2 ***	2.1	-8.4 *	5.0	8.0 *
Poland	-11.5 ***	-3.6	-1.9	3.8	9.3 ***	-10.5 ***	-2.8	-2.5	2.5	7.5 *
Slovak Republic	-9.3 **	-7.6	0.9	2.8	5.8 *	-9.0 **	-8.7	-0.7	-0.3	0.5
Spain	m	m	m	m	m	m	m	m	m	m
Sweden	-23.3 **	-9.0	-8.7 *	5.3	10.5 ***	-19.7 **	-4.0	-13.5 **	-3.2	-4.9
United States	-18.9 ***	-11.7 **	-9.2 ***	3.1	4.4	-16.9 ***	-10.4 **	-10.0 ***	0.6	-0.1
Sub-national entities										
Flanders (Belgium)	-21.0 ***	-7.6	-3.5	1.0	5.2	-21.8 ***	-9.8	-6.9	-2.8	-1.3
England (UK)	-32.4 ***	-5.1	0.4	5.1	11.1 ***	-31.0 ***	-4.4	0.6	3.6	8.8 *
Northern Ireland (UK)	-9.4	1.4	-16.6	3.3	13.0 **	-10.1	0.2	-19.3 *	-1.4	5.2
England/N. Ireland (UK)	-31.4 ***	-4.9	0.3	5.1	11.2 ***	-30.1 ***	-4.3	0.4	3.5	8.8 *
Average[1]	-16.2 ***	-3.7 ***	-3.6 ***	4.2 ***	9.3 ***	-15.7 ***	-3.3 ***	-5.0 ***	1.4	5.1 ***
Average-22[2]	m	m	m	m	m	m	m	m	m	m
Partners										
Cyprus[3]	m	m	m	m	m	m	m	m	m	m
Russian Federation[4]	3.9	-11.7	2.7	6.6	9.0	-0.1	-15.0 *	-3.2	1.9	-0.6

1. Average of 19 participating OECD countries and entities.
2. Average of 22 OECD countries and entities: average of 19 countries with France, Italy and Spain.
3. See notes at the beginning of this Annex.
4. See note at the beginning of this Annex.
* Significant estimate p ≤ 0.10.
** Significant estimate p ≤ 0.05.
*** Significant estimate p ≤ 0.01.

Notes: The reference category for problem solving in rich-environment is Below Level 1 and low users for use of e-mail. Version 1 adjusts for socio-demographic characteristics (age, gender, foreign-born status, years of education and marital status). Version 2 adds literacy and numeracy proficiency to the regression of Version 1. Version 3 adds frequency of ICT use (e-mail) in everyday life as an adjustment to Version 2. Version 4 adds use of reading/writing/numeracy skills in everyday life as an additional adjustment to Version 3. Regression coefficients of the versions are available in Table B4.12 in Annex B.

Source: Survey of Adult Skills (PIAAC) (2012).

StatLink ⟨⟩ http://dx.doi.org/10.1787/888933232221

[Part 2/2]

Table A4.14 **Differences in the rate of labour force participation between various groups after accounting for various characteristics**

OECD	Versions 3 (Version 2 + e-mail use in everyday life)						Version 4 (Version 3 + reading/writing/numeracy use in everyday life)					
	No computer experience	Failed ICT core	Opted out	Level 1	Level 2/3	Frequent use of e-mail	No computer experience	Failed ICT core	Opted out	Level 1	Level 2/3	Frequent use of e-mail
	% point	% point	% point	% point	% point	% point	% point	% point	% point	% point	% point	% point
National entities												
Australia	-20.8 ***	-11.8 *	-1.8	0.3	5.2	3.2	-28.2 ***	-10.7	-3.1	0.7	4.9	9.7 ***
Austria	-15.6 ***	-7.4	-10.7 *	-0.8	-0.9	-1.4	-25.0 ***	-9.2	-12.0 **	-1.6	-1.5	2.6
Canada	-11.0 ***	-6.3 **	-4.7	-0.3	2.7	-0.6	-17.0 ***	-5.6 *	-5.9 *	-0.4	2.8	3.8 *
Czech Republic	-14.6 **	7.4	5.6	-1.4	3.8	1.5	-13.0 *	9.2	4.9	-1.1	4.0	8.1
Denmark	-27.7 ***	-6.7	-11.9 **	2.2	7.2	-1.2	-25.5 ***	-5.4	-11.1 **	3.1	8.9	3.8
Estonia	-20.6 ***	-5.4	-5.0 *	-0.1	2.0	7.4 ***	-17.9 ***	-8.0 *	-4.9	0.3	1.9	7.9 ***
Finland	-22.0 ***	-13.6 ***	-11.6 ***	6.1 *	10.0 **	7.4 **	-21.4 ***	-17.8 ***	-9.7 **	5.6	9.0 *	12.9 ***
France	m	m	m	m	m	m	m	m	m	m	m	m
Germany	-6.8	2.4	-8.8 *	-1.0	-1.1	-2.7	-7.2	2.5	-9.0 *	0.0	1.5	-0.7
Ireland	-9.9 **	4.7	-4.8	5.0	11.5 **	2.7	-9.8 *	5.7	-6.8	4.5	11.7 **	6.3 *
Italy	m	m	m	m	m	m	m	m	m	m	m	m
Japan	-9.2 **	-2.8	-2.2	-0.1	4.1	-2.4	-12.5 **	-3.8	-4.4	-1.1	4.0	-3.4
Korea	-6.3 **	-4.6	-0.9	-1.6	3.9	1.8	-5.7	-2.4	-3.3	-3.3	3.6	4.5
Netherlands	-2.0	0.8	-4.6	9.0 **	15.8 ***	9.9 **	1.5	-1.2	-7.4	8.4	16.8 ***	15.0 **
Norway	-28.2 ***	2.2	-7.5 *	4.8	7.9 *	2.4	-32.0 ***	6.0	-4.3	7.5 *	11.3 **	5.2
Poland	-6.5 **	-2.5	-0.7	1.9	6.9 *	9.1 ***	-8.8 *	-2.7	-0.6	1.6	6.8	12.4 ***
Slovak Republic	-4.0	-7.3	1.6	-0.7	-0.3	9.3 **	-3.6	-9.2	2.2	-0.8	0.0	9.8 **
Spain	m	m	m	m	m	m	m	m	m	m	m	m
Sweden	-25.3 **	-4.6	-16.5 ***	-2.4	-3.8	-6.8 *	-7.2	-2.4	-15.4 **	-2.8	-4.6	-4.3
United States	-18.8 ***	-11.2 **	-11.3 ***	0.8	0.1	-3.2	-30.7 ***	-13.9 **	-12.3 ***	0.2	-2.1	1.4
Sub-national entities												
Flanders (Belgium)	-28.8 ***	-11.3 *	-9.8 *	-2.0	-0.3	-9.4 **	-25.7 ***	-13.3	-13.3 *	-1.6	1.0	-5.4
England (UK)	-29.1 ***	-4.1	1.4	3.4	8.5 *	2.6	-34.5 ***	-2.4	4.4	5.0	11.3 **	7.4 **
Northern Ireland (UK)	-7.7	1.1	-18.1	-2.0	4.2	4.3	-9.2	-0.2	-13.3	-1.8	3.7	8.5 **
England/N. Ireland (UK)	-28.0 ***	-3.9	1.2	3.2	8.5 *	2.8	-33.2 ***	-2.4	4.3	4.9	11.2 **	7.6 **
Average[1]	-14.4 ***	-3.2 ***	-4.4 ***	1.4	5.0 ***	2.1 ***	-14.6 ***	-2.6 *	-4.7 ***	1.5	5.6 ***	5.8 ***
Average-22[2]	m	m	m	m	m	m	m	m	m	m	m	m

Partners

Cyprus[3]	m	m	m	m	m	m	m	m	m	m	m	m
Russian Federation[4]	-0.1	-15.0 *	-3.2	1.9	-0.6	0.1	8.3	-13.9	-0.9	6.5	4.3	4.7

1. Average of 19 participating OECD countries and entities.
2. Average of 22 OECD countries and entities: average of 19 countries with France, Italy and Spain.
3. See notes at the beginning of this Annex.
4. See note at the beginning of this Annex.
* Significant estimate p ≤ 0.10.
** Significant estimate p ≤ 0.05.
*** Significant estimate p ≤ 0.01.

Notes: The reference category for problem solving in rich-environment is Below Level 1 and low users for use of e-mail. Version 1 adjusts for socio-demographic characteristics (age, gender, foreign-born status, years of education and marital status). Version 2 adds literacy and numeracy proficiency to the regression of Version 1. Version 3 adds frequency of ICT use (e-mail) in everyday life as an adjustment to Version 2. Version 4 adds use of reading/writing/numeracy skills in everyday life as an additional adjustment to Version 3. Regression coefficients of the versions are available in Table B4.12 in Annex B.
Source: Survey of Adult Skills (PIAAC) (2012).

StatLink ᓚ http://dx.doi.org/10.1787/888933232221

[Part 1/2]
Differences in the rate of unemployment between various groups after accounting for various characteristics

Table A4.15

OECD	Version 1 (socio-demographic controls)					Version 2 (Model 1 + literacy and numeracy)				
	No computer experience	Failed ICT core	Opted out	Level 1	Level 2/3	No computer experience	Failed ICT core	Opted out	Level 1	Level 2/3
	% point	% point	% point	% point	% point	% point	% point	% point	% point	% point
National entities										
Australia	-4.3	-2.2	-0.9	-2.7	-4.4 **	-4.2	-2.4	-1.3	-3.1	-4.8 **
Austria	-2.3	-1.7	-2.1	-0.2	-2.2	-2.0	-1.5	-1.4	0.4	-1.3
Canada	4.1 *	2.8 *	-0.2	0.0	-0.5	2.9	2.4	-0.5	0.8	1.2
Czech Republic	3.3	1.8	4.7	2.8	1.2	3.2	1.5	5.9	5.3	5.0
Denmark	-3.3	0.2	3.4	0.6	2.9	-3.4	-0.2	3.3	3.2	10.2 **
Estonia	7.6 ***	0.7	3.3 **	1.2	-1.8	7.8 ***	0.9	4.3 ***	2.8 *	0.0
Finland	1.6	2.8	-0.3	0.1	0.1	1.5	0.7	-1.2	1.0	2.6
France	m	m	m	m	m	m	m	m	m	m
Germany	0.9	1.4	5.0 **	0.9	-1.6	-0.3	-0.4	4.8 *	2.8	0.9
Ireland	0.7	-3.1	-1.4	1.0	-3.2	0.6	-3.0	-0.3	3.7	1.0
Italy	m	m	m	m	m	m	m	m	m	m
Japan	-2.4	-0.5	-1.6	-1.0	-2.1	-3.0 **	-2.6	-2.8 *	-2.1	-3.1 **
Korea	0.1	0.7	0.1	0.1	0.0	-0.4	-0.1	-0.8	0.1	0.0
Netherlands	-5.8	-4.1	-0.2	-3.5	-4.8 **	-6.3	-4.3	-1.1	-3.7	-5.1
Norway	-3.1	1.9	-1.5	0.9	-0.7	-3.1	0.8	-1.4	2.6	1.7
Poland	5.0 *	1.4	2.0	0.8	-1.6	4.6 *	1.2	2.1	1.1	-1.2
Slovak Republic	5.7 *	0.4	-1.8	-4.0	-3.4	4.9	1.1	-2.0	-3.4	-1.9
Spain	m	m	m	m	m	m	m	m	m	m
Sweden	16.2	5.5	6.6	-0.4	-3.9 **	16.5	5.1	7.6 *	0.6	-3.0
United States	-6.8 ***	-1.5	-1.4	-1.4	-3.7	-7.3 ***	-2.7	-1.2	1.4	1.0
Sub-national entities										
Flanders (Belgium)	-1.8	-1.4	-0.5	-0.7	-1.0	-1.8	-1.2	0.1	-0.4	-0.5
England (UK)	-0.3	3.7	-3.7	-2.1	-4.9 **	-1.0	3.0	-3.6	-0.2	-2.3
Northern Ireland (UK)	2.3	-3.5	-4.9	-3.1	-4.2 *	2.3	-3.6	-5.0	-2.3	-2.8
England/N. Ireland (UK)	-0.1	3.5	-3.7	-2.2	-4.8 **	-0.8	2.8	-3.6	-0.3	-2.3
Average[1]	1.0	0.8	0.7	-0.2	-1.6 ***	0.6	0.0	0.7	1.0	0.5
Average-22[2]	m	m	m	m	m	m	m	m	m	m

Partners

Cyprus[3]	m	m	m	m	m	m	m	m	m	m
Russian Federation[4]	2.8	-1.7	0.5	3.3	6.2	0.1	-2.3	-1.8	0.3	-0.2

1. Average of 19 participating OECD countries and entities.
2. Average of 22 OECD countries and entities: average of 19 countries with France, Italy and Spain.
3. See notes at the beginning of this Annex.
4. See note at the beginning of this Annex.
* Significant estimate p ≤ 0.10.
** Significant estimate p ≤ 0.05.
*** Significant estimate p ≤ 0.01.

Notes: The reference category for problem solving in rich-environment is Below Level 1 and low users for use of e-mail. Version 1 adjusts for socio-demographic characteristics (age, gender, foreign-born status, years of education and marital status). Version 2 adds literacy and numeracy proficiency to the regression of Version 1. Version 3 adds frequency of ICT use (e-mail) in everyday life as an adjustment to Version 2. Version 4 adds use of reading/writing/numeracy skills in everyday life as an additional adjustment to Version 3. Regression coefficients of the versions are available in Table B4.13 in Annex B.
Source: Survey of Adult Skills (PIAAC) (2012).
StatLink http://dx.doi.org/10.1787/888933232233

[Part 2/2]

Differences in the rate of unemployment between various groups after accounting for various characteristics

Table A4.15

OECD	Version 3 (Version 2 + e-mail use in everyday life)						Version 4 (Version 3 + reading/writing/numeracy use in everyday life)					
	No computer experience	Failed ICT core	Opted out	Level 1	Level 2/3	Frequent use of e-mail	No computer experience	Failed ICT core	Opted out	Level 1	Level 2/3	Frequent use of e-mail
	% point	% point	% point	% point	% point	% point	% point	% point	% point	% point	% point	% point
National entities												
Australia	-3.7	-2.3	-1.0	-3.1	-4.8 **	1.2	-0.7	-1.6	0.7	-3.4	-4.6 *	0.1
Austria	-2.0	-1.5	-1.4	0.4	-1.3	0.0	-1.0	-1.7	-2.0	-0.3	-2.3	-1.3
Canada	5.3 *	2.7	0.1	0.7	1.1	2.5 **	11.4 **	5.0 **	1.3	1.0	1.7	0.7
Czech Republic	3.2	1.5	5.9	5.3	5.0	0.1	3.9	1.9	5.3	5.2	4.5	-1.9
Denmark	-3.3	-0.2	3.3	3.2	10.2 **	0.2	-5.5	0.2	1.8	3.7	11.1 **	-2.3
Estonia	10.0 ***	1.2	5.0 ***	2.8 *	0.1	2.3	11.0 ***	2.2	5.9 ***	3.6 **	1.1	-0.6
Finland	4.2	0.9	-0.7	0.8	2.2	2.8 **	9.4 *	2.2	-0.3	1.4	2.5	-0.3
France	m	m	m	m	m	m	m	m	m	m	m	m
Germany	-0.3	-0.4	4.8 *	2.8	0.9	0.1	1.8	0.3	5.4 *	1.9	0.0	0.0
Ireland	2.0	-3.1	0.3	3.2	0.5	2.5	4.8	-3.9	0.9	3.6	0.2	-2.4
Italy	m	m	m	m	m	m	m	m	m	m	m	m
Japan	-2.9 **	-2.6	-2.8 *	-2.2	-3.1 **	0.3	-3.2 **	-3.0 **	-3.0 **	-2.4	-3.3 **	-0.2
Korea	-0.2	-0.2	-0.7	0.1	0.0	0.7	0.4	-0.1	-1.1	-0.2	-0.2	0.0
Netherlands	-4.0	-4.1	0.3	-3.9	-5.1	7.8 **	-8.2	-4.6	0.5	-3.2	-4.6	2.5
Norway	-3.1	0.7	-1.4	2.5	1.6	0.3	-3.1	0.8	-0.9	3.1	1.3	0.2
Poland	4.2	1.2	2.0	1.2	-1.1	-0.8	7.6 **	1.7	2.4	0.8	-1.3	-2.7
Slovak Republic	3.2	0.9	-2.5	-3.3	-1.6	-2.4	7.1 *	2.5	-2.7	-2.8	-1.1	-3.2
Spain	m	m	m	m	m	m	m	m	m	m	m	m
Sweden	24.2	5.0	9.5 *	0.0	-3.4	3.9	-6.7	6.6	6.9	-1.1	-4.0 *	4.2
United States	-6.6 **	-2.1	0.3	1.1	0.7	3.6 *	-3.9	-0.5	4.3	3.3	5.1	-1.0
Sub-national entities												
Flanders (Belgium)	-1.5	-1.1	0.4	-0.4	-0.6	0.8	-1.8	-1.7	3.3	-0.6	-0.5	0.3
England (UK)	-0.4	3.1	-3.4	-0.3	-2.4	1.0	11.0	7.3 *	-1.1	0.3	-2.1	-1.2
Northern Ireland (UK)	1.7	-3.6	-5.1	-2.2	-2.6	-0.9	1.5	-3.6	-5.3	-2.5	-3.0	-3.5 **
England/N. Ireland (UK)	-0.2	2.9	-3.4	-0.4	-2.4	0.9	10.4	6.9 *	-1.2	0.2	-2.2	-1.3
Average[1]	1.9	0.1	1.1	0.9	0.4	1.9 ***	2.2	0.8	1.7	1.0	0.5	-0.1
Average-22[2]	m	m	m	m	m	m	m	m	m	m	m	m
Partners												
Cyprus[3]	m	m	m	m	m	m	m	m	m	m	m	m
Russian Federation[4]	0.9	-2.4	-1.5	0.1	-0.5	2.7	-0.5	-2.7	-3.9	1.9	-0.6	1.8

1. Average of 19 participating OECD countries and entities.
2. Average of 22 OECD countries and entities: average of 19 countries with France, Italy and Spain.
3. See notes at the beginning of this Annex.
4. See note at the beginning of this Annex.
* Significant estimate p ≤ 0.10.
** Significant estimate p ≤ 0.05.
*** Significant estimate p ≤ 0.01.

Notes: The reference category for problem solving in rich-environment is Below Level 1 and low users for use of e-mail. Version 1 adjusts for socio-demographic characteristics (age, gender, foreign-born status, years of education and marital status). Version 2 adds literacy and numeracy proficiency to the regression of Version 1. Version 3 adds frequency of ICT use (e-mail) in everyday life as an adjustment to Version 2. Version 4 adds use of reading/writing/numeracy skills in everyday life as an additional adjustment to Version 3. Regression coefficients of the versions are available in Table B4.13 in Annex B.

Source: Survey of Adult Skills (PIAAC) (2012).

StatLink ⟶ http://dx.doi.org/10.1787/888933232233

[Part 1/4]

Table A4.16 **Percentage differences in wages between various groups, before and after accounting for various characteristics**

OECD	Version 1 (socio-demographic controls)					Version 2 (Version 1 + literacy and numeracy)				
	No computer experience	Failed ICT core	Opted out	Level 1	Level 2/3	No computer experience	Failed ICT core	Opted out	Level 1	Level 2/3
	ß	ß	ß	ß	ß	ß	ß	ß	ß	ß
National entities										
Australia	-0.07	0.03	-0.03	0.04	0.12 ***	-0.05	0.01	-0.06	-0.01	0.02
Austria	-0.09 **	0.04	-0.04	0.09 ***	0.20 ***	-0.11 ***	0.02	-0.09 **	0.04	0.10 ***
Canada	-0.10 **	0.00	-0.03	0.09 ***	0.18 ***	-0.09 **	-0.03	-0.08 ***	0.02	0.04
Czech Republic	-0.14 **	-0.09	-0.06	0.08 ***	0.17 ***	-0.16 ***	-0.13 *	-0.11 **	0.05	0.11 ***
Denmark	-0.10 **	0.00	-0.04	0.04 *	0.11 ***	-0.11 **	0.00	-0.05	0.02	0.06 **
Estonia	-0.30 ***	-0.07	-0.06 **	0.08 ***	0.20 ***	-0.30 ***	-0.08	-0.09 ***	0.04	0.11 **
Finland	-0.09	-0.01	-0.03	0.07 ***	0.13 ***	-0.10 *	-0.01	-0.05	0.04 *	0.08 **
France	m	m	m	m	m	m	m	m	m	m
Germany	-0.16 ***	-0.01	-0.08 *	0.08 **	0.19 ***	-0.19 ***	-0.03	-0.13 ***	0.03	0.09 **
Ireland	-0.11	0.06	0.00	0.12 ***	0.20 ***	-0.11	0.04	-0.03	0.06	0.09 *
Italy	m	m	m	m	m	m	m	m	m	m
Japan	-0.19 ***	-0.03	-0.05	0.06	0.15 ***	-0.20 ***	-0.09 *	-0.10 *	0.00	0.05
Korea	-0.10	-0.09	-0.02	0.06	0.09	-0.12 *	-0.13 **	-0.07	0.02	0.02
Netherlands	-0.16 **	0.03	-0.02	0.09 ***	0.18 ***	-0.16 **	0.00	-0.06	0.04	0.08 *
Norway	-0.11	-0.02	-0.01	0.09 ***	0.17 ***	-0.10	-0.01	-0.02	0.06 **	0.11 ***
Poland	-0.09 *	0.07	0.04	0.09 **	0.18 ***	-0.11 **	0.04	-0.01	0.05	0.11 **
Slovak Republic	-0.10 **	0.19 **	0.05	0.13 **	0.23 ***	-0.12 **	0.16 *	0.01	0.08	0.15 **
Spain	m	m	m	m	m	m	m	m	m	m
Sweden	-0.03	0.06	-0.04	0.05 ***	0.14 ***	-0.02	0.07	-0.05	0.02	0.06 **
United States	-0.10 *	0.04	-0.05	0.13 ***	0.25 ***	-0.08	0.03	-0.09 *	0.06	0.12 **
Sub-national entities										
Flanders (Belgium)	-0.10 **	-0.05	-0.06	0.09 ***	0.14 ***	-0.10 **	-0.06	-0.08 *	0.05 **	0.07 **
England (UK)	-0.15 **	-0.02	0.04	0.13 ***	0.30 ***	-0.16 **	-0.07	-0.04	0.03	0.10 **
Northern Ireland (UK)	-0.11 *	-0.04	0.00	0.11 ***	0.21 ***	-0.12 *	-0.07	-0.05	0.06	0.09 *
England/N. Ireland (UK)	-0.15 **	-0.02	0.04	0.13 ***	0.30 ***	-0.15 **	-0.07	-0.04	0.03	0.10 **
Average[1]	-0.12 ***	0.01	-0.03 ***	0.08 ***	0.18 ***	-0.12 ***	-0.01	-0.06 ***	0.04 ***	0.08 ***
Average-22[2]	m	m	m	m	m	m	m	m	m	m

Partners

Cyprus[3]	m	m	m	m	m	m	m	m	m	m
Russian Federation[4]	-0.05	0.26 ***	0.08	0.13	0.26 ***	-0.07	0.23 **	0.05	0.11	0.22 *

1. Average of 19 participating OECD countries and entities.
2. Average of 22 OECD countries and entities: average of 19 countries with France, Italy and Spain.
3. See notes at the beginning of this Annex.
4. See note at the beginning of this Annex.
* Significant estimate p ≤ 0.10.
** Significant estimate p ≤ 0.05.
*** Significant estimate p ≤ 0.01.

Notes: The reference category for problem solving in rich-environment is Below Level 1. Version 1 adjusts for socio-demographic characteristics (age, gender, foreign-born status, years of education, marital status and years of experience). Version 2 adds literacy and numeracy proficiency to the regression of Version 1. Version 3 adds the frequency of ICT use (e-mail) at work, the two adequacy measures of computer skills for work and the frequency of complex problem solving at work as an adjustment to Version 2. Version 4 adds use of reading/writing/numeracy skills at work as an additional adjustment to Version 3. Version 5 adds occupation as an additional adjustment to Version 4.

Source: Survey of Adult Skills (PIAAC) (2012).

StatLink ᴍ╤ http://dx.doi.org/10.1787/888933232243

[Part 2/4]

Percentage differences in wages between various groups, before and after accounting for various characteristics

Table A4.16

OECD	Version 3 (Version 2 + e-mail use, adequacy of ICT skills and frequency of complex problem solving at work)								
	No computer experience	Failed ICT core	Opted out	Level 1	Level 2/3	Frequent use of e-mail	Computer workers without computer skills to do the job well	Computer workers whose skills have affected employment	Regular users of complex problem solving
	ß	ß	ß	ß	ß	ß	ß	ß	ß
National entities									
Australia	0.01	0.01	-0.04	-0.03	-0.02	0.16 ***	-0.02	-0.05 **	0.09 ***
Austria	-0.01	0.06	-0.04	0.01	0.06 *	0.14 ***	0.00	-0.09 **	0.10 ***
Canada	0.00	-0.01	-0.03	-0.01	-0.01	0.21 ***	0.05 *	-0.08 ***	0.11 ***
Czech Republic	-0.07	-0.10	-0.09 **	0.01	0.03	0.10 ***	-0.06	0.00	0.04 *
Denmark	-0.06	0.00	-0.03	0.00	0.03	0.10 ***	-0.04 ***	-0.02	0.05 ***
Estonia	-0.24 ***	-0.06	-0.07 **	0.01	0.05	0.17 ***	0.00	-0.08 **	0.10 ***
Finland	-0.04	0.00	-0.01	0.03	0.06 **	0.08 ***	-0.03	-0.01	0.07 ***
France	m	m	m	m	m	m	m	m	m
Germany	-0.06	0.05	-0.06	-0.01	0.03	0.13 ***	-0.03	-0.09 *	0.09 ***
Ireland	0.01	0.08	0.02	0.03	0.05	0.15 ***	0.06 *	-0.10 ***	0.06 ***
Italy	m	m	m	m	m	m	m	m	m
Japan	-0.10 **	-0.09 *	-0.07	-0.03	-0.02	0.19 ***	-0.03	-0.03	0.07 ***
Korea	-0.05	-0.09	-0.02	0.01	-0.03	0.24 ***	0.00	-0.15 *	0.08 ***
Netherlands	-0.05	0.02	-0.02	0.01	0.04	0.20 ***	0.02	-0.05	0.09 ***
Norway	-0.08	-0.01	-0.01	0.04	0.09 ***	0.08 ***	0.01	-0.06 **	0.06 ***
Poland	-0.06	0.04	0.01	0.04	0.09 *	0.12 ***	0.06	0.01	0.08 ***
Slovak Republic	-0.03	0.15 *	0.05	0.07	0.12 **	0.14 ***	-0.07	0.06	0.09 ***
Spain	m	m	m	m	m	m	m	m	m
Sweden	0.03	0.07	-0.02	0.01	0.04	0.06 ***	0.02	-0.07 **	0.08 ***
United States	-0.02	0.06	-0.04	0.02	0.06	0.26 ***	-0.03	-0.03	0.11 ***
Sub-national entities									
Flanders (Belgium)	-0.03	-0.03	-0.05	0.03	0.04	0.09 ***	0.00	-0.07 ***	0.03 ***
England (UK)	-0.01	-0.01	0.03	-0.01	0.04	0.24 ***	-0.03	-0.16 ***	0.13 ***
Northern Ireland (UK)	-0.05	-0.04	-0.01	0.04	0.05	0.16 ***	0.07	-0.08 *	0.11 ***
England/N. Ireland (UK)	-0.01	-0.01	0.03	-0.01	0.04	0.23 ***	-0.02	-0.15 ***	0.13 ***
Average¹	-0.05	0.01 ***	-0.03	0.01 ***	0.04	0.15	-0.01 ***	-0.06	0.08
Average-22²	m	m	m	m	m	m	m	m	m
Partners									
Cyprus³	m	m	m	m	m	m	m	m	m
Russian Federation⁴	-0.05	0.21 **	0.05	0.08	0.14	0.28 **	-0.15	0.16	0.10 *

1. Average of 19 participating OECD countries and entities.
2. Average of 22 OECD countries and entities: average of 19 countries with France, Italy and Spain.
3. See notes at the beginning of this Annex.
4. See note at the beginning of this Annex.
* Significant estimate p ≤ 0.10.
** Significant estimate p ≤ 0.05.
*** Significant estimate p ≤ 0.01.

Notes: The reference category for problem solving in rich-environment is Below Level 1. Version 1 adjusts for socio-demographic characteristics (age, gender, foreign-born status, years of education, marital status and years of experience). Version 2 adds literacy and numeracy proficiency to the regression of Version 1. Version 3 adds the frequency of ICT use (e-mail) at work, the two adequacy measures of computer skills for work and the frequency of complex problem solving at work as an adjustment to Version 2. Version 4 adds use of reading/writing/numeracy skills at work as an additional adjustment to Version 3. Version 5 adds occupation as an additional adjustment to Version 4.
Source: Survey of Adult Skills (PIAAC) (2012).

StatLink ⬛⬛ http://dx.doi.org/10.1787/888933232243

[Part 3/4]
Percentage differences in wages between various groups, before and after accounting for various characteristics

Table A4.16

	Version 4 (Version 3 + reading/writing/numeracy use at work)								
	No computer experience	Failed ICT core	Opted out	Level 1	Level 2/3	Frequent use of e-mail	Computer workers without computer skills to do the job well	Computer workers whose skills have affected employment	Regular users of complex problem solving
OECD	ß	ß	ß	ß	ß	ß	ß	ß	ß
National entities									
Australia	0,06	-0,07	-0,04	-0,04	-0,03	0,11 ***	-0,02	-0,05 **	0,07 ***
Austria	0,03	0,03	-0,12 **	0,00	0,04	0,08 ***	-0,02	-0,12 **	0,09 ***
Canada	-0,02	0,00	-0,06	-0,01	-0,02	0,16 ***	0,05 **	-0,06 ***	0,09 ***
Czech Republic	0,09	-0,13	-0,05	0,00	0,03	0,08 ***	-0,07	-0,04	0,03
Denmark	-0,04	0,02	-0,08 **	0,01	0,02	0,08 ***	-0,04 ***	0,00	0,06 ***
Estonia	-0,25 ***	-0,13 *	-0,06	-0,02	0,02	0,09 ***	-0,03	-0,07 **	0,09 ***
Finland	0,09	0,01	-0,02	0,03	0,05 *	0,03	-0,02	0,00	0,05 ***
France	m	m	m	m	m	m	m	m	m
Germany	-0,16 **	0,01	-0,12 *	-0,03	-0,02	0,11 ***	-0,01	-0,14 **	0,06 ***
Ireland	0,19 **	-0,03	-0,02	0,02	0,01	0,05	0,05	-0,09 ***	0,02
Italy	m	m	m	m	m	m	m	m	m
Japan	-0,16 **	-0,08	-0,09	-0,03	-0,02	0,12 ***	-0,04 *	-0,03	0,01
Korea	-0,12	-0,05	0,00	0,00	-0,07	0,17 ***	-0,01	-0,12	0,07 **
Netherlands	-0,01	0,08	-0,01	0,01	0,04	0,16 ***	0,00	-0,07 **	0,09 ***
Norway	-0,21	-0,05	-0,06	0,01	0,05	0,05 **	0,01	-0,06 **	0,04 ***
Poland	-0,04	-0,01	0,03	0,05	0,09	0,04	0,03	0,01	0,04
Slovak Republic	0,04	0,14	0,03	0,05	0,09	0,11 ***	-0,10	0,07	0,08 ***
Spain	m	m	m	m	m	m	m	m	m
Sweden	-0,14 *	0,19 **	-0,03	0,02	0,06 *	0,04	0,01	-0,09 ***	0,06 ***
United States	-0,11	0,11	-0,05	0,01	0,04	0,21 ***	-0,07	-0,04	0,09 ***
Sub-national entities									
Flanders (Belgium)	-0,17 **	-0,12 **	-0,10 *	0,01	0,01	0,05 **	0,00	-0,04	0,02
England (UK)	0,09	-0,06	-0,02	0,01	0,05	0,18 ***	-0,02	-0,17 ***	0,08 ***
Northern Ireland (UK)	-0,19 *	-0,04	-0,09	0,03	0,03	0,04	0,05	-0,06	0,09 ***
England/N. Ireland (UK)	0,08	-0,06	-0,02	0,01	0,05	0,17 ***	-0,02	-0,16 ***	0,09 ***
Average[1]	-0,04 ***	-0,01	-0,04 ***	0,00	0,02	0,10 ***	-0,02 ***	-0,06 ***	0,06 ***
Average-22[2]		m	m	m	m	m	m	m	m
Partners									
Cyprus[3]	m	m	m	m	m	m	m	m	m
Russian Federation[4]	0,05	0,10	0,07	0,03	0,07	0,28 ***	0,03	0,16	0,12

1. Average of 19 participating OECD countries and entities.
2. Average of 22 OECD countries and entities: average of 19 countries with France, Italy and Spain.
3. See notes at the beginning of this Annex.
4. See note at the beginning of this Annex.
* Significant estimate p ≤ 0.10.
** Significant estimate p ≤ 0.05.
*** Significant estimate p ≤ 0.01.

Notes: The reference category for problem solving in rich-environment is Below Level 1. Version 1 adjusts for socio-demographic characteristics (age, gender, foreign-born status, years of education, marital status and years of experience). Version 2 adds literacy and numeracy proficiency to the regression of Version 1. Version 3 adds the frequency of ICT use (e-mail) at work, the two adequacy measures of computer skills for work and the frequency of complex problem solving at work as an adjustment to Version 2. Version 4 adds use of reading/writing/numeracy skills at work as an additional adjustment to Version 3. Version 5 adds occupation as an additional adjustment to Version 4.

Source: Survey of Adult Skills (PIAAC) (2012).

StatLink http://dx.doi.org/10.1787/888933232243

[Part 4/4]

Percentage differences in wages between various groups, before and after accounting for various characteristics

Table A4.16

OECD	Version 5 (Version 4 + occupation)								
	No computer experience	Failed ICT core	Opted out	Level 1	Level 2/3	Frequent use of e-mail	Computer workers without computer skills to do the job well	Computer workers whose skills have affected employment	Regular users of complex problem solving
	ß	ß	ß	ß	ß	ß	ß	ß	ß
National entities									
Australia	0.05	-0.08	-0.03	-0.04	-0.04	0.09 ***	-0.03	-0.05 **	0.06 ***
Austria	0.02	0.04	-0.13 **	-0.01	0.04	0.08 ***	-0.02	-0.11 **	0.07 ***
Canada	-0.05	0.01	-0.05	-0.01	-0.01	0.13 ***	0.05 *	-0.06 **	0.07 ***
Czech Republic	0.07	-0.12	-0.04	-0.01	0.02	0.09 ***	-0.08	-0.03	0.01
Denmark	-0.04	0.03	-0.07 *	0.01	0.02	0.07 ***	-0.04 ***	0.00	0.05 ***
Estonia	-0.26 ***	-0.14 **	-0.07	-0.01	0.02	0.08 **	-0.04	-0.07 **	0.08 ***
Finland	0.04	0.01	-0.02	0.03	0.05	0.02	-0.03	0.00	0.03 ***
France	m	m	m	m	m	m	m	m	m
Germany	-0.17 ***	0.00	-0.12 *	-0.04	-0.03	0.11 ***	-0.01	-0.13 **	0.05 ***
Ireland	0.15 *	-0.02	-0.02	0.02	0.01	0.05	0.02	-0.08 **	0.00
Italy	m	m	m	m	m	m	m	m	m
Japan	-0.16 **	-0.07	-0.07	-0.03	-0.02	0.11 ***	-0.05 **	-0.03 *	0.00
Korea	-0.14	-0.06	-0.02	-0.01	-0.08	0.16 ***	-0.01	-0.10	0.06 *
Netherlands	-0.02	0.06	-0.02	0.00	0.03	0.15 ***	0.00	-0.08 **	0.07 ***
Norway	-0.22	-0.04	-0.05	0.02	0.05	0.03	0.01	-0.05 **	0.03 *
Poland	-0.07	-0.02	0.03	0.05	0.07	0.04	0.03	0.00	0.02
Slovak Republic	0.02	0.13	0.03	0.04	0.08	0.11 ***	-0.10 *	0.07	0.06 **
Spain	m	m	m	m	m	m	m	m	m
Sweden	-0.15 **	0.16 **	-0.04	0.02	0.04	0.00	0.00	-0.08 ***	0.04 ***
United States	-0.11	0.11	-0.03	0.00	0.03	0.19 ***	-0.07	-0.03	0.05
Sub-national entities									
Flanders (Belgium)	-0.16 **	-0.10 *	-0.09	0.01	0.01	0.05 **	0.00	-0.04	0.02
England (UK)	0.12	-0.02	0.00	0.01	0.05	0.13 ***	0.00	-0.15 ***	0.07 **
Northern Ireland (UK)	-0.18 *	-0.06	-0.12 *	0.02	0.01	0.03	0.03	-0.05	0.07 ***
England/N. Ireland (UK)	0.10	-0.02	0.00	0.01	0.05	0.12 ***	0.00	-0.15 ***	0.07 ***
Average¹	-0.06 ***	-0.01	-0.04 ***	0.00	0.02	0.09 ***	-0.02 ***	-0.05 ***	0.04 ***
Average-22²	m	m	m	m	m	m	m	m	m
Partners									
Cyprus³	m	m	m	m	m	m	m	m	m
Russian Federation⁴	0.06	0.11	0.06	0.04	0.07	0.28 ***	0.03	0.16	0.12

1. Average of 19 participating OECD countries and entities.
2. Average of 22 OECD countries and entities: average of 19 countries with France, Italy and Spain.
3. See notes at the beginning of this Annex.
4. See note at the beginning of this Annex.
* Significant estimate p ≤ 0.10.
** Significant estimate p ≤ 0.05.
*** Significant estimate p ≤ 0.01.

Notes: The reference category for problem solving in rich-environment is Below Level 1. Version 1 adjusts for socio-demographic characteristics (age, gender, foreign-born status, years of education, marital status and years of experience). Version 2 adds literacy and numeracy proficiency to the regression of Version 1. Version 3 adds the frequency of ICT use (e-mail) at work, the two adequacy measures of computer skills for work and the frequency of complex problem solving at work as an adjustment to Version 2. Version 4 adds use of reading/writing/numeracy skills at work as an additional adjustment to Version 3. Version 5 adds occupation as an additional adjustment to Version 4.
Source: Survey of Adult Skills (PIAAC) (2012).

StatLink http://dx.doi.org/10.1787/888933232243

Annex B

ADDITIONAL TABLES

All tables in Annex B are available on line.

Notes regarding Cyprus

Note by Turkey: The information in this document with reference to "Cyprus" relates to the southern part of the Island. There is no single authority representing both Turkish and Greek Cypriot people on the Island. Turkey recognises the Turkish Republic of Northern Cyprus (TRNC). Until a lasting and equitable solution is found within the context of the United Nations, Turkey shall preserve its position concerning the "Cyprus issue".

Note by all the European Union Member States of the OECD and the European Union: The Republic of Cyprus is recognised by all members of the United Nations with the exception of Turkey. The information in this document relates to the area under the effective control of the Government of the Republic of Cyprus.

A note regarding the Russian Federation

Readers should note that the sample for the Russian Federation does not include the population of the Moscow municipal area. The data published, therefore, do not represent the entire resident population aged 16-65 in Russia but rather the population of Russia *excluding* the population residing in the Moscow municipal area.

More detailed information re garding the data from the Russian Federation as well as that of other countries can be found in the *Technical Report of the Survey of Adult Skills* (OECD, 2014).

[Part 1/1]

Table B1.1 **Percentage of households with access to a computer at home (including PC, portable, handheld), 2000 to 2011**

OECD	2000	2001	2002	2003	2004	2005	2006	2007	2008	2009	2010	2011
Australia	53.0	58.0	61.0	66.0	67.0	70.0	73.0	75.0	78.0	m	82.6	m
Austria	34.0	m	49.2	50.8	58.6	63.1	67.1	70.7	75.9	74.5	76.2	78.1
Belgium	m	m	m	m	m	m	57.5	67.2	70.0	71.1	76.7	78.9
Canada	55.2	59.8	64.1	66.6	68.7	72.0	75.4	78.4	79.4	81.7	82.7	m
Chile	17.9	m	m	25.5	m	m	34.5	m	m	43.9	m	m
Czech Republic	m	m	m	23.8	29.5	30.0	39.0	43.4	52.4	59.6	64.1	69.9
Denmark	65.0	69.6	72.2	78.5	79.3	83.8	85.0	83.0	85.5	86.2	88.0	90.4
Estonia	m	m	m	m	36.0	43.0	52.4	57.2	59.6	65.1	69.2	71.4
Finland	47.0	52.9	54.5	57.4	57.0	64.0	71.1	74.0	75.8	80.1	82.0	85.1
France	27.0	32.4	36.6	45.7	49.8	m	m	65.6	68.4	74.2	76.5	78.2
Germany	47.3	53.0	61.0	65.2	68.7	69.9	76.9	78.6	81.8	84.1	85.7	86.9
Greece	m	m	25.3	28.7	29.0	32.6	36.7	40.2	44.0	47.3	53.4	57.2
Hungary	m	m	m	m	31.9	42.3	49.6	53.5	58.8	63.0	66.4	69.7
Iceland	m	m	m	m	85.7	89.3	84.6	89.1	91.9	92.5	93.1	94.7
Ireland	32.4	m	m	42.2	46.3	54.9	58.6	65.5	70.3	72.8	76.5	80.6
Israel	47.1	49.8	53.8	54.6	59.2	62.4	65.8	68.9	71.0	74.4	76.7	m
Italy	29.4	m	39.9	47.7	47.4	45.7	51.6	53.4	56.0	61.3	64.8	66.2
Japan	50.5	58.0	71.7	78.2	77.5	80.5	80.8	85.0	85.9	87.2	83.4	77.4
Korea	71.0	76.9	78.6	77.9	77.8	78.9	79.6	80.4	80.9	81.4	81.8	81.9
Luxembourg	m	m	52.6	58.0	67.3	74.5	77.3	80.0	82.8	87.9	90.2	91.7
Mexico	m	11.8	15.2	m	18.0	18.6	20.6	22.1	25.7	26.8	29.9	30.0
Netherlands	m	m	69.0	70.8	74.0	77.9	80.0	86.3	87.7	90.8	92.0	94.2
New Zealand	m	46.6	m	62.0	m	m	72.0	m	m	80.0	m	m
Norway	m	m	m	71.2	71.5	74.2	75.4	82.4	85.8	87.6	90.9	91.0
Poland	m	m	m	m	36.1	40.1	45.4	53.7	58.9	66.1	69.0	71.3
Portugal	27.0	39.0	26.8	38.3	41.3	42.5	45.6	48.3	49.8	56.0	59.5	63.7
Slovak Republic	m	m	m	m	38.5	46.7	50.1	55.4	63.2	64.0	72.2	75.4
Slovenia	m	m	m	m	58.0	61.0	65.3	66.0	65.1	71.2	70.5	74.4
Spain	30.4	m	m	47.1	52.1	54.6	57.2	60.4	63.6	66.3	68.7	71.5
Sweden	59.9	69.2	m	m	m	79.7	82.5	82.9	87.1	87.6	89.5	91.6
Switzerland	57.7	62.2	65.4	68.9	70.6	76.5	77.4	79.2	81.4	82.5	m	m
Turkey	m	m	m	m	10.2	12.2	m	27.3	33.4	37.4	44.2	m
United Kingdom	38.0	49.0	57.9	63.2	65.3	70.0	71.5	75.4	78.0	81.2	82.6	84.6
United States	51.0	56.2	m	61.8	m	m	m	m	m	m	77.0	m
OECD average	45.7	52.8	53.0	57.6	54.2	59.0	64.2	66.1	69.3	71.4	74.7	77.2

Partners

	2000	2001	2002	2003	2004	2005	2006	2007	2008	2009	2010	2011
Brazil	m	12.6	14.2	15.3	16.3	18.5	22.1	26.5	31.2	32.3	34.9	45.4
China	m	m	10.2	14.3	20.0	25.0	27.0	29.0	31.8	34.4	35.4	38.0
India	m	m	0.3	1.0	1.5	2.0	3.0	3.7	4.4	5.3	6.1	6.9
Indonesia	m	m	2.5	3.0	2.8	3.7	4.4	5.9	8.3	10.2	10.8	12.0
Russian Federation	m	m	7.0	11.0	13.0	14.0	15.1	35.0	43.0	49.0	55.0	57.1
South Africa	m	8.6	9.9	11.0	12.0	13.0	13.9	14.8	15.9	17.1	18.3	19.5

Source: OECD, ICT database; Eurostat, Community Survey on ICT usage in households and by individuals, June 2012; and for non-OECD countries: International Telecommunication Union (ITU), World Telecommunication/ICT Indicators 2012 database, June 2012.

StatLink ⏴⏵ http://dx.doi.org/10.1787/888933232257

[Part 1/1]

Table B1.2 Percentage of households with access to the Internet, 2000-2011

OECD	2000	2001	2002	2003	2004	2005	2006	2007	2008	2009	2010	2011
Australia	32.0	42.0	46.0	53.0	56.0	60.0	64.0	67.0	72.0	m	78.9	m
Austria	19.0	m	33.5	37.4	44.6	46.7	52.3	59.6	68.9	69.8	72.9	75.4
Belgium	m	m	m	m	m	50.2	54.0	60.2	63.6	67.4	72.7	76.5
Canada	42.6	49.9	54.5	56.9	59.8	64.3	68.1	72.7	74.6	77.8	78.4	m
Chile	8.7	m	m	12.8	m	m	19.7	m	m	30.0	m	m
Czech Republic	m	m	m	14.8	19.4	19.1	29.3	35.1	45.9	54.2	60.5	66.6
Denmark	46.0	59.0	55.6	64.2	69.4	74.9	78.7	78.1	81.9	82.5	86.1	90.1
Estonia	m	m	m	m	30.8	38.7	45.6	52.9	58.1	63.0	67.8	70.8
Finland	30.0	39.5	44.3	47.4	50.9	54.1	64.7	68.8	72.4	77.8	80.5	84.2
France	11.9	18.1	23.0	31.0	33.6	m	40.9	55.1	62.3	68.9	73.6	75.9
Germany	16.4	36.0	46.1	54.1	60.0	61.6	67.1	70.7	74.9	79.1	82.5	83.3
Greece	m	m	12.2	16.3	16.5	21.7	23.1	25.4	31.0	38.1	46.4	50.2
Hungary	m	m	m	m	14.2	22.1	32.3	38.4	48.4	55.1	60.5	65.2
Iceland	m	m	m	m	80.6	84.4	83.0	83.7	87.7	89.6	92.0	92.6
Ireland	20.4	m	m	35.6	39.7	47.2	50.0	57.3	63.0	66.7	71.7	78.1
Israel	19.8	22.5	25.4	30.8	40.7	48.9	54.6	59.3	61.8	66.3	68.1	m
Italy	18.8	m	33.7	32.1	34.1	38.6	40.0	43.4	46.9	53.5	59.0	61.6
Japan	m	m	48.8	53.6	55.8	57.0	60.5	62.1	63.9	67.1	m	m
Korea	49.8	63.2	70.2	68.8	86.0	92.7	94.0	94.1	94.3	95.9	96.8	97.2
Luxembourg	m	m	39.9	45.4	58.6	64.6	70.2	74.6	80.1	87.2	90.3	90.6
Mexico	m	6.2	7.5	m	8.7	9.0	10.1	12.0	13.5	18.4	22.3	23.3
Netherlands	41.0	m	58.0	60.5	65.0	78.3	80.3	82.9	86.1	89.7	90.9	93.6
New Zealand	m	37.4	m	m	m	m	65.0	m	m	75.0	m	m
Norway	m	m	m	60.5	60.1	64.0	68.8	77.6	84.0	85.6	89.8	92.2
Poland	m	m	11.0	14.0	26.0	30.4	35.9	41.0	47.6	58.6	63.4	66.6
Portugal	8.0	18.0	15.1	21.7	26.2	31.5	35.2	39.6	46.0	47.9	53.7	58.0
Slovak Republic	m	m	m	m	23.3	23.0	26.6	46.1	58.3	62.2	67.5	70.8
Slovenia	m	m	m	m	46.9	48.2	54.4	57.6	58.9	63.9	68.1	72.6
Spain	m	m	m	27.5	33.6	35.5	39.1	44.6	51.0	54.0	59.1	63.9
Sweden	48.2	53.3	m	m	m	72.5	77.4	78.5	84.4	86.0	88.3	90.6
Switzerland	m	m	m	m	61.0	m	70.5	73.9	77.0	79.4	85.0	m
Turkey	6.9	m	m	m	7.0	7.7	m	19.7	25.4	30.0	41.6	m
United Kingdom	19.0	40.0	49.7	55.1	55.9	60.2	62.6	66.7	71.1	76.7	79.6	82.7
United States	41.5	50.3	m	54.6	m	m	m	61.7	m	68.7	71.1	m
OECD average	27.7	38.2	37.5	42.5	43.6	48.5	54.8	58.1	63.1	66.2	71.6	74.9

Partners	2000	2001	2002	2003	2004	2005	2006	2007	2008	2009	2010	2011
Brazil	m	8.6	10.3	11.5	12.4	13.6	16.8	20.0	23.8	23.9	27.1	37.8
China	m	m	5.0	7.0	9.0	11.0	13.4	16.4	18.3	20.3	23.7	30.9
India	m	m	0.2	0.7	1.4	1.6	2.9	3.0	3.4	3.5	4.2	6.0
Indonesia	m	m	m	m	m	1.0	1.2	1.3	1.9	2.7	4.6	7.0
Russian Federation	m	m	3.5	5.0	6.0	7.0	8.2	25.0	29.0	36.0	41.3	46.0
South Africa	m	m	1.9	2.1	2.5	3.0	3.6	4.8	6.5	8.8	10.1	9.8

Source: OECD, ICT database; Eurostat, Community Survey on ICT usage in households and by individuals, June 2012; and for non-OECD countries: International Telecommunication Union (ITU), World Telecommunication/ICT Indicators 2012 database, June 2012.

StatLink ⟨⟩ http://dx.doi.org/10.1787/888933232265

[Part 1/1]
Table B1.3 **Percentage of individuals aged 16-74 using any handheld device to access the Internet**

OECD	2012
Austria	36
Belgium	30
Czech Republic	14
Denmark	51
Estonia	18
Finland	45
France	33
Germany	24
Greece	16
Hungary	12
Iceland	44
Ireland	29
Italy	12
Luxembourg	48
Netherlands	44
Norway	58
Poland	15
Portugal	13
Slovak Republic	27
Slovenia	22
Spain	31
Sweden	60
United Kingdom	57
Average	32

Source: Eurostat, Community Survey on ICT usage in households and by individuals.
StatLink http://dx.doi.org/10.1787/888933232272

[Part 1/1]
Table B1.4 **Percentage of Individuals using the Internet in middle income and developing countries**

	2013
Albania	60
Argentina	60
Bahrain	90
Bermuda	95
Bhutan	30
Brazil	52
Canada	86
China	46
Costa Rica	46
Egypt	50
India	15
Indonesia	16
Jordan	44
Kazakhstan	54
Lebanon	71
Malaysia	67
Morocco	56
Nigeria	38
Qatar	85
Romania	50
Russian Federation	61
Saudi Arabia	61
South Africa	49
Tunisia	44
Ukraine	42
United Arab Emirates	88

Source: International Telecommunication Union (ITU) estimate.
StatLink http://dx.doi.org/10.1787/888933232286

[Part 1/1]
Table B1.5 Percentage of individuals aged 16-74 using online banking

OECD	2005	2013	2014
Austria	22	49	48
Belgium	23	58	61
Czech Republic	5	41	46
Denmark	49	82	84
Estonia	45	72	77
Finland	56	84	86
France[1]	19	58	58
Germany[1]	32	47	49
Greece	1	11	13
Hungary	6	26	30
Iceland	61	87	91
Ireland	13	46	48
Italy	8	22	26
Luxembourg	37	63	67
Netherlands	50	82	83
Norway	62	87	89
Poland	6	32	33
Portugal	8	23	25
Slovak Republic	10	39	41
Slovenia	12	32	32
Spain	14	33	37
Sweden	51	82	82
Turkey	2	11	m
United Kingdom	27	54	57
Average	26	51	55

1. Year of reference 2006.
Notes: Within the three months prior to the survey. Internet banking includes electronic transactions with a bank for payment etc. or for looking up account information.
Source: Eurostat, Community Survey on ICT usage in households and by individuals.
StatLink ᴍ⃝ http://dx.doi.org/10.1787/888933232290

[Part 1/1]
Table B1.6 Percentage of individuals aged 16-74 using the Internet for sending and/or receiving e-mails

OECD	2005	2013	2014
Austria	48	74	73
Belgium	49	76	77
Czech Republic	27	70	74
Denmark	69	88	90
Estonia	49	67	72
Finland	63	83	86
France[1]	34	74	73
Germany[1]	60	78	80
Greece	14	46	50
Hungary	31	69	71
Iceland	75	93	93
Ireland	31	67	67
Italy	26	51	53
Luxembourg	63	88	89
Netherlands	73	90	90
Norway	68	88	90
Poland	24	51	53
Portugal	26	53	54
Slovak Republic	42	71	69
Slovenia	36	63	62
Spain	34	62	64
Sweden	67	87	86
Switzerland	m	m	84
Turkey	9	27	m
United Kingdom	57	79	80
Average	45	71	74

1. Year of reference 2006.
Notes: Within the three months prior to the survey.
Source: Eurostat, Community Survey on ICT usage in households and by individuals.
StatLink ᴍ⃝ http://dx.doi.org/10.1787/888933232303

 ADULTS, COMPUTERS AND PROBLEM SOLVING: WHAT'S THE PROBLEM?

[Part 1/1]

Table B1.7 **Percentage of enterprises (with at least 10 employees) sending and/or receiving e-invoices**

OECD	2007	2008	2009	2010
Austria	18	17	12	18
Belgium	31	36	39	39
Czech Republic	33	17	18	17
Denmark	37	43	38	39
Estonia	25	39	40	39
Finland	27	25	24	36
France	10	20	21	36
Germany	19	27	31	36
Greece	10	15	11	16
Hungary	4	5	6	8
Iceland	m	20	m	25
Ireland	26	22	21	28
Italy	34	29	34	56
Luxembourg	23	24	20	37
Netherlands	11	29	34	35
Norway	29	31	31	47
Poland	8	11	12	16
Portugal	14	24	23	27
Slovak Republic	14	23	30	34
Slovenia	7	8	9	10
Spain	9	12	17	25
Sweden	18	17	25	28
Turkey	5	m	m	13
United Kingdom	15	11	8	11
Average	19	22	23	28

Source: Eurostat, Community Survey on ICT usage in households and by individuals.

StatLink ╓═╖ http://dx.doi.org/10.1787/888933232312

[Part 1/3]

Table B2.1 **Percentage of adults who opted out of taking the computer-based assessment by various characteristics**

	Age										Education					
	16-24 year-olds		25-34 year-olds		35-44 year-olds		45-54 year-olds		55-65 year-olds		Lower than upper secondary		Upper secondary		Tertiary	
OECD	%	S.E.	%	S.E.	%	S.E.	%	S.E.	%	S.E.	%	S.E.	%	S.E.	%	S.E.
National entities																
Australia	6.9	(1.1)	9.5	(1.1)	13.5	(1.2)	16.8	(1.1)	22.3	(1.5)	21.9	(1.3)	13.9	(0.9)	7.4	(0.7)
Austria	4.6	(0.8)	7.8	(1.1)	10.5	(1.0)	14.4	(1.0)	17.3	(1.2)	15.6	(1.2)	11.3	(0.6)	6.6	(0.8)
Canada	1.9	(0.3)	3.0	(0.4)	6.0	(0.6)	8.1	(0.6)	11.5	(0.7)	10.6	(0.9)	7.2	(0.4)	4.3	(0.3)
Czech Republic	4.0	(0.9)	6.0	(0.9)	11.4	(1.5)	19.5	(2.7)	18.5	(1.7)	13.5	(1.7)	13.3	(1.0)	6.5	(1.4)
Denmark	2.5	(0.5)	3.7	(0.5)	4.3	(0.6)	7.3	(0.7)	12.7	(0.8)	11.7	(0.8)	5.9	(0.6)	2.8	(0.3)
Estonia	3.7	(0.5)	8.2	(0.7)	14.6	(0.9)	23.2	(1.1)	28.5	(1.1)	12.4	(0.8)	18.6	(0.6)	14.2	(0.7)
Finland	1.8	(0.5)	1.6	(0.4)	4.7	(0.8)	10.9	(0.9)	24.2	(1.3)	14.8	(1.1)	12.4	(0.7)	3.8	(0.4)
France	3.9	(0.5)	8.4	(0.7)	10.8	(0.8)	15.2	(1.0)	17.7	(1.0)	16.1	(0.8)	11.7	(0.6)	6.8	(0.6)
Germany	1.3	(0.4)	3.2	(0.8)	6.3	(0.9)	7.9	(1.0)	9.9	(1.1)	7.0	(1.1)	6.9	(0.7)	4.4	(0.6)
Ireland	7.2	(1.1)	12.0	(1.2)	16.7	(1.1)	24.6	(1.6)	29.1	(1.7)	25.5	(1.2)	19.0	(1.1)	8.4	(0.6)
Italy	6.3	(1.4)	11.7	(1.4)	16.7	(1.2)	18.2	(1.5)	17.0	(1.7)	16.2	(1.1)	15.0	(1.1)	7.6	(1.2)
Japan	12.9	(1.6)	12.3	(1.5)	13.9	(1.4)	16.1	(1.3)	22.2	(1.5)	17.4	(1.6)	20.1	(1.3)	11.5	(0.9)
Korea	0.8	(0.3)	1.6	(0.3)	4.2	(0.5)	9.4	(0.8)	10.6	(0.9)	8.0	(0.7)	6.8	(0.5)	2.1	(0.3)
Netherlands	1.6	(0.5)	1.8	(0.5)	3.0	(0.5)	5.8	(0.7)	9.0	(0.9)	8.2	(0.7)	3.7	(0.4)	2.1	(0.4)
Norway	1.1	(0.4)	2.9	(0.6)	5.6	(0.6)	6.5	(0.8)	17.0	(1.4)	12.0	(0.9)	7.0	(0.5)	2.5	(0.4)
Poland	12.4	(0.7)	19.3	(1.3)	28.1	(1.6)	30.3	(1.8)	28.5	(1.4)	14.7	(1.2)	28.3	(0.9)	18.8	(1.1)
Slovak Republic	6.9	(0.7)	9.9	(0.8)	10.8	(0.9)	14.6	(1.2)	18.6	(1.3)	9.1	(0.8)	14.4	(0.6)	8.6	(1.0)
Spain	3.5	(0.6)	7.7	(0.8)	11.1	(0.9)	12.6	(0.9)	15.4	(1.3)	13.2	(0.7)	11.6	(1.0)	6.1	(0.6)
Sweden	0.7	(0.3)	2.0	(0.6)	4.3	(0.8)	7.0	(1.0)	13.0	(1.0)	10.3	(1.1)	4.9	(0.5)	2.9	(0.4)
United States	3.0	(0.7)	4.7	(0.9)	5.0	(0.7)	7.0	(0.9)	12.0	(1.2)	11.9	(1.4)	8.2	(1.0)	2.2	(0.4)
Sub-national entities																
Flanders (Belgium)	1.8	(0.4)	2.2	(0.5)	3.4	(0.5)	5.5	(0.7)	8.9	(0.8)	7.8	(0.8)	5.5	(0.5)	2.6	(0.4)
England (UK)	0.8	(0.4)	2.5	(0.5)	3.7	(0.6)	6.3	(0.9)	9.4	(1.1)	8.0	(0.9)	3.8	(0.6)	3.0	(0.5)
Northern Ireland (UK)	0.3	(0.3)	1.5	(0.5)	1.9	(0.5)	2.1	(0.6)	6.1	(1.2)	4.4	(0.6)	1.7	(0.4)	0.6	(0.2)
England/N. Ireland (UK)	0.8	(0.4)	2.4	(0.5)	3.6	(0.6)	6.1	(0.9)	9.3	(1.0)	7.9	(0.9)	3.7	(0.5)	3.0	(0.4)
Average[1]	4.0	(0.2)	6.0	(0.2)	8.9	(0.2)	12.7	(0.3)	17.0	(0.3)	12.6	(0.3)	11.1	(0.2)	6.0	(0.2)
Average-22[2]	4.1	(0.2)	6.5	(0.2)	9.5	(0.2)	13.1	(0.3)	17.0	(0.3)	13.0	(0.2)	11.3	(0.2)	6.1	(0.2)
Partners																
Cyprus[3]	12.8	(1.5)	15.4	(1.2)	20.3	(1.3)	22.7	(1.4)	19.5	(1.5)	7.8	(0.8)	21.9	(1.0)	20.8	(1.0)
Russian Federation[4]	6.6	(1.3)	12.5	(1.7)	14.6	(2.9)	13.6	(1.9)	16.2	(2.1)	3.2	(1.0)	11.3	(1.5)	14.7	(2.3)

1. Average of 19 participating OECD countries and entities.
2. Average of 22 OECD countries and entities: average of 19 countries with France, Italy and Spain.
3. See notes at the beginning of this Annex.
4. See notes at the beginning of this Annex.
Source: Survey of Adult Skills (PIAAC) (2012).
StatLink ᵐᵃᵖ http://dx.doi.org/10.1787/888933232321

[Part 2/3]

Table B2.1 Percentage of adults who opted out of taking the computer-based assessment by various characteristics

OECD	Gender				Parents' Education						Immigrant and language background							
	Men		Women		Neither parent attained upper secondary		At least one parent attained upper secondary		At least one parent attained tertiary		Native-born and native language		Native-born and foreign language		Foreign-born and native language		Foreign-born and foreign language	
	%	S.E.	%	S.E.	%	S.E.	%	S.E.	%	S.E.	%	S.E.	%	S.E.	%	S.E.	%	S.E.
National entities																		
Australia	13.1	(0.8)	14.3	(0.7)	18.6	(0.9)	12.1	(1.1)	7.1	(0.8)	13.7	(0.7)	12.3	(2.8)	12.6	(1.3)	17.1	(1.6)
Austria	9.9	(0.6)	12.5	(0.7)	16.4	(1.2)	10.3	(0.7)	7.5	(1.0)	10.9	(0.5)	9.6	(3.3)	9.4	(2.5)	16.2	(1.9)
Canada	6.0	(0.4)	6.6	(0.3)	11.2	(0.7)	6.2	(0.5)	3.1	(0.2)	5.5	(0.3)	5.6	(0.8)	8.0	(1.2)	9.1	(0.8)
Czech Republic	10.4	(0.9)	13.8	(1.1)	20.6	(3.0)	11.6	(0.9)	5.8	(1.3)	12.0	(0.9)	c	c	7.8	(4.7)	18.5	(6.3)
Denmark	6.5	(0.4)	6.3	(0.4)	9.9	(0.6)	6.7	(0.5)	2.6	(0.4)	5.6	(0.3)	6.0	(3.1)	2.3	(0.9)	13.8	(1.0)
Estonia	14.4	(0.5)	17.1	(0.6)	24.8	(1.1)	14.4	(0.7)	9.5	(0.7)	14.7	(0.5)	19.5	(2.4)	23.1	(1.6)	21.7	(3.9)
Finland	9.4	(0.6)	10.0	(0.6)	17.3	(0.8)	5.8	(0.5)	2.1	(0.4)	9.8	(0.4)	4.1	(2.0)	2.8	(2.7)	18.0	(4.1)
France	11.4	(0.5)	11.8	(0.6)	16.0	(0.7)	7.5	(0.6)	7.1	(0.7)	10.5	(0.4)	9.5	(2.3)	21.0	(1.9)	18.9	(1.8)
Germany	4.9	(0.5)	7.3	(0.7)	10.7	(2.0)	6.0	(0.6)	4.0	(0.7)	5.5	(0.5)	3.6	(2.3)	8.0	(2.4)	11.2	(1.8)
Ireland	17.1	(0.8)	17.7	(0.9)	24.1	(1.0)	12.1	(1.1)	8.6	(0.9)	17.3	(0.7)	41.7	(7.9)	14.3	(1.5)	20.5	(2.7)
Italy	14.6	(1.0)	14.6	(1.1)	16.7	(1.0)	10.8	(1.4)	7.1	(1.9)	14.0	(0.9)	22.9	(6.7)	9.3	(3.9)	22.8	(3.1)
Japan	13.2	(0.9)	18.7	(1.2)	19.0	(1.3)	17.1	(1.3)	12.8	(1.2)	16.2	(0.9)	c	c	c	c	c	c
Korea	5.5	(0.4)	5.3	(0.4)	7.8	(0.5)	2.9	(0.5)	2.4	(0.4)	5.2	(0.3)	c	c	7.3	(3.6)	18.9	(6.7)
Netherlands	3.8	(0.4)	5.2	(0.4)	6.2	(0.5)	3.4	(0.5)	2.1	(0.4)	3.7	(0.3)	3.8	(2.9)	5.4	(1.9)	12.2	(1.6)
Norway	5.9	(0.5)	7.5	(0.6)	14.1	(1.0)	5.4	(0.6)	2.4	(0.4)	6.6	(0.4)	8.2	(4.2)	5.1	(2.9)	8.6	(1.2)
Poland	21.5	(0.8)	26.0	(0.9)	26.8	(1.3)	24.4	(0.8)	14.7	(1.3)	23.7	(0.7)	29.1	(5.8)	c	c	c	c
Slovak Republic	11.5	(0.7)	12.9	(0.6)	13.6	(0.8)	12.3	(0.7)	8.5	(1.0)	11.9	(0.4)	16.8	(2.2)	17.1	(4.8)	11.4	(4.8)
Spain	9.4	(0.6)	11.9	(0.8)	12.0	(0.7)	7.8	(1.3)	6.7	(1.0)	10.5	(0.6)	13.4	(3.0)	11.8	(1.8)	11.6	(2.1)
Sweden	5.2	(0.5)	6.2	(0.5)	9.5	(0.8)	3.4	(0.7)	2.2	(0.4)	5.1	(0.4)	3.6	(2.1)	2.8	(2.2)	9.4	(1.1)
United States	6.3	(0.8)	6.4	(0.6)	13.8	(1.6)	6.2	(0.8)	3.4	(0.7)	6.2	(0.7)	5.9	(2.4)	4.3	(1.4)	10.6	(1.2)
Sub-national entities																		
Flanders (Belgium)	4.7	(0.5)	4.7	(0.4)	8.1	(0.6)	2.8	(0.4)	2.2	(0.4)	4.5	(0.3)	9.6	(2.3)	5.9	(1.9)	11.7	(2.4)
England (UK)	4.1	(0.5)	5.0	(0.6)	8.1	(1.0)	3.5	(0.5)	2.2	(0.5)	4.4	(0.4)	3.6	(2.4)	5.2	(1.5)	6.2	(1.5)
Northern Ireland (UK)	2.1	(0.4)	2.5	(0.4)	3.8	(0.6)	1.6	(0.4)	0.6	(0.4)	2.4	(0.3)	c	c	2.0	(1.4)	0.8	(0.8)
England/N. Ireland (UK)	4.1	(0.5)	4.9	(0.5)	7.8	(1.0)	3.4	(0.5)	2.2	(0.5)	4.4	(0.4)	3.6	(2.4)	5.1	(1.5)	6.1	(1.5)
Average[1]	9.1	(0.1)	10.7	(0.2)	14.7	(0.3)	8.8	(0.2)	5.4	(0.2)	9.6	(0.1)	11.4	(0.9)	8.3	(0.6)	13.8	(0.8)
Average-22[2]	9.5	(0.1)	11.0	(0.2)	14.8	(0.3)	8.8	(0.2)	5.6	(0.2)	9.9	(0.1)	12.0	(0.8)	9.2	(0.6)	14.4	(0.7)
Partners																		
Cyprus[3]	17.5	(0.8)	18.5	(0.8)	24.6	(1.0)	19.8	(1.2)	16.6	(1.3)	21.4	(0.6)	c	c	23.3	(2.9)	28.2	(4.1)
Russian Federation[4]	10.8	(1.7)	14.6	(2.4)	17.3	(2.2)	10.8	(1.7)	12.1	(2.1)	m	m	m	m	m	m	m	m

1. Average of 19 participating OECD countries and entities.
2. Average of 22 OECD countries and entities: average of 19 countries with France, Italy and Spain.
3. See notes at the beginning of this Annex.
4. See note at the beginning of this Annex.
Notes: Results for the Russian Federation are missing as no language variables are available for the Russian Federation.
Source: Survey of Adult Skills (PIAAC) (2012).

StatLink ⟪⟫ http://dx.doi.org/10.1787/888933232321

[Part 3/3]

Table B2.1   **Percentage of adults who opted out of taking the computer-based assessment by various characteristics**

	Participation in adult education				E-mail use				Literacy proficiency							
	Did not participate in AET		Did participate in AET		Low frequency of e-mail use (less than monthly or no use)		High frequency of e-mail use (at least monthly use)		At or below Level 1		Level 2		Level 3		Level 4/5	
OECD	%	S.E.	%	S.E.	%	S.E.	%	S.E.	%	S.E.	%	S.E.	%	S.E.	%	S.E.
National entities																
Australia	21.4	(1.0)	9.9	(0.7)	31.4	(1.5)	8.9	(0.6)	22.7	(2.3)	15.9	(1.3)	11.9	(0.9)	9.0	(1.2)
Austria	15.6	(0.8)	9.0	(0.7)	24.7	(1.1)	5.8	(0.4)	14.5	(1.6)	14.3	(0.9)	8.5	(0.8)	6.3	(1.6)
Canada	10.8	(0.5)	4.3	(0.3)	18.1	(0.8)	3.5	(0.2)	9.6	(0.9)	7.0	(0.5)	5.2	(0.5)	4.2	(0.7)
Czech Republic	16.7	(1.1)	9.8	(1.1)	23.2	(2.0)	8.1	(0.9)	9.4	(1.8)	13.1	(1.4)	12.3	(1.3)	10.8	(3.2)
Denmark	12.8	(0.7)	4.2	(0.3)	23.4	(1.4)	3.6	(0.2)	15.1	(1.2)	7.6	(0.7)	3.2	(0.4)	1.1	(0.6)
Estonia	22.1	(0.8)	13.7	(0.6)	31.7	(1.1)	10.7	(0.4)	11.7	(1.3)	15.8	(0.9)	17.0	(0.8)	16.5	(1.6)
Finland	20.0	(1.0)	6.1	(0.4)	31.0	(1.6)	5.0	(0.4)	15.5	(1.8)	13.4	(1.1)	11.0	(0.7)	4.8	(0.8)
France	15.5	(0.6)	8.0	(0.6)	22.5	(1.0)	7.5	(0.4)	11.1	(1.0)	12.2	(0.8)	11.0	(0.7)	14.0	(1.7)
Germany	9.5	(0.9)	4.3	(0.5)	16.7	(1.4)	2.4	(0.3)	8.2	(1.4)	7.6	(0.9)	4.8	(0.7)	2.9	(1.1)
Ireland	24.1	(1.0)	15.1	(1.0)	30.9	(1.1)	10.7	(0.8)	17.8	(1.8)	19.8	(1.3)	16.5	(1.0)	11.2	(1.9)
Italy	16.8	(1.1)	12.7	(1.3)	21.7	(1.3)	8.8	(0.9)	11.5	(1.4)	16.6	(1.2)	15.1	(1.5)	15.3	(3.9)
Japan	20.2	(1.2)	11.7	(1.0)	23.5	(1.3)	10.8	(1.0)	12.9	(2.8)	18.6	(1.6)	16.8	(1.1)	12.7	(1.4)
Korea	8.1	(0.6)	4.1	(0.4)	9.1	(0.6)	2.7	(0.3)	5.3	(1.0)	6.9	(0.6)	4.7	(0.5)	2.6	(1.0)
Netherlands	8.3	(0.8)	3.1	(0.3)	18.6	(1.8)	2.9	(0.2)	10.8	(1.4)	5.8	(0.9)	3.1	(0.4)	2.3	(0.6)
Norway	14.9	(1.0)	3.7	(0.4)	26.7	(1.7)	3.8	(0.3)	11.5	(1.6)	8.7	(0.8)	5.3	(0.6)	3.1	(1.0)
Poland	29.3	(0.8)	19.4	(1.2)	31.5	(1.0)	18.1	(0.9)	20.6	(1.6)	24.8	(1.4)	23.3	(1.2)	27.8	(3.1)
Slovak Republic	14.8	(0.7)	10.1	(0.8)	19.0	(0.9)	8.0	(0.5)	7.4	(1.3)	12.9	(0.8)	13.2	(0.8)	10.6	(2.4)
Spain	13.9	(0.9)	8.4	(0.6)	17.8	(1.1)	6.2	(0.5)	9.0	(1.0)	12.2	(0.9)	10.7	(1.1)	9.4	(2.9)
Sweden	11.4	(0.8)	3.7	(0.4)	23.4	(1.7)	2.4	(0.3)	14.0	(1.7)	7.7	(1.0)	3.4	(0.5)	0.9	(0.4)
United States	11.3	(1.0)	4.5	(0.7)	17.8	(1.5)	2.7	(0.4)	10.3	(1.4)	8.7	(1.0)	4.5	(0.7)	1.4	(0.6)
Sub-national entities																
Flanders (Belgium)	7.9	(0.6)	2.7	(0.4)	13.7	(1.1)	2.8	(0.3)	6.7	(1.2)	5.9	(0.8)	4.4	(0.5)	2.2	(0.7)
England (UK)	6.7	(0.7)	3.8	(0.5)	13.8	(1.3)	2.1	(0.3)	5.3	(1.0)	5.1	(0.7)	4.1	(0.6)	3.9	(1.1)
Northern Ireland (UK)	3.6	(0.5)	1.5	(0.3)	5.3	(0.7)	0.7	(0.2)	2.9	(0.8)	2.8	(0.6)	1.8	(0.6)	1.4	(1.0)
England/N. Ireland (UK)	6.6	(0.6)	3.8	(0.5)	13.4	(1.2)	2.0	(0.3)	5.2	(1.0)	5.0	(0.7)	4.1	(0.6)	3.8	(1.0)
Average[1]	15.0	(0.2)	7.5	(0.2)	22.5	(0.3)	6.1	(0.1)	12.1	(0.4)	11.5	(0.2)	9.0	(0.2)	7.1	(0.4)
Average-22[2]	15.1	(0.2)	7.8	(0.2)	22.3	(0.3)	6.2	(0.1)	11.9	(0.3)	11.8	(0.2)	9.4	(0.2)	7.9	(0.4)
Partners																
Cyprus[3]	23.3	(1.0)	23.9	(1.1)	24.9	(1.0)	18.8	(0.9)	11.3	(1.9)	17.2	(1.2)	26.4	(1.2)	47.1	(4.0)
Russian Federation[4]	14.0	(1.7)	12.3	(3.4)	16.1	(1.8)	8.5	(1.7)	9.3	(3.3)	11.6	(1.8)	14.4	(2.5)	14.6	(3.8)

1. Average of 19 participating OECD countries and entities.
2. Average of 22 OECD countries and entities: average of 19 countries with France, Italy and Spain.
3. See notes at the beginning of this Annex.
4. See note at the beginning of this Annex.
Source: Survey of Adult Skills (PIAAC) (2012).

StatLink 🔗 http://dx.doi.org/10.1787/888933232321

[Part 1/1]

Table B2.2 Percentage of individuals aged 16-74 using the Internet for seeking health-related information

OECD	2005	2013
Austria	16	49
Belgium	19	43
Czech Republic	3	41
Denmark	24	54
Estonia	16	39
Finland	39	60
France[1]	13	49
Germany[1]	34	58
Greece	2	34
Hungary	10	49
Iceland	39	65
Ireland	10	38
Italy	9	32
Luxembourg	41	58
Netherlands	41	57
Norway	26	54
Poland	7	27
Portugal	10	42
Slovak Republic	9	44
Slovenia	15	50
Spain	13	44
Sweden	23	56
Turkey	3	26
United Kingdom	25	45
Average	19	46

1. Year of reference 2006.

Note: Within the 3 months prior to the Eurostat Community Survey.

Source: Eurostat, Community Survey on ICT usage in households and by individuals.

StatLink http://dx.doi.org/10.1787/888933232336

[Part 1/3]

Table B3.1 **Likelihood of adults scoring at Level 2 or 3 in problem solving in technology-rich environments, by socio-demographic characteristics (Version 1)**

| OECD | Age (reference 55-65 year-olds) | | | | | | | | | | | |
| | 16-24 year-olds | | | 25-34 year-olds | | | 35-44 year-olds | | | 45-54 year-olds | | |
	ß	S.E.	p-value	ß	S.E.	p-value	ß	S.E.	p-value	ß	S.E.	p-value
National entities												
Australia	0.9	(0.2)	0.000	1.1	(0.1)	0.000	0.9	(0.1)	0.000	0.6	(0.2)	0.000
Austria	2.1	(0.2)	0.000	2.3	(0.2)	0.000	1.8	(0.2)	0.000	1.1	(0.2)	0.000
Canada	1.0	(0.2)	0.000	1.2	(0.1)	0.000	1.0	(0.1)	0.000	0.5	(0.1)	0.000
Czech Republic	1.4	(0.3)	0.000	1.7	(0.2)	0.000	0.9	(0.2)	0.000	0.3	(0.2)	0.246
Denmark	1.7	(0.2)	0.000	2.1	(0.1)	0.000	1.7	(0.1)	0.000	1.0	(0.1)	0.000
Estonia	2.3	(0.2)	0.000	2.2	(0.2)	0.000	1.5	(0.2)	0.000	0.8	(0.2)	0.000
Finland	2.7	(0.2)	0.000	2.8	(0.2)	0.000	2.1	(0.2)	0.000	1.2	(0.1)	0.000
France	m	m	m	m	m	m	m	m	m	m	m	m
Germany	2.0	(0.2)	0.000	2.1	(0.2)	0.000	1.5	(0.2)	0.000	0.8	(0.2)	0.000
Ireland	1.9	(0.3)	0.000	1.8	(0.2)	0.000	1.5	(0.2)	0.000	0.9	(0.2)	0.000
Italy	m	m	m	m	m	m	m	m	m	m	m	m
Japan	1.6	(0.2)	0.000	2.1	(0.2)	0.000	1.8	(0.2)	0.000	1.0	(0.1)	0.000
Korea	2.8	(0.3)	0.000	2.3	(0.2)	0.000	1.6	(0.2)	0.000	0.7	(0.2)	0.001
Netherlands	1.5	(0.2)	0.000	1.7	(0.1)	0.000	1.5	(0.2)	0.000	0.8	(0.1)	0.000
Norway	2.0	(0.2)	0.000	2.1	(0.1)	0.000	1.7	(0.2)	0.000	1.1	(0.1)	0.000
Poland	1.9	(0.3)	0.000	1.9	(0.3)	0.000	1.6	(0.3)	0.000	0.8	(0.3)	0.008
Slovak Republic	0.9	(0.3)	0.001	1.1	(0.2)	0.000	0.8	(0.2)	0.000	0.4	(0.2)	0.097
Spain	m	m	m	m	m	m	m	m	m	m	m	m
Sweden	1.7	(0.2)	0.000	1.7	(0.1)	0.000	1.4	(0.1)	0.000	0.8	(0.1)	0.000
United States	0.8	(0.3)	0.013	0.9	(0.2)	0.000	0.7	(0.2)	0.000	0.3	(0.2)	0.041
Sub-national entities												
Flanders (Belgium)	1.8	(0.2)	0.000	1.7	(0.2)	0.000	1.2	(0.1)	0.000	0.6	(0.1)	0.000
England (UK)	0.6	(0.2)	0.009	1.2	(0.1)	0.000	0.9	(0.2)	0.000	0.5	(0.2)	0.004
Northern Ireland (UK)	1.4	(0.3)	0.000	1.4	(0.3)	0.000	1.0	(0.2)	0.000	0.5	(0.3)	0.068
England/N. Ireland (UK)	0.7	(0.2)	0.006	1.2	(0.1)	0.000	0.9	(0.2)	0.000	0.5	(0.2)	0.003
Average[1]	1.7	(0.1)	0.000	1.8	(0.0)	0.000	1.4	(0.0)	0.000	0.8	(0.0)	0.000
Average-22[2]	m	m	m	m	m	m	m	m	m	m	m	m
Partners												
Cyprus[3]	m	m	m	m	m	m	m	m	m	m	m	m
Russian Federation[4]	m	m	m	m	m	m	m	m	m	m	m	m

1. Average of 19 participating OECD countries and entities.
2. Average of 22 OECD countries and entities: average of 19 countries with France, Italy and Spain.
3. See notes at the beginning of this Annex.
4. See note at the beginning of this Annex.
Note: Results for the Russian Federation are missing due to the lack of the language variables.
Source: Survey of Adult Skills (PIAAC) (2012).
StatLink ⟨≡⟩ http://dx.doi.org/10.1787/888933232345

[Part 2/3]

Likelihood of adults scoring at Level 2 or 3 in problem solving in technology-rich environments, by socio-demographic characteristics (Version 1)

Table B3.1

OECD	Immigrant and language background (reference foreign-born and foreign language)									Educational attainment (reference lower than upper secondary)					
	Native-born and native language			Native-born and foreign language			Foreign-born and native language			Upper secondary			Tertiary		
	ß	S.E.	p-value	ß	S.E.	p-value	ß	S.E.	p-value	ß	S.E.	p-value	ß	S.E.	p-value
National entities															
Australia	1.2	(0.1)	0.000	1.0	(0.3)	0.001	1.1	(0.2)	0.000	0.6	(0.1)	0.000	1.4	(0.1)	0.000
Austria	1.4	(0.2)	0.000	0.9	(0.3)	0.004	1.5	(0.3)	0.000	1.1	(0.2)	0.000	1.8	(0.2)	0.000
Canada	1.0	(0.1)	0.000	1.0	(0.2)	0.000	0.5	(0.1)	0.000	0.8	(0.1)	0.000	1.6	(0.1)	0.000
Czech Republic	1.0	(0.5)	0.246	c	c	c	1.3	(0.7)	0.089	0.5	(0.2)	0.005	1.7	(0.2)	0.000
Denmark	1.7	(0.1)	0.000	1.3	(0.4)	0.002	1.4	(0.3)	0.000	0.8	(0.1)	0.000	1.7	(0.1)	0.000
Estonia	0.2	(0.4)	0.000	0.0	(0.4)	0.972	-0.2	(0.4)	0.627	0.8	(0.1)	0.000	1.5	(0.1)	0.000
Finland	1.5	(0.4)	0.000	0.8	(0.4)	0.082	1.7	(0.5)	0.001	0.7	(0.1)	0.000	2.0	(0.2)	0.000
France	m	m	m	m	m	m	m	m	m	m	m	m	m	m	m
Germany	1.6	(0.2)	0.000	0.9	(0.4)	0.032	1.2	(0.3)	0.000	0.8	(0.2)	0.000	1.8	(0.2)	0.000
Ireland	0.9	(0.2)	0.000	0.4	(0.5)	0.388	1.0	(0.2)	0.000	1.0	(0.2)	0.000	2.0	(0.2)	0.000
Italy	m	m	m	m	m	m	m	m	m	m	m	m	m	m	m
Japan	c	c	0.000	c	c	c	c	c	c	0.9	(0.2)	0.000	1.7	(0.2)	0.000
Korea	4.8	(9.5)	0.001	c	c	c	3.9	(9.5)	0.680	0.7	(0.2)	0.000	1.8	(0.2)	0.000
Netherlands	1.5	(0.2)	0.000	0.4	(0.6)	0.449	1.2	(0.3)	0.000	1.0	(0.1)	0.000	2.0	(0.1)	0.000
Norway	1.6	(0.1)	0.000	0.8	(0.4)	0.024	1.2	(0.3)	0.001	0.7	(0.1)	0.000	1.9	(0.1)	0.000
Poland	c	c	0.008	c	c	c	c	c	c	0.2	(0.1)	0.125	1.4	(0.2)	0.000
Slovak Republic	0.6	(0.6)	0.097	0.0	(0.7)	0.941	0.0	(0.8)	0.978	0.7	(0.1)	0.000	1.6	(0.2)	0.000
Spain	m	m	m	m	m	m	m	m	m	m	m	m	m	m	m
Sweden	1.8	(0.2)	0.000	1.3	(0.3)	0.000	1.2	(0.3)	0.001	1.2	(0.2)	0.000	2.2	(0.2)	0.000
United States	1.3	(0.2)	0.041	1.3	(0.4)	0.001	0.6	(0.3)	0.094	0.9	(0.2)	0.000	2.0	(0.2)	0.000
Sub-national entities															
Flanders (Belgium)	1.6	(0.3)	0.000	1.2	(0.4)	0.003	1.5	(0.4)	0.000	0.8	(0.2)	0.000	2.0	(0.2)	0.000
England (UK)	1.2	(0.2)	0.004	1.0	(0.4)	0.011	0.7	(0.3)	0.017	1.0	(0.1)	0.000	1.8	(0.2)	0.000
Northern Ireland (UK)	1.0	(0.4)	0.068	c	c	c	0.7	(0.6)	0.252	1.1	(0.3)	0.000	2.0	(0.3)	0.000
England/N. Ireland (UK)	1.2	(0.2)	0.003	1.0	(0.4)	0.010	0.7	(0.3)	0.014	1.0	(0.1)	0.000	1.8	(0.2)	0.000
Average[1]	1.5	(0.6)	0.000	0.8	(0.1)	0.000	1.2	(0.6)	0.040	0.8	(0.0)	0.000	1.8	(0.0)	0.000
Average-22[2]	m	m	m	m	m	m	m	m	m	m	m	m	m	m	m
Partners															
Cyprus[3]	m	m	m	m	m	m	m	m	m	m	m	m	m	m	m
Russian Federation[4]	m	m	m	m	m	m	m	m	m	m	m	m	m	m	m

1. Average of 19 participating OECD countries and entities.
2. Average of 22 OECD countries and entities: average of 19 countries with France, Italy and Spain.
3. See notes at the beginning of this Annex.
4. See note at the beginning of this Annex.
Note: Results for the Russian Federation are missing due to the lack of the language variables.
Source: Survey of Adult Skills (PIAAC) (2012).

StatLink http://dx.doi.org/10.1787/888933232345

[Part 3/3]

Table B3.1 Likelihood of adults scoring at Level 2 or 3 in problem solving in technology-rich environments, by socio-demographic characteristics (Version 1)

OECD	Gender (reference women) Men			Parents' educational attainment (reference neither parent attained upper secondary) At least one parent attained upper secondary			At least one parent attained tertiary			Participation in adult education and training (reference did not participate) Participated		
	ß	S.E.	p-value	ß	S.E.	p-value	ß	S.E.	p-value	ß	S.E.	p-value
National entities												
Australia	0.1	(0.1)	0.397	0.5	(0.1)	0.000	0.7	(0.1)	0.000	0.8	(0.1)	0.000
Austria	0.4	(0.1)	0.000	0.6	(0.1)	0.000	1.0	(0.1)	0.000	0.6	(0.1)	0.000
Canada	0.1	(0.1)	0.155	0.6	(0.1)	0.000	0.8	(0.1)	0.000	0.7	(0.1)	0.000
Czech Republic	0.2	(0.1)	0.049	0.8	(0.3)	0.006	1.4	(0.3)	0.000	0.6	(0.1)	0.000
Denmark	0.3	(0.1)	0.000	0.1	(0.1)	0.345	0.6	(0.1)	0.000	0.6	(0.1)	0.000
Estonia	0.2	(0.1)	0.032	0.5	(0.1)	0.001	1.1	(0.1)	0.000	0.9	(0.1)	0.000
Finland	0.3	(0.1)	0.001	0.5	(0.1)	0.000	1.0	(0.1)	0.000	0.5	(0.1)	0.000
France	m	m	m	m	m	m	m	m	m	m	m	m
Germany	0.3	(0.1)	0.002	0.8	(0.2)	0.000	1.2	(0.2)	0.000	0.7	(0.1)	0.000
Ireland	0.4	(0.1)	0.001	0.5	(0.1)	0.000	1.0	(0.1)	0.000	0.6	(0.1)	0.000
Italy	m	m	m	m	m	m	m	m	m	m	m	m
Japan	0.6	(0.1)	0.000	0.0	(0.1)	0.906	0.4	(0.1)	0.001	0.6	(0.1)	0.000
Korea	0.3	(0.1)	0.000	0.3	(0.1)	0.021	0.6	(0.1)	0.000	0.6	(0.1)	0.000
Netherlands	0.4	(0.1)	0.000	0.3	(0.1)	0.010	0.5	(0.1)	0.000	0.4	(0.1)	0.000
Norway	0.5	(0.1)	0.000	0.5	(0.1)	0.000	0.8	(0.1)	0.000	0.5	(0.1)	0.000
Poland	0.4	(0.1)	0.001	0.6	(0.2)	0.004	1.3	(0.2)	0.000	0.7	(0.1)	0.000
Slovak Republic	0.1	(0.1)	0.261	0.8	(0.1)	0.000	1.1	(0.2)	0.000	0.9	(0.1)	0.000
Spain	m	m	m	m	m	m	m	m	m	m	m	m
Sweden	0.3	(0.1)	0.004	0.5	(0.1)	0.000	0.8	(0.1)	0.000	0.7	(0.1)	0.000
United States	0.2	(0.1)	0.019	1.0	(0.2)	0.000	1.4	(0.2)	0.000	0.6	(0.1)	0.000
Sub-national entities												
Flanders (Belgium)	0.4	(0.1)	0.000	0.5	(0.1)	0.000	0.8	(0.1)	0.000	0.5	(0.1)	0.000
England (UK)	0.5	(0.1)	0.000	0.8	(0.1)	0.000	1.2	(0.1)	0.000	0.6	(0.1)	0.000
Northern Ireland (UK)	0.6	(0.1)	0.000	0.7	(0.2)	0.000	1.1	(0.2)	0.000	0.5	(0.1)	0.000
England/N. Ireland (UK)	0.5	(0.1)	0.000	0.8	(0.1)	0.000	1.2	(0.1)	0.000	0.6	(0.1)	0.000
Average[1]	0.3	(0.0)	0.000	0.5	(0.0)	0.000	0.9	(0.0)	0.000	0.6	(0.0)	0.000
Average-22[2]	m	m	m	m	m	m	m	m	m	m	m	m
Partners												
Cyprus[3]	m	m	m	m	m	m	m	m	m	m	m	m
Russian Federation[4]	m	m	m	m	m	m	m	m	m	m	m	m

1. Average of 19 participating OECD countries and entities.
2. Average of 22 OECD countries and entities: average of 19 countries with France, Italy and Spain.
3. See notes at the beginning of this Annex.
4. See note at the beginning of this Annex.
Note: Results for the Russian Federation are missing due to the lack of the language variables.
Source: Survey of Adult Skills (PIAAC) (2012).
StatLink http://dx.doi.org/10.1787/888933232345

[Part 1/3]

Likelihood of adults scoring at Level 2 or 3 in problem solving in technology-rich environments, by socio-demographic characteristics and ICT use (Version 2)

Table B3.2

OECD	Age (reference 55-65 year-olds)											
	16-24 year-olds			25-34 year-olds			35-44 year-olds			45-54 year-olds		
	ß	S.E.	p-value	ß	S.E.	p-value	ß	S.E.	p-value	ß	S.E.	p-value
National entities												
Australia	0.8	(0.2)	0.000	1.0	(0.1)	0.000	0.9	(0.1)	0.000	0.6	(0.2)	0.000
Austria	1.9	(0.2)	0.000	2.1	(0.2)	0.000	1.7	(0.2)	0.000	1.0	(0.2)	0.000
Canada	0.8	(0.2)	0.000	1.1	(0.1)	0.000	0.9	(0.1)	0.000	0.5	(0.1)	0.000
Czech Republic	1.0	(0.3)	0.001	1.4	(0.2)	0.000	0.7	(0.2)	0.007	0.2	(0.3)	0.510
Denmark	1.7	(0.2)	0.000	2.1	(0.1)	0.000	1.6	(0.1)	0.000	1.0	(0.1)	0.000
Estonia	1.9	(0.2)	0.000	1.9	(0.2)	0.000	1.3	(0.2)	0.000	0.6	(0.2)	0.000
Finland	2.5	(0.2)	0.000	2.6	(0.2)	0.000	2.0	(0.2)	0.000	1.2	(0.1)	0.000
France	m	m	m	m	m	m	m	m	m	m	m	m
Germany	1.6	(0.2)	0.000	1.9	(0.2)	0.000	1.3	(0.2)	0.000	0.7	(0.2)	0.000
Ireland	1.6	(0.3)	0.000	1.6	(0.2)	0.000	1.4	(0.2)	0.000	0.9	(0.2)	0.000
Italy	m	m	m	m	m	m	m	m	m	m	m	m
Japan	1.5	(0.2)	0.000	1.9	(0.2)	0.000	1.6	(0.2)	0.000	0.9	(0.1)	0.000
Korea	2.6	(0.3)	0.000	2.1	(0.2)	0.000	1.5	(0.2)	0.000	0.6	(0.2)	0.004
Netherlands	1.4	(0.2)	0.000	1.7	(0.1)	0.000	1.5	(0.2)	0.000	0.8	(0.1)	0.000
Norway	1.9	(0.2)	0.000	2.0	(0.2)	0.000	1.6	(0.2)	0.000	1.0	(0.1)	0.000
Poland	1.4	(0.3)	0.000	1.6	(0.3)	0.000	1.3	(0.3)	0.000	0.8	(0.3)	0.017
Slovak Republic	0.4	(0.3)	0.174	0.6	(0.2)	0.001	0.4	(0.2)	0.076	0.2	(0.2)	0.354
Spain	m	m	m	m	m	m	m	m	m	m	m	m
Sweden	1.6	(0.2)	0.000	1.6	(0.1)	0.000	1.3	(0.2)	0.000	0.8	(0.1)	0.000
United States	0.7	(0.3)	0.042	0.7	(0.2)	0.000	0.6	(0.2)	0.000	0.3	(0.2)	0.067
Sub-national entities												
Flanders (Belgium)	1.6	(0.2)	0.000	1.6	(0.2)	0.000	1.1	(0.1)	0.000	0.6	(0.1)	0.000
England (UK)	0.6	(0.2)	0.022	1.1	(0.2)	0.000	0.8	(0.2)	0.000	0.5	(0.2)	0.004
Northern Ireland (UK)	1.3	(0.3)	0.000	1.3	(0.3)	0.000	0.9	(0.2)	0.000	0.5	(0.3)	0.068
England/N. Ireland (UK)	0.6	(0.2)	0.015	1.1	(0.2)	0.000	0.8	(0.2)	0.000	0.5	(0.2)	0.004
Average[1]	1.5	(0.1)	0.000	1.6	(0.0)	0.000	1.2	(0.0)	0.000	0.7	(0.0)	0.000
Average-22[2]	m	m	m	m	m	m	m	m	m	m	m	m
Partners												
Cyprus[3]	m	m	m	m	m	m	m	m	m	m	m	m
Russian Federation[4]	m	m	m	m	m	m	m	m	m	m	m	m

1. Average of 19 participating OECD countries and entities.
2. Average of 22 OECD countries and entities: average of 19 countries with France, Italy and Spain.
3. See notes at the beginning of this Annex.
4. See note at the beginning of this Annex.
Note: Results for the Russian Federation are missing due to the lack of the language variables.
Source: Survey of Adult Skills (PIAAC) (2012).
StatLink ᴬᴹˢᴸ http://dx.doi.org/10.1787/888933232357

[Part 2/3]
Likelihood of adults scoring at Level 2 or 3 in problem solving in technology-rich environments, by socio-demographic characteristics and ICT use (Version 2)

Table B3.2

| OECD | Immigrant and language background (reference foreign-born and foreign language) | | | | | | | | | Educational attainment (reference lower than upper secondary) | | | | | |
| | Native-born and native language | | | Native-born and foreign language | | | Foreign-born and native language | | | Upper secondary | | | Tertiary | | |
	ß	S.E.	p-value	ß	S.E.	p-value	ß	S.E.	p-value	ß	S.E.	p-value	ß	S.E.	p-value
National entities															
Australia	1.2	(0.1)	0.000	1.0	(0.3)	0.001	1.0	(0.2)	0.000	0.4	(0.1)	0.001	1.1	(0.1)	0.000
Austria	1.4	(0.2)	0.000	0.8	(0.3)	0.008	1.4	(0.3)	0.000	0.9	(0.2)	0.000	1.5	(0.2)	0.000
Canada	1.0	(0.1)	0.000	0.9	(0.2)	0.000	0.5	(0.1)	0.000	0.7	(0.1)	0.000	1.4	(0.2)	0.000
Czech Republic	1.0	(0.5)	0.042	c	c	c	1.4	(0.7)	0.050	0.4	(0.2)	0.029	1.4	(0.2)	0.000
Denmark	1.7	(0.1)	0.000	1.2	(0.4)	0.003	1.4	(0.3)	0.000	0.7	(0.1)	0.000	1.6	(0.1)	0.000
Estonia	0.2	(0.4)	0.600	0.0	(0.5)	0.990	-0.2	(0.4)	0.692	0.7	(0.1)	0.000	1.4	(0.1)	0.000
Finland	1.5	(0.4)	0.001	0.8	(0.4)	0.084	1.7	(0.5)	0.000	0.7	(0.2)	0.000	1.9	(0.2)	0.000
France	m	m	m	m	m	m	m	m	m	m	m	m	m	m	m
Germany	1.5	(0.2)	0.000	0.8	(0.4)	0.054	1.2	(0.3)	0.001	0.7	(0.2)	0.000	1.6	(0.2)	0.000
Ireland	1.0	(0.2)	0.000	0.7	(0.5)	0.181	1.0	(0.2)	0.000	0.8	(0.2)	0.000	1.7	(0.2)	0.000
Italy	m	m	m	m	m	m	m	m	m	0.8	(0.2)	0.000	1.6	(0.2)	0.000
Japan	c	c	c	c	c	c	c	c	c	0.5	(0.2)	0.004	1.5	(0.2)	0.000
Korea	4.8	(9.5)	0.613	c	c	c	4.1	(9.5)	0.668	0.5	(0.2)	0.004	1.9	(0.1)	0.000
Netherlands	1.4	(0.2)	0.000	0.4	(0.6)	0.539	1.2	(0.3)	0.000	0.9	(0.1)	0.000	1.9	(0.1)	0.000
Norway	1.6	(0.1)	0.000	0.9	(0.4)	0.019	1.2	(0.4)	0.001	0.7	(0.1)	0.000	1.8	(0.1)	0.000
Poland	c	c	c	c	c	c	c	c	c	0.1	(0.1)	0.682	1.0	(0.2)	0.000
Slovak Republic	0.6	(0.6)	0.314	0.1	(0.7)	0.911	0.0	(0.8)	0.994	0.4	(0.2)	0.008	1.1	(0.2)	0.000
Spain	m	m	m	m	m	m	m	m	m	m	m	m	m	m	m
Sweden	1.8	(0.2)	0.000	1.2	(0.3)	0.000	1.3	(0.3)	0.000	1.1	(0.2)	0.000	2.0	(0.2)	0.000
United States	1.3	(0.2)	0.000	1.3	(0.4)	0.001	0.5	(0.3)	0.142	0.7	(0.2)	0.000	1.6	(0.2)	0.000
Sub-national entities															
Flanders (Belgium)	1.6	(0.3)	0.000	1.2	(0.4)	0.002	1.5	(0.4)	0.000	0.7	(0.2)	0.000	1.8	(0.2)	0.000
England (UK)	1.3	(0.2)	0.000	1.0	(0.4)	0.018	0.6	(0.3)	0.021	0.9	(0.1)	0.000	1.5	(0.2)	0.000
Northern Ireland (UK)	1.1	(0.4)	0.002	c	c	c	0.7	(0.6)	0.249	1.0	(0.3)	0.001	1.7	(0.3)	0.000
England/N. Ireland (UK)	1.3	(0.2)	0.000	1.0	(0.4)	0.017	0.6	(0.3)	0.018	0.9	(0.1)	0.000	1.5	(0.2)	0.000
Average[1]	1.5	(0.6)	0.009	0.8	(0.1)	0.000	1.2	(0.6)	0.039	0.7	(0.0)	0.000	1.5	(0.0)	0.000
Average-22[2]	m	m	m	m	m	m	m	m	m	m	m	m	m	m	m
Partners															
Cyprus[3]	m	m	m	m	m	m	m	m	m	m	m	m	m	m	m
Russian Federation[4]	m	m	m	m	m	m	m	m	m	m	m	m	m	m	m

1. Average of 19 participating OECD countries and entities.
2. Average of 22 OECD countries and entities: average of 19 countries with France, Italy and Spain.
3. See notes at the beginning of this Annex.
4. See note at the beginning of this Annex.
Note: Results for the Russian Federation are missing due to the lack of the language variables.
Source: Survey of Adult Skills (PIAAC) (2012).
StatLink ⟐⟐ http://dx.doi.org/10.1787/888933232357

[Part 3/3]
Likelihood of adults scoring at Level 2 or 3 in problem solving in technology-rich environments,
Table B3.2 **by socio-demographic characteristics and ICT use (Version 2)**

OECD	Gender (reference women)			Parents' educational attainment (reference neither parent attained upper secondary)						Participation in adult education and training (reference did not participate)			E-mail use (reference not high/regular use of e-mail)		
	Men			At least one parent attained upper secondary			At least one parent attained tertiary			Participated			High/regular use of e-mail		
	ß	S.E.	p-value	ß	S.E.	p-value	ß	S.E.	p-value	ß	S.E.	p-value	ß	S.E.	p-value
National entities															
Australia	0.2	(0.1)	0.097	0.4	(0.1)	0.002	0.6	(0.1)	0.000	0.7	(0.1)	0.000	1.4	(0.1)	0.000
Austria	0.4	(0.1)	0.000	0.5	(0.1)	0.000	0.8	(0.2)	0.000	0.5	(0.1)	0.000	1.8	(0.2)	0.000
Canada	0.1	(0.1)	0.026	0.5	(0.1)	0.000	0.7	(0.1)	0.000	0.6	(0.1)	0.000	1.5	(0.2)	0.000
Czech Republic	0.2	(0.1)	0.111	0.7	(0.3)	0.023	1.3	(0.3)	0.000	0.5	(0.1)	0.001	1.6	(0.2)	0.000
Denmark	0.3	(0.1)	0.000	0.1	(0.1)	0.492	0.5	(0.1)	0.000	0.5	(0.1)	0.000	1.5	(0.2)	0.000
Estonia	0.2	(0.1)	0.015	0.4	(0.2)	0.005	1.0	(0.1)	0.000	0.8	(0.1)	0.000	1.5	(0.2)	0.000
Finland	0.4	(0.1)	0.000	0.4	(0.1)	0.000	1.0	(0.1)	0.000	0.4	(0.1)	0.000	1.4	(0.2)	0.000
France	m	m	m	m	m	m	m	m	m	m	m	m	m	m	m
Germany	0.3	(0.1)	0.002	0.7	(0.2)	0.002	1.1	(0.2)	0.000	0.5	(0.1)	0.000	1.6	(0.1)	0.000
Ireland	0.4	(0.1)	0.001	0.4	(0.1)	0.000	0.9	(0.1)	0.000	0.5	(0.1)	0.000	1.5	(0.2)	0.000
Italy	m	m	m	m	m	m	m	m	m	m	m	m	m	m	m
Japan	0.5	(0.1)	0.000	0.0	(0.1)	0.735	0.3	(0.1)	0.028	0.5	(0.1)	0.000	1.2	(0.1)	0.000
Korea	0.3	(0.1)	0.001	0.2	(0.1)	0.069	0.5	(0.1)	0.000	0.5	(0.1)	0.000	0.8	(0.1)	0.000
Netherlands	0.4	(0.1)	0.000	0.3	(0.1)	0.016	0.5	(0.1)	0.000	0.3	(0.1)	0.003	1.8	(0.2)	0.000
Norway	0.5	(0.1)	0.000	0.4	(0.1)	0.000	0.8	(0.1)	0.000	0.5	(0.1)	0.000	1.2	(0.2)	0.000
Poland	0.4	(0.1)	0.001	0.3	(0.2)	0.131	0.9	(0.2)	0.000	0.5	(0.1)	0.000	1.7	(0.2)	0.000
Slovak Republic	0.1	(0.1)	0.157	0.5	(0.1)	0.000	0.9	(0.2)	0.000	0.7	(0.1)	0.000	1.7	(0.2)	0.000
Spain	m	m	m	m	m	m	m	m	m	m	m	m	m	m	m
Sweden	0.3	(0.1)	0.005	0.4	(0.1)	0.000	0.7	(0.1)	0.000	0.6	(0.1)	0.000	1.6	(0.1)	0.000
United States	0.3	(0.1)	0.003	0.9	(0.2)	0.000	1.3	(0.2)	0.000	0.5	(0.1)	0.000	1.5	(0.2)	0.000
Sub-national entities															
Flanders (Belgium)	0.4	(0.1)	0.000	0.5	(0.1)	0.002	0.8	(0.1)	0.000	0.4	(0.1)	0.001	1.8	(0.2)	0.000
England (UK)	0.5	(0.1)	0.000	0.8	(0.1)	0.000	1.0	(0.2)	0.000	0.5	(0.1)	0.000	1.7	(0.2)	0.000
Northern Ireland (UK)	0.6	(0.1)	0.000	0.6	(0.2)	0.001	1.0	(0.2)	0.000	0.4	(0.2)	0.009	1.4	(0.2)	0.000
England/N. Ireland (UK)	0.5	(0.1)	0.000	0.8	(0.1)	0.000	1.0	(0.1)	0.000	0.5	(0.1)	0.000	1.7	(0.2)	0.000
Average[1]	0.3	(0.0)	0.000	0.4	(0.0)	0.000	0.8	(0.0)	0.000	0.5	(0.0)	0.000	1.5	(0.0)	0.000
Average-22[2]	m	m	m	m	m	m	m	m	m	m	m	m	m	m	m
Partners															
Cyprus[3]	m	m	m	m	m	m	m	m	m	m	m	m	m	m	m
Russian Federation[4]	m	m	m	m	m	m	m	m	m	m	m	m	m	m	m

1. Average of 19 participating OECD countries and entities.
2. Average of 22 OECD countries and entities: average of 19 countries with France, Italy and Spain.
3. See notes at the beginning of this Annex.
4. See note at the beginning of this Annex.
Note: Results for the Russian Federation are missing due to the lack of the language variables.
Source: Survey of Adult Skills (PIAAC) (2012).
StatLink ᗂᗂ᙮ http://dx.doi.org/10.1787/888933232357

[Part 1/4]

Likelihood of adults scoring at Level 2 or 3 in problem solving in technology-rich environments, by socio-demographic characteristics, e-mail use and cognitive skills (Version 3)

Table B3.3

OECD	Age (reference 55-65 year-olds)											
	16-24 year-olds			25-34 year-olds			35-44 year-olds			45-54 year-olds		
	ß	S.E.	p-value	ß	S.E.	p-value	ß	S.E.	p-value	ß	S.E.	p-value
National entities												
Australia	1.3	(0.3)	0.000	1.1	(0.2)	0.000	0.8	(0.2)	0.000	0.6	(0.2)	0.006
Austria	1.7	(0.3)	0.000	1.8	(0.2)	0.000	1.3	(0.2)	0.000	0.8	(0.2)	0.001
Canada	1.4	(0.2)	0.000	1.2	(0.1)	0.000	1.0	(0.1)	0.000	0.6	(0.1)	0.000
Czech Republic	1.3	(0.4)	0.001	1.4	(0.3)	0.000	0.7	(0.3)	0.011	0.3	(0.3)	0.401
Denmark	1.7	(0.3)	0.000	2.0	(0.2)	0.000	1.4	(0.1)	0.000	0.8	(0.2)	0.000
Estonia	2.0	(0.3)	0.000	2.0	(0.2)	0.000	1.4	(0.2)	0.000	0.7	(0.2)	0.001
Finland	2.2	(0.3)	0.000	2.2	(0.2)	0.000	1.7	(0.2)	0.000	0.9	(0.2)	0.000
France	m	m	m	m	m	m	m	m	m	m	m	m
Germany	1.7	(0.3)	0.000	1.7	(0.2)	0.000	1.1	(0.2)	0.000	0.6	(0.2)	0.010
Ireland	2.0	(0.3)	0.000	1.7	(0.2)	0.000	1.3	(0.2)	0.000	0.9	(0.2)	0.000
Italy	m	m	m	m	m	m	m	m	m	m	m	m
Japan	1.3	(0.2)	0.000	1.7	(0.2)	0.000	1.4	(0.2)	0.000	0.7	(0.2)	0.000
Korea	2.6	(0.3)	0.000	1.9	(0.3)	0.000	1.3	(0.2)	0.000	0.6	(0.2)	0.009
Netherlands	1.4	(0.3)	0.000	1.4	(0.2)	0.000	1.0	(0.2)	0.000	0.5	(0.2)	0.001
Norway	2.2	(0.3)	0.000	1.8	(0.2)	0.000	1.3	(0.2)	0.000	0.8	(0.2)	0.000
Poland	1.6	(0.3)	0.000	1.7	(0.3)	0.000	1.4	(0.3)	0.000	0.7	(0.3)	0.035
Slovak Republic	0.7	(0.4)	0.055	0.7	(0.2)	0.001	0.4	(0.3)	0.181	0.3	(0.3)	0.267
Spain	m	m	m	m	m	m	m	m	m	m	m	m
Sweden	1.7	(0.3)	0.000	1.5	(0.2)	0.000	1.1	(0.2)	0.000	0.6	(0.2)	0.001
United States	1.2	(0.4)	0.006	0.9	(0.2)	0.000	0.8	(0.2)	0.000	0.3	(0.2)	0.121
Sub-national entities												
Flanders (Belgium)	1.6	(0.3)	0.000	1.4	(0.2)	0.000	1.0	(0.2)	0.000	0.4	(0.2)	0.017
England (UK)	1.3	(0.3)	0.000	1.4	(0.2)	0.000	0.9	(0.2)	0.000	0.5	(0.2)	0.025
Northern Ireland (UK)	1.8	(0.3)	0.000	1.5	(0.3)	0.000	0.9	(0.3)	0.001	0.5	(0.3)	0.072
England/N. Ireland (UK)	1.3	(0.3)	0.000	1.4	(0.2)	0.000	0.9	(0.2)	0.000	0.5	(0.2)	0.023
Average[1]	1.6	(0.1)	0.000	1.6	(0.0)	0.000	1.1	(0.0)	0.000	0.6	(0.0)	0.000
Average-22[2]	m	m	m	m	m	m	m	m	m	m	m	m
Partners												
Cyprus[3]	m	m	m	m	m	m	m	m	m	m	m	m
Russian Federation[4]	m	m	m	m	m	m	m	m	m	m	m	m

1. Average of 19 participating OECD countries and entities.
2. Average of 22 OECD countries and entities: average of 19 countries with France, Italy and Spain.
3. See notes at the beginning of this Annex.
4. See note at the beginning of this Annex.
Note: Results for the Russian Federation are missing due to the lack of the language variables.
Source: Survey of Adult Skills (PIAAC) (2012).

StatLink ᴬᴵᴾ http://dx.doi.org/10.1787/888933232364

[Part 2/4]

Likelihood of adults scoring at Level 2 or 3 in problem solving in technology-rich environments by socio-demographic characteristics, e-mail use and cognitive skills (Version 3)

Table B3.3

OECD	Immigrant and language background (reference foreign-born and foreign language)									Educational attainment (reference lower than upper secondary)					
	Native-born and native language			Native-born and foreign language			Foreign-born and native language			Upper secondary			Tertiary		
	ß	S.E.	p-value	ß	S.E.	p-value	ß	S.E.	p-value	ß	S.E.	p-value	ß	S.E.	p-value
National entities															
Australia	0.6	(0.2)	0.002	0.6	(0.3)	0.110	0.4	(0.2)	0.061	0.0	(0.2)	0.902	0.5	(0.1)	0.003
Austria	0.8	(0.2)	0.000	0.7	(0.4)	0.089	0.9	(0.4)	0.025	0.6	(0.2)	0.005	0.6	(0.2)	0.013
Canada	0.4	(0.2)	0.015	0.4	(0.2)	0.058	0.3	(0.2)	0.093	0.0	(0.2)	0.853	0.3	(0.2)	0.249
Czech Republic	1.0	(0.5)	0.052	c	c	c	1.6	(0.9)	0.063	0.1	(0.2)	0.666	0.6	(0.3)	0.031
Denmark	1.0	(0.2)	0.000	0.7	(0.6)	0.204	0.8	(0.4)	0.043	0.3	(0.1)	0.063	0.7	(0.2)	0.000
Estonia	-0.2	(0.4)	0.573	-0.3	(0.5)	0.510	-0.1	(0.5)	0.871	0.3	(0.1)	0.034	0.6	(0.2)	0.001
Finland	0.5	(0.7)	0.473	0.0	(0.7)	0.964	0.7	(0.6)	0.248	0.3	(0.2)	0.171	1.0	(0.2)	0.000
France	m	m	m	m	m	m	m	m	m	m	m	m	m	m	m
Germany	1.0	(0.3)	0.001	0.7	(0.5)	0.199	0.8	(0.4)	0.033	0.1	(0.2)	0.617	0.5	(0.3)	0.051
Ireland	0.5	(0.2)	0.027	-0.1	(0.6)	0.915	0.6	(0.3)	0.030	0.4	(0.2)	0.103	0.9	(0.2)	0.000
Italy	m	m	m	m	m	m	m	m	m	m	m	m	m	m	m
Japan	c	c	c	c	c	c	c	c	c	0.6	(0.2)	0.001	1.0	(0.2)	0.000
Korea	4.2	(9.8)	0.670	c	c	c	3.7	(9.8)	0.706	0.3	(0.2)	0.278	0.9	(0.2)	0.000
Netherlands	0.6	(0.2)	0.016	0.3	(0.7)	0.696	1.1	(0.4)	0.011	0.3	(0.2)	0.064	0.8	(0.1)	0.000
Norway	0.8	(0.2)	0.000	0.5	(0.5)	0.370	0.5	(0.5)	0.322	0.5	(0.2)	0.004	1.0	(0.2)	0.000
Poland	c	c	c	c	c	c	c	c	c	-0.1	(0.2)	0.469	0.4	(0.2)	0.092
Slovak Republic	0.6	(0.7)	0.412	0.1	(0.9)	0.910	0.0	(0.9)	0.965	0.1	(0.2)	0.524	0.6	(0.3)	0.048
Spain	m	m	m	m	m	m	m	m	m	m	m	m	m	m	m
Sweden	0.8	(0.2)	0.000	0.3	(0.4)	0.343	0.6	(0.5)	0.225	0.7	(0.2)	0.001	0.9	(0.2)	0.000
United States	0.8	(0.3)	0.010	0.8	(0.5)	0.102	0.1	(0.4)	0.789	0.2	(0.2)	0.319	0.5	(0.2)	0.030
Sub-national entities															
Flanders (Belgium)	0.7	(0.5)	0.149	0.5	(0.6)	0.393	0.8	(0.6)	0.169	0.3	(0.2)	0.267	0.6	(0.2)	0.006
England (UK)	0.6	(0.2)	0.008	0.7	(0.5)	0.188	0.2	(0.3)	0.507	0.2	(0.2)	0.277	0.7	(0.2)	0.002
Northern Ireland (UK)	0.3	(0.4)	0.475	c	c	c	0.0	(0.7)	0.953	0.3	(0.3)	0.432	0.6	(0.3)	0.032
England/N. Ireland (UK)	0.6	(0.2)	0.008	0.7	(0.5)	0.189	0.2	(0.3)	0.503	0.2	(0.2)	0.257	0.7	(0.2)	0.001
Average[1]	0.9	(0.6)	0.137	0.4	(0.1)	0.006	0.8	(0.6)	0.187	0.3	(0.0)	0.000	0.7	(0.1)	0.000
Average-22[2]	m	m	m	m	m	m	m	m	m	m	m	m	m	m	m
Partners															
Cyprus[3]	m	m	m	m	m	m	m	m	m	m	m	m	m	m	m
Russian Federation[4]	m	m	m	m	m	m	m	m	m	m	m	m	m	m	m

1. Average of 19 participating OECD countries and entities.
2. Average of 22 OECD countries and entities: average of 19 countries with France, Italy and Spain.
3. See notes at the beginning of this Annex.
4. See note at the beginning of this Annex.
Note: Results for the Russian Federation are missing due to the lack of the language variables.
Source: Survey of Adult Skills (PIAAC) (2012).

StatLink ⟨⟨⟨ http://dx.doi.org/10.1787/888933232364

[Part 3/4]

Likelihood of adults scoring at Level 2 or 3 in problem solving in technology-rich environments,
Table B3.3 **by socio-demographic characteristics, e-mail use and cognitive skills (Version 3)**

OECD	Gender (reference women) Men			Parents' educational attainment (reference neither parent attained upper secondary) At least one parent attained upper secondary			At least one parent attained tertiary			Participation in adult education and training (reference did not participate) Participated			E-mail use (reference not high/regular use of e-mail) High/regular use of e-mail		
	ß	S.E.	p-value	ß	S.E.	p-value	ß	S.E.	p-value	ß	S.E.	p-value	ß	S.E.	p-value
National entities															
Australia	0.1	(0.1)	0.391	0.3	(0.1)	0.024	0.3	(0.1)	0.011	0.5	(0.1)	0.000	1.0	(0.2)	0.000
Austria	0.5	(0.1)	0.001	0.2	(0.1)	0.092	0.4	(0.2)	0.070	0.4	(0.1)	0.010	1.6	(0.2)	0.000
Canada	0.1	(0.1)	0.482	0.4	(0.1)	0.001	0.4	(0.1)	0.001	0.4	(0.1)	0.000	1.2	(0.1)	0.000
Czech Republic	0.2	(0.1)	0.219	0.6	(0.3)	0.067	1.0	(0.4)	0.007	0.4	(0.1)	0.015	1.3	(0.2)	0.000
Denmark	0.3	(0.1)	0.005	0.0	(0.1)	0.804	0.1	(0.1)	0.259	0.4	(0.1)	0.004	1.1	(0.2)	0.000
Estonia	0.2	(0.1)	0.054	0.4	(0.2)	0.033	0.8	(0.1)	0.000	0.6	(0.1)	0.000	1.5	(0.2)	0.000
Finland	0.5	(0.1)	0.000	0.4	(0.1)	0.003	0.6	(0.2)	0.001	0.3	(0.1)	0.038	1.1	(0.2)	0.000
France	m	m	m	m	m	m	m	m	m	m	m	m	m	m	m
Germany	0.3	(0.1)	0.005	0.5	(0.3)	0.093	0.6	(0.3)	0.043	0.3	(0.1)	0.046	1.3	(0.2)	0.000
Ireland	0.3	(0.1)	0.033	0.3	(0.1)	0.083	0.6	(0.2)	0.001	0.3	(0.2)	0.025	1.3	(0.2)	0.000
Italy	m	m	m	m	m	m	m	m	m	m	m	m	m	m	m
Japan	0.6	(0.1)	0.000	-0.2	(0.1)	0.253	0.1	(0.1)	0.293	0.4	(0.1)	0.000	1.1	(0.1)	0.000
Korea	0.3	(0.1)	0.027	0.1	(0.1)	0.454	0.3	(0.1)	0.019	0.4	(0.1)	0.005	0.6	(0.1)	0.000
Netherlands	0.3	(0.1)	0.001	0.1	(0.1)	0.449	0.2	(0.1)	0.112	0.2	(0.2)	0.110	1.3	(0.3)	0.000
Norway	0.4	(0.1)	0.000	0.4	(0.1)	0.014	0.5	(0.2)	0.002	0.5	(0.2)	0.003	1.1	(0.2)	0.000
Poland	0.4	(0.1)	0.002	0.2	(0.2)	0.522	0.6	(0.3)	0.038	0.4	(0.1)	0.002	1.4	(0.3)	0.000
Slovak Republic	0.2	(0.1)	0.127	0.4	(0.2)	0.042	0.5	(0.2)	0.008	0.6	(0.1)	0.000	1.7	(0.2)	0.000
Spain	m	m	m	m	m	m	m	m	m	m	m	m	m	m	m
Sweden	0.3	(0.1)	0.047	0.4	(0.1)	0.007	0.5	(0.1)	0.000	0.6	(0.2)	0.000	1.4	(0.2)	0.000
United States	0.2	(0.1)	0.040	0.6	(0.3)	0.016	0.6	(0.2)	0.006	0.3	(0.1)	0.025	0.9	(0.2)	0.000
Sub-national entities															
Flanders (Belgium)	0.3	(0.1)	0.016	0.3	(0.2)	0.075	0.4	(0.2)	0.024	0.4	(0.2)	0.018	1.6	(0.3)	0.000
England (UK)	0.5	(0.1)	0.000	0.4	(0.2)	0.015	0.4	(0.2)	0.030	0.4	(0.1)	0.006	1.4	(0.2)	0.000
Northern Ireland (UK)	0.5	(0.2)	0.003	0.5	(0.2)	0.025	0.7	(0.2)	0.008	0.3	(0.2)	0.151	1.3	(0.2)	0.000
England/N. Ireland (UK)	0.5	(0.1)	0.000	0.4	(0.2)	0.010	0.4	(0.2)	0.021	0.4	(0.1)	0.006	1.4	(0.2)	0.000
Average[1]	0.3	(0.0)	0.000	0.3	(0.0)	0.000	0.5	(0.0)	0.000	0.4	(0.0)	0.000	1.3	(0.0)	0.000
Average-22[2]	m	m	m	m	m	m	m	m	m	m	m	m	m	m	m
Partners															
Cyprus[3]	m	m	m	m	m	m	m	m	m	m	m	m	m	m	m
Russian Federation[4]	m	m	m	m	m	m	m	m	m	m	m	m	m	m	m

1. Average of 19 participating OECD countries and entities.
2. Average of 22 OECD countries and entities: average of 19 countries with France, Italy and Spain.
3. See notes at the beginning of this Annex.
4. See note at the beginning of this Annex.
Note: Results for the Russian Federation are missing due to the lack of the language variables.
Source: Survey of Adult Skills (PIAAC) (2012).
StatLink ⫘ http://dx.doi.org/10.1787/888933232364

[Part 4/4]

Likelihood of adults scoring at Level 2 or 3 in problem solving in technology-rich environments, by socio-demographic characteristics, e-mail use and cognitive skills (Version 3)

Table B3.3

OECD	Literacy levels (reference Level 2)								
	Below Level 1 and Level 1			Level 3			Level 4 and Level 5		
	ß	S.E.	p-value	ß	S.E.	p-value	ß	S.E.	p-value
National entities									
Australia	-4.2	(6.6)	0.529	2.0	(0.1)	0.000	3.4	(0.2)	0.000
Austria	-4.6	(6.8)	0.498	2.0	(0.2)	0.000	3.4	(0.3)	0.000
Canada	-3.1	(0.5)	0.000	2.1	(0.1)	0.000	3.6	(0.2)	0.000
Czech Republic	-2.8	(1.4)	0.041	1.8	(0.2)	0.000	2.8	(0.3)	0.000
Denmark	-3.5	(3.6)	0.332	2.1	(0.1)	0.000	4.0	(0.3)	0.000
Estonia	-2.3	(0.8)	0.005	2.0	(0.2)	0.000	3.3	(0.1)	0.000
Finland	-2.9	(7.2)	0.692	2.1	(0.2)	0.000	3.8	(0.2)	0.000
France	m	m	m	m	m	m	m	m	m
Germany	-3.0	(0.7)	0.000	1.9	(0.1)	0.000	3.4	(0.3)	0.000
Ireland	-2.9	(1.0)	0.004	1.8	(0.2)	0.000	3.1	(0.2)	0.000
Italy	m	m	m	m	m	m	m	m	m
Japan	-6.9	(12.7)	0.590	1.8	(0.2)	0.000	2.8	(0.2)	0.000
Korea	-6.6	(11.0)	0.551	2.0	(0.1)	0.000	3.3	(0.2)	0.000
Netherlands	-5.2	(10.0)	0.604	2.3	(0.1)	0.000	4.1	(0.2)	0.000
Norway	-2.4	(0.6)	0.000	2.1	(0.2)	0.000	3.9	(0.3)	0.000
Poland	-2.1	(0.6)	0.001	1.8	(0.1)	0.000	2.5	(0.2)	0.000
Slovak Republic	-2.2	(0.7)	0.003	1.9	(0.2)	0.000	3.2	(0.3)	0.000
Spain	m	m	m	m	m	m	m	m	m
Sweden	-2.8	(3.9)	0.478	2.0	(0.2)	0.000	4.1	(0.3)	0.000
United States	-4.6	(5.7)	0.416	2.2	(0.2)	0.000	4.2	(0.3)	0.000
Sub-national entities									
Flanders (Belgium)	-3.0	(3.6)	0.407	2.1	(0.1)	0.000	3.9	(0.2)	0.000
England (UK)	-2.2	(0.6)	0.000	1.9	(0.2)	0.000	3.5	(0.2)	0.000
Northern Ireland (UK)	-2.3	(0.9)	0.009	2.0	(0.3)	0.000	3.7	(0.3)	0.000
England/N. Ireland (UK)	-2.2	(0.6)	0.000	1.9	(0.2)	0.000	3.5	(0.2)	0.000
Average[1]	-3.6	(1.3)	0.006	2.0	(0.0)	0.000	3.5	(0.1)	0.000
Average-22[2]	m	m	m	m	m	m	m	m	m
Partners									
Cyprus[3]	m	m	m	m	m	m	m	m	m
Russian Federation[4]	m	m	m	m	m	m	m	m	m

1. Average of 19 participating OECD countries and entities.
2. Average of 22 OECD countries and entities: average of 19 countries with France, Italy and Spain.
3. See notes at the beginning of this Annex.
4. See note at the beginning of this Annex.
Note: Results for the Russian Federation are missing due to the lack of the language variables.
Source: Survey of Adult Skills (PIAAC) (2012).
StatLink 🔗 http://dx.doi.org/10.1787/888933232364

[Part 1/3]
Table B3.4 **Likelihood of adults having no computer experience, by socio-demographic characteristics (Version 1)**

	Age (reference 55-65 year-olds)											
	16-24 year-olds			25-34 year-olds			35-44 year-olds			45-54 year-olds		
OECD	ß	S.E.	p-value	ß	S.E.	p-value	ß	S.E.	p-value	ß	S.E.	p-value
National entities												
Australia	-2.0	(0.9)	0.031	-2.0	(0.4)	0.000	-1.5	(0.2)	0.000	-0.8	(0.2)	0.000
Austria	-4.4	(12.0)	0.719	-2.7	(0.3)	0.000	-1.7	(0.2)	0.000	-0.9	(0.1)	0.000
Canada	-2.7	(0.9)	0.002	-2.1	(0.3)	0.000	-1.6	(0.2)	0.000	-0.5	(0.1)	0.000
Czech Republic	-3.1	(0.6)	0.000	-2.0	(0.4)	0.000	-2.3	(0.2)	0.000	-0.6	(0.2)	0.001
Denmark	-8.0	(11.7)	0.499	-1.3	(0.4)	0.002	-1.5	(0.4)	0.000	-0.9	(0.2)	0.000
Estonia	-7.8	(10.3)	0.451	-3.7	(0.3)	0.000	-1.8	(0.1)	0.000	-0.8	(0.1)	0.000
Finland	-18.4	(17.2)	0.289	-17.8	(17.2)	0.305	-3.2	(0.9)	0.000	-0.6	(0.2)	0.021
France	m	m	m	m	m	m	m	m	m	m	m	m
Germany	-3.7	(0.9)	0.000	-3.2	(0.5)	0.000	-1.7	(0.2)	0.000	-0.8	(0.1)	0.000
Ireland	-2.5	(0.5)	0.000	-2.3	(0.2)	0.000	-1.3	(0.2)	0.000	-0.6	(0.2)	0.000
Italy	m	m	m	m	m	m	m	m	m	m	m	m
Japan	-2.9	(0.5)	0.000	-2.6	(0.3)	0.000	-2.0	(0.2)	0.000	-0.9	(0.1)	0.000
Korea	-4.1	(0.6)	0.000	-3.5	(0.3)	0.000	-2.2	(0.2)	0.000	-0.8	(0.1)	0.000
Netherlands	-15.7	(16.9)	0.356	-2.1	(0.5)	0.000	-1.5	(0.3)	0.000	-1.1	(0.3)	0.003
Norway	-2.4	(0.8)	0.005	-3.3	(14.0)	0.817	-1.9	(0.5)	0.000	-0.4	(0.1)	0.002
Poland	-3.7	(0.3)	0.000	-2.3	(0.2)	0.000	-1.3	(0.2)	0.000	-0.6	(0.1)	0.000
Slovak Republic	-2.2	(0.2)	0.000	-2.0	(0.1)	0.000	-1.1	(0.1)	0.000	-0.6	(0.1)	0.000
Spain	m	m	m	m	m	m	m	m	m	m	m	m
Sweden	-1.2	(0.7)	0.078	-2.1	(0.6)	0.001	-4.5	(0.8)	0.000	-1.5	(0.4)	0.000
United States	-2.6	(0.5)	0.000	-2.1	(0.3)	0.000	-1.0	(0.3)	0.000	-0.5	(0.2)	0.009
Sub-national entities												
Flanders (Belgium)	-3.3	(0.6)	0.000	-1.5	(0.3)	0.000	-1.4	(0.2)	0.000	-0.7	(0.1)	0.000
England (UK)	-2.9	(1.6)	0.082	-3.5	(0.5)	0.000	-1.7	(0.3)	0.000	-0.5	(0.2)	0.026
Northern Ireland (UK)	-1.9	(0.5)	0.000	-1.7	(0.3)	0.000	-1.0	(0.2)	0.000	-0.3	(0.2)	0.125
England/N. Ireland (UK)	-2.7	(1.1)	0.013	-3.2	(0.4)	0.000	-1.6	(0.3)	0.000	-0.4	(0.2)	0.027
Average[1]	-4.9	(1.6)	0.003	-3.3	(1.2)	0.006	-1.9	(0.1)	0.000	-0.7	(0.0)	0.000
Average-22[2]	m	m	m	m	m	m	m	m	m	m	m	m
Partners												
Cyprus[3]	m	m	m	m	m	m	m	m	m	m	m	m
Russian Federation[4]	m	m	m	m	m	m	m	m	m	m	m	m

1. Average of 19 participating OECD countries and entities.
2. Average of 22 OECD countries and entities: average of 19 countries with France, Italy and Spain.
3. See notes at the beginning of this Annex.
4. See note at the beginning of this Annex.
Note: Results for the Russian Federation are missing due to the lack of the language variables.
Source: Survey of Adult Skills (PIAAC) (2012).
StatLink ⟨⟩ http://dx.doi.org/10.1787/888933232376

[Part 2/3]

Table B3.4   **Likelihood of adults having no computer experience, by socio-demographic characteristics (Version 1)**

OECD	Immigrant and language background (reference foreign-born and foreign language)									Educational attainment (reference lower than upper secondary)					
	Native-born and native language			Native-born and foreign language			Foreign-born and native language			Upper secondary			Tertiary		
	ß	S.E.	p-value	ß	S.E.	p-value	ß	S.E.	p-value	ß	S.E.	p-value	ß	S.E.	p-value
National entities															
Australia	-1.2	(0.2)	0.000	-1.2	(0.7)	0.102	-1.2	(0.3)	0.000	-0.7	(0.2)	0.000	-2.1	(0.3)	0.000
Austria	-0.7	(0.2)	0.001	-2.1	(1.2)	0.074	-1.0	(0.5)	0.060	-1.2	(0.1)	0.000	-2.6	(0.3)	0.000
Canada	-1.0	(0.1)	0.000	-1.5	(0.3)	0.000	-0.8	(0.2)	0.001	-1.3	(0.1)	0.000	-2.5	(0.2)	0.000
Czech Republic	0.3	(0.4)	0.484	c	c	c	1.1	(0.5)	0.050	-1.1	(0.2)	0.000	-4.0	(0.5)	0.000
Denmark	-1.1	(0.2)	0.000	-0.3	(12.1)	0.978	-0.3	(1.0)	0.791	-1.3	(0.2)	0.000	-4.6	(1.1)	0.000
Estonia	-0.5	(0.3)	0.078	-0.3	(0.5)	0.522	-0.3	(0.3)	0.295	-1.1	(0.1)	0.000	-2.6	(0.2)	0.000
Finland	-0.5	(1.1)	0.624	0.3	(1.2)	0.819	0.7	(1.5)	0.627	-1.1	(0.2)	0.000	-4.3	(0.8)	0.000
France	m	m	m	m	m	m	m	m	m	m	m	m	m	m	m
Germany	-0.6	(0.2)	0.023	-0.8	(0.7)	0.266	-0.2	(0.4)	0.635	-1.1	(0.2)	0.000	-2.1	(0.3)	0.000
Ireland	0.8	(0.4)	0.042	1.3	(0.5)	0.013	-0.1	(0.5)	0.906	-1.6	(0.1)	0.000	-3.0	(0.3)	0.000
Italy	m	m	m	m	m	m	m	m	m	m	m	m	m	m	m
Japan	c	c	c	c	c	c	c	c	c	-1.6	(0.1)	0.000	-2.5	(0.2)	0.000
Korea	-2.1	(0.7)	0.002	c	c	c	-0.9	(0.8)	0.248	-1.6	(0.1)	0.000	-3.3	(0.2)	0.000
Netherlands	-1.4	(0.3)	0.000	0.3	(1.1)	0.761	-0.7	(0.5)	0.172	-1.7	(0.3)	0.000	-2.5	(0.5)	0.000
Norway	-1.4	(0.4)	0.001	-15.8	(20.4)	0.442	-15.1	(20.2)	0.459	-1.4	(0.3)	0.000	-3.0	(0.6)	0.000
Poland	c	c	c	c	c	c	c	c	c	-1.4	(0.1)	0.000	-3.8	(0.3)	0.000
Slovak Republic	-1.0	(0.5)	0.063	-1.0	(0.5)	0.067	-0.3	(0.6)	0.666	-1.8	(0.1)	0.000	-4.7	(0.3)	0.000
Spain	m	m	m	m	m	m	m	m	m	m	m	m	m	m	m
Sweden	-1.8	(0.4)	0.000	-15.6	(21.6)	0.472	-1.2	(13.2)	0.926	-0.9	(0.3)	0.003	-2.4	(1.1)	0.032
United States	-1.5	(0.3)	0.000	-0.6	(0.5)	0.192	-1.2	(0.6)	0.063	-1.8	(0.2)	0.000	-3.0	(0.2)	0.000
Sub-national entities															
Flanders (Belgium)	-0.9	(0.3)	0.001	-1.3	(0.4)	0.004	-1.6	(0.7)	0.017	-0.9	(0.1)	0.000	-2.7	(0.4)	0.000
England (UK)	-1.0	(0.3)	0.004	-0.9	(13.0)	0.945	-0.5	(0.4)	0.190	-1.1	(0.2)	0.000	-1.9	(0.4)	0.000
Northern Ireland (UK)	0.2	(0.7)	0.774	c	c	c	0.3	(0.7)	0.717	-1.2	(0.2)	0.000	-2.9	(0.5)	0.000
England/N. Ireland (UK)	-0.9	(0.3)	0.006	-0.8	(1.8)	0.643	-0.5	(0.4)	0.202	-1.1	(0.2)	0.000	-2.0	(0.3)	0.000
Average[1]	-0.9	(0.1)	0.000	-2.6	(2.1)	0.221	-1.4	(1.4)	0.332	-1.3	(0.0)	0.000	-3.0	(0.1)	0.000
Average-22[2]	m	m	m	m	m	m	m	m	m	m	m	m	m	m	m
Partners															
Cyprus[3]	m	m	m	m	m	m	m	m	m	m	m	m	m	m	m
Russian Federation[4]	m	m	m	m	m	m	m	m	m	m	m	m	m	m	m

1. Average of 19 participating OECD countries and entities.
2. Average of 22 OECD countries and entities: average of 19 countries with France, Italy and Spain.
3. See notes at the beginning of this Annex.
4. See note at the beginning of this Annex.
Note: Results for the Russian Federation are missing due to the lack of the language variables.
Source: Survey of Adult Skills (PIAAC) (2012).

StatLink http://dx.doi.org/10.1787/888933232376

[Part 3/3]

Table B3.4 **Likelihood of adults having no computer experience, by socio-demographic characteristics (Version 1)**

OECD	Gender (reference women)			Parents' educational attainment (reference neither parent attained upper secondary)						Participation in adult education and training (reference did not participate)		
	Men			At least one parent attained upper secondary			At least one parent attained tertiary			Participated		
	ß	S.E.	p-value	ß	S.E.	p-value	ß	S.E.	p-value	ß	S.E.	p-value
National entities												
Australia	-1.0	(0.3)	0.002	-1.0	(0.3)	0.002	-0.6	(0.3)	0.049	-1.6	(0.3)	0.000
Austria	-0.9	(0.2)	0.000	-0.9	(0.2)	0.000	-1.7	(0.4)	0.000	-1.4	(0.2)	0.000
Canada	-0.5	(0.1)	0.000	-0.5	(0.1)	0.000	-1.1	(0.2)	0.000	-1.2	(0.1)	0.000
Czech Republic	-0.5	(0.2)	0.018	-0.5	(0.2)	0.018	-0.7	(0.4)	0.094	-1.1	(0.2)	0.000
Denmark	-0.1	(0.2)	0.552	-0.1	(0.2)	0.552	-1.2	(0.4)	0.003	-1.6	(0.2)	0.000
Estonia	-0.6	(0.1)	0.000	-0.6	(0.1)	0.000	-0.8	(0.2)	0.000	-1.8	(0.1)	0.000
Finland	-0.2	(0.3)	0.501	-0.2	(0.3)	0.501	-1.8	(0.7)	0.015	-1.5	(0.3)	0.000
France	m	m	m	m	m	m	m	m	m	m	m	m
Germany	-0.6	(0.2)	0.004	-0.6	(0.2)	0.004	-1.3	(0.2)	0.000	-1.4	(0.2)	0.000
Ireland	-0.9	(0.2)	0.000	-0.9	(0.2)	0.000	-1.4	(0.4)	0.001	-1.1	(0.1)	0.000
Italy	m	m	m	m	m	m	m	m	m	m	m	m
Japan	-0.1	(0.2)	0.582	-0.1	(0.2)	0.582	-0.6	(0.2)	0.015	-1.4	(0.2)	0.000
Korea	-0.2	(0.1)	0.143	-0.2	(0.1)	0.143	-0.5	(0.2)	0.029	-0.9	(0.1)	0.000
Netherlands	-1.0	(0.3)	0.006	-1.0	(0.3)	0.006	-0.4	(0.5)	0.420	-1.4	(0.3)	0.000
Norway	-0.1	(0.3)	0.863	-0.1	(0.3)	0.863	0.1	(0.4)	0.765	-1.2	(0.3)	0.000
Poland	-1.0	(0.1)	0.000	-1.0	(0.1)	0.000	-1.6	(0.3)	0.000	-1.2	(0.2)	0.000
Slovak Republic	-0.9	(0.1)	0.000	-0.9	(0.1)	0.000	-2.0	(0.3)	0.000	-1.0	(0.1)	0.000
Spain	m	m	m	m	m	m	m	m	m	m	m	m
Sweden	0.1	(0.5)	0.777	0.1	(0.5)	0.777	-1.1	(1.7)	0.549	-2.1	(0.4)	0.000
United States	-0.6	(0.2)	0.004	-0.6	(0.2)	0.004	-1.2	(0.3)	0.000	-1.4	(0.2)	0.000
Sub-national entities												
Flanders (Belgium)	-1.1	(0.2)	0.000	-1.1	(0.2)	0.000	-1.2	(0.4)	0.003	-1.5	(0.2)	0.000
England (UK)	-0.3	(0.2)	0.167	-0.3	(0.2)	0.167	-0.5	(0.5)	0.333	-1.5	(0.3)	0.000
Northern Ireland (UK)	-0.9	(0.2)	0.000	-0.9	(0.2)	0.000	-1.1	(0.5)	0.019	-1.0	(0.2)	0.000
England/N. Ireland (UK)	0.0	(0.2)	0.902	-0.4	(0.2)	0.078	-0.5	(0.4)	0.251	-1.5	(0.2)	0.000
Average[1]	-0.5	(0.1)	0.000	-0.6	(0.1)	0.000	-1.0	(0.1)	0.000	-1.4	(0.1)	0.000
Average-22[2]	m	m	m	m	m	m	m	m	m	m	m	m
Partners												
Cyprus[3]	m	m	m	m	m	m	m	m	m	m	m	m
Russian Federation[4]	m	m	m	m	m	m	m	m	m	m	m	m

1. Average of 19 participating OECD countries and entities.
2. Average of 22 OECD countries and entities: average of 19 countries with France, Italy and Spain.
3. See notes at the beginning of this Annex.
4. See note at the beginning of this Annex.
Note: Results for the Russian Federation are missing due to the lack of the language variables.
Source: Survey of Adult Skills (PIAAC) (2012).
StatLink ⟐⟐⟐ http://dx.doi.org/10.1787/888933232376

 ADULTS, COMPUTERS AND PROBLEM SOLVING: WHAT'S THE PROBLEM?

[Part 1/4]

Table B3.5 **Likelihood of adults having no computer experience, by socio-demographic characteristics and cognitive skills (Version 3)**

OECD	Age (reference 55-65 year-olds)											
	16-24 year-olds			25-34 year-olds			35-44 year-olds			45-54 year-olds		
	ß	S.E.	p-value	ß	S.E.	p-value	ß	S.E.	p-value	ß	S.E.	p-value
National entities												
Australia	-2.2	(0.9)	0.016	-2.0	(0.4)	0.000	-1.4	(0.2)	0.000	-0.7	(0.2)	0.001
Austria	-4.3	(12.0)	0.719	-2.6	(0.3)	0.000	-1.7	(0.2)	0.000	-0.8	(0.1)	0.000
Canada	-2.8	(0.9)	0.002	-2.1	(0.3)	0.000	-1.6	(0.2)	0.000	-0.5	(0.1)	0.000
Czech Republic	-3.1	(0.6)	0.000	-2.0	(0.4)	0.000	-2.3	(0.2)	0.000	-0.7	(0.2)	0.000
Denmark	-7.9	(12.5)	0.528	-1.1	(0.4)	0.007	-1.3	(0.4)	0.001	-0.8	(0.2)	0.003
Estonia	-7.9	(10.2)	0.440	-3.7	(0.3)	0.000	-1.8	(0.1)	0.000	-0.8	(0.1)	0.000
Finland	-17.8	(18.7)	0.344	-17.4	(18.7)	0.355	-3.1	(0.9)	0.001	-0.5	(0.3)	0.071
France	m	m	m	m	m	m	m	m	m	m	m	m
Germany	-3.6	(0.9)	0.000	-3.1	(0.5)	0.000	-1.7	(0.3)	0.000	-0.7	(0.1)	0.000
Ireland	-2.5	(0.5)	0.000	-2.3	(0.2)	0.000	-1.3	(0.2)	0.000	-0.6	(0.2)	0.000
Italy	m	m	m	m	m	m	m	m	m	m	m	m
Japan	-2.8	(0.5)	0.000	-2.4	(0.3)	0.000	-1.8	(0.2)	0.000	-0.7	(0.2)	0.000
Korea	-4.1	(0.6)	0.000	-3.5	(0.3)	0.000	-2.2	(0.2)	0.000	-0.8	(0.1)	0.000
Netherlands	-16.3	(19.0)	0.393	-2.0	(0.5)	0.001	-1.4	(0.3)	0.000	-0.6	(0.2)	0.002
Norway	-2.5	(0.8)	0.004	-3.2	(14.0)	0.819	-1.8	(0.5)	0.001	-1.0	(0.4)	0.008
Poland	-3.7	(0.3)	0.000	-2.3	(0.2)	0.000	-1.3	(0.2)	0.000	-0.4	(0.1)	0.004
Slovak Republic	-2.4	(0.2)	0.000	-2.1	(0.1)	0.000	-1.2	(0.1)	0.000	-0.6	(0.1)	0.000
Spain	m	m	m	m	m	m	m	m	m	m	m	m
Sweden	-1.0	(0.6)	0.142	-2.0	(0.6)	0.003	-4.4	(0.8)	0.000	-1.4	(0.4)	0.001
United States	-2.4	(0.5)	0.000	-2.1	(0.3)	0.000	-1.0	(0.3)	0.000	-0.6	(0.2)	0.010
Sub-national entities												
Flanders (Belgium)	-3.2	(0.6)	0.000	-1.4	(0.3)	0.000	-1.3	(0.2)	0.000	-0.7	(0.1)	0.000
England (UK)	-3.1	(1.6)	0.064	-3.6	(0.5)	0.000	-1.7	(0.3)	0.000	-0.5	(0.2)	0.017
Northern Ireland (UK)	-1.9	(0.5)	0.000	-1.7	(0.3)	0.000	-1.0	(0.2)	0.000	-0.3	(0.2)	0.114
England/N. Ireland (UK)	-2.9	(1.1)	0.008	-3.3	(0.4)	0.000	-1.6	(0.3)	0.000	-0.5	(0.2)	0.018
Average[1]	-4.9	(1.8)	0.005	-3.2	(1.2)	0.010	-1.8	(0.1)	0.000	-0.7	(0.0)	0.000
Average-22[2]	m	m	m	m	m	m	m	m	m	m	m	m
Partners												
Cyprus[3]	m	m	m	m	m	m	m	m	m	m	m	m
Russian Federation[4]	m	m	m	m	m	m	m	m	m	m	m	m

1. Average of 19 participating OECD countries and entities.
2. Average of 22 OECD countries and entities: average of 19 countries with France, Italy and Spain.
3. See notes at the beginning of this Annex.
4. See note at the beginning of this Annex.
Note: Results for the Russian Federation are missing due to the lack of the language variables.
Source: Survey of Adult Skills (PIAAC) (2012).
StatLink http://dx.doi.org/10.1787/888933232386

[Part 2/4]
Likelihood of adults having no computer experience, by socio-demographic characteristics and cognitive skills (Version 3)

Table B3.5

OECD	Immigrant and language background (reference foreign-born and foreign language)									Educational attainment (reference lower than upper secondary)					
	Native-born and native language			Native-born and foreign language			Foreign-born and native language			Upper secondary			Tertiary		
	ß	S.E.	p-value	ß	S.E.	p-value	ß	S.E.	p-value	ß	S.E.	p-value	ß	S.E.	p-value
National entities															
Australia	-0.6	(0.2)	0.003	-1.0	(0.7)	0.175	-0.8	(0.3)	0.029	-0.4	(0.2)	0.036	-1.4	(0.3)	0.000
Austria	-0.5	(0.2)	0.032	-2.0	(1.2)	0.086	-0.8	(0.5)	0.120	-1.1	(0.1)	0.000	-2.4	(0.3)	0.000
Canada	-0.8	(0.1)	0.000	-1.2	(0.3)	0.000	-0.7	(0.2)	0.005	-1.0	(0.1)	0.000	-2.1	(0.2)	0.000
Czech Republic	0.3	(0.5)	0.485	c	c	c	1.0	(0.5)	0.060	-1.0	(0.2)	0.000	-3.6	(0.5)	0.000
Denmark	-0.7	(0.2)	0.003	0.1	(12.1)	0.992	0.0	(1.0)	0.984	-1.1	(0.2)	0.000	-4.1	(1.1)	0.000
Estonia	-0.4	(0.3)	0.166	-0.2	(0.4)	0.621	-0.3	(0.3)	0.295	-1.0	(0.1)	0.000	-2.4	(0.2)	0.000
Finland	-0.2	(1.1)	0.864	0.5	(1.2)	0.680	1.3	(1.4)	0.370	-1.0	(0.2)	0.000	-3.9	(0.8)	0.000
France	m	m	m	m	m	m	m	m	m	m	m	m	m	m	m
Germany	-0.4	(0.3)	0.089	-0.7	(0.7)	0.315	-0.1	(0.4)	0.800	-0.9	(0.2)	0.000	-1.8	(0.3)	0.000
Ireland	1.1	(0.4)	0.012	1.6	(0.5)	0.003	0.2	(0.5)	0.742	-1.4	(0.1)	0.000	-2.8	(0.3)	0.000
Italy	m	m	m	m	m	m	m	m	m	m	m	m	m	m	m
Japan	c	c	c	c	c	c	c	c	c	-1.4	(0.2)	0.000	-2.1	(0.2)	0.000
Korea	-1.8	(0.7)	0.007	c	c	c	-0.8	(0.8)	0.326	-1.4	(0.1)	0.000	-3.0	(0.2)	0.000
Netherlands	-0.9	(0.3)	0.001	0.4	(1.1)	0.756	-0.5	(0.5)	0.300	-1.4	(0.3)	0.000	-1.9	(0.6)	0.001
Norway	-1.1	(0.4)	0.007	-15.9	(22.3)	0.478	-15.0	(22.1)	0.501	-1.3	(0.3)	0.000	-2.8	(0.6)	0.000
Poland	c	c	c	c	c	c	c	c	c	-1.3	(0.1)	0.000	-3.5	(0.3)	0.000
Slovak Republic	-1.0	(0.5)	0.070	-1.1	(0.6)	0.060	-0.3	(0.7)	0.704	-1.7	(0.1)	0.000	-4.5	(0.4)	0.000
Spain	m	m	m	m	m	m	m	m	m	m	m	m	m	m	m
Sweden	-1.2	(0.5)	0.011	-15.8	(23.2)	0.496	-0.8	(13.6)	0.954	-0.6	(0.3)	0.037	-1.9	(1.2)	0.116
United States	-1.2	(0.3)	0.000	-0.3	(0.4)	0.459	-0.9	(0.6)	0.168	-1.5	(0.2)	0.000	-2.2	(0.3)	0.000
Sub-national entities															
Flanders (Belgium)	-0.5	(0.3)	0.036	-1.1	(0.5)	0.014	-1.3	(0.7)	0.050	-0.7	(0.1)	0.000	-2.3	(0.4)	0.000
England (UK)	-0.5	(0.3)	0.100	-0.7	(13.0)	0.959	-0.1	(0.4)	0.731	-0.8	(0.2)	0.000	-1.5	(0.4)	0.000
Northern Ireland (UK)	0.2	(0.7)	0.715	c	c	c	0.3	(0.7)	0.670	-1.1	(0.2)	0.000	-2.7	(0.5)	0.000
England/N. Ireland (UK)	-0.5	(0.3)	0.126	-0.6	(1.8)	0.726	-0.1	(0.4)	0.735	-0.8	(0.2)	0.000	-1.5	(0.3)	0.000
Average[1]	-0.6	(0.1)	0.000	-2.5	(2.3)	0.278	-1.2	(1.5)	0.449	-1.1	(0.0)	0.000	-2.6	(0.1)	0.000
Average-22[2]	m	m	m	m	m	m	m	m	m	m	m	m	m	m	m
Partners															
Cyprus[3]	m	m	m	m	m	m	m	m	m	m	m	m	m	m	m
Russian Federation[4]	m	m	m	m	m	m	m	m	m	m	m	m	m	m	m

1. Average of 19 participating OECD countries and entities.
2. Average of 22 OECD countries and entities: average of 19 countries with France, Italy and Spain.
3. See notes at the beginning of this Annex.
4. See note at the beginning of this Annex.
Note: Results for the Russian Federation are missing due to the lack of the language variables.
Source: Survey of Adult Skills (PIAAC) (2012).
StatLink ▄▄▄▄ http://dx.doi.org/10.1787/888933232386

[Part 3/4]

Table B3.5 **Likelihood of adults having no computer experience, by socio-demographic characteristics and cognitive skills (Version 3)**

OECD	Gender (reference women)			Parents' educational attainment (reference neither parent attained upper secondary)						Participation in adult education and training (reference did not participate)		
	Men			At least one parent attained upper secondary			At least one parent attained tertiary			Participated		
	ß	S.E.	p-value	ß	S.E.	p-value	ß	S.E.	p-value	ß	S.E.	p-value
National entities												
Australia	-0.9	(0.3)	0.005	-0.9	(0.3)	0.005	-0.5	(0.3)	0.102	-1.4	(0.3)	0.000
Austria	-0.9	(0.2)	0.000	-0.9	(0.2)	0.000	-1.6	(0.4)	0.000	-1.3	(0.2)	0.000
Canada	-0.5	(0.1)	0.001	-0.5	(0.1)	0.001	-1.0	(0.2)	0.000	-1.1	(0.1)	0.000
Czech Republic	-0.5	(0.2)	0.031	-0.5	(0.2)	0.031	-0.6	(0.4)	0.114	-1.1	(0.2)	0.000
Denmark	-0.1	(0.2)	0.710	-0.1	(0.2)	0.710	-1.0	(0.4)	0.019	-1.4	(0.2)	0.000
Estonia	-0.6	(0.1)	0.000	-0.6	(0.1)	0.000	-0.8	(0.2)	0.000	-1.7	(0.1)	0.000
Finland	-0.1	(0.3)	0.726	-0.1	(0.3)	0.726	-1.7	(0.7)	0.019	-1.4	(0.3)	0.000
France	m	m	m	m	m	m	m	m	m	m	m	m
Germany	-0.6	(0.2)	0.009	-0.6	(0.2)	0.009	-1.2	(0.3)	0.000	-1.3	(0.2)	0.000
Ireland	-0.9	(0.2)	0.000	-0.9	(0.2)	0.000	-1.3	(0.4)	0.002	-1.1	(0.1)	0.000
Italy	m	m	m	m	m	m	m	m	m	m	m	m
Japan	0.0	(0.2)	0.902	0.0	(0.2)	0.902	-0.5	(0.3)	0.075	-1.3	(0.2)	0.000
Korea	-0.2	(0.1)	0.191	-0.2	(0.1)	0.191	-0.5	(0.2)	0.043	-0.8	(0.1)	0.000
Netherlands	-0.8	(0.4)	0.019	-0.8	(0.4)	0.019	-0.2	(0.6)	0.743	-1.3	(0.3)	0.000
Norway	0.1	(0.3)	0.835	0.1	(0.3)	0.835	0.3	(0.4)	0.477	-1.1	(0.3)	0.000
Poland	-0.9	(0.1)	0.000	-0.9	(0.1)	0.000	-1.6	(0.3)	0.000	-1.2	(0.2)	0.000
Slovak Republic	-0.8	(0.1)	0.000	-0.8	(0.1)	0.000	-1.9	(0.3)	0.000	-1.0	(0.1)	0.000
Spain	m	m	m	m	m	m	m	m	m	m	m	m
Sweden	0.4	(0.5)	0.428	0.4	(0.5)	0.428	-0.8	(1.8)	0.664	-1.9	(0.4)	0.000
United States	-0.4	(0.2)	0.050	-0.4	(0.2)	0.050	-0.9	(0.3)	0.012	-1.4	(0.2)	0.000
Sub-national entities												
Flanders (Belgium)	-1.1	(0.2)	0.000	-1.1	(0.2)	0.000	-1.0	(0.4)	0.013	-1.5	(0.2)	0.000
England (UK)	-0.2	(0.2)	0.499	-0.2	(0.2)	0.499	-0.2	(0.4)	0.692	-1.4	(0.3)	0.000
Northern Ireland (UK)	-0.8	(0.2)	0.000	-0.8	(0.2)	0.000	-1.0	(0.5)	0.027	-1.0	(0.2)	0.000
England/N. Ireland (UK)	0.0	(0.2)	0.899	-0.2	(0.2)	0.299	-0.2	(0.4)	0.549	-1.4	(0.2)	0.000
Average[1]	-0.5	(0.1)	0.000	-0.5	(0.1)	0.000	-0.9	(0.1)	0.000	-1.3	(0.1)	0.000
Average-22[2]	m	m	m	m	m	m	m	m	m	m	m	m
Partners												
Cyprus[3]	m	m	m	m	m	m	m	m	m	m	m	m
Russian Federation[4]	m	m	m	m	m	m	m	m	m	m	m	m

1. Average of 19 participating OECD countries and entities.
2. Average of 22 OECD countries and entities: average of 19 countries with France, Italy and Spain.
3. See notes at the beginning of this Annex.
4. See note at the beginning of this Annex.

Note: Results for the Russian Federation are missing due to the lack of the language variables.

Source: Survey of Adult Skills (PIAAC) (2012).

StatLink ⟹ http://dx.doi.org/10.1787/888933232386

[Part 4/4]
Likelihood of adults having no computer experience, by socio-demographic characteristics and cognitive skills (Version 3)

Table B3.5

OECD	Literacy levels (reference Level 2)								
	Below Level 1 and Level 1			Level 3			Level 4 and Level 5		
	ß	S.E.	p-value	ß	S.E.	p-value	ß	S.E.	p-value
National entities									
Australia	1.2	(0.2)	0.000	-0.9	(0.3)	0.002	-2.0	(3.7)	0.583
Austria	0.5	(0.2)	0.038	-0.3	(0.3)	0.283	-2.5	(8.8)	0.780
Canada	0.5	(0.1)	0.000	-0.6	(0.2)	0.009	-1.0	(0.6)	0.126
Czech Republic	0.3	(0.3)	0.327	-0.5	(0.2)	0.039	-1.9	(1.1)	0.083
Denmark	0.9	(0.3)	0.001	-1.0	(0.6)	0.145	-9.4	(25.3)	0.712
Estonia	0.4	(0.1)	0.005	-0.4	(0.1)	0.008	-0.7	(0.3)	0.031
Finland	0.7	(0.3)	0.009	-0.3	(0.3)	0.276	-5.4	(13.3)	0.687
France	m	m	m	m	m	m	m	m	m
Germany	0.4	(0.2)	0.047	-0.3	(0.3)	0.284	-1.0	(0.8)	0.212
Ireland	0.5	(0.2)	0.008	-0.2	(0.2)	0.366	-1.1	(1.0)	0.277
Italy	m	m	m	m	m	m	m	m	m
Japan	0.9	(0.2)	0.000	-0.6	(0.2)	0.001	-1.2	(0.3)	0.000
Korea	0.7	(0.2)	0.000	-0.2	(0.2)	0.250	-0.2	(0.5)	0.770
Netherlands	0.8	(0.3)	0.008	-0.8	(0.4)	0.061	-2.7	(11.0)	0.807
Norway	0.8	(0.3)	0.025	-0.3	(0.5)	0.578	-3.7	(13.9)	0.791
Poland	0.5	(0.2)	0.001	-0.3	(0.2)	0.063	-0.9	(0.6)	0.148
Slovak Republic	0.7	(0.2)	0.000	-0.3	(0.1)	0.019	-0.3	(0.4)	0.443
Spain	m	m	m	m	m	m	m	m	m
Sweden	0.9	(0.5)	0.094	-1.8	(6.3)	0.776	-14.8	(23.1)	0.524
United States	1.0	(0.2)	0.000	-1.0	(0.6)	0.065	-12.8	(14.0)	0.363
Sub-national entities									
Flanders (Belgium)	0.6	(0.2)	0.003	-0.5	(0.2)	0.074	-2.5	(7.1)	0.730
England (UK)	0.7	(0.2)	0.001	-0.7	(0.3)	0.035	-2.1	(5.7)	0.708
Northern Ireland (UK)	0.0	(0.2)	0.995	-0.4	(0.3)	0.197	-0.5	(1.2)	0.659
England/N. Ireland (UK)	0.7	(0.2)	0.001	-0.7	(0.3)	0.025	-2.0	(1.2)	0.092
Average[1]	0.7	(0.1)	0.000	-0.6	(0.3)	0.091	-3.5	(2.4)	0.141
Average-22[2]	m	m	m	m	m	m	m	m	m
Partners									
Cyprus[3]	m	m	m	m	m	m	m	m	m
Russian Federation[4]	m	m	m	m	m	m	m	m	m

1. Average of 19 participating OECD countries and entities.
2. Average of 22 OECD countries and entities: average of 19 countries with France, Italy and Spain.
3. See notes at the beginning of this Annex.
4. See note at the beginning of this Annex.
Note: Results for the Russian Federation are missing due to the lack of the language variables.
Source: Survey of Adult Skills (PIAAC) (2012).
StatLink ⟟⟟⟟ http://dx.doi.org/10.1787/888933232386

[Part 1/1]

Table B3.6

Percentage of adults scoring at Level 2 or 3 in problem solving in technology-rich environments or have no computer experience, by participation in adult education and training (formal and non-formal)

OECD	Did not participate in adult education and training				Did participate in adult education and training			
	No computer experience		Level 2/3		No computer experience		Level 2/3	
	%	S.E.	%	S.E.	%	S.E.	%	S.E.
National entities								
Australia	9.0	(0.7)	21.3	(1.4)	0.9	0.2	47.9	(1.3)
Austria	18.8	(1.0)	18.6	(1.0)	2.4	0.4	42.9	(1.3)
Canada	10.4	(0.4)	19.7	(0.8)	1.4	0.1	44.3	(0.8)
Czech Republic	19.2	(1.1)	19.8	(1.5)	3.7	0.6	39.7	(1.6)
Denmark	7.0	(0.6)	19.8	(1.1)	0.6	0.1	44.3	(1.0)
Estonia	21.8	(0.7)	11.0	(0.8)	2.0	0.2	34.2	(1.1)
Finland	10.1	(0.8)	20.0	(1.1)	0.8	0.2	47.6	(1.1)
France	16.9	(0.6)	m	m	3.0	0.3	m	m
Germany	16.6	(1.1)	19.9	(1.1)	2.3	0.4	44.9	(1.4)
Ireland	19.3	(0.8)	12.4	(0.9)	4.1	0.5	32.4	(1.3)
Italy	34.0	(1.0)	m	m	6.3	1.0	m	m
Japan	17.0	(0.8)	24.3	(0.9)	3.1	0.4	45.7	(1.3)
Korea	28.9	(0.9)	13.9	(0.9)	6.9	0.4	35.6	(1.3)
Netherlands	8.2	(0.8)	23.5	(1.3)	0.8	0.2	48.0	(1.2)
Norway	4.1	(0.5)	23.1	(1.4)	0.6	0.1	47.9	(1.0)
Poland	31.8	(0.9)	7.8	(0.6)	4.9	0.6	28.9	(1.7)
Slovak Republic	33.7	(1.0)	14.0	(0.8)	7.2	0.8	39.8	(1.6)
Spain	29.7	(0.9)	m	m	5.4	0.5	m	m
Sweden	4.6	(0.7)	23.1	(1.5)	c	c	50.4	(1.2)
United States	13.1	(1.0)	17.3	(1.1)	1.6	0.3	40.1	(1.5)
Sub-national entities								
Flanders (Belgium)	15.5	(0.7)	20.9	(1.1)	1.6	0.3	45.1	(1.4)
England (UK)	8.9	(0.7)	20.7	(1.1)	1.2	0.3	43.3	(1.3)
Northern Ireland (UK)	19.2	(1.1)	15.2	(1.4)	3.7	0.6	37.4	(2.0)
England/N. Ireland (UK)	9.3	(0.7)	20.5	(1.1)	1.3	0.3	43.1	(1.2)
Average[1]	15.7	(0.2)	18.5	(0.3)	2.6	(0.1)	42.3	(0.3)
Average-22[2]	17.2	(0.2)	m	m	2.9	(0.1)	m	m

Partners

Cyprus[3]	36.2	(0.9)	m	m	7.8	0.8	m	m
Russian Federation[4]	24.9	(2.3)	21.3	(2.1)	5.1	1.1	33.1	(3.1)

1. Average of 19 participating OECD countries and entities.
2. Average of 22 OECD countries and entities: average of 19 countries with France, Italy and Spain.
3. See notes at the beginning of this Annex.
4. See note at the beginning of this Annex.
Source: Survey of Adult Skills (PIAAC) (2012).

StatLink ⎯⎯ http://dx.doi.org/10.1787/888933232390

[Part 1/1]

Percentage of adults scoringe at Level 2 or 3 in problem solving in technology-rich environments or have no computer experience, by parents' educational attainment

Table B3.7

OECD	Neither parent attained upper secondary				At least one parent attained upper secondary				At least one parent attained tertiary			
	No computer experience		Level 2/3		No computer experience		Level 2/3		No computer experience		Level 2/3	
	%	S.E.	%	S.E.	%	S.E.	%	S.E.	%	S.E.	%	S.E.
National entities												
Australia	6.8	(0.7)	26.7	(1.3)	1.2	(0.3)	45.2	(2.1)	0.9	0.3	56.7	(1.8)
Austria	23.8	(1.3)	13.8	(1.1)	5.2	(0.5)	36.6	(1.2)	1.6	0.5	52.1	(2.2)
Canada	11.9	(0.6)	17.0	(1.0)	2.7	(0.3)	37.8	(1.1)	0.7	0.1	50.9	(0.9)
Czech Republic	29.3	(3.5)	7.9	(1.8)	8.9	(0.6)	32.4	(1.3)	2.8	0.9	59.7	(3.2)
Denmark	5.2	(0.5)	23.2	(1.2)	2.1	(0.4)	36.5	(1.3)	0.3	0.1	56.4	(1.3)
Estonia	24.4	(1.1)	7.4	(0.8)	5.4	(0.4)	26.9	(1.3)	2.4	0.3	46.2	(1.4)
Finland	7.2	(0.6)	20.7	(0.9)	1.4	(0.3)	50.0	(1.4)	c	c	67.8	(2.0)
France	19.5	(0.7)	m	m	3.5	(0.4)	m	m	1.2	0.3	53.0	(1.3)
Germany	25.4	(2.5)	9.4	(1.7)	7.8	(0.8)	33.8	(1.2)	2.1	0.4	47.8	(1.9)
Ireland	17.8	(0.7)	13.3	(0.9)	2.7	(0.4)	31.8	(1.8)	0.6	0.2	47.8	(1.9)
Italy	32.8	(1.1)	m	m	3.5	(0.8)	m	m	c	c	m	m
Japan	22.0	(1.6)	17.7	(1.4)	7.9	(0.7)	32.9	(1.2)	2.4	0.4	52.3	(1.4)
Korea	26.0	(0.7)	16.0	(0.9)	5.3	(0.5)	41.2	(1.6)	2.3	0.4	54.3	(1.9)
Netherlands	5.1	(0.4)	29.5	(1.2)	0.7	(0.2)	49.5	(1.6)	0.5	0.2	63.5	(1.6)
Norway	3.6	(0.6)	19.9	(1.2)	1.2	(0.3)	41.9	(1.3)	0.6	0.2	59.6	(1.5)
Poland	48.2	(1.3)	3.9	(0.7)	9.3	(0.6)	20.7	(1.0)	2.3	0.7	45.2	(2.4)
Slovak Republic	51.4	(1.4)	7.7	(0.7)	12.3	(0.6)	29.2	(1.1)	1.6	0.4	50.6	(2.5)
Spain	21.9	(0.6)	m	m	4.2	(0.8)	m	m	1.6	0.5	m	m
Sweden	3.2	(0.5)	24.8	(1.1)	1.0	(0.4)	50.9	(1.7)	c	c	62.6	(1.4)
United States	18.3	(2.0)	8.1	(1.4)	3.3	(0.5)	31.2	(1.7)	0.9	0.2	47.8	(1.8)
Sub-national entities												
Flanders (Belgium)	16.3	(0.8)	17.0	(1.3)	2.2	(0.3)	42.6	(1.5)	0.7	0.3	61.3	(1.5)
England (UK)	9.5	(0.9)	15.6	(1.4)	2.6	(0.5)	43.5	(1.5)	1.2	0.5	57.6	(2.2)
Northern Ireland (UK)	20.9	(1.4)	12.4	(1.3)	4.4	(0.6)	36.3	(2.0)	1.2	0.5	57.0	(3.6)
England/N. Ireland (UK)	10.1	(0.8)	15.4	(1.4)	2.7	(0.5)	43.2	(1.5)	1.2	0.4	57.6	(2.2)
Average[1]	18.7	(0.3)	15.8	(0.3)	4.4	(0.1)	37.6	(0.3)	1.4	(0.1)	55.0	(0.4)
Average-22[2]	19.5	(0.3)	m	m	4.3	(0.1)	m	m	1.4	(0.1)	m	m
Partners												
Cyprus[3]	35.3	(0.9)	m	m	6.2	(0.9)	m	m	2.4	0.8	m	m
Russian Federation[4]	40.5	(3.0)	11.4	(2.3)	14.5	(1.3)	26.7	(2.8)	4.1	1.0	36.0	(3.4)

1. Average of 19 participating OECD countries and entities.
2. Average of 22 OECD countries and entities: average of 19 countries with France, Italy and Spain.
3. See notes at the beginning of this Annex.
4. See note at the beginning of this Annex.
Source: Survey of Adult Skills (PIAAC) (2012).

StatLink ⧉ http://dx.doi.org/10.1787/888933232406

[Part 1/1]

Percentage of adults scoring at Level 2 or 3 in problem solving in technology-rich environments or have no computer experience, by frequency of e-mail use

Table B3.8

OECD	Low frequency of e-mail use (less than monthly or no use)				High frequency of e-mail use (at least monthly use)			
	No computer experience		Level 2/3		No computer experience		Level 2/3	
	%	S.E.	%	S.E.	%	S.E.	%	S.E.
National entities								
Australia	17.9	(1.2)	10.6	(1.2)	a	a	46.9	(1.2)
Austria	32.5	(1.5)	6.2	(0.8)	a	a	44.7	(1.1)
Canada	23.1	(0.8)	8.4	(0.9)	a	a	43.9	(0.7)
Czech Republic	39.0	(1.9)	6.7	(1.3)	a	a	43.0	(1.4)
Denmark	17.7	(1.3)	7.7	(1.3)	a	a	43.8	(0.8)
Estonia	40.6	(1.1)	2.9	(0.5)	a	a	35.8	(0.9)
Finland	19.4	(1.4)	7.4	(1.0)	a	a	49.2	(0.9)
France	37.4	(1.0)	m	m	a	a	m	m
Germany	31.0	(1.9)	7.6	(0.9)	a	a	46.7	(1.1)
Ireland	30.0	(1.2)	5.2	(0.6)	a	a	35.7	(1.2)
Italy	53.2	(1.4)	m	m	a	a	m	m
Japan	24.8	(1.1)	15.2	(1.0)	a	a	49.2	(1.3)
Korea	36.8	(0.9)	11.3	(0.9)	a	a	44.6	(1.2)
Netherlands	28.3	(2.0)	5.1	(1.1)	a	a	47.0	(0.8)
Norway	12.4	(1.3)	10.2	(1.3)	a	a	46.7	(0.9)
Poland	46.0	(1.1)	2.3	(0.5)	a	a	31.6	(1.2)
Slovak Republic	57.2	(1.4)	4.6	(0.7)	a	a	39.0	(1.0)
Spain	43.5	(1.1)	m	m	a	a	m	m
Sweden	10.1	(1.4)	9.4	(1.1)	a	a	50.4	(0.8)
United States	21.3	(1.6)	7.0	(1.1)	a	a	41.4	(1.3)
Sub-national entities								
Flanders (Belgium)	40.2	(1.5)	4.5	(0.9)	a	a	44.1	(1.0)
England (UK)	19.2	(1.2)	7.2	(1.1)	a	a	43.4	(1.1)
Northern Ireland (UK)	29.4	(1.4)	7.4	(1.2)	a	a	41.2	(1.7)
England/N. Ireland (UK)	19.7	(1.2)	7.2	(1.1)	a	a	43.3	(1.0)
Average[1]	28.8	(0.3)	7.3	(0.2)	a	a	43.5	(0.2)
Average-22[2]	31.0	(0.3)	m	m	a	a	m	m

Partners

Cyprus[3]	44.3	(1.1)	m	m	a	a	m	m
Russian Federation[4]	32.5	(3.8)	12.3	(1.5)	a	a	43.5	(2.9)

1. Average of 19 participating OECD countries and entities.
2. Average of 22 OECD countries and entities: average of 19 countries with France, Italy and Spain.
3. See notes at the beginning of this Annex.
4. See note at the beginning of this Annex.
Source: Survey of Adult Skills (PIAAC) (2012).

StatLink ᴍ⒮ᴾ http://dx.doi.org/10.1787/888933232412

[Part 1/1]

Table B4.1 **Percentage of adults scoring at Level 2 or 3 in problem solving in technology-rich environments or having no computer experience, by occupation type**

OECD	Skilled occupations				Semi-skilled white-collar occupations				Semi-skilled blue-collar occupations				Elementary occupations			
	No computer experience		Level 2/3		No computer experience		Level 2/3		No computer experience		Level 2/3		No computer experience		Level 2/3	
	%	S.E.	%	S.E.	%	S.E.	%	S.E.	%	S.E.	%	S.E.	%	S.E.	%	S.E.
National entities																
Australia	0.5	(0.1)	55.6	(1.4)	1.4	(0.3)	37.7	(2.0)	7.2	(1.0)	22.1	(2.0)	4.9	(0.9)	25.4	(3.4)
Austria	1.2	(0.3)	49.5	(1.5)	3.4	(0.5)	31.3	(1.6)	17.8	(1.3)	20.0	(1.6)	27.2	(2.9)	11.8	(2.0)
Canada	1.0	(0.2)	49.2	(0.9)	3.4	(0.4)	34.0	(1.2)	8.7	(0.7)	20.7	(1.3)	9.4	(1.0)	25.0	(1.8)
Czech Republic	1.0	(0.2)	50.2	(2.3)	4.2	(0.9)	33.1	(2.6)	14.8	(1.5)	19.3	(2.0)	21.4	(3.1)	19.3	(2.9)
Denmark	0.1	(0.1)	53.7	(1.0)	1.2	(0.3)	37.5	(1.4)	4.3	(0.6)	23.9	(1.7)	3.6	(0.7)	27.9	(2.4)
Estonia	0.6	(0.1)	42.0	(1.2)	5.1	(0.6)	26.7	(1.5)	14.6	(0.9)	12.5	(1.0)	19.3	(1.4)	18.3	(1.9)
Finland	0.1	(0.1)	57.9	(1.2)	1.4	(0.4)	40.5	(1.6)	5.3	(0.7)	26.4	(1.8)	5.0	(1.2)	33.4	(2.3)
France	2.0	(0.3)	m	m	5.3	(0.6)	m	m	17.0	(1.0)	m	m	23.4	(1.4)	m	m
Germany	1.4	(0.4)	54.8	(1.8)	5.1	(0.6)	34.3	(1.5)	10.3	(1.2)	22.0	(1.8)	20.4	(2.5)	17.4	(2.3)
Ireland	1.9	(0.3)	40.7	(1.5)	5.9	(0.7)	25.8	(1.7)	15.5	(1.4)	14.3	(1.5)	15.0	(1.7)	13.8	(2.1)
Italy	3.7	(0.7)	m	m	14.9	(1.5)	m	m	31.7	(2.2)	m	m	44.7	(2.8)	m	m
Japan	1.7	(0.3)	51.9	(1.7)	6.6	(0.7)	34.1	(1.4)	17.7	(1.3)	23.7	(1.8)	22.5	(3.2)	18.8	(2.7)
Korea	2.7	(0.5)	44.8	(1.9)	9.5	(0.7)	32.0	(1.3)	26.9	(1.3)	15.9	(1.3)	33.9	(2.1)	16.0	(1.9)
Netherlands	0.2	(0.1)	57.2	(1.2)	0.7	(0.2)	40.7	(1.6)	6.4	(1.0)	24.5	(2.4)	7.8	(1.4)	26.9	(2.7)
Norway	0.3	(0.1)	57.8	(1.5)	0.8	(0.3)	37.1	(1.5)	2.3	(0.6)	28.2	(1.9)	2.7	(1.2)	22.9	(3.3)
Poland	2.7	(0.5)	33.4	(1.7)	8.5	(0.9)	19.0	(1.5)	28.5	(1.2)	8.9	(0.9)	30.0	(2.3)	12.5	(1.7)
Slovak Republic	3.3	(0.5)	38.9	(1.6)	14.7	(1.2)	25.9	(2.3)	31.4	(1.4)	16.0	(1.3)	47.7	(2.6)	14.6	(2.6)
Spain	2.5	(0.6)	m	m	9.8	(0.7)	m	m	27.1	(1.2)	m	m	26.4	(1.8)	m	m
Sweden	0.1	(0.1)	60.5	(1.3)	1.2	(0.4)	41.0	(1.8)	1.6	(0.5)	29.2	(2.1)	3.2	(1.5)	27.5	(3.3)
United States	0.6	(0.2)	47.9	(1.6)	3.0	(0.7)	29.1	(1.6)	10.7	(1.3)	17.2	(1.9)	13.6	(2.4)	16.8	(2.9)
Sub-national entities																
Flanders (Belgium)	1.0	(0.2)	51.6	(1.3)	3.5	(0.6)	31.7	(1.9)	12.9	(1.1)	20.1	(1.8)	18.2	(1.8)	14.4	(2.0)
England (UK)	0.6	(0.2)	57.3	(1.7)	2.3	(0.5)	33.1	(1.5)	4.8	(0.9)	19.4	(2.2)	7.6	(1.4)	17.5	(2.5)
Northern Ireland (UK)	1.1	(0.4)	52.1	(1.9)	6.9	(0.9)	30.8	(2.4)	15.7	(2.1)	12.9	(2.4)	17.7	(2.7)	18.2	(3.6)
England/N. Ireland (UK)	0.6	(0.2)	57.1	(1.6)	2.4	(0.5)	33.0	(1.4)	5.2	(0.9)	19.2	(2.2)	7.9	(1.4)	17.5	(2.4)
Average[1]	1.1	(0.1)	50.3	(0.4)	4.3	(0.1)	32.9	(0.4)	12.7	(0.2)	20.2	(0.4)	16.5	(0.5)	20.0	(0.6)
Average-22[2]	1.3	(0.1)	50.3	(0.4)	5.1	(0.1)	32.9	(0.4)	14.5	(0.2)	20.2	(0.4)	18.5	(0.4)	20.0	(0.6)

Partners

Cyprus[3]	6.3	(0.8)	m	m	17.4	(1.3)	m	m	43.8	(2.1)	m	m	55.2	(3.1)	m	m
Russian Federation[4]	6.7	(1.0)	33.4	(2.3)	16.4	(2.8)	24.3	(2.3)	23.2	(2.7)	18.9	(2.6)	39.4	(4.1)	16.9	(4.6)

1. Average of 19 participating OECD countries and entities.
2. Average of 22 OECD countries and entities: average of 19 countries with France, Italy and Spain.
3. See notes at the beginning of this Annex.
4. See note at the beginning of this Annex.
Source: Survey of Adult Skills (PIAAC) (2012).

StatLink http://dx.doi.org/10.1787/888933232424

[Part 1/1]
Table B4.2 **Frequency of e-mail use at work and in everyday life**

OECD	Regular use at work and in everyday life		Regular use at work and irregular use in everyday life		Irregular use at work and regular use in everyday life		Irregular use at work and in everyday life		Missing	
National entities	%	S.E.	%	S.E.	%	S.E.	%	S.E.	%	S.E.
Australia	55.6	(0.8)	6.0	(0.3)	23.6	(0.8)	12.6	(0.5)	2.3	(0.2)
Austria	50.0	(0.8)	5.8	(0.4)	21.7	(0.6)	20.0	(0.6)	2.4	(0.2)
Canada	55.2	(0.6)	4.6	(0.2)	26.4	(0.5)	12.5	(0.4)	1.2	(0.1)
Czech Republic	48.8	(1.2)	4.8	(0.6)	28.3	(1.2)	17.2	(1.0)	0.9	(0.3)
Denmark	62.9	(0.6)	3.6	(0.3)	25.6	(0.6)	7.3	(0.4)	0.6	(0.1)
Estonia	49.1	(0.7)	3.6	(0.2)	30.6	(0.6)	15.9	(0.4)	0.8	(0.1)
Finland	63.0	(0.6)	5.0	(0.3)	23.0	(0.6)	8.9	(0.4)	0.1	(0.1)
France	46.8	(0.6)	5.4	(0.3)	27.2	(0.5)	19.4	(0.5)	1.2	(0.1)
Germany	49.2	(0.8)	4.8	(0.4)	25.7	(0.8)	18.4	(0.7)	1.9	(0.2)
Ireland	44.3	(1.0)	7.1	(0.4)	26.8	(1.0)	21.1	(0.7)	0.6	(0.2)
Italy	34.0	(0.8)	6.2	(0.5)	25.1	(1.0)	33.6	(1.1)	1.1	(0.3)
Japan	35.4	(0.8)	11.0	(0.6)	23.2	(0.7)	28.6	(0.7)	1.9	(0.2)
Korea	40.2	(0.7)	6.4	(0.3)	18.6	(0.6)	34.3	(0.7)	0.5	(0.1)
Netherlands	66.3	(0.6)	2.1	(0.2)	23.2	(0.6)	5.6	(0.3)	2.9	(0.2)
Norway	65.6	(0.6)	4.1	(0.3)	21.4	(0.5)	6.3	(0.3)	2.7	(0.2)
Poland	39.1	(0.8)	3.6	(0.4)	25.0	(0.7)	31.9	(0.7)	0.4	(0.1)
Slovak Republic	40.7	(1.0)	4.8	(0.4)	26.3	(0.8)	27.6	(0.8)	0.5	(0.1)
Spain	37.5	(0.7)	5.7	(0.4)	26.9	(0.7)	28.4	(0.8)	1.5	(0.2)
Sweden	62.4	(0.8)	5.9	(0.4)	23.8	(0.7)	7.6	(0.4)	0.3	(0.1)
United States	51.7	(1.2)	5.7	(0.4)	21.4	(0.8)	16.1	(0.8)	5.2	(0.7)
Sub-national entities										
Flanders (Belgium)	56.3	(0.9)	3.9	(0.3)	21.5	(0.7)	11.4	(0.5)	7.0	(0.3)
England (UK)	56.0	(0.9)	5.6	(0.4)	24.1	(0.8)	12.4	(0.6)	1.9	(0.2)
Northern Ireland (UK)	46.7	(1.2)	8.7	(0.7)	21.4	(1.1)	20.1	(0.8)	3.2	(0.4)
England/N. Ireland (UK)	55.7	(0.9)	5.7	(0.4)	24.1	(0.7)	12.7	(0.6)	1.9	(0.2)
Average[1]	52.2	(0.2)	5.2	(0.1)	24.2	(0.2)	16.6	(0.1)	1.8	(0.1)
Average-22[2]	50.4	(0.2)	5.3	(0.1)	24.5	(0.2)	18.1	(0.1)	1.7	(0.1)
Partners										
Cyprus[3]	23.8	(0.6)	6.7	(0.5)	14.2	(0.6)	31.5	(0.8)	23.8	(0.5)
Russian Federation[4]	23.9	(1.9)	5.4	(0.5)	23.4	(1.2)	47.0	(2.3)	0.3	(0.1)

1. Average of 19 participating OECD countries and entities.
2. Average of 22 OECD countries and entities: average of 19 countries with France, Italy and Spain.
3. See notes at the beginning of this Annex.
4. See notes at the beginning of this Annex.
Source: Survey of Adult Skills (PIAAC) (2012).

StatLink http://dx.doi.org/10.1787/888933232436

[Part 1/1]

Table B4.3 **Frequency of Internet use to better understand issues related to work and to everyday life**

OECD	Regular use at work and in everyday life		Regular use at work and irregular use in everyday life		Irregular use at work and regular use in everyday life		Irregular use at work and in everyday life		Missing	
	%	S.E.	%	S.E.	%	S.E.	%	S.E.	%	S.E.
National entities										
Australia	50.7	(0.8)	7.1	(0.4)	23.8	(0.8)	16.1	(0.5)	2.3	(0.2)
Austria	46.5	(0.8)	4.6	(0.4)	27.5	(0.7)	19.1	(0.6)	2.4	(0.2)
Canada	49.2	(0.5)	6.7	(0.3)	27.0	(0.4)	16.0	(0.4)	1.2	(0.1)
Czech Republic	45.4	(1.4)	3.8	(0.4)	33.9	(1.4)	16.0	(1.1)	0.9	(0.3)
Denmark	56.1	(0.7)	6.1	(0.3)	27.1	(0.6)	10.1	(0.4)	0.6	(0.1)
Estonia	45.8	(0.7)	6.1	(0.3)	30.2	(0.6)	17.1	(0.5)	0.8	(0.1)
Finland	57.6	(0.7)	4.9	(0.3)	26.5	(0.6)	10.9	(0.5)	0.2	(0.1)
France	39.6	(0.6)	3.8	(0.2)	34.2	(0.6)	21.3	(0.6)	1.2	(0.1)
Germany	45.3	(0.9)	5.1	(0.4)	30.1	(0.7)	17.5	(0.7)	2.0	(0.2)
Ireland	39.1	(0.9)	8.5	(0.4)	27.9	(0.8)	23.9	(0.7)	0.6	(0.2)
Italy	29.1	(1.0)	8.1	(0.6)	26.4	(1.0)	35.3	(1.2)	1.1	(0.3)
Japan	33.5	(0.8)	16.3	(0.7)	16.7	(0.6)	31.7	(0.7)	1.9	(0.2)
Korea	42.4	(0.7)	8.8	(0.4)	19.9	(0.7)	28.3	(0.7)	0.5	(0.1)
Netherlands	53.1	(0.7)	6.7	(0.3)	26.3	(0.6)	11.1	(0.4)	2.9	(0.2)
Norway	58.9	(0.6)	5.6	(0.3)	24.3	(0.5)	8.5	(0.4)	2.7	(0.2)
Poland	38.4	(0.7)	4.7	(0.4)	27.3	(0.8)	29.2	(0.8)	0.5	(0.1)
Slovak Republic	36.5	(0.9)	5.7	(0.4)	27.9	(0.8)	29.3	(0.9)	0.6	(0.1)
Spain	33.1	(0.8)	7.1	(0.5)	28.3	(0.7)	30.1	(0.7)	1.5	(0.2)
Sweden	53.1	(0.8)	6.5	(0.4)	29.0	(0.7)	11.0	(0.6)	0.4	(0.1)
United States	46.8	(1.0)	7.8	(0.5)	22.1	(0.6)	18.0	(0.9)	5.2	(0.7)
Sub-national entities										
Flanders (Belgium)	47.4	(0.8)	6.1	(0.4)	25.2	(0.7)	14.3	(0.6)	7.0	(0.3)
England (UK)	48.1	(0.9)	8.1	(0.5)	25.2	(0.9)	16.7	(0.7)	1.9	(0.2)
Northern Ireland (UK)	39.6	(1.1)	11.3	(0.7)	21.9	(1.1)	24.1	(0.9)	3.2	(0.4)
England/N. Ireland (UK)	47.9	(0.9)	8.2	(0.5)	25.1	(0.9)	16.9	(0.7)	1.9	(0.2)
Average[1]	47.0	(0.2)	6.8	(0.1)	26.2	(0.2)	18.2	(0.2)	1.8	(0.1)
Average-22[2]	45.2	(0.2)	6.7	(0.1)	26.7	(0.2)	19.6	(0.1)	1.7	(0.1)
Partners										
Cyprus[3]	21.7	(0.6)	5.6	(0.5)	17.4	(0.7)	31.5	(0.8)	23.8	(0.5)
Russian Federation[4]	23.0	(1.3)	6.8	(0.6)	29.7	(1.4)	40.2	(1.2)	0.3	(0.1)

1. Average of 19 participating OECD countries and entities.
2. Average of 22 OECD countries and entities: average of 19 countries with France, Italy and Spain.
3. See notes at the beginning of this Annex.
4. See note at the beginning of this Annex.
Note: Regular use is defined as a frequency of at least monthly use. Irregular use is defined as a frequency of less than monthly use.
Source: Survey of Adult Skills (PIAAC) (2012).
StatLink 🔗 http://dx.doi.org/10.1787/888933232443

[Part 1/1]

Frequency of Internet use for conducting transactions (e.g. buying or selling products or services, or banking) at work and in everyday life

Table B4.4

OECD	Regular use at work and in everyday life		Regular use at work and irregular use in everyday life		Irregular use at work and regular use in everyday life		Irregular use at work and in everyday life		Missing	
	%	S.E.	%	S.E.	%	S.E.	%	S.E.	%	S.E.
National entities										
Australia	25.3	(0.8)	4.2	(0.3)	40.6	(0.7)	27.7	(0.7)	2.3	(0.2)
Austria	15.9	(0.5)	4.4	(0.3)	32.6	(0.7)	44.7	(0.7)	2.4	(0.2)
Canada	20.4	(0.5)	4.3	(0.2)	42.2	(0.5)	31.9	(0.5)	1.2	(0.1)
Czech Republic	17.0	(1.0)	4.8	(0.5)	36.6	(1.4)	40.6	(1.3)	0.9	(0.3)
Denmark	25.3	(0.5)	3.2	(0.3)	51.6	(0.7)	19.3	(0.5)	0.6	(0.1)
Estonia	26.3	(0.6)	2.7	(0.2)	47.6	(0.6)	22.7	(0.6)	0.8	(0.1)
Finland	24.5	(0.6)	1.9	(0.2)	60.3	(0.7)	13.1	(0.5)	0.2	(0.1)
France	9.3	(0.4)	4.2	(0.3)	36.0	(0.7)	49.3	(0.7)	1.2	(0.1)
Germany	14.4	(0.6)	3.5	(0.3)	38.7	(0.9)	41.4	(0.8)	1.9	(0.2)
Ireland	17.2	(0.7)	4.4	(0.4)	36.9	(0.9)	40.9	(0.9)	0.6	(0.2)
Italy	8.0	(0.5)	5.1	(0.5)	15.7	(0.8)	70.1	(1.0)	1.1	(0.3)
Japan	7.5	(0.5)	4.3	(0.3)	22.4	(0.7)	63.9	(0.8)	1.9	(0.2)
Korea	27.9	(0.7)	4.8	(0.3)	28.5	(0.7)	38.3	(0.8)	0.5	(0.1)
Netherlands	21.1	(0.6)	2.4	(0.2)	57.1	(0.8)	16.4	(0.6)	2.9	(0.2)
Norway	25.7	(0.6)	2.1	(0.2)	56.8	(0.7)	12.7	(0.5)	2.7	(0.2)
Poland	14.4	(0.7)	3.1	(0.3)	29.9	(0.8)	52.1	(0.8)	0.4	(0.1)
Slovak Republic	15.6	(0.6)	4.2	(0.4)	27.5	(0.7)	52.2	(0.8)	0.5	(0.1)
Spain	9.0	(0.4)	4.4	(0.3)	20.3	(0.6)	64.9	(0.8)	1.5	(0.2)
Sweden	21.0	(0.6)	2.3	(0.2)	58.6	(0.8)	17.8	(0.6)	0.3	(0.1)
United States	22.5	(0.8)	5.4	(0.4)	35.0	(0.8)	31.9	(0.9)	5.2	(0.7)
Sub-national entities										
Flanders (Belgium)	17.5	(0.7)	3.5	(0.3)	44.3	(0.7)	27.7	(0.6)	7.0	(0.3)
England (UK)	22.9	(0.9)	3.2	(0.3)	45.1	(1.0)	26.8	(0.8)	1.9	(0.2)
Northern Ireland (UK)	16.1	(0.9)	5.1	(0.5)	40.0	(1.1)	35.7	(1.1)	3.2	(0.4)
England/N. Ireland (UK)	22.7	(0.8)	3.3	(0.3)	45.0	(1.0)	27.1	(0.8)	1.9	(0.2)
Average[1]	20.1	(0.2)	3.6	(0.1)	41.7	(0.2)	32.8	(0.2)	1.8	(0.1)
Average-22[2]	18.6	(0.1)	3.8	(0.1)	39.3	(0.2)	36.7	(0.2)	1.7	(0.1)
Partners										
Cyprus[3]	5.5	(0.3)	3.3	(0.3)	11.9	(0.6)	55.5	(0.8)	23.8	(0.5)
Russian Federation[4]	4.0	(0.3)	4.3	(0.6)	6.8	(0.5)	84.5	(0.8)	0.5	(0.1)

1. Average of 19 participating OECD countries and entities.
2. Average of 22 OECD countries and entities: average of 19 countries with France, Italy and Spain.
3. See notes at the beginning of this Annex.
4. See note at the beginning of this Annex.
Note: Regular use is defined as a frequency of at least monthly use. Irregular use is defined as a frequency of less than monthly use.
Source: Survey of Adult Skills (PIAAC) (2012).

StatLink ⬛🔨⬛ http://dx.doi.org/10.1787/888933232458

[Part 1/1]

Table B4.5 **Frequency of spreadsheet software use (e.g. Excel) at work and in everyday life**

OECD	Regular use at work and in everyday life		Regular use at work and irregular use in everyday life		Irregular use at work and regular use in everyday life		Irregular use at work and in everyday life		Missing	
	%	S.E.	%	S.E.	%	S.E.	%	S.E.	%	S.E.
National entities										
Australia	15.0	(0.6)	30.5	(0.7)	4.1	(0.4)	47.9	(0.8)	2.4	(0.2)
Austria	15.8	(0.5)	22.6	(0.7)	5.4	(0.4)	53.7	(0.8)	2.4	(0.2)
Canada	16.5	(0.5)	25.9	(0.4)	6.8	(0.3)	49.5	(0.6)	1.2	(0.1)
Czech Republic	17.7	(1.2)	25.0	(1.2)	6.4	(0.6)	50.0	(1.3)	1.0	(0.3)
Denmark	18.4	(0.5)	20.4	(0.6)	9.6	(0.5)	51.0	(0.6)	0.7	(0.1)
Estonia	14.9	(0.5)	23.6	(0.5)	7.3	(0.3)	53.4	(0.7)	0.8	(0.1)
Finland	13.7	(0.5)	23.7	(0.5)	6.2	(0.4)	56.1	(0.7)	0.3	(0.1)
France	12.5	(0.4)	24.4	(0.5)	5.0	(0.3)	56.9	(0.7)	1.3	(0.1)
Germany	16.9	(0.7)	21.1	(0.7)	6.7	(0.5)	53.3	(0.8)	2.0	(0.2)
Ireland	9.6	(0.5)	26.6	(0.7)	5.7	(0.4)	57.4	(0.9)	0.6	(0.2)
Italy	11.9	(0.6)	18.9	(0.8)	5.2	(0.4)	62.8	(0.9)	1.2	(0.3)
Japan	10.5	(0.5)	32.9	(0.6)	3.5	(0.3)	51.2	(0.8)	1.9	(0.2)
Korea	16.5	(0.5)	22.9	(0.7)	5.5	(0.3)	54.6	(0.7)	0.5	(0.1)
Netherlands	19.4	(0.6)	27.1	(0.7)	8.2	(0.4)	42.4	(0.8)	2.9	(0.2)
Norway	15.6	(0.6)	22.7	(0.7)	6.5	(0.4)	52.5	(0.7)	2.7	(0.2)
Poland	12.6	(0.6)	16.1	(0.6)	5.2	(0.3)	65.7	(0.7)	0.4	(0.1)
Slovak Republic	16.7	(0.7)	20.0	(0.8)	5.9	(0.4)	56.8	(1.1)	0.6	(0.1)
Spain	11.3	(0.6)	19.2	(0.6)	5.5	(0.3)	62.5	(0.8)	1.5	(0.2)
Sweden	14.0	(0.6)	24.4	(0.7)	5.9	(0.4)	55.5	(0.7)	0.3	(0.1)
United States	14.8	(0.6)	25.1	(0.7)	6.3	(0.3)	48.5	(1.0)	5.3	(0.7)
Sub-national entities										
Flanders (Belgium)	18.0	(0.6)	23.8	(0.8)	5.6	(0.4)	45.7	(0.8)	7.0	(0.3)
England (UK)	16.1	(0.7)	29.7	(0.9)	5.1	(0.4)	47.3	(0.9)	1.8	(0.2)
Northern Ireland (UK)	9.8	(0.7)	29.9	(1.0)	4.1	(0.5)	53.0	(1.2)	3.2	(0.4)
England/N. Ireland (UK)	16.0	(0.7)	29.7	(0.8)	5.0	(0.4)	47.5	(0.9)	1.9	(0.2)
Average[1]	15.4	(0.1)	24.4	(0.2)	6.1	(0.1)	52.2	(0.2)	1.8	(0.1)
Average-22[2]	14.9	(0.1)	23.9	(0.2)	6.0	(0.1)	53.4	(0.2)	1.8	(0.1)

Partners

Cyprus[3]	6.6	(0.4)	15.5	(0.6)	2.6	(0.3)	51.5	(0.8)	23.8	(0.5)
Russian Federation[4]	8.8	(0.9)	17.0	(0.8)	5.1	(0.7)	68.7	(1.1)	0.3	(0.1)

1. Average of 19 participating OECD countries and entities.
2. Average of 22 OECD countries and entities: average of 19 countries with France, Italy and Spain.
3. See notes at the beginning of this Annex.
4. See note at the beginning of this Annex.
Note: Regular use is defined as a frequency of at least monthly use. Irregular use is defined as a frequency of less than monthly use.
Source: Survey of Adult Skills (PIAAC) (2012).
StatLink ⬛📊 http://dx.doi.org/10.1787/888933232469

[Part 1/1]

Table B4.6 **Frequency of a word processor use (e.g. Word) at work and in everyday life**

OECD	Regular use at work and in everyday life		Regular use at work and irregular use in everyday life		Irregular use at work and regular use in everyday life		Irregular use at work and in everyday life		Missing	
National entities	%	S.E.	%	S.E.	%	S.E.	%	S.E.	%	S.E.
Australia	30.7	(0.8)	20.8	(0.6)	13.1	(0.7)	33.1	(0.8)	2.3	(0.2)
Austria	32.1	(0.7)	17.0	(0.6)	13.7	(0.5)	34.9	(0.8)	2.4	(0.2)
Canada	29.8	(0.6)	19.9	(0.4)	15.8	(0.4)	33.2	(0.6)	1.2	(0.1)
Czech Republic	31.0	(1.2)	17.3	(0.8)	13.9	(0.8)	36.9	(1.2)	1.0	(0.3)
Denmark	41.1	(0.7)	15.5	(0.5)	19.6	(0.6)	23.1	(0.6)	0.7	(0.1)
Estonia	25.8	(0.5)	17.3	(0.6)	12.1	(0.4)	44.0	(0.7)	0.8	(0.1)
Finland	30.4	(0.7)	23.2	(0.6)	12.9	(0.5)	33.1	(0.5)	0.3	(0.1)
France	20.6	(0.4)	21.5	(0.5)	10.2	(0.4)	46.4	(0.6)	1.2	(0.1)
Germany	36.2	(0.9)	14.4	(0.5)	15.6	(0.7)	31.8	(0.8)	2.0	(0.2)
Ireland	22.2	(0.8)	22.4	(0.7)	13.2	(0.7)	41.5	(1.0)	0.7	(0.2)
Italy	20.5	(0.8)	15.4	(0.7)	11.7	(0.6)	51.3	(1.0)	1.1	(0.3)
Japan	10.6	(0.5)	31.5	(0.6)	5.7	(0.4)	50.4	(0.8)	1.9	(0.2)
Korea	22.1	(0.7)	20.3	(0.7)	8.5	(0.4)	48.7	(0.6)	0.5	(0.1)
Netherlands	43.4	(0.8)	15.4	(0.6)	16.7	(0.5)	21.6	(0.6)	2.9	(0.2)
Norway	37.6	(0.6)	19.5	(0.6)	16.1	(0.5)	24.1	(0.5)	2.7	(0.2)
Poland	28.0	(0.7)	11.0	(0.6)	12.5	(0.5)	48.0	(0.8)	0.5	(0.1)
Slovak Republic	30.3	(0.9)	13.2	(0.7)	13.7	(0.7)	42.1	(1.0)	0.6	(0.1)
Spain	23.7	(0.8)	14.4	(0.7)	13.1	(0.5)	47.4	(0.8)	1.5	(0.2)
Sweden	30.3	(0.8)	22.4	(0.6)	16.5	(0.7)	30.6	(0.8)	0.2	(0.1)
United States	29.5	(0.9)	17.2	(0.5)	14.5	(0.6)	33.6	(0.9)	5.2	(0.7)
Sub-national entities										
Flanders (Belgium)	32.3	(0.7)	18.5	(0.6)	10.2	(0.4)	32.1	(0.8)	7.0	(0.3)
England (UK)	32.5	(0.8)	22.2	(0.7)	12.5	(0.7)	31.0	(0.8)	1.9	(0.2)
Northern Ireland (UK)	24.3	(1.0)	24.5	(0.9)	10.9	(0.8)	37.1	(1.2)	3.2	(0.4)
England/N. Ireland (UK)	32.2	(0.8)	22.3	(0.7)	12.4	(0.7)	31.2	(0.7)	1.9	(0.2)
Average[1]	30.3	(0.2)	18.9	(0.1)	13.5	(0.1)	35.5	(0.2)	1.8	(0.1)
Average-22[2]	29.1	(0.2)	18.7	(0.1)	13.3	(0.1)	37.2	(0.2)	1.7	(0.1)
Partners										
Cyprus[3]	15.1	(0.5)	14.2	(0.6)	6.2	(0.5)	40.7	(0.9)	23.8	(0.5)
Russian Federation[4]	19.0	(1.4)	14.6	(0.7)	12.1	(0.8)	54.0	(1.4)	0.3	(0.1)

1. Average of 19 participating OECD countries and entities.
2. Average of 22 OECD countries and entities: average of 19 countries with France, Italy and Spain.
3. See notes at the beginning of this Annex.
4. See note at the beginning of this Annex.
Note: Regular use is defined as a frequency of at least monthly use. Irregular use is defined as a frequency of less than monthly use.
Source: Survey of Adult Skills (PIAAC) (2012).
StatLink http://dx.doi.org/10.1787/888933232479

[Part 1/1]

Table B4.7 **Percentage of workers, by frequency of complex problem solving**

OECD	Less than monthly or never		At least monthly	
	%	S.E.	%	S.E.
National entities				
Australia	52.7	(0.8)	44.9	(0.9)
Austria	65.3	(0.7)	32.3	(0.7)
Canada	60.7	(0.5)	37.9	(0.5)
Czech Republic	60.5	(1.5)	38.5	(1.4)
Denmark	64.9	(0.7)	34.4	(0.7)
Estonia	69.3	(0.6)	29.7	(0.6)
Finland	69.3	(0.7)	29.9	(0.7)
France	65.8	(0.7)	32.0	(0.7)
Germany	64.3	(0.8)	33.7	(0.8)
Ireland	62.5	(0.9)	36.8	(0.8)
Italy	60.0	(1.3)	38.9	(1.3)
Japan	76.5	(0.6)	21.4	(0.6)
Korea	76.3	(0.8)	23.1	(0.7)
Netherlands	67.6	(0.7)	29.4	(0.7)
Norway	64.9	(0.7)	32.1	(0.7)
Poland	70.6	(0.8)	28.5	(0.8)
Slovak Republic	60.5	(0.9)	38.5	(0.9)
Spain	64.4	(0.8)	33.9	(0.8)
Sweden	65.5	(0.8)	33.8	(0.8)
United States	51.7	(0.7)	43.0	(0.9)
Sub-national entities				
Flanders (Belgium)	60.6	(0.8)	32.3	(0.8)
England (UK)	54.7	(0.9)	43.4	(0.9)
Northern Ireland (UK)	58.9	(1.2)	37.9	(1.1)
England/N. Ireland (UK)	54.8	(0.9)	43.2	(0.9)
Average[1]	64.1	(0.2)	33.9	(0.2)
Average-22[2]	64.0	(0.2)	34.0	(0.2)
Partners				
Cyprus[3]	49.3	(0.7)	26.7	(0.7)
Russian Federation[4]	59.0	(1.2)	39.5	(1.4)

1. Average of 19 participating OECD countries and entities.
2. Average of 22 OECD countries and entities: average of 19 countries with France, Italy and Spain.
3. See notes at the beginning of this Annex.
4. See note at the beginning of this Annex.
Note: Complex problems are defined as problems that take at least 30 minutes to find a good solution.
Source: Survey of Adult Skills (PIAAC) (2012).
StatLink ⏭ http://dx.doi.org/10.1787/888933232483

Table B4.8   **Percentage of workers who reported lack of computer skills to do their job well, by age**

OECD	16-24 year-olds		25-34 year-olds		35-44 year-olds		45-54 year-olds		55-65 year-olds	
	%	S.E.	%	S.E.	%	S.E.	%	S.E.	%	S.E.
National entities										
Australia	1.0	(0.4)	4.0	(0.7)	6.9	(0.9)	9.0	(1.0)	11.4	(1.3)
Austria	1.0	(0.4)	1.9	(0.5)	1.7	(0.4)	5.3	(0.7)	5.5	(1.1)
Canada	1.1	(0.3)	2.4	(0.4)	3.7	(0.4)	7.7	(0.6)	7.0	(0.7)
Czech Republic	0.1	(0.1)	1.9	(0.4)	2.3	(0.8)	4.3	(1.2)	2.8	(0.6)
Denmark	1.1	(0.4)	4.4	(0.9)	9.6	(0.9)	11.7	(1.2)	11.8	(0.9)
Estonia	2.2	(0.6)	4.3	(0.6)	7.6	(0.7)	10.5	(0.9)	9.2	(0.8)
Finland	0.8	(0.4)	4.1	(0.7)	9.0	(1.0)	14.6	(1.3)	18.9	(1.3)
France	1.8	(0.5)	5.5	(0.5)	9.5	(0.8)	12.1	(0.8)	11.1	(1.0)
Germany	0.6	(0.3)	2.9	(0.7)	3.6	(0.6)	6.1	(1.0)	4.4	(0.8)
Ireland	1.0	(0.6)	1.7	(0.4)	7.8	(0.8)	7.5	(1.0)	8.7	(1.4)
Italy	0.2	(0.3)	2.3	(0.8)	3.9	(0.6)	4.4	(0.8)	8.4	(1.7)
Japan	14.2	(1.9)	26.1	(1.7)	29.2	(1.3)	28.7	(1.5)	24.1	(1.2)
Korea	9.4	(1.5)	13.0	(1.1)	15.9	(1.1)	15.3	(1.1)	10.0	(1.2)
Netherlands	1.9	(0.6)	3.4	(0.7)	4.9	(0.6)	6.5	(0.8)	6.7	(0.8)
Norway	2.5	(0.6)	8.4	(0.9)	15.0	(1.0)	20.2	(1.3)	19.4	(1.6)
Poland	1.1	(0.2)	2.4	(0.6)	3.8	(0.8)	7.5	(1.3)	7.7	(1.5)
Slovak Republic	1.4	(0.6)	1.8	(0.5)	2.5	(0.5)	3.3	(0.6)	5.1	(1.0)
Spain	1.6	(0.7)	2.2	(0.5)	5.0	(0.8)	6.3	(0.7)	9.6	(1.5)
Sweden	1.3	(0.5)	3.7	(0.7)	7.2	(0.9)	10.5	(1.0)	13.7	(1.2)
United States	1.3	(0.6)	2.3	(0.5)	4.0	(0.8)	5.7	(0.8)	8.6	(0.9)
Sub-national entities										
Flanders (Belgium)	1.1	(0.5)	2.9	(0.6)	7.6	(0.8)	8.8	(1.0)	8.8	(1.2)
England (UK)	0.6	(0.3)	3.1	(0.6)	7.2	(1.0)	9.2	(1.2)	7.7	(1.1)
Northern Ireland (UK)	0.9	(0.5)	3.2	(1.1)	4.9	(0.9)	6.7	(1.2)	8.2	(1.6)
England/N. Ireland (UK)	0.7	(0.3)	3.1	(0.6)	7.1	(1.0)	9.2	(1.2)	7.7	(1.1)
Average[1]	2.3	(0.2)	5.0	(0.2)	7.9	(0.2)	10.1	(0.2)	10.1	(0.3)
Average-22[2]	2.2	(0.1)	4.8	(0.2)	7.6	(0.2)	9.8	(0.2)	10.0	(0.2)

Partners

Cyprus[3]	0.4	(0.2)	1.4	(0.3)	5.9	(0.8)	5.0	(0.9)	3.8	(0.8)
Russian Federation[4]	1.8	(0.6)	2.5	(0.6)	4.2	(0.9)	4.1	(0.8)	3.0	(0.5)

1. Average of 19 participating OECD countries and entities.
2. Average of 22 OECD countries and entities: average of 19 countries with France, Italy and Spain.
3. See notes at the beginning of this Annex.
4. See note at the beginning of this Annex.
Source: Survey of Adult Skills (PIAAC) (2012).

StatLink ⬛⬛ http://dx.doi.org/10.1787/888933232497

[Part 1/1]

Percentage of workers whose lack of computer skills have affected their chances of getting a job, promotion or pay raise, by age

Table B4.9

OECD	16-24 year-olds %	S.E.	25-34 year-olds %	S.E.	35-44 year-olds %	S.E.	45-54 year-olds %	S.E.	55-65 year-olds %	S.E.
National entities										
Australia	2.8	(0.7)	5.7	(0.8)	6.9	(0.9)	8.7	(1.0)	6.9	(0.9)
Austria	2.2	(0.6)	2.8	(0.6)	3.6	(0.6)	4.0	(0.6)	1.3	(0.6)
Canada	2.9	(0.5)	5.5	(0.5)	8.0	(0.6)	7.2	(0.5)	6.1	(0.7)
Czech Republic	3.0	(0.9)	4.2	(1.0)	2.0	(0.7)	1.3	(0.4)	2.3	(0.8)
Denmark	1.6	(0.5)	3.8	(0.7)	5.6	(0.8)	4.2	(0.6)	3.3	(0.4)
Estonia	5.3	(0.7)	4.8	(0.6)	5.2	(0.6)	6.1	(0.6)	5.6	(0.7)
Finland	1.5	(0.5)	4.7	(0.8)	4.4	(0.6)	2.6	(0.5)	3.5	(0.6)
France	3.0	(0.7)	5.4	(0.7)	4.8	(0.6)	5.7	(0.6)	3.5	(0.6)
Germany	1.5	(0.5)	3.2	(0.7)	3.5	(0.7)	2.9	(0.6)	2.3	(0.5)
Ireland	2.2	(0.7)	2.8	(0.5)	6.3	(0.7)	4.7	(0.8)	6.1	(0.9)
Italy	3.7	(1.2)	4.3	(0.9)	3.9	(0.6)	2.7	(0.6)	3.4	(0.8)
Japan	14.1	(1.8)	17.4	(1.3)	19.0	(1.1)	16.5	(1.2)	13.1	(1.3)
Korea	0.4	(0.2)	1.9	(0.4)	2.8	(0.6)	1.4	(0.3)	0.7	(0.3)
Netherlands	1.8	(0.5)	3.1	(0.6)	3.7	(0.6)	3.0	(0.6)	3.0	(0.7)
Norway	2.5	(0.6)	4.8	(0.7)	5.2	(0.5)	5.7	(0.7)	4.0	(0.8)
Poland	5.4	(0.5)	6.8	(0.7)	5.8	(0.9)	4.1	(0.8)	3.5	(0.9)
Slovak Republic	2.7	(0.9)	3.9	(0.6)	3.2	(0.6)	2.4	(0.4)	2.5	(0.8)
Spain	3.0	(1.0)	2.8	(0.5)	4.5	(0.6)	3.9	(0.7)	4.0	(1.1)
Sweden	1.8	(0.6)	4.7	(0.9)	3.0	(0.7)	3.4	(0.6)	4.2	(0.7)
United States	4.2	(1.0)	5.5	(0.8)	7.7	(0.9)	8.6	(0.9)	8.0	(1.1)
Sub-national entities										
Flanders (Belgium)	2.1	(0.6)	4.1	(0.7)	4.1	(0.6)	3.9	(0.5)	5.2	(1.1)
England (UK)	1.0	(0.5)	5.1	(0.9)	6.1	(0.8)	5.6	(0.8)	4.7	(0.9)
Northern Ireland (UK)	2.5	(1.1)	3.8	(0.9)	3.8	(0.7)	3.5	(0.8)	4.5	(1.2)
England/N. Ireland (UK)	1.0	(0.5)	5.1	(0.8)	6.1	(0.8)	5.5	(0.8)	4.7	(0.9)
Average[1]	3.1	(0.2)	5.0	(0.2)	5.6	(0.2)	5.1	(0.2)	4.5	(0.2)
Average-22[2]	3.1	(0.2)	4.9	(0.2)	5.4	(0.2)	4.9	(0.1)	4.4	(0.2)

Partners

	16-24 year-olds %	S.E.	25-34 year-olds %	S.E.	35-44 year-olds %	S.E.	45-54 year-olds %	S.E.	55-65 year-olds %	S.E.
Cyprus[3]	4.5	(1.5)	4.1	(0.7)	5.9	(0.8)	3.9	(0.8)	2.9	(0.8)
Russian Federation[4]	6.6	(1.4)	6.5	(1.2)	5.9	(1.0)	3.1	(0.9)	2.6	(0.7)

1. Average of 19 participating OECD countries and entities.
2. Average of 22 OECD countries and entities: average of 19 countries with France, Italy and Spain.
3. See notes at the beginning of this Annex.
4. See note at the beginning of this Annex.
Source: Survey of Adult Skills (PIAAC) (2012).

StatLink 🔗 http://dx.doi.org/10.1787/888933232509

 ADULTS, COMPUTERS AND PROBLEM SOLVING: WHAT'S THE PROBLEM?

[Part 1/1]

Percentage of workers who reported that they lack the computer skills to do the job well, by proficiency in problem solving in technology-rich environments

Table B4.10

OECD	No computer experience		Failed ICT core		Opted out		Below Level 1		Level 1		Level 2/3	
	%	S.E.	%	S.E.	%	S.E.	%	S.E.	%	S.E.	%	S.E.
National entities												
Australia	a	a	3.7	(1.3)	9.4	(1.5)	10.4	(1.8)	7.8	(0.9)	4.3	(0.6)
Austria	a	a	6.0	(1.9)	4.6	(1.0)	5.1	(1.3)	3.1	(0.6)	2.4	(0.5)
Canada	a	a	8.1	(1.3)	9.4	(1.3)	6.9	(1.0)	4.6	(0.6)	2.8	(0.4)
Czech Republic	a	a	1.9	(1.0)	5.0	(1.7)	6.6	(1.8)	2.1	(0.8)	0.9	(0.4)
Denmark	a	a	7.5	(1.5)	10.1	(2.1)	15.2	(1.5)	8.8	(0.8)	5.6	(0.7)
Estonia	a	a	7.9	(1.9)	9.6	(0.9)	10.1	(1.2)	7.5	(0.7)	4.7	(0.7)
Finland	a	a	12.1	(2.4)	18.2	(2.1)	20.3	(2.4)	11.8	(1.2)	5.2	(0.6)
France	a	a	11.3	(1.7)	10.2	(1.0)	m	m	m	m	m	m
Germany	a	a	6.9	(2.3)	9.0	(2.1)	8.0	(1.4)	4.3	(0.6)	2.0	(0.4)
Ireland	a	a	4.7	(1.9)	10.2	(1.4)	10.1	(1.8)	4.9	(0.8)	2.2	(0.5)
Italy	a	a	2.5	(1.9)	7.9	(1.2)	m	m	m	m	m	m
Japan	a	a	34.8	(2.3)	34.1	(1.9)	30.1	(2.9)	29.3	(2.0)	23.5	(1.3)
Korea	a	a	17.6	(1.9)	27.9	(3.3)	22.2	(2.7)	17.1	(1.6)	9.7	(1.2)
Netherlands	a	a	8.6	(2.8)	14.2	(3.1)	5.9	(1.3)	5.4	(0.7)	3.7	(0.6)
Norway	a	a	6.2	(1.8)	18.5	(2.5)	20.3	(2.3)	16.2	(1.1)	11.1	(0.7)
Poland	a	a	4.8	(1.5)	6.4	(1.1)	5.9	(1.3)	4.4	(1.0)	3.8	(0.9)
Slovak Republic	a	a	2.0	(1.5)	6.2	(1.4)	3.7	(1.6)	3.6	(0.7)	1.7	(0.5)
Spain	a	a	8.5	(1.5)	7.9	(1.5)	m	m	m	m	m	m
Sweden	a	a	12.1	(3.0)	12.4	(2.4)	12.4	(2.1)	9.7	(1.0)	4.5	(0.5)
United States	a	a	8.9	(2.7)	8.5	(2.0)	5.2	(1.1)	5.3	(0.7)	3.1	(0.5)
Sub-national entities												
Flanders (Belgium)	a	a	4.3	(1.9)	10.0	(2.7)	11.2	(1.5)	7.1	(0.9)	5.9	(0.8)
England (UK)	a	a	7.7	(2.5)	11.6	(3.5)	8.5	(1.6)	6.2	(0.8)	4.4	(0.7)
Northern Ireland (UK)	a	a	4.5	(2.1)	8.8	(4.5)	8.9	(2.2)	5.3	(0.9)	3.3	(0.7)
England/N. Ireland (UK)	a	a	7.6	(2.4)	11.5	(3.4)	8.5	(1.6)	6.1	(0.8)	4.4	(0.7)
Average[1]	a	a	8.7	(0.5)	12.4	(0.5)	11.5	(0.4)	8.4	(0.2)	5.3	(0.2)
Average-22[2]	a	a	8.5	(0.4)	11.9	(0.4)	m	m	m	m	m	m

Partners

Cyprus[3]	a	a	9.8	(3.5)	8.6	(1.0)	m	m	m	m	m	m
Russian Federation[4]	a	a	1.4	(1.2)	5.3	(1.2)	5.1	(1.1)	3.5	(1.1)	3.0	(1.2)

1. Average of 19 participating OECD countries and entities.
2. Average of 22 OECD countries and entities: average of 19 countries with France, Italy and Spain.
3. See notes at the beginning of this Annex.
4. See note at the beginning of this Annex.

Source: Survey of Adult Skills (PIAAC) (2012).

StatLink http://dx.doi.org/10.1787/888933232511

[Part 1/1]

Table B4.11

Percentage of workers who reported that their lack of computer skills has affected the chances of getting a job, promotion or pay raise, by proficiency in problem solving in technology-rich environments

OECD	No computer experience		Failed ICT core		Opted out		Below Level 1		Level 1		Level 2/3	
	%	S.E.	%	S.E.	%	S.E.	%	S.E.	%	S.E.	%	S.E.
National entities												
Australia	a	a	5.3	(1.9)	9.4	(1.4)	9.2	(1.9)	7.1	(0.9)	4.9	(0.6)
Austria	a	a	3.4	(1.7)	2.5	(0.8)	5.4	(1.7)	3.5	(0.7)	2.9	(0.5)
Canada	a	a	9.3	(1.5)	7.7	(1.2)	8.4	(0.9)	6.5	(0.5)	5.0	(0.5)
Czech Republic	a	a	0.4	(0.4)	2.0	(0.8)	1.5	(0.8)	2.4	(0.8)	4.0	(0.9)
Denmark	a	a	3.7	(1.0)	3.8	(1.4)	4.6	(1.0)	4.0	(0.5)	3.6	(0.5)
Estonia	a	a	4.3	(1.5)	4.5	(0.7)	7.1	(0.9)	5.9	(0.6)	5.7	(0.6)
Finland	a	a	3.7	(1.7)	2.0	(0.9)	3.9	(1.0)	2.5	(0.5)	4.3	(0.5)
France	a	a	2.3	(0.9)	4.3	(0.8)	m	m	m	m	m	m
Germany	a	a	1.8	(1.1)	2.4	(1.0)	4.2	(1.1)	3.1	(0.6)	2.8	(0.4)
Ireland	a	a	6.6	(2.2)	5.8	(1.0)	7.0	(1.6)	4.7	(0.8)	3.0	(0.5)
Italy	a	a	4.0	(2.2)	1.7	(0.4)	m	m	m	m	m	m
Japan	a	a	14.1	(1.8)	10.9	(1.3)	20.5	(2.4)	19.4	(1.6)	20.9	(1.1)
Korea	a	a	1.3	(0.5)	3.7	(1.5)	2.9	(0.8)	2.0	(0.5)	1.5	(0.4)
Netherlands	a	a	5.5	(2.5)	3.1	(1.6)	3.0	(1.1)	3.4	(0.6)	2.8	(0.5)
Norway	a	a	8.0	(2.0)	6.5	(1.7)	7.0	(1.3)	5.1	(0.7)	3.4	(0.4)
Poland	a	a	6.5	(1.8)	4.9	(1.0)	5.9	(1.2)	5.9	(0.9)	8.0	(1.0)
Slovak Republic	a	a	4.5	(3.1)	2.3	(0.8)	4.5	(1.3)	3.8	(0.6)	3.7	(0.7)
Spain	a	a	4.4	(1.4)	3.5	(1.1)	m	m	m	m	m	m
Sweden	a	a	6.2	(2.1)	4.5	(1.8)	3.1	(1.2)	4.1	(0.8)	2.9	(0.5)
United States	a	a	16.7	(3.9)	6.2	(1.7)	9.1	(1.5)	7.8	(0.9)	5.8	(0.8)
Sub-national entities												
Flanders (Belgium)	a	a	7.4	(2.2)	4.0	(1.6)	6.3	(1.3)	4.6	(0.8)	3.6	(0.6)
England (UK)	a	a	8.1	(2.7)	2.9	(1.2)	5.3	(1.2)	5.0	(0.8)	4.6	(0.7)
Northern Ireland (UK)	a	a	3.0	(1.7)	9.5	(5.1)	6.3	(1.7)	4.3	(0.8)	2.6	(0.8)
England/N. Ireland (UK)	a	a	7.9	(2.6)	2.9	(1.2)	5.3	(1.2)	4.9	(0.8)	4.6	(0.7)
Average[1]	a	a	6.1	(0.5)	4.7	(0.3)	6.3	(0.3)	5.3	(0.2)	4.9	(0.1)
Average-22[2]	a	a	5.8	(0.4)	4.5	(0.3)	m	m	m	m	m	m

Partners

Cyprus[3]	a	a	13.9	(3.8)	7.4	(1.1)	m	m	m	m	m	m
Russian Federation[4]	a	a	12.4	(3.8)	7.4	(2.1)	4.2	(1.2)	6.0	(1.3)	5.5	(1.1)

1. Average of 19 participating OECD countries and entities.
2. Average of 22 OECD countries and entities: average of 19 countries with France, Italy and Spain.
3. See notes at the beginning of this Annex.
4. See note at the beginning of this Annex.
Source: Survey of Adult Skills (PIAAC) (2012).

StatLink 🔗 http://dx.doi.org/10.1787/888933232526

[Part 1/2]
Table B4.12
Likelihood of participating in the labour force, by proficiency in problem solving in technology-rich environments and use of e-mail in everyday life

OECD	Version 1 (socio-demographic controls)					Version 2 (Version 1 + literacy and numeracy)				
	No computer experience	Failed ICT core	Opted out	Level 1	Level 2/3	No computer experience	Failed ICT core	Opted out	Level 1	Level 2/3
	ß	ß	ß	ß	ß	ß	ß	ß	ß	ß
National entities										
Australia	-1.1 ***	-0.6 *	-0.1	0.1	0.5 *	-1.0 ***	-0.6 *	-0.1	0.0	0.3
Austria	-0.7 **	-0.3	-0.4	0.2	0.3	-0.7 ***	-0.4	-0.5 *	-0.1	-0.1
Canada	-0.6 ***	-0.3 **	-0.2	0.2	0.5 ***	-0.5 ***	-0.3 **	-0.2	0.0	0.2
Czech Republic	-0.8 ***	0.5	0.4	0.0	0.3	-0.8 ***	0.5	0.3	-0.1	0.2
Denmark	-1.1 ***	-0.3	-0.5 **	0.4 **	0.9 ***	-1.1 ***	-0.3	-0.5 **	0.1	0.4
Estonia	-1.4 ***	-0.4 *	-0.4 ***	0.2	0.5 **	-1.5 ***	-0.5 *	-0.5 ***	0.0	0.2
Finland	-1.1 ***	-0.6 ***	-0.3 **	0.6 ***	1.2 ***	-1.1 ***	-0.7 ***	-0.6 ***	0.3 **	0.6 **
France	m	m	m	m	m	m	m	m	m	m
Germany	-0.3	0.1	-0.3	0.3	0.5 **	-0.3	0.2	-0.4 *	-0.1	-0.1
Ireland	-0.5 ***	0.2	-0.2	0.4 *	0.8 ***	-0.5 ***	0.2	-0.2	0.3	0.7 **
Italy	m	m	m	m	m	m	m	m	m	m
Japan	-0.4 *	-0.2	-0.1	0.0	0.2	-0.4 *	-0.1	-0.1	0.0	0.2
Korea	-0.4 ***	-0.3	-0.1	-0.1	0.3	-0.4 **	-0.3	-0.1	-0.1	0.3
Netherlands	-0.4 *	-0.1	-0.4 *	0.4 **	0.7 ***	-0.4	0.0	-0.3	0.5 **	0.9 ***
Norway	-1.3 ***	0.0	-0.4 *	0.5 **	1.0 ***	-1.3 ***	0.1	-0.4 *	0.3	0.5 *
Poland	-0.6 ***	-0.2	-0.1	0.2	0.7 ***	-0.5 ***	-0.2	-0.1	0.2	0.5 *
Slovak Republic	-0.5 **	-0.4	0.1	0.2	0.4 *	-0.5 **	-0.5	0.0	0.0	0.0
Spain	m	m	m	m	m	m	m	m	m	m
Sweden	-1.1 **	-0.5	-0.4 *	0.3	0.7 ***	-0.9 **	-0.2	-0.7 **	-0.2	-0.3
United States	-1.0 ***	-0.7 **	-0.5 ***	0.2	0.3	-0.9 ***	-0.6 **	-0.6 ***	0.0	0.0
Sub-national entities										
Flanders (Belgium)	-0.9 ***	-0.4	-0.2	0.1	0.3	-0.9 ***	-0.4	-0.3	-0.1	-0.1
England (UK)	-1.4 ***	-0.2	0.0	0.3	0.7 ***	-1.3 ***	-0.2	0.0	0.2	0.5 *
Northern Ireland (UK)	-0.4	0.1	-0.7	0.2	0.7 **	-0.4	0.0	-0.8 *	-0.1	0.2
England/N. Ireland (UK)	-1.3 ***	-0.2	0.0	0.3	0.7 ***	-1.3 ***	-0.2	0.0	0.2	0.5 *
Average[1]	-0.8 *	-0.2 ***	-0.2	0.2 ***	0.58 ***	-0.8 ***	-0.2 ***	-0.3	0.1	0.3 ***
Average-22[2]	m	m	m	m	m	m	m	m	m	m
Partners										
Cyprus[3]	m	m	m	m	m	m	m	m	m	m
Russian Federation[4]	0.2	-0.5	0.1	0.3	0.4	0.0	-0.6 *	-0.1	0.1	0.0

1. Average of 19 participating OECD countries and entities.
2. Average of 22 OECD countries and entities: average of 19 countries with France, Italy and Spain.
3. See notes at the beginning of this Annex.
4. See note at the beginning of this Annex.
* Significant estimate p ≤ 0.10.
** Significant estimate p ≤ 0.05.
*** Significant estimate p ≤ 0.01.

Notes: The reference category for problem solving in rich-environment is Below Level 1 and low users for use of e-mail. Version 1 adjusts for socio-demographic characteristics (age, gender, foreign-born status, years of education and marital status). Version 2 adds literacy and numeracy proficiency to the regression of Version 1. Version 3 adds frequency of ICT use (e-mail) in everyday life as an adjustment to Version 2. Version 4 adds use of reading/writing/numeracy skills in everyday life as an additional adjustment to Version 3.
Source: Survey of Adult Skills (PIAAC) (2012).

StatLink ⬛🔗 http://dx.doi.org/10.1787/888933232539

[Part 2/2]

Table B4.12 **Likelihood of participating in the labour force, by proficiency in problem solving in technology-rich environments and use of e-mail in everyday life**

OECD	Version 3 (Version 2 + e-mail use in everyday life)						Version 4 (Version 3 + reading/writing/numeracy use in everyday life)					
	No computer experience	Failed ICT core	Opted out	Level 1	Level 2/3	Frequent use of e-mail	No computer experience	Failed ICT core	Opted out	Level 1	Level 2/3	Frequent use of e-mail
	ß	ß	ß	ß	ß	ß	ß	ß	ß	ß	ß	ß
National entities												
Australia	-0.9 ***	-0.6 *	-0.1	0.0	0.3	0.1	-1.2 ***	-0.5	-0.2	0.0	0.3	0.5 ***
Austria	-0.8 ***	-0.4	-0.5 *	0.0	-0.1	-0.1	-1.1 ***	-0.5	-0.6 **	-0.1	-0.1	0.1
Canada	-0.6 ***	-0.3 **	-0.3	0.0	0.2	0.0	-0.8 ***	-0.3 *	-0.3 *	0.0	0.2	0.2 *
Czech Republic	-0.7 **	0.5	0.4	-0.1	0.2	0.1	-0.7 *	0.7	0.3	-0.1	0.3	0.4
Denmark	-1.2 ***	-0.3	-0.5 **	0.1	0.4	-0.1	-1.1 ***	-0.3	-0.5 **	0.2	0.5	0.2
Estonia	-1.2 ***	-0.4	-0.4 *	0.0	0.2	0.3 ***	-1.1 ***	-0.6 *	-0.4	0.0	0.2	0.4 ***
Finland	-0.9 ***	-0.6 ***	-0.5 ***	0.3 *	0.6 **	0.3 **	-0.9 ***	-0.8 ***	-0.4 **	0.3	0.5 *	0.6 ***
France	m	m	m	m	m	m	m	m	m	m	m	m
Germany	-0.4	0.2	-0.5 *	-0.1	-0.1	-0.1	-0.4	0.2	-0.5 *	0.0	0.1	0.0
Ireland	-0.4 **	0.2	-0.2	0.3	0.6 **	0.1	-0.4 *	0.3	-0.3	0.2	0.7 **	0.3 *
Italy	m	m	m	m	m	m	m	m	m	m	m	m
Japan	-0.5 **	-0.2	-0.1	0.0	0.3	-0.1	-0.6 **	-0.2	-0.2	-0.1	0.2	-0.2
Korea	-0.3 **	-0.3	-0.1	-0.1	0.3	0.1	-0.3	-0.1	-0.2	-0.2	0.2	0.2
Netherlands	-0.1	0.0	-0.2	0.5 **	0.9 ***	0.4 **	0.1	-0.1	-0.3	0.4	1.0 ***	0.7 **
Norway	-1.2 ***	0.1	-0.4 *	0.3	0.5 *	0.1	-1.4 ***	0.4	-0.2	0.5 *	0.8 **	0.2
Poland	-0.4 **	-0.1	0.0	0.1	0.5 *	0.4 ***	-0.5 *	-0.2	0.0	0.1	0.5	0.6 ***
Slovak Republic	-0.2	-0.4	0.1	0.0	0.0	0.4 **	-0.2	-0.5	0.1	-0.1	0.0	0.4 **
Spain	m	m	m	m	m	m	m	m	m	m	m	m
Sweden	-1.1 **	-0.2	-0.8 ***	-0.1	-0.2	-0.3 *	-0.4	-0.1	-0.7 **	-0.2	-0.2	-0.2
United States	-1.0 ***	-0.6 **	-0.7 ***	0.1	0.0	-0.2	-1.5 ***	-0.8 **	-0.7 ***	0.0	-0.1	0.1
Sub-national entities												
Flanders (Belgium)	-1.2 ***	-0.5 *	-0.4 *	-0.1	0.0	-0.4 **	-1.1 ***	-0.6	-0.6 *	-0.1	0.0	-0.2
England (UK)	-1.2 ***	-0.2	0.1	0.2	0.5 *	0.1	-1.5 ***	-0.1	0.2	0.3	0.7 **	0.4 **
Northern Ireland (UK)	-0.3	0.1	-0.8	-0.1	0.2	0.2	-0.4	0.0	-0.6	-0.1	0.2	0.4 **
England/N. Ireland (UK)	-1.2 ***	-0.2	0.1	0.2	0.5 *	0.1	-1.4 ***	-0.1	0.2	0.3	0.7 **	0.4 **
Average[1]	-0.8 ***	-0.2	-0.3	0.1	0.3 ***	0.1 ***	-0.79 ***	-0.2 **	-0.3	0.1	0.3 ***	0.2 ***
Average-22[2]	m	m	m	m	m	m	m	m	m	m	m	m
Partners												
Cyprus[3]	m	m	m	m	m	m	m	m	m	m	m	m
Russian Federation[4]	0.0	-0.6 *	-0.1	0.1	0.0	0.0	0.4	-0.6	0.0	0.3	0.2	0.2

1. Average of 19 participating OECD countries and entities.
2. Average of 22 OECD countries and entities: average of 19 countries with France, Italy and Spain.
3. See notes at the beginning of this Annex.
4. See note at the beginning of this Annex.
* Significant estimate p ≤ 0.10.
** Significant estimate p ≤ 0.05.
*** Significant estimate p ≤ 0.01.
Notes: The reference category for problem solving in rich-environment is Below Level 1 and low users for use of e-mail. Version 1 adjusts for socio-demographic characteristics (age, gender, foreign-born status, years of education and marital status). Version 2 adds literacy and numeracy proficiency to the regression of Version 1. Version 3 adds frequency of ICT use (e-mail) in everyday life as an adjustment to Version 2. Version 4 adds use of reading/writing/numeracy skills in everyday life as an additional adjustment to Version 3.
Source: Survey of Adult Skills (PIAAC) (2012).

StatLink ᴍᴀᴘ http://dx.doi.org/10.1787/888933232539

[Part 1/2]

Likelihood of being unemployed, by proficiency in problem solving in technology-rich environments and e-mail use in everyday life

Table B4.13

OECD	Version 1 (socio-demographic controls)					Version 2 (Version 1 + literacy and numeracy)				
	No computer experience	Failed ICT core	Opted out	Level 1	Level 2/3	No computer experience	Failed ICT core	Opted out	Level 1	Level 2/3
	ß	ß	ß	ß	ß	ß	ß	ß	ß	ß
National entities										
Australia	-1.0	-0.4	-0.1	-0.5	-1.0 **	-1.0	-0.4	-0.2	-0.6	-1.2 **
Austria	-0.5	-0.4	-0.5	0.0	-0.5	-0.4	-0.3	-0.3	0.1	-0.3
Canada	0.7 *	0.5 *	-0.1	0.0	-0.1	0.5	0.5	-0.1	0.2	0.3
Czech Republic	0.6	0.4	0.8	0.5	0.2	0.6	0.3	0.9	0.8	0.8
Denmark	-0.9	0.0	0.5	0.1	0.5	-1.0	0.0	0.5	0.5	1.2 **
Estonia	0.9 ***	0.1	0.5 **	0.2	-0.4	0.9 ***	0.2	0.6 ***	0.4 *	0.0
Finland	0.3	0.5	-0.1	0.0	0.0	0.3	0.2	-0.4	0.2	0.5
France	m	m	m	m	m	m	m	m	m	m
Germany	0.2	0.3	0.8 **	0.2	-0.4	-0.1	-0.1	0.8 *	0.5	0.2
Ireland	0.1	-0.3	-0.1	0.1	-0.3	0.1	-0.3	0.0	0.3	0.1
Italy	m	m	m	m	m	m	m	m	m	m
Japan	-1.0	-0.1	-0.6	-0.3	-0.8	-1.6 **	-1.2	-1.4 *	-0.9	-1.7 **
Korea	0.0	0.2	0.0	0.0	0.0	-0.2	0.0	-0.4	0.0	0.0
Netherlands	-1.3	-0.8	0.0	-0.6	-0.9 **	-1.5	-0.8	-0.2	-0.7	-1.0
Norway	-12.3	0.5	-0.7	0.3	-0.2	-12.1	0.2	-0.6	0.6	0.5
Poland	0.6 *	0.2	0.3	0.1	-0.3	0.6 *	0.2	0.3	0.2	-0.2
Slovak Republic	0.5 *	0.0	-0.2	-0.5	-0.4	0.4	0.1	-0.2	-0.4	-0.2
Spain	m	m	m	m	m	m	m	m	m	m
Sweden	1.4	0.7	0.8	-0.1	-0.9 **	1.4	0.6	0.8 *	0.1	-0.6
United States	-1.2 ***	-0.2	-0.2	-0.2	-0.5	-1.4 ***	-0.3	-0.1	0.1	0.1
Sub-national entities										
Flanders (Belgium)	-1.0	-0.7	-0.2	-0.3	-0.4	-1.1	-0.6	0.0	-0.1	-0.2
England (UK)	0.0	0.4	-0.6	-0.3	-0.9 **	-0.1	0.3	-0.6	0.0	-0.3
Northern Ireland (UK)	0.3	-0.7	-1.2	-0.6	-1.0 *	0.3	-0.7	-1.3	-0.4	-0.5
England/N. Ireland (UK)	0.0	0.4	-0.6	-0.3	-0.9 **	-0.1	0.3	-0.6	0.0	-0.3
Average¹	-0.7	0.1	0.0	-0.1	-0.4	-0.8	-0.1	0.0	0.1	-0.1
Average-22²	m	m	m	m	m	m	m	m	m	m
Partners										
Cyprus³	m	m	m	m	m	m	m	m	m	m
Russian Federation⁴	0.6	-0.6	0.1	0.6	1.0	0.0	-0.9	-0.6	0.1	-0.1

1. Average of 19 participating OECD countries and entities.
2. Average of 22 OECD countries and entities: average of 19 countries with France, Italy and Spain.
3. See notes at the beginning of this Annex.
4. See note at the beginning of this Annex.
*   Significant estimate p ≤ 0.10.
** Significant estimate p ≤ 0.05.
*** Significant estimate p ≤ 0.01.

Notes: The reference category for problem solving in rich-environment is Below Level 1 and low users for use of e-mail. Version 1 adjusts for socio-demographic characteristics (age, gender, foreign-born status, years of education and marital status). Version 2 adds literacy and numeracy proficiency to the regression of Version 1. Version 3 adds frequency of ICT use (e-mail) in everyday life as an adjustment to Version 2. Version 4 adds use of reading/writing/numeracy skills in everyday life as an additional adjustment to Version 3.
Source: Survey of Adult Skills (PIAAC) (2012).

StatLink ᴍᴄ℩ http://dx.doi.org/10.1787/888933232540

[Part 2/2]

Likelihood of being unemployed, by proficiency in problem solving in technology-rich environments and e-mail use in everyday life

Table B4.13

	Version 3 (Version 2 + e-mail use in everyday life)						Version 4 (Version 3 + reading/writing/numeracy use in everyday life)					
	No computer experience	Failed ICT core	Opted out	Level 1	Level 2/3	Frequent use of e-mail	No computer experience	Failed ICT core	Opted out	Level 1	Level 2/3	Frequent use of e-mail
OECD	ß	ß	ß	ß	ß	ß	ß	ß	ß	ß	ß	ß
National entities												
Australia	-0.8	-0.4	-0.2	-0.6	-1.2 **	0.2	-0.1	-0.3	0.1	-0.7	-1.1 *	0.0
Austria	-0.4	-0.3	-0.3	0.1	-0.3	0.0	-0.2	-0.3	-0.4	0.0	-0.5	-0.5
Canada	0.8 *	0.5	0.0	0.1	0.2	0.5 **	1.4 **	0.8 **	0.3	0.2	0.3	0.1
Czech Republic	0.6	0.3	0.9	0.8	0.8	0.0	0.7	0.4	0.8	0.8	0.7	-0.3
Denmark	-1.0	0.0	0.5	0.5	1.2 **	0.0	-12.7	0.0	0.3	0.6	1.2 **	-0.5
Estonia	1.1 ***	0.2	0.7 ***	0.4 *	0.0	0.2	1.2 ***	0.3	0.8 ***	0.5 **	0.2	-0.1
Finland	0.7	0.2	-0.2	0.2	0.5	0.6 **	1.3 *	0.4	-0.1	0.3	0.5	-0.1
France	m	m	m	m	m	m	m	m	m	m	m	m
Germany	-0.1	-0.1	0.8 *	0.5	0.2	0.0	0.3	0.1	0.8 *	0.4	0.0	0.0
Ireland	0.2	-0.3	0.0	0.3	0.0	0.2	0.4	-0.4	0.1	0.3	0.0	-0.3
Italy	m	m	m	m	m	m	m	m	m	m	m	m
Japan	-1.5 **	-1.2	-1.4 *	-0.9	-1.7 **	0.1	-1.9 **	-1.6 **	-1.7 **	-1.0	-2.0 **	-0.1
Korea	-0.1	-0.1	-0.3	0.0	0.0	0.3	-0.2	-0.1	-0.6	-0.1	-0.1	0.0
Netherlands	-0.7	-0.7	0.0	-0.7	-1.0	1.0 **	-13.1	-0.9	0.1	-0.5	-0.9	0.4
Norway	-12.0	0.2	-0.6	0.6	0.4	0.1	-10.1	0.3	-0.3	0.7	0.4	0.1
Poland	0.5	0.2	0.3	0.2	-0.2	-0.1	0.9 **	0.2	0.3	0.1	-0.2	-0.3
Slovak Republic	0.3	0.1	-0.3	-0.4	-0.2	-0.2	0.6 *	0.2	-0.3	-0.3	-0.1	-0.3
Spain	m	m	m	m	m	m	m	m	m	m	m	m
Sweden	1.8	0.6	1.0 *	0.0	-0.7	0.6	-12.3	0.8	0.8	-0.2	-1.0 *	0.6
United States	-1.2 **	-0.3	0.0	0.1	0.1	0.4 *	-0.5	-0.1	0.4	0.3	0.5	-0.2
Sub-national entities												
Flanders (Belgium)	-0.8	-0.5	0.1	-0.2	-0.3	0.4	-1.0	-0.9	0.8	-0.2	-0.2	0.2
England (UK)	-0.1	0.3	-0.5	0.0	-0.4	0.1	1.0	0.7 *	-0.1	0.0	-0.3	-0.2
Northern Ireland (UK)	0.2	-0.8	-1.3	-0.4	-0.5	-0.2	0.2	-0.7	-1.4	-0.5	-0.6	-0.8 **
England/N. Ireland (UK)	0.0	0.3	-0.5	0.0	-0.4	0.1	0.9	0.7 *	-0.2	0.0	-0.3	-0.2
Average[1]	-0.66	-0.07	0.03	0.06	-0.13	0.24 ***	-2.34	-0.02	0.10	0.06	-0.14 **	-0.06
Average-22[2]	m	m	m	m	m	m	m	m	m	m	m	m
Partners												
Cyprus[3]	m	m	m	m	m	m	m	m	m	m	m	m
Russian Federation[4]	0.2	-0.9	-0.5	0.0	-0.1	0.5	-0.1	-1.1	-3.3	0.4	-0.2	0.4

1. Average of 19 participating OECD countries and entities.
2. Average of 22 OECD countries and entities: average of 19 countries with France, Italy and Spain.
3. See notes at the beginning of this Annex.
4. See note at the beginning of this Annex.
* Significant estimate p ≤ 0.10.
** Significant estimate p ≤ 0.05.
*** Significant estimate p ≤ 0.01.

Notes: The reference category for problem solving in rich-environment is Below Level 1 and low users for use of e-mail. Version 1 adjusts for socio-demographic characteristics (age, gender, foreign-born status, years of education and marital status). Version 2 adds literacy and numeracy proficiency to the regression of Version 1. Version 3 adds frequency of ICT use (e-mail) in everyday life as an adjustment to Version 2. Version 4 adds use of reading/writing/numeracy skills in everyday life as an additional adjustment to Version 3.

Source: Survey of Adult Skills (PIAAC) (2012).

StatLink http://dx.doi.org/10.1787/888933232540

[Part 1/1]

Table B4.14 **Percentage of adults aged 16-65 who worked during previous five years, by type of occupation**

OECD	Skilled occupations		Semi-skilled white-collar occupations		Semi-skilled blue-collar occupations		Elementary occupations		Missing	
	%	S.E.	%	S.E.	%	S.E.	%	S.E.	%	S.E.
National entities										
Australia	41.6	(0.8)	27.4	(0.6)	18.6	(0.6)	9.7	(0.5)	2.6	(0.3)
Austria	38.3	(0.8)	27.4	(0.7)	21.8	(0.7)	8.6	(0.4)	4.0	(0.3)
Canada	49.4	(0.5)	25.0	(0.4)	15.9	(0.4)	7.6	(0.3)	2.0	(0.1)
Czech Republic	33.8	(0.9)	24.3	(0.9)	31.8	(0.9)	8.6	(0.5)	1.5	(0.3)
Denmark	41.8	(0.6)	27.2	(0.6)	17.5	(0.5)	11.7	(0.5)	1.8	(0.2)
Estonia	40.8	(0.6)	19.4	(0.5)	28.1	(0.5)	10.2	(0.4)	1.4	(0.1)
Finland	38.0	(0.6)	28.6	(0.6)	23.6	(0.6)	9.1	(0.4)	0.8	(0.1)
France	38.0	(0.5)	25.7	(0.5)	22.9	(0.5)	11.6	(0.4)	1.8	(0.1)
Germany	35.8	(0.6)	30.1	(0.7)	22.4	(0.6)	8.7	(0.5)	3.1	(0.3)
Ireland	34.7	(0.7)	33.4	(0.7)	21.6	(0.7)	9.3	(0.5)	1.0	(0.2)
Italy	29.5	(0.7)	28.8	(0.9)	28.0	(1.0)	11.8	(0.7)	1.9	(0.3)
Japan	31.2	(0.7)	34.6	(0.6)	18.9	(0.7)	6.0	(0.3)	9.4	(0.4)
Korea	27.5	(0.6)	39.1	(0.8)	20.6	(0.6)	11.4	(0.5)	1.4	(0.2)
Netherlands	48.6	(0.6)	28.3	(0.6)	11.1	(0.4)	8.9	(0.4)	3.1	(0.2)
Norway	38.9	(0.6)	29.8	(0.6)	14.2	(0.5)	4.7	(0.3)	12.5	(0.4)
Poland	34.7	(0.7)	23.4	(0.6)	31.2	(0.6)	9.3	(0.5)	1.4	(0.2)
Slovak Republic	38.5	(0.8)	22.4	(0.7)	28.7	(0.7)	8.8	(0.5)	1.5	(0.2)
Spain	29.3	(0.7)	32.4	(0.7)	21.3	(0.6)	15.3	(0.5)	1.7	(0.2)
Sweden	41.9	(0.5)	29.6	(0.7)	20.6	(0.5)	6.3	(0.4)	1.6	(0.2)
United States	41.2	(0.8)	29.3	(0.6)	15.1	(0.7)	8.6	(0.5)	5.8	(0.7)
Sub-national entities										
Flanders (Belgium)	42.2	(0.8)	23.8	(0.7)	17.2	(0.5)	8.6	(0.4)	8.3	(0.4)
England (UK)	36.4	(0.7)	34.5	(0.7)	15.5	(0.6)	10.5	(0.5)	3.1	(0.3)
Northern Ireland (UK)	31.5	(0.9)	35.3	(0.9)	17.3	(0.8)	8.2	(0.6)	7.6	(0.5)
England/N. Ireland (UK)	36.2	(0.7)	34.5	(0.7)	15.6	(0.6)	10.4	(0.5)	3.2	(0.3)
Average[1]	38.7	(0.2)	28.3	(0.1)	20.8	(0.1)	8.8	(0.1)	3.5	(0.1)
Average-22[2]	37.8	(0.1)	28.4	(0.1)	21.2	(0.1)	9.3	(0.1)	3.3	(0.1)

Partners

Cyprus[3]	28.5	(0.6)	28.5	(0.7)	13.0	(0.5)	5.8	(0.4)	24.2	(0.5)
Russian Federation[4]	35.9	(1.5)	19.1	(0.7)	23.2	(0.8)	4.3	(0.3)	17.6	(1.6)

1. Average of 19 participating OECD countries and entities.
2. Average of 22 OECD countries and entities: average of 19 countries with France, Italy and Spain.
3. See notes at the beginning of this Annex.
4. See note at the beginning of this Annex.
Source: Survey of Adult Skills (PIAAC) (2012).
StatLink ⬛ http://dx.doi.org/10.1787/888933232554

ORGANISATION FOR ECONOMIC CO-OPERATION AND DEVELOPMENT

The OECD is a unique forum where governments work together to address the economic, social and environmental challenges of globalisation. The OECD is also at the forefront of efforts to understand and to help governments respond to new developments and concerns, such as corporate governance, the information economy and the challenges of an ageing population. The Organisation provides a setting where governments can compare policy experiences, seek answers to common problems, identify good practice and work to co-ordinate domestic and international policies.

The OECD member countries are: Australia, Austria, Belgium, Canada, Chile, the Czech Republic, Denmark, Estonia, Finland, France, Germany, Greece, Hungary, Iceland, Ireland, Israel, Italy, Japan, Korea, Luxembourg, Mexico, the Netherlands, New Zealand, Norway, Poland, Portugal, the Slovak Republic, Slovenia, Spain, Sweden, Switzerland, Turkey, the United Kingdom and the United States. The European Union takes part in the work of the OECD.

OECD Publishing disseminates widely the results of the Organisation's statistics gathering and research on economic, social and environmental issues, as well as the conventions, guidelines and standards agreed by its members.

OECD PUBLISHING, 2, rue André-Pascal, 75775 PARIS CEDEX 16
(978-92-64-23683-7) ISBN